CW01269477

Modernism and the New Spain

MODERNIST LITERATURE & CULTURE
Kevin J. H. Dettmar and Mark Wollaeger, Series Editors

Consuming Traditions
Elizabeth Outka

Machine-Age Comedy
Michael North

The Art of Scandal
Sean Latham

The Hypothetical Mandarin
Eric Hayot

Nations of Nothing But Poetry
Matthew Hart

Modernism & Copyright
Paul K. Saint-Amour

Accented America
Joshua L. Miller

Criminal Ingenuity
Ellen Levy

Modernism's Mythic Pose
Carrie J. Preston

Pragmatic Modernism
Lisi Schoenbach

World Views
Jon Hegglund

Unseasonable Youth
Jed Esty

Americanizing Britain
Genevieve Abravanel

At the Violet Hour
Sarah Cole

Modernism and the New Spain
Gayle Rogers

Modernism and the New Spain

Britain, Cosmopolitan Europe, and Literary History

Gayle Rogers

OXFORD
UNIVERSITY PRESS

OXFORD
UNIVERSITY PRESS

Oxford University Press is a department of the University of Oxford.
It furthers the University's objective of excellence in research,
scholarship, and education by publishing worldwide.

Oxford   New York
Auckland   Cape Town   Dar es Salaam   Hong Kong   Karachi
Kuala Lumpur   Madrid   Melbourne   Mexico City   Nairobi
New Delhi   Shanghai   Taipei   Toronto

With offices in
Argentina   Austria   Brazil   Chile   Czech Republic   France   Greece
Guatemala   Hungary   Italy   Japan   Poland   Portugal   Singapore
South Korea   Switzerland   Thailand   Turkey   Ukraine   Vietnam

Oxford is a registered trade mark of Oxford University Press in the UK and certain other countries.

Published in the United States of America by Oxford University Press
198 Madison Avenue, New York, NY 10016

© Oxford University Press 2012

All rights reserved. No part of this publication may be reproduced,
stored in a retrieval system, or transmitted, in any form or by any means, without
the prior permission in writing of Oxford University Press, or as expressly
permitted by law, by license, or under terms agreed with the appropriate
reproduction rights organization. Inquiries concerning reproduction outside the
scope of the above should be sent to the Rights Department, Oxford University Press,
at the address above.

You must not circulate this work in any other form and you must impose this
same condition on any acquirer.

Library of Congress Cataloging-in-Publication Data
Rogers, Gayle, 1978–
Modernism and the new Spain : Britain, cosmopolitan Europe,
and literary history / Gayle Rogers.
   p. cm.—(Modernist literature & culture)
ISBN 978-0-19-991497-5
1. Spanish literature—20th century—History and criticism.
2. English literature—20th century—History and criticism.
3. European literature—20th century—History and criticism.
4. Modernism (Literature)—Spain. 5. Spain—In literature.
6. Difference (Psychology) in literature. I. Title.
PQ6073.M6R64   2012
860.9'112—dc23   2012006291

9 8 7 6 5 4 3 2 1

Printed in the United States of America
on acid-free paper

Contents

Series Editors' Foreword ix
Acknowledgments xiii

Introduction: The Problem of Spain and the Cultural Map of Interwar Europe   3

Spain, the Idea of Europe, and Modernist Literary History   10
The New Spain, Southern Europe, and Kantian Cosmopolitanism   13
Ortega in Public: The Reformist Critique and the Plan for a New Spain   16
Spengler and the *Revista de Occidente*'s Cosmopolitanism   19
Spain's New Europeanizers   21
Organization and Argument   25

1. An Anglo-Spanish Vanguard: The *Criterion*, the *Revista de Occidente*, and the Periodical Project of the New Europe   29

    An "Unborn Quarterly of Unknown Qualities": The *Criterion*'s Europe   32
    Rediscovering Spain   35
    Windows onto the New Spain: Marichalar and Trend   38
    An "Older European Nation" and its New *Revista de Occidente*   42
    Translation, Not "Treasure"   43
    British Writing and Ortega's New Europe   46
    The Young Generation/*La generación joven*: British Modernism in the *Revista de Occidente*'s Spain   47
    The Margins of the Occident, Spanish Exceptionalism, and the Future of Europe   51

Spain and the Constitution of the West in the *Criterion*   56
European Writing, War, and Demise: Revaluating England and the British Empire   59

2. Joyce and the Spanish *Ulysses*   65

Molly's "Spanish Type" and Cultural Decadence   67
The "European Family" and the End of Empires   72
Joyce, Ortega, and the Cultural Politics of Gibraltar   74
Marichalar's Spanish Joyce   77
Translating Joyce and Hispanophone Vanguardism   82
Joyce's Cosmopolitanism in Anglo- and Hispanophone Literary-Critical History   85
"Joyce est un peu espagnol—pas?": Re-reading *Ulysses* and the Afterlife of Marichalar's Joyce   88

3. Lytton Strachey and *La nueva biografía* in Spain: Avant-garde Literature, the New Liberalism, and the Ruins of the Nineteenth Century   95

Modernist Critique and Strachey's New Biography   98
Power and "Inevitable Destruction" in "The End of General Gordon"   101
Strachey's "Lives," Vanguard Writing, and *La nueva biografía* in Spain   105
Reform, Reconstruction, and the Liberal Project in Spain   110
Aristocracy and the Self-destruction of "the Greatest Fortune in Spain": Marichalar's *Osuna*   113
Not Don Juan, but Don Quixote—The Dandy   118
Decline, Disillusion, and the Fate of *La nueva biografía*   121

4. Virginia Woolf and the Spanish Civil War: *Three Guineas*, Victoria Ocampo, and International Feminism   125

Woolf's "Innumerable, Indescribable, Unthinkable" Spain   128
Spain's Woolf   131
Ocampo, Frank, and "Our America"   133
Sur, the Intersection of Europe and the Americas   136
"Living History": Woolf, Ocampo, Misogyny, and Fascism   139
The Republic at War, British Literary Politics, and the Contexts of Woolf's Activism   144
The Meaning of Death in Spain   148
"Dead Bodies and Ruined Houses": Spain, War, and Feminism   151
Woolf's Hispanic "Outsiders"   157

5. Spain in Translation and Revision: Spender, Altolaguirre, and Lorca in British Literary Culture   163

   Speaking for Spain, Misreading Ortega   166
   An Anglo-Spanish Literary History: Altolaguirre's *1616*   170
   From Disgust to Sympathy: The Evolution of Spender's Spain   174
   New Writing and *Poems for Spain*: Translation, Sympathy, and Solidarity   178
   Romances, Lorca, and the Fall of the Republic   182
   The Spanish Cause, Through Lorca   184
   The Logic of Attachment: Spender, Lorca, and Spain's European Fate   189
   Another Lorca, Another Spain: The Battle Continues   192

Conclusion: Modernism, War, and the Memory of Spain after 1939   199

Appendix: "James Joyce in His Labyrinth [*Revista de Occidente*, 1924]" by Antonio Marichalar, translated by Gayle Rogers   209

Notes   221
Index   273

Series Editors' Foreword

Seemingly out of joint with time, Spain has posed a challenge to the idea of Europe for many years. Today the European Union sees it as a domino poised to topple in response to possible financial defaults in Greece, Italy, and Ireland. The nineteenth century had less rational concerns. Under the influence of Hispanist fantasies, Kant viewed Spain as a backward region of demented hotheads whose excessive pride, recalcitrant insularity, and innate cruelty inclined them to ignite heretics and torture bulls. Nor has twentieth-century Spain, at once historically premature in its loss of empire and belated with respect to social reform and secularism, found a secure spot in Anglophone studies of modernism.

In *Modernism and the New Spain*, Gayle Rogers breaks new ground by providing a richly textured cultural and literary history of a mutually constitutive dialogue between British and Hispanophone modernisms in the interwar years. Rogers's transnational study thus contributes to a paradigm shift taking place in modernist studies, and takes its place alongside two related books in this series, Matthew Hart's *Nations of Nothing But Poetry: Modernism, Transnationalism, and Synthetic Vernacular Writing* (2010) and Jon Hegglund's *World Views: Metageographies of Modernist Fiction* (2012). Like Hart and Hegglund, Rogers thinks beyond the nation; but whereas Hart and Hegglund focus respectively on the border-crossing of poetic idiom ("synthetic vernacular") and the supra-national mapping performed by modern novels ("metageographies"), *Modernism and the New Spain* recovers an important nexus of collaborative exchanges that took place through the agency of transnational periodical culture.

Central here is José Ortega y Gasset's interwar project of attempting to rebuild European community by rethinking it through its Spanish margins. Perceived as too close to Africa, too Islamic, too backward, Spain was not even part of Europe for Kant; but Ortega believed that Spain was uniquely situated to serve as the locus for an interwar reconceptualization of European culture that would emphasize, in Rogers's words, "a new synthetic Spanish-European modernity"—a new brand of cosmopolitanism drawing on Spain's multicultural hybridity in order to regenerate a continent ruined by the Great War. The margin, in other words, would provide a new center.

Ultimately the dialogue is more a polylogue that extends beyond Britain and Spain to North and South America and Ireland. Anglophone scholars will gain new insight into familiar figures, including T. S. Eliot, James Joyce, Lytton Strachey, and Virginia Woolf, while also learning a great deal about less familiar figures, such as Ortega (too often known in English only as the author of *The Dehumanization of Art* or *The Revolt of the Masses*), Antonio Marichalar, Victoria Ocampo, Manuel Altolaguirre, and Waldo Frank. But Rogers speaks to both sides of the disciplinary divide: in departments of English, Federico García Lorca is probably known mainly as a martyr to the Republican cause in the Spanish Civil War but rarely surfaces in discussions of modernism, vanguardism, or even poetry in general; in Spanish Departments, Lorca is widely discussed, of course, but Rogers offers a fresh account of the complex battles over the cultural and political significance of his assassination that played out in the efforts of Stephen Spender and Altolaguirre to use Lorca to establish connections between the Auden Generation and the Spanish Generation of '27.

Ortega, who became an enormously influential broker of culture, serves as the focal point for Rogers's cognate project of recovering the cultural idealism of interwar modernist culture. Ortega's Anglo-American (not quite) double in this classically modernist project of rebirth was T. S. Eliot, who founded the *Criterion* in 1922 in order to renovate European intellectual community from the English margin. Chapter 1 tells the story of how Eliot came to see Spain as crucial to his project of generating cross-cultural dialogues that would introduce important continental writers to the English reading public, and how he discovered in Ortega's literary journal—the *Revista de Occidente*, founded in 1923—a periodical equally invested in a regenerative project of Europeanization. In 1929, the *Criterion* and the *Revista* "embarked enthusiastically on a shared circulation scheme built around a new international literary competition": "one piece of short fiction would be selected by a jury to be translated and published simultaneously in five different reviews [English, Spanish, French, Italian, and German] . . . across

Europe." Such collaboration, it was hoped, might contribute to the formation of a post-nationalist Europe.

How and why these idealistic aims ultimately were defeated is a sad part of the story that Rogers tells, but the surge of cultural energies that came to be known as Spain's Silver Age (1898–1939) and the productive collaborations that linked Spain, Britain, and the Americas in this period provide an invigorating set of counter-narratives about vital transnational communities in which innovative aesthetic practices were directed toward a common cultural good. Eliot, for instance, was extraordinarily fortunate to find a Spanish intermediary in Antonio Marichalar, who not only was instrumental in bringing previously unknown and untranslated Spanish writers to the attention of the *Criterion*'s readership but also wrote the first article on Joyce in Spanish for the *Revista* in 1924 (translated into English for the first time by Rogers and included in an appendix). In addition to initiating an interpretation of the Spanish-Irish connections that pervade *Ulysses*—a project that Rogers updates through brilliant readings of Gibraltar, the Blooms, and Joyce's narratives on imperial decline—Marichalar also was largely responsible for circulating the works of William Faulkner, Lytton Strachey, Liam O'Flaherty, Hart Crane, and D. H. Lawrence among Hispanophone audiences. Manuel Altolaguirre, whose bilingual journal, *1616: English and Spanish Poetry*, blurred boundaries between British and Spanish modernisms, will also be a revelation for British modernists.

Much more remains beyond the scope of our summary here: Rogers's recovery of cultural narratives occluded by the dominant Anglophone accounts of the Spanish Civil War provided by Ernest Hemingway and George Orwell (who, it turns out, initially despised Stephen Spender, whose efforts to reshape Anglophone understanding of the war Rogers recounts); the ways in which Virginia Woolf's friendship with the Argentine Ocampo, too easily scanted as a minor figure in Woolf's life, contributed to her thinking in *Three Guineas* and thus to the emergence of international feminism; the synergy among Ortega's philosophy, Strachey's *Eminent Victorians*, and Marichalar's translation that catalyzed Spain's *nueva biografía*, or New Biography, movement; the seemingly incomprehensible poetic connection between the fascist writer Roy Campbell, who in the 1930s praised the murder of Lorca and once punched Spender during a poetry reading, and Lorca himself, whose poetry Campbell later decided to translate, beautifully; and Rogers's closing discussion of post-1939 Spain, featuring an epilogic treatment of Andalusian philosopher and author María Zambrano, whose autobiography *Delirium and Destiny* (1984), unpublished for nearly four decades, bespeaks, in Rogers's words, "Spain's delayed and difficult journey" toward the kind of European statehood that Ortega had hoped to bring about after the loss of its empire. A new world of transnational exploration awaits readers of this exemplary contribution to Modernist Literature & Culture.

—MARK WOLLAEGER AND KEVIN J. H. DETTMAR

Acknowledgments

My research has been generously supported by the National Endowment for the Humanities; the Hewlett Foundation; the Program for Cultural Cooperation between the Spanish Ministry of Culture and United States Universities; the Keck Foundation of the Huntington Library; at the University of Pittsburgh: the European Union Center of Excellence/European Studies Center, the School of Arts and Sciences, the Department of English; at Northwestern University: the Department of English, the Graduate School, the Weinberg College of Arts and Sciences, the Brady Travel Fund, and the Virgil Heltzel Fellowship. And though not directly toward this project, the generosity of Martha Rivers Ingram and the Ingram Scholarship Program enabled this work to begin before I could even have known where it would lead. I am grateful for the assistance I received during my research in Madrid from the staff and directors of the Fundación Ortega y Gasset-Gregorio Marañón—in particular, Asención Uña and Javier Zamora Bonilla—the Real Academia de la Historia, the library of the Residencia de Estudiantes (especially Miguel Jiménez), the Biblioteca Nacional, and the Hemeroteca Municipal. I am also thankful for the support and aid from the Fundación María Zambrano (Vélez-Málaga), the Special Collections library at Northwestern, the Newberry Library (Chicago), the Huntington Library (San Marino, CA), the Harry Ransom Humanities Research Center at the University of Texas at Austin, the Houghton Library at Harvard University, the Department of Special Collections and University Archives at the University of Tulsa, the Special Collections of the University at Buffalo, and the library of the University of Pittsburgh.

Portions of this book were presented at the conferences, conventions, and symposia of the following associations, where I benefited from invaluable feedback and discussions: Modern Language Association, Modernist Studies Association, American Comparative Literature Association, International James Joyce Foundation, Mediamorphosis: Print Culture and Transatlantic Public Sphere(s), 1880–1940, Society for the Study of Narrative Literature, Mellon Dissertation Forum at the Alice Berline Kaplan Center for the Humanities, Midwestern Modern Language Association, the Literature Program Work-in-Progress colloquium at the University of Pittsburgh, and the Magazine Modernisms Seminar (NEH/University of Tulsa). My students at the University of Pittsburgh and at Northwestern University have provided the critical questions and innovative ideas that have kept these topics fresh and exciting for me through the years, and for that I am thankful. They have continually reshaped the ways I think about modernism, about the authors we've discussed, and about theories of cosmopolitanism as they influence our readings of world literatures.

Behind all of these lists—which feel hopelessly impersonal—are friendships, collegiality, conversations, and memories that have made the labor of this project continually enjoyable and engaging at every turn. I cannot help but be astounded by the number of gracious, altruistic, and intellectually generous people who helped make this book a truly collaborative effort. Nearly every faculty member of the Department of English at Northwestern, at some point, assisted me with this project when it was a dissertation. I thank the department for supporting me as a member of their scholarly community. My interactions with my graduate colleagues at Northwestern helped me work through the early phases of this project. They are too many to name, but Joanne Diaz in particular deserves more thanks than I can offer her. To my dissertation committee, Paul Breslin, Reginald Gibbons, Darío Fernández-Morera, and Jordana Mendelson, I owe my heartfelt appreciation for guiding me through countless missteps and revisions that clarified the future direction of this study. Along the way, Brian Edwards, Julia Stern, Christopher Lane, Patrick Paul Garlinger, and Kevin Bell offered substantial advice that enriched this project. Jules Law went out of his way to help me frame and articulate my work at numerous points, providing the kind of sharp, analytic, and schematic commentaries that I sorely needed along the way. More important, he has been a caring mentor, and his friendship has sustained my work in both direct and indirect ways. Christine Froula saw my work through from start to finish, even returning to read the introduction in its final phases of revision—and doing so with the same incredible eye that she brought to shepherding my graduate work. With enthusiastic engagement, patient guidance, and unwavering dedication, she had the foresight that this project needed for years. For her profound, encouraging aid across nearly a decade now, I offer her my deepest thanks and my wish that she can take a measure of pride in this finished product.

I have happily accrued a number of other debts to colleagues and friends in the process of writing this book—debts that I hope to repay in time. Greg Downs read this manuscript in draft and brought a brilliant, insightful sense of methodology and argument to it that reoriented my thinking on a number of issues. Chapters and sections of this manuscript benefited immensely from the suggestions and critiques offered to me by Sean Latham, Eurie Dahn, Aarti Smith Madan, Juan Herrero-Senés, Lori Cole, and Leah Flack. I owe Sean also for leading our seminar on periodical studies, which, along with many conversations and much counsel, altered the nature and direction of my arguments for the better, and for pointing me to *Horizon*, which had been only on the periphery of my consciousness. Eurie provided criticism and feedback with amazing precision and detail. Lori and Juan knew the material for my first and third chapters, respectively, quite masterfully, and I am glad for their insights on them, and Leah has long been a perfect interlocutor on this and other projects. My colleagues at the University of Pittsburgh have provided a lively, supportive environment that has been perfect for developing this project—though any attempt to single out every member of our large institutional family would surely fail. Dan Morgan, Jonathan Arac, Nancy Glazener, Colin MacCabe, Shalini Puri, Adam Lowenstein, Hannah Johnson, and Bill Scott all read parts of this work and/or the proposal, for which I am very grateful.

Much of my work would have been, frankly, impossible without the invaluable information, support, and contacts that have been generously shared with me by Domingo Ródenas de Moya. I hope this book does justice to his exemplary level of scholarship and generosity. Alessandra Chiriboga has been a wonderful and informative proofreader. Numerous other conversations and exchanges have clarified issues both big and small for me, and for those I thank the following friends: the Magazine Modernisms seminar: Bart Brinkman, Lori Cole, N. C. Christopher Couch, Eurie Dahn, Jeff Drouin, David Earle, Mark Gaipa, Lindsey Gilbert, Rob Hurd, Verna Kale, Sean Latham, James Murphy, Michael Rozendal, Bob Scholes, Carey Snyder, Daniel Worden, Clifford Wulfman, and Justine Price, whom we all miss dearly; Bruce Robbins and the members of the seminar on Cosmopolitanism at the University of Pittsburgh's Humanities Center; Rebecca Walkowitz, Lisa Weihman, and the members of the seminar on Literary History at West Virginia University; Ann Ardis, Dan Balderston, Jessica Berman, John Beverley, John Bishop, María Teresa Caneda Cabrera, Ted Cachey, Bill Chase, Norman Cheadle, Patrick Collier, Erik Gellman, Juan Gómez, Barbara Green, Faye Hammill, Jason Harding, Gabriele Hayden, Karen Leick, Ben Lerner, Dennis Looney, Josh Lund, Jenny

Mann, Celia Marshik, Guy Ortolano, Libby Otto, Carrie Preston, Brian Price, Antonio Raúl de Toro Santos, César Salgado, Alberta Sbragia, David Smith, Ania Spyra, Judy Suh, Abram Van Engen, and Mark Wollaeger. I would like to conclude by extending my very warm thanks to Kevin Dettmar for his generous readings and advice, Brendan O'Neill for his celerity and acumen in guiding me through production, the production staff at Oxford University Press for their indefatigable work, and the anonymous readers of the manuscript for their impeccable insights.

This book is dedicated above all to my family. My parents, Britt and Alice Rogers, provided the model of unconditional, selfless support that I hope to follow throughout my life. Britt, Laura, Meghan, and Dustin have shown me patience and encouragement for years and have helped in more ways than they likely recognize. The same is true for my in-laws Debbie, Eric, Tracy, Pat, and Jordan. This entire task would have been empty were it not for my constant feeling that every piece of energy I put into it was somehow for Audrey—and now for Aiden, too. The fact that our family is an ever-present source of joy has, in short, made this worthwhile.

I am incredibly grateful to Don Luis Ignacio Marichalar de Silva, who has generously allowed me to quote and translate from Antonio Marichalar's many unpublished writings. I would like to thank the estate of Gerald Heard for permission to quote from his letters.

A version of chapter 2 appeared as "Joyce and the Spanish *Ulysses*" in *Modernism/modernity*. A portion of chapter 5 appeared as "1616, Bilingual Modernism, and Anglo-Spanish Literary History" in the *Journal of Modern Periodical Studies* 3:1. A version of the appendix appeared as "James Joyce in His Labyrinth," by Antonio Marichalar, trans. Gayle Rogers, in *Publications of the Modern Language Association (PMLA)*. I am grateful to each of these publications, and to Johns Hopkins University Press, The Pennsylvania State University Press, and the Modern Language Association of America, respectively, for permission to reprint or incorporate this material.

All translations, and their faults, are mine unless otherwise noted. Whenever possible, I refer to available English translations of the texts cited in this study; modifications are noted. I have silently emended Spanish words and names when quoting from Anglophone sources, and English words and names in Spanish-language sources, except when noted.

Modernism and the New Spain

Introduction: The Problem of Spain and the Cultural Map of Interwar Europe

> Spain is a grotesque deformation of European civilization.[1]
> —Ramón del Valle-Inclán, *Luces de Bohemia* [*Bohemian Lights*] (1920)
>
> In Spain the veil is torn.
>
> In Spain is Europe. England also is in Spain.[2]
> —Rex Warner, "The Tourist Looks at Spain" (1937)

When José Ortega y Gasset sought to draw figures from across Europe into the project of renovating in twentieth-century Spain Immanuel Kant's pioneering, yet problematic, vision of a continental community, he took up an enormous historical burden. In his typological study of national characters, *Anthropology from a Pragmatic Point of View* (1798), Kant groups Spaniards with Italians, Indians, and Chinese as people "who brood over revenge in their rage or are persistent in their love to the point of dementia." He writes that "the *Spaniard*, who arose from the mixture of European with Arabian (Moorish) blood," has a perilously "noble national pride" and an irrational devotion to his "ancient religion." But his even "worse side" is that

> he does not learn from foreigners; does not travel in order to get to know other peoples; remains centuries behind in the sciences; resists any reform;

is proud of not having to work; is of a romantic temperament of spirit, as the bullfight shows; is cruel, as the former *Auto da Fé* proves; and shows in his taste an origin that is partly non-European.

Kant draws on a centuries-old set of tropes of Spaniards as Europe's African contagion, marked by backwardness, sloth, vengeance, retrogressive Catholicism, and recalcitrant insularity. Furthermore, they can never be Kant's ideal cosmopolitans, for they have no "disinterested curiosity to get to know the outside world," and "still less to be transplanted there (as citizens of the world)."[3] For Kant, as for Hegel after him, Spain lies on the periphery of European modernity, in the past, beyond an enlightened awakening. These northern European images of Spain and of Hispanic peoples had been prevalent since the Black Legend of Spain's barbarisms during the Inquisition and the conquest of the New World, and they were revived around the time of the Spanish-American War of 1898, when Spain's once-mighty empire all but collapsed after a long decline. Just eight years later, the young Madrileño Ortega traveled to Germany for his postgraduate studies with the Neo-Kantian philosophers Hermann Cohen and Paul Natorp. For Ortega, who would soon become Spain's leading intellectual, this experience was the beginning of a decades-long, controversial venture to transform his unevenly developed native country into the locus for a new synthetic Spanish-European modernity. He would regenerate it into what he called the "New Spain," and would make his compatriots "citizens of the world," not by refuting Kant's denigrations or embracing Spain's African heritage, but by claiming the right to forge a cosmopolitan union from Europe's southwestern edge. The foundation of this sweeping project, which ranged from public philosophy and social pedagogy to periodical cooperations and book translations, was a transnational public sphere through which Spanish modernists could collaborate with their foreign counterparts. These included the partners they found among cosmopolitan, reform-minded British modernists, including T. S. Eliot, James Joyce, Virginia Woolf, Lytton Strachey, and Stephen Spender, who were working from multifariously connected spaces on the continent's various margins. Across several interlaced literary generations, two modernist movements—one based in Spain and the other in Britain, but stretching at important moments to the literary landscapes of Ireland and North and South America—joined one another in a largely overlooked effort of idealism and critique to revise a Europe in crisis through its notoriously paradoxical, inscrutable corner.

Modernism and the New Spain is an international literary and critical history of why the multifaceted "Spanish problem"—especially as Ortega framed and updated it—shifts our present-day understandings of modernism across languages and borders.[4] With this term, I mean to gather the profound stakes of several debates within Spain and beyond about whether or not the country should, could, or ever did belong to Europe. Ortega's ambitious endeavor to resolve these long-standing cultural questions through a Europeanizing modernist movement was at the heart of the explosion of creativity known as the *Edad de Plata* [Silver Age, 1898–1939], especially after the Great War. In this era, seen by scholars as the modern heir to the *Siglo de Oro* [Golden Age, roughly 1490s to early 1600s], when Spain was at the forefront of European culture, Ortega was a towering presence—the "Duke of this Renaissance," as a colleague dubbed him.[5] He provided a significant amount of the intellectual and material resources for imbricating domestic and foreign modernisms in a manner that necessitates a comparative scope to recover. This book reconstructs and analyzes an expansive archive of meditations on and defenses of the implications of a Spanish-European modernity as they were registered in multiform exchanges among Eliot, Joyce, Strachey, Woolf, and Spender, and Ortega and his colleagues, including Antonio Marichalar, Victoria Ocampo, Manuel Altolaguirre, and Federico García Lorca. This archive includes works in five genres—the novel, the biography, the public epistle, poetry, and the translation—and the interwoven journals, newspapers, philosophical essays, manifestos, and correspondence that remade all of them.

Excavating and interpreting this archive fully requires conceiving of these transformations (critical, creative, or otherwise) as robustly as these modernist figures did, understanding them as vitally engaged across spaces and media in ways that contemporary scholars have not explored completely. Thus, bringing together Anglophone and Hispanophone documents and criticism in each case, I begin by detailing the relationship between two Europeanist periodicals, the English *Criterion* (1922–1939) and the Spanish *Revista de Occidente* [*Review of the West*, 1923–1936] (chapter 1). Chapter 2 intertwines a close reading of *Ulysses* (1922) with an analysis of its circulation in Spain from the 1920s to the present. I compare and link Strachey's and Marichalar's biographical studies in the rapidly changing political contexts of post-monarchic, democratic Spain in chapter 3, then explicate in chapter 4, through a textual history of *Three Guineas* (1938), the international feminist cultural politics that Woolf developed with Ocampo. Finally, employing the mode of bilingual literary history exemplified by Altolaguirre's journal *1616: English and Spanish Poetry* (1934–1935), I argue in chapter 5 that *Poems for Spain* (1939) and the politics surrounding Spender's translations of Lorca represent a high point in the broad-ranging Anglo-Spanish defense of Spain's European culture that Ortega voiced. Taken together, these studies demonstrate that across Europe's traditional divisions of language, religion, ethnicity, and national history, writers in English and in Spanish depended on one another's politics, stereotypes, and, most important, peers and critics for their evolution and dissemination, entering into cooperative interchanges that were larger than any author, text, or movement.[6]

What makes these collaborations surprising are the ways in which they triangulated their shared work onto the third space of Europe. As Kant's characterizations make clear, Spain could not easily be reintegrated with the modern continent. The reciprocal dialogues among the writers in *Modernism and the New Spain*, moreover, blossomed when the notion of a unified political or cultural entity of "Europe" might have seemed dead (or at best dubious) in the wake of the Great War, which had, as Ezra Pound wrote, exposed a "botched civilization." These writers instead allied their modified sketches of Europe with the reemergence of Spain—as an actual or an imagined site—as the microcosm and the animating model for the regeneration of the ruined post-war continent. They interpreted and adapted one another's works as crucial documents not only in revising domestic cultures, but also in rebuilding an unsettled continent after the age of warring nationalisms and empires. This Europe and its letters would be rebuilt not in its familiar core, but from the political, racial, geographical, gendered, and other margins, many of which intersected in Spain. Throughout the interwar era, Spain's relationship to the continent was negotiated from within (Ortega, Marichalar, Lorca), from an adoptive imperial metropolis (Eliot), from another marginal European nation coming into being (Joyce), from the perspective of a feminist who "ha[s] no country" (Woolf), from the American periphery (Ocampo, Waldo Frank), from the view of witnesses to its fight against fascism (Spender, Altolaguirre), and later from England during World War II (Cyril Connolly) and from transatlantic exile (María Zambrano). Whether Spain represented the British empire's disruption of continental unity or global poetic freedoms threatened by the Spanish Civil War, these figures' agendas of provocative cultural politics were attached to the reconfiguration of Europe's universalisms around a New Spain. This Spain would be a liberal-democratic, post-imperial, multicultural, secular, pro-European site with a commitment to women's rights and vanguard arts—a dream that many hoped the Spanish Second Republic (1931–1939) would fulfill. In the process of Spain's rebirth, the local, the national, and the international would be reconceived, cohered, and revitalized together, through literary traffic across multidirectional pathways.

Since these authors did not tackle these questions or carry out their work in isolation, I make the case that the Spanish, British, and other associated Europeanizing modernist movements treated here are best understood as mutually constitutive.

Reinventing the continent *through* the New Spain meant fashioning connections among what Ortega called the "trinity of England, France, [and] Germany" and the amazingly heterogeneous "cultural awakening" in interwar Spain that the German humanist and comparatist E. R. Curtius described.[7] The reasons why Ortega and his circle looked to writers in Britain—seen as both a bastion of liberal democracy and a brutal, boorish empire—in their dual quest to Europeanize Spain and to Hispanize Europe perhaps are not intuitively obvious, nor are the reasons why Britons imagined Europe through a remote Spain and its cultural figures. The two countries had few long-standing literary relations, almost none among writers at the time, and each had strong, complex anti-European movements domestically, though for much different reasons. Their writers wedded their cultural authority and reputations to one another's, however, through a symbiosis between the production and the reception of texts. Literary histories have tended to privilege production, typically in a single language, but modernist cultural-political visions were lodged in formal techniques and in book reviews alike. Apparently oblique moments became presiding themes, paratexts became primary texts as writers drew on one another. That is to say, these writers transported the universalist elements and poetics of modernist texts, from *Ulysses* and *Three Guineas* to Lorca's *Poems*, to environments beyond their national, linguistic, and temporal origins. And this occurred dialogically but unequally, without balance between London and Madrid, for instance, in ways that implicitly hierarchical studies of influence, themes, origins, or similarities alone do not reveal. The lateral view of the material shapes of these emergent modernist formations in fact calls into question where one movement ends and another begins: Altolaguirre's *1616*, like several texts in this study, belongs simultaneously to both English- and Spanish-language literary modernisms, as they are generally figured.[8] Marichalar's essay/translation "James Joyce in His Labyrinth" is at once a reading of the affinities between Ireland and Spain that Joyce resurrects in his works and an adaptation of Joyce's Irish Europeanism to the burgeoning Spanish-European avant-garde. His text, in turn, further illuminates the alliances that Joyce posits in his novel as a post-imperial, transnational epic. Similarly, I argue that Eliot and Ortega used one another's reviews to authorize their own marginal national-Europeanist agendas, and that Ocampo's writings and activism extend, clarify, and amplify the stakes of the cosmopolitan feminism that Woolf ties to the Spanish Civil War.

The forms of collaboration and open-ended "authorship" employed in these texts ranged from conventional (such as mutual translations) to less studied forms, such as the reception of Lorca's works in England, which inspired debates on Spain's Europeanness during its civil war. To delineate these shifting linguistic, cultural, generic, textual, and geographical contours of British, Spanish, and European modernisms, I re-create the models of space and belonging, literary histories and international genealogies, intertextual exchange, and cross-cultural networks offered by the figures in this book. Cosmopolitan thought, with its sympathetic declarations of collectivity and supranationality, provided the common language and the sensibilities that brought them together. The writers treated in *Modernism and the New Spain* thus suffuse their works with an ethos that is captured best in Ocampo's public "Letter to Virginia Woolf": "By defending your causes, . . . Virginia, . . . I defend my own, too. . . . May my efforts join with others by all women, unknown or famous, working throughout the world."[9] Whether in the quest to form a "united European front" of cosmopolitan writers or the attempts of Britain's Auden Generation and Spain's Generation of '27 to express anti-fascist solidarity, modernist writers redefined Europe's cosmopolitan spirit not by detachment and distance, but by rescripting national identity to entail attachment and engagement abroad.[10] In a moment of the widespread politicization of culture in Europe, the writers in this book believed that literature, culture, and foreign cooperation were the spaces and means for critique, and that they could foster large-scale historical change in a way that party politics or state structures could not. As they did so, the shared cosmopolitanisms that originated uniquely in these Anglo-Spanish interchanges—as opposed to those with their French or German colleagues, for instance—fell between Eurocentric universalisms inherited from Enlightenment and twentieth-century postcolonial ideals of planetary justice.

In many cases, modernist periodicals, which thrived in Britain and in Spain and which factor heavily into this book, were essential media for transmitting these variegated flows of new literature and thought. They allowed writers to bridge cultural gaps by channeling their reformist collaborations throughout Europe, through its margins, and even beyond Europe, in places such as Buenos Aires or New York.[11] When Eliot wrote in 1930 of the groundbreaking partnership between his *Criterion*, Ortega's *Revista de Occidente*, and several other journals that shared staff writers and a circulation scheme, he employed the multivalent metaphor of "circulation." Such cooperation, he believed, had revived and "ke[pt] the intellectual blood of Europe" in healthy "circulation" among Europe's "higher community," which had disintegrated after the war.[12] His figure for the continent's "circulation" crosses the journalistic, biological, and intellectual realms, and it underscores my approach to an archive in which texts, ideas, and aesthetic practices traveled widely, expanding their "evolving radi[i] of literary action" across radically different contexts.[13] The reviews featured in this study—Eliot's *Criterion*, Ortega's *Revista de Occidente*, Ocampo's *Sur* [*South*], Spender and John Lehmann's

New Writing, Altolaguirre's *1616*, and Connolly's *Horizon*, to name a few—composed public spheres in which literary experimentation, translations, chronicles, and more converged fantastically. Woolf's claim that "literature is no one's private ground; literature is common ground. It is not cut up into nations; there are no wars there," captures this belief in the inherent transnationalism of texts.[14] In periodical spheres, domestic ventures also gained both their local and international prestige by trading on the currency of authorial reputations such as Joyce's or Ramón Gómez de la Serna's. As both privileged zones of intercultural contact and the mobile, constantly updated media of Spain's and Europe's rejuvenation, these reviews brought together the print spheres of these literary economies to record, whether in conversations on concepts such as "tradition" or in debates on the League of Nations, the vigorous discourses on Spain's possible modernity.

There was not univocality among the figures I treat, nor were all involved in Ortega's New Spain. Instead, the answers to the plans and calls for literary internationalism relied on the versatile labor of a loose, widespread corps of Hispanophilic Europeanists who served as intermediaries, including Curtius, Frank, Valery Larbaud, J. B. Trend, F. S. Flint, and Ricardo Baeza. These figures joined their peers in integrating a body of thought on "Europe"—however idealized or mythical that thought might have been—that nationalist rhetoric had provincialized. Their energy originated among a moderate, disaffected minority, and in the conflicts that I trace through each chapter, its diverse manifestations were pitted against the perceived anti-Europeanism of nationalism, imperialism, anti-liberalism, patriarchal capitalism, and fascism, respectively. Ortega's unfinished Kantian project, I argue, grew out of a critique of what he described in his first publication in English as "the most abnormal nation of Europe" to become a modernist vision of international arts and letters.[15] This vision forms the initial context for the works this book treats. These writers ask, in innovative ways, a prismatic array of interrelated questions: How could Ortega's vision of Spain as the "spiritual promontory of Europe, . . . the prow of the continental soul in the broad expanse of the globe," be enacted, revised, and challenged by colleagues and adversaries, both locally and abroad?[16] How might Europe and Britain be altered by an embrace of Spain, the internal Other against which the continent had defined itself, in this uncertain and unstable post-war moment? What are the implications of thinking of Spain not as Europe's problem, but as part of its solution for a new, amended unity? If Spanish culture were not "dead beyond resurrection,"[17] as a consensus of British scholars held, what role would its new writing, arts, and philosophy—in particular, its ties to its Anglophone counterparts—play in shaping the culture of a future Europe and its reconstructed nations? And what would become of Ortega's schematics and vocabulary over the course of an era in which, as the epigraphs above indicate, Spain underwent seismic changes and moved from the continent's forgotten sidelines to the center of debates over its soul during the Spanish Civil War? The archive of international modernisms and of interwar European modernity that developed around the responses to these questions brings into focus this era's struggles over the physical and metaphysical borders of Europe (historical and present), over the competing definitions of modernity and race between its north and south, over the imbalances of power between its "advanced" and "benighted" nations and their major and minor languages, and over the very status of culture and literature between two cataclysmically violent wars. This book argues that these modernisms must be recast critically in order to account for the conjunctions of complex reform movements that shaped one another and, ultimately, ended in failures that were ominous signals for the whole of Europe.

Spain, the Idea of Europe, and Modernist Literary History

While the revaluations of Anglophone modernist studies in the past two decades have produced rich studies of texts, practices, and ideologies as they were formulated and reformulated globally in Ireland, India, China, the Caribbean, Indonesia, the Pacific Rim, or various parts of Africa and Latin America, Spain remains, as it was for Kant, an ambiguous space on the scholarly map.[18] Important work to reconsider Spanish modernism internationally has come from scholars including Anthony L. Geist and José B. Monleón, C. Christopher Soufas, Mary Lee Bretz, Jordana Mendelson, Jessica Berman, José-Carlos Mainer, and Domingo Ródenas de Moya, all of whom have shown compellingly that Spanish writing indeed revises the predominantly Anglo-American critical narratives of the modernist era.[19] And they have demonstrated this by tracing, for instance, common intellectual and philosophical pursuits or influences, affinities among literary experiments, and the foreign artistic engagements of many Spanish figures—and by pointing out the flaws in prevailing conceptions of modernism that have excluded Spain. Spanish modernism, however, is still widely viewed by critics in Europe and the Americas as an object of study distinct from (and too often, belated, secondary, or derivative with regard to) its counterparts and as bounded essentially by the Spanish nation and the discipline of Hispanic studies.[20] English-language global modernist studies and Spanish literary history have not yet actualized their potential to recalibrate one another's bearings.

This book probes our critical sense of what Eliot called the "cultural map . . . of Europe" and asks why such maps have been drawn as they are.[21] The writers addressed here continually asserted that local spaces depend on the constant circulation of foreign ideas, texts, and cultural figures through them, that nation-states are pluri-national, multiethnic, multilingual, and always in flux. Anglo- and Hispanophone scholars have not looked far enough beyond traditional geographies to account fully for the critical histories built around authors from the other's language, from the 1920s to the present—whether Spanish readings of Strachey or British understandings of Ortega. To redress these gaps, *Modernism and the New Spain* moves beyond the nation-based, area studies–style approach to global modernisms common in Anglophone scholarship. Space—national and colonial spaces in particular—remains fundamental to this comparative literary history, but my aim is not to affirm Spanish modernism's place in European modernism (or to situate it in African, transatlantic, or other groupings to which Spain theoretically might belong); nor will I add its cultural productions to an implicitly Anglocentric sphere. I propose instead a set of fluid maps of modernist cultures derived from the interlocking constellations such as London-Madrid-Berlin or Dublin-Paris-Madrid that Ortega, Eliot, Ocampo, Frank, Joyce, Larbaud, and their peers projected around their sympathetic work. The cultural traffic among these and other sites expands the geographies of this book through converging critiques that alternately opposed or attempted to exist apart from the crises and political realities of the interwar era.[22]

Modernist writers inscribed their literary histories into international and translingual spheres of which Spain was a key component: the *Criterion* and the *Revista de Occidente* participated in a fiction competition across five European countries and languages; Marichalar placed Joyce, Proust, and Spanish Jesuit thinkers together in his "History of World Literature"; Ocampo worked with Waldo Frank to establish a bilingual pan-American literary tradition rooted in transatlantic thought; and *1616* traced Anglo-Spanish literary affiliations from early modern sonneteers to university students of the 1930s. Within these spheres, Madrid, for instance, was one of the incredibly vibrant, understudied sites of the "polycentric" modernisms that Susan Stanford Friedman has described, and yet all "centers" and all "modernisms" are not equal.[23] Not unlike spaces such as Russia, Turkey, or Greece, Spain was at once a vital *and* a marginal site for the renovation of multiple modernisms. It *de*-centers, displaces, defamiliarizes, challenges, and further pluralizes our ideas of the means by which modernism operated. Spain's European exceptionality both revises the maps of modernisms and grounds the heuristics and methodologies that this book employs. (Indeed, its presence alters the usual boundaries of "interwar literature" itself, as it was neutral in the Great War, and its civil war began in 1936.) Its archives also introduce new texts into consideration, aid in recuperating phenomena such as the international New Biography, and flesh out the ways in which modernists invoked the memories of Napoleon and his invasion of Spain, for one, whether as an archetype for modern tyranny or as a prototypical cause that rallied the British Romantics to Spain's defense.

Furthermore, twentieth-century Spain was, as revisionist historians have shown, both "an integral part of a European and international process [of modernization] and indeed a regional variant of that process," sometimes preceding the continent's trends (the decline of empire, the battle between fascism and communism), other times trailing them (secularism and social reforms, liberalism, modern education systems).[24] The country's relationship to Britain in particular—neither colony nor competing metropole, but a former imperial adversary now barely considered European—does not fit the typical paradigms given by global modernist studies. Their cultural relations bear out this transitional, in-between, and sometimes paradoxical portrait of its "semi-peripheral" status, in the terms of world-systems theory. Spain's literary relations with Britain had been uneven for some time: more British literature had been translated into Spanish than vice versa, for instance.[25] The disproportionate reciprocity between these literatures presented a challenge that writers inside and outside Spain foregrounded in the moment, when a considerable body of the Anglo-American imaginary still viewed Spain, in "Hispanist" fantasies, as a country with a "rickety monarchy, obscurantist clergy, and ... primitive bullfights, ... a twelfth-century holdover from the dark ages."[26] It was, moreover, "geographically and culturally remote from the mainstream of European life, ... inherently politically unstable," and "comic and incomprehensible ... inhabited by bomb-throwing anarchists and pistol-waving generals all readily disposed to revolution."[27] Even to putatively enlightened observers such as a *TLS* reviewer of Ortega's work, Spain was an unknowable "*cul-de-sac* of Europe and Africa."[28]

Spain's European marginality and its proximity to Africa have been geographical features that fed myths such as its allegedly sanguinary Catholicism and its "qualified Westernness" throughout its cultural history.[29] The writers studied here do not reject Eurocentrism wholesale; rather, this book intends to shift the Eurocentric balance of modernist studies by contextualizing and historicizing it through the changing notions of Hispanicity/*hispanidad* at the time. In the early twentieth century, "Europe" was identified most centrally with Paris, which does figure into this study. But "Paris," Ortega insisted after the war, "is an abstraction.... It is Nowhere, it is 'Utopia.'"[30] Europe could not be revived simply by reviving its long-time core; it had to be indelibly altered, and Ortega succeeded instead in convincing many of

Spain's leading intellectuals, writers, artists, and other vanguardists not to emigrate from the periphery to Paris—as Luis Buñuel, Salvador Dalí, and Pablo Picasso had, in addition to figures like Joyce and Stein—but, for the first time in generations, to remain in Spain and to Europeanize visibly their own capital, Madrid.

Somewhat ossified notions of "Europe" and its historical continuity, combined with post-Franco Spain's place in the continent, can obscure the degree to which, as Michael P. Iarocci writes regarding postcolonial historiography, modern Europe and its ideal *république des lettres* were "born out of the material and discursive defeat of early modern Spain," especially its humiliations by Britain and the Netherlands.[31] Spain had the distinctive heritage of having launched Europe's New World colonial era and having become the subject of denigrating tropes associated with colonialism's logic. The expanding countries and empires of northern, Germanic, and Reformed Protestant Europe defined and continually redefined both "Europe" and their own national characters, Roberto M. Dainotto has shown, against the "defective Europeanness" of their contracting southern, Latin, Catholic neighbors—Spain, Portugal, and Italy.[32] The French, many of whom still claimed that "Africa begins at the Pyrenees," often allied themselves with the Germans and British on this count. Voltaire famously commented that Spain may as well belong to the "savage parts of Africa," while Montesquieu's pseudo-scientific climatological reading of European characters offered a Hispanophobic account of the inferiority of France's southern neighbor.[33]

The New Spain, Southern Europe, and Kantian Cosmopolitanism

Ortega's reorientation of Europe's axes, his revision of its syncretistic heritage, and his acute attention to foreign representations of Spain offer an exemplary adumbration of the theoretical work necessary to envisage European modernisms through a network that featured Madrid. To a degree, the philosopher believed in the myths that had made northern Europe the ideal of progress and post-Renaissance modernity, and southern Europe the site of retrogression and anti-modernity. His first plan was to import this modern Europe into a backward Spain, replicating his intellectual path from his studies in Germany. Spaniards must "absorb" European culture, "swallow it whole," he wrote, and for him it was best represented not by the French arts that ruled in Spain, but by the "world" of German philosophy that he had "received."[34] The scion of a famous publishing family in Madrid, he founded the short-lived continentalist reviews *Faro* [*Beacon*, or *Lighthouse*, 1908] and

Europa (1910), both of which he used, along with daily newspapers, to translate and circulate this "world" throughout Iberia. The bar for his cultural renaissance was European modernity: "only seen from Europe is Spain possible," he insisted in 1910, "all of Spain's afflictions begin and end with this one word: . . . [Europe]."³⁵ And Europeans see Spaniards, he added, as "objects of ridicule."³⁶

While in Germany, Ortega had found Kant's *Critique of Pure Reason* "enormously difficult for the Latin mind." Though he called himself "a pure Celto-Iberian flame burning, glittering with enthusiasm in German universities," he always felt "rooted in Spain," writes his pupil Julián Marías. He never had "the illusion of . . . 'cosmopolitanism,' the illusion of the man who feels like a 'citizen of the world' because he could not escape his Hispanic origins," Marías explains.³⁷ This sense of racial and cultural difference was accentuated when he encountered Kant's exclusions of Spain from Europe's cosmopolitan community, though he sympathized to some degree with the characterizations. When he looked back to his distant mentor, Ortega, one of the most important modernist figures to engage Kant's work, saw that "Kant's *Anthropologie* contains an observation on Spain so profound and so true that it makes one shudder. Kant says that the Turks when they travel usually describe the character of a country according to its typical vice." They called Spain the "Land of ancestors," Ortega writes, for "those who have gone before continue to rule us and form an oligarchy of the dead, which oppresses us" (*MQ* 48). "We cannot follow tradition," he insisted; "on the contrary, we must go against tradition, beyond tradition, . . . [and] dominate the past" (*MQ* 106, 49). But Ortega soon realized that bringing German clarity, interiority, and rationalism alone to Spanish superficiality, exteriority, and confusion would not foster Spain's long-delayed Enlightenment.³⁸ His interrogation of Spain's past became a concomitant interrogation of the history of how the formative enunciations of Europe's division into "characters" had marginalized or excluded Spain.

The philosopher's public work evolved into a proposal of a new understanding of Spain and Europe as he came to see that the continent, even before the war, was in a perilous state itself. Northern Europe did not represent modernization, liberalism, and rationalism unproblematically; Germans had become "crude, philistine, and materialistic," absorbed with imperialism and opposed to the arts, he believed.³⁹ Europe's dominant modernity must be modified, he argued, and Spain has synthesized northern European and Mediterranean qualities *already*—with an additional "Celtic" character. Ortega writes that

> my thought . . . tends to combine all my ancestral heritage in one firm integration. . . . I am not Mediterranean only. I am not willing to confine myself

within the Iberian corner of myself. . . . Why does the Spaniard persist in living anachronistically within himself? Why does he forget his Germanic inheritance? . . . I try to make peace among my inner personalities and I urge them toward collaboration.

For Kant, the typical Spaniard's ethnic hybridity and his aversion to foreign influence excluded the possibility of his being a cosmopolitan European. For Hegel, the mixed German-Roman blood of Europe's Latin nations led to disharmony. Ortega sees Spain's "Germanic inheritance," brought by the Visigoths and sustained in contemporary Spaniards who embrace continental thought, in Italy and France, too; they are not "Mediterranean" only, but also are "steeped in Germanic blood."[40] Indeed, Ortega redraws the Germanic portraits of Spain and Europe by arguing that there was no real "Europe" until northern and southern characters combined politically, culturally, ethnically, and otherwise. Recognizing, recovering, and reanimating this heritage, he believes, is the first step toward creating a pan-European culture of which Spain would be an integral part.

Extending his critiques of Kant, Ortega posits that the German philosopher has defined modern man, but that his definition is incomplete. He has provided, that is, the most powerful philosophical revolution of the modern era and the one most in need of revision. "Modern man . . . is Western European, which is to say, more or less, Germanic [*germánico*]," Ortega writes. When Kant universalized his own Germanic perspective and being, he did not see that in "Southern Europe [*la Europa meridional*], the Germanic man has taken on a Mediterranean character."[41] This myopia is clearest, Ortega claims, in Kant's idealism, which the Spaniard took to be the pinnacle of the philosophical tradition of Europe's modern era. As a mode of inquiry and thought, Ortega argues, idealism "alone justifies . . . the existence of the European continent. . . . With great audacity and perseverance, during the past four centuries the Western white man has explored the world from an idealist's point of view," and yet he has not comprehended or accounted for his own (white, Germanic) body.[42] Ortega instead emphasizes a multiperspectival cosmopolitanism to account phenomenologically for racial difference. His best-known statement, "I am myself and my circumstances," is a pithy, early form of his theory of ratio-vitalism, which sought to overcome the mind/body split through a blend of (northern European) rationalist idealism with (southern European) vitalism grounded in embodied experience and perception (*MQ* 53, 45).

Ortega's task was to revise the revolution in thought that Kant initiated, following from the way in which the German philosopher had recast the notion of "life, which was classically conceived as an *adaptation* of the subject to the universe, . . . into the *reform* of the universe."⁴³ That is, Kant developed the abstract notions of justice and universality into principles through which Europe would achieve its "universal cosmopolitan condition" through a unifying "reformative revolution"—first of sensibilities, then of governments.⁴⁴ As Walter Mignolo notes, "when Kant thinks in terms of 'all nations of the earth,' he assumes that the entire planet eventually will be organized by the terms he has envisioned for Western Europe and will be defined by his description of national characters."⁴⁵ Ortega, who both incorporated and resisted Kant's thought throughout his career, underscores the necessity of overhauling Kant's static typologies and his principles alike when revising Enlightenment Eurocentrism. His ideal of free mobility across a European federation, or a "United States of Europe," as he would call it, was clearly Kantian in origins (*RM* 139). He saw modern Europe through Kant because "in Kantian criticism we contemplate the gigantic projection of the modern bourgeois soul that has governed the destinies of Europe increasingly since the Renaissance."⁴⁶ And the reformism posited as inherent in cosmopolitan sensibilities enabled modernist writers to detach intellectuals from imperialist and nationalist projects and to reclaim their Europeanist roots through a series of new alliances. This work continued as the writers featured in this book constantly rethought prevailing models of foreign affiliation, altering such elements as Ortega's pitting Europe against northern Africa in racialized terms (a move that Lorca, for one, would contest sharply) and his willful inattention to the Semitic or "Asiatic" heritage of Spain, to the diversity of the country's provinces, or to Latin America's ties to Iberia. Cosmopolitanism thus was mobilized to transform "Europe" into a liberatory political entity, but often with a failure to conceive of Europe in terms completely extricated from the exclusivity of the pre-war era.

Ortega in Public: The Reformist Critique and the Plan for a New Spain

The cultural moment of Ortega's reformism in Silver Age Spain was defined by the country's responses to the former empire's loss to America in 1898, known locally as "The Disaster," which intensified the centuries-old debates about *el Ser de España*, or the very nature, or essence, of Spain and Spanishness. There were bitter contestations among the competing plans for a future Spain, most of which shared a broad agreement that the country had been for some time in steep decline that was only worsening. Proposals for twentieth-century Spain included the possibilities of a powerful central Castilian state that dominated Catalonia, Galicia, Andalusia, and the other provinces; a resurgent empire of the pan-Hispanic race; a loose amalgam of autonomous, diverse states that embraced their extra-Iberian elements; a multicultural, socialist workers' state, or even a satellite of the Soviet Union; or a European liberal democracy guided by an intelligentsia, as Ortega would have it. The philosopher's program took hold at the same time that the writer and intellectual Ramiro de Maeztu, for instance, was achieving renown as an anti-liberal Catholic reactionary, and Ernesto Giménez Caballero's case for an Italian-style fascist state was gathering force.[47] To liberate his country from its "oligarchy of the dead," Ortega would have it turn neither inward nor outward, but both. Dissatisfied with the strategies of *regeneracionismo* ["regenerationism"] offered by his predecessors in the Generation of '98, the precocious young philosopher sparred with his one-time mentor Miguel de Unamuno—a major voice in the Europeanism debates—over the latter's turn toward mysticism and nativism. Ortega was angry and merciless in his domestic critiques, calling his country "invertebrate" and "a slum of humanity."[48] He urged his compatriots that Spain's only hope was to re-create the Europeanism of the Golden Age without a corollary neo-imperial or neo-colonial era, and without worshipping the national past. He positioned himself as the corrective to the Generation of '98, which had culminated "the gradual annihilation of Spain as a possibility" in Europe that had begun with the Counter-Reformation (*MQ* 106).

In the first half of 1914, just before the Great War, came Ortega's prominent public articulation of his plan for a New Spain. Ortega organized the new Liga de Educación Política [League of Political Education], a national party headed by over one hundred reformist liberal intellectuals, professionals, writers, and artists. In March, with his domestic stature beginning to peak, Ortega marked the founding of the League with an ambitious public address that garnered great national attention, "Vieja y nueva política" ["Old and new politics," 1914]. Here, he reframed the cultural debate on regeneration and modernity through the long-disputed question of *las dos Españas* [The Two Spains], and he did so in terms and metaphors that fit his ideals. The Two Spains—one reactionary and conservative, the other progressive and reformist—epitomized the country's cultural "conflict between tradition and modernity," writes Thomas Mermall, and inevitably brought into focus "the theme of Spain's relation to Europe, known as the project of *europeización*."[49] To be sure, this characterization was overly extreme and general, and was often unfavorable to the "old" side, but the language prevailed (in no small part thanks to a famous 1913 poem on the two Spains by Antonio Machado). Ortega capitalized upon it, placing himself at the forefront of the secularizing forces in Spain that the church long had suppressed. At only 30 years old, he exhorted his countrymen to dismantle Old Spain—"Official Spain," a vision of

Spanish nationality promulgated by the monarchic state of the Restoration and the electoral system of "organized corruption" rigged by the powerful politician Antonio Cánovas. Official Spain, he claimed, clings to *caciquismo* [bossism] and feudalistic religious and aristocratic traditions, "encompasses ... all organisms of our society, from Parliament to newspapers and from rural schools to universities," and is "an immense skeleton of a vanished organism." In place of that, Ortega argues, must come a "New Spain," which would be a "Vital Spain," a "spontaneous, diffuse, evolving organism of the nation ... [with] an interconnected network" of culture and society. Ortega appropriated this term (*Nueva España*) from the former empire's name for its New World holdings and infused it with his own sense of international social order. An elite, broad-minded vanguard would dedicate all of its "conscious, deliberate, and organic powers" to navigating between the "brains" and the fragmented body politic throughout Spain—to operating, as he would characterize it later, as neither political leaders nor priests, but as an "aristocracy organizing a *pueblo*."[50]

Drawing also on his readings of Renan, Ortega broadened Spain's public sphere and opened it to new European influences that had been foreclosed previously, bringing the bourgeois Madrileño (implicitly masculine) into contact with ideas that would expand his provincial sensibilities. A ubiquitous public figure, Ortega would spend decades working to expand this sphere—with its connections to the rise of liberal democracy in Europe implied—through his journals, newspaper columns, book series, lectures, university courses, *tertulias* [intellectual conversation groups], and education initiatives. He made his case by conducting philosophical "experiments on a new Spain" in his popular *Meditaciones del Quijote* [*Meditations on Quixote*, 1914], which appeared only two weeks before the outbreak of the war. A series of media initiatives followed: he launched the review *España* (1915) as the League of Political Education's official organ (financed with aid from liberal British investors), then his "one-man review" *El Espectador* (1916–1934), and then co-founded the Madrid daily *El Sol* in 1917. While serializing his works in these outlets, Ortega extended his critiques across to the continent: "I believe that in the whole of Europe, but more particularly in Spain, the present generation is ... derelict.... Our institutions, like our theatres, are anachronisms. We have ... lacked the courage to break resolutely with such devitalized accretions of the past."[51] The remedy, for Ortega, was to have his colleagues and his readers see themselves as invested in the same projects as their European peers, and thus to cohere them into an international vanguard. "To be English, German, or French," he later wrote, "is to be provincial.... Every 'intellectual' to-day ... feels suffocated within the boundaries of his country; feels his nationality as an absolute limitation" (*RM* 149, 146–147).

Spengler and the *Revista de Occidente*'s Cosmopolitanism

While Kant, who wrote in an era of incipient nationalisms, was Ortega's primary imagined German interlocutor, the Spaniard also engaged the thought of other Germans ranging from Dilthey and Simmel to Hegel and Heidegger. The one who partially inspired the *Revista de Occidente* was Oswald Spengler. In his *Decline of the West* (1918–1922), Spengler claims that writers and thinkers should no longer refer to a

> Continent of Europe . . . [or] draw an ideal frontier corresponding to the physical frontier between "Europe" and "Asia." The word "Europe" ought to be struck out of history. . . . [It is an] empty sound. . . . There is historically no "European" type, and it is sheer delusion to speak of the Hellenes as "European antiquity." . . . "East" and "West" are notions that contain real history.[52]

Spengler's pronouncement of the death of Europe reverberated across the continent, only gaining further traction after the war. The Great War had extended the pervasive debates between Spain's nativist *hispanizantes* and the continentalist *europeizantes*, and Ortega, decried for allegedly wanting to import German hegemony, was forced to contrast his controversial brand of Europeanism with what he deemed the naïve version of it that his forebears had proclaimed. He was forced to revise his own faith in the curative power of European thought for Spain, too. Europe and Spain both needed one another to redefine themselves, and they needed a new relationship for this. Worse still, Ortega feared that Spain might be read as the emblem of the death of Europe and the West. But while he felt some sympathy with Spengler's argument, the Spaniard found his prognosis for the demise of the West premature and finally unconvincing. His new periodical, the *Revista de Occidente*, would reclaim from Spengler both the life of the West and the integration of a new Europe through a Spanish synthesis that would remain at the root, even as the journal's interests eventually branched beyond Ortega's intellectual ambit, throughout the Americas, to Russia, and to the "East."

The *Revista de Occidente*, which figures centrally into the first three chapters of this book and into parts of the final two, was Ortega's broadest, most extensively collaborative, most internationalist, and final major periodical. The product of his life's work in cultural politics, as Evelyne López Campillo characterizes it, the *Revista* was also the most influential Hispanophone periodical of the interwar era.[53] The review's title signaled its challenge to Spengler: Ortega helped Manuel García Morente translate Spengler's *Decline of the West* into Spanish in 1923 as *La decadencia de*

Occidente. In his "Propósitos" ["Propositions," or "Purposes"] of the inaugural issue, Ortega foresees that the *Revista* in fact will rejuvenate in Spain "the most vital, most natural curiosity" among alert, active readers. Despite having been neutral in the war, Spain now feels the "post-war climate" of dread and hopelessness, even in its villages, he writes. He believes that his new journal, by cooperating with its European counterparts, will "efface . . . the old modes of existence," foster "the widespread germination of life" and "reveal the plane of a new architecture on which Western life [*la vida occidental*] is being reconstructed." Embracing the marginal vantage that Spain offered, the *Revista de Occidente*, he says, will "present to its readers the essential panorama of European and American life."

Tying together his critiques of Kant and Spengler, Ortega outlined his plan to wrest European cosmopolitanism back from oligarchs who had been masquerading in its supranational garb, and from those who used it as an epithet for stateless groups such as European Jews. The spirit of a new post-war cosmopolitanism will allow the *Revista*, in terms similar to Eliot's aspirations for the *Criterion*, "to tend to Spanish matters, but at the same time, . . . to bring to our pages collaborative work from men throughout the West whose exemplary words capture the interests pulsing in the contemporary soul." He argued against the logic that had allowed aristocrats in Britain and in Spain, for instance, to feel sympathy for their German peers during the war:

> Before the war, an internationalism of words and gestures existed—a deceitful, abstract cosmopolitanism that cancelled national peculiarities a priori. It was the cosmopolitanism of workers and bankers, of the Ritz Hotel and the sleeping-car. . . . But the cosmopolitanism of today is better, for instead of requiring us to abandon our characters and ethnic destinies, it recognizes and appreciates their engagement.[54]

While also castigating the League of Nations, Ortega offers a "complementary" vision of international harmony and cosmopolitan ethics—a critique of nationalisms as having corrupted Europe's integrity that many of his counterparts in this study shared.[55] Bringing cosmopolitan European sensibilities to Spain meant, for Ortega, that Spaniards must see their history and culture as much in the works of Proust, Goethe, Shakespeare, and Joyce as in Cervantes, St. John of the Cross, Góngora, Goya, and Lorca. Madrid would be part of a new pan-European periodical network and community, and as Germany moved toward fascism, Ortega emphasized that country's Europeanism less and his journal's version much more. Not only Spaniards like Ortega and Marichalar, but also E. R. Curtius, the English musicologist J. B. Trend, and a number of other figures believed that Spain should emerge from its second-class citizenship in the European republic of letters to become a *privileged* site for rethinking the continent after the Great War. To Trend, who plays a large role in chapter 1, Spain "seem[ed] not a country of war and lechery, but of a new Age of Reason."[56] The publisher Samuel Putnam, who disseminated Spanish works in translation, went so far as to write that the Great War, "for [Spain], removed the mental Pyrenees, made her a part of Europe" and thus ideal for representing "the after-War spirit in European literature" as expressed by a "new generation" of authors.[57] Recovering the history of such voices and visions reveals the means by which the stereotypical tourist's gaze was converted into sympathetic attachment across this era—by which ingrained "types" were transformed into model subjectivities for the future.

When Spanish modernism burst forth in a range of cultural and political journals, from the fascist *Gaceta Literaria* [*Literary Gazette*] to the communist *Octubre*, this project would be challenged on multiple fronts. An array of *casticista* [racial purists], nativist, nationalist, clericist, fascist, and other movements—many of them led by figures whom Ortega knew, whether as one-time colleagues or as adversaries—gained momentum and allied forcefully with one another throughout the 1920s and 1930s. These same figures, in fact, had rejected the arrival of the cosmopolitan Spanish American *modernismo* in Spain in the early 1900s. The hardening line encapsulated by the claim that Spain should embody "one faith, one baptism, one flock, one shepherd, one Church, one crusade, a legion of saints" manifesting "greatness" and national "unity" (from Marcelino Menéndez Pelayo, the nineteenth-century apologist for the Inquisition) proved a nearly intractable ideological opponent for Spain's secular Europeanists.[58]

Spain's New Europeanizers

Ortega himself focused sparingly on British literature, though he pointed out Kant's debt to English thinkers and linked it to England's capitalist development. Instead, he opened that door and many others, then pointed the way for his collaborators, through institutions and through media such as the *Revista de Occidente*. A resource of enormous depth and breadth, the *Revista* featured not only literature, philosophy, and criticism, but also biology, physics, sociology, psychology, history, archaeology, economics, and anthropology in its foreign intellectual commerce. Spain's brightest and most creative minds, who confronted and revised anti-European attitudes among their compatriots and dismissals of Spain abroad, worked with what Ortega characterized as an enlightened minority, including Joyce, Valéry,

Eliot, Borges, Curtius, Count Keyserling, and others across Europe and the Americas. To his student Benjamín Jarnés, Ortega represented a "living refutation of that part of the Black Legend which argued that Spain was culturally backward with regard to Europe."[59] The philosopher found fertile ground for his staff in a progressive Spanish university that figures into this book: Madrid's Residencia de Estudiantes [Students' Residence]. The first residential college in Spain, the Residencia opened in 1910 as a place where, as Amparo Hurtado Díaz writes, "to 'Europeanize' oneself was the keyword of the day."[60] Outside the control of church or state—except when future Spanish dictators would intervene—"the Resi," as it was known, provided young Spaniards with a new form of liberal, secular education. Spain's most pro-European and specifically Anglophilic center for thought, it was (and remains) a school modeled directly on Oxford and Cambridge, where its founders had studied the English educational system. The school, which added a Residencia de Señoritas in 1915, derived its reformist ethos from the sensibilities of the philosopher Karl Friedrich Christian Krause, himself a disciple of Kant. With extensive programs of cultural pedagogy, the Resi extended the work of Spain's famous Institución Libre de Enseñanza [Independent Institute for Instruction], which stressed the "individual's civic responsibility, and ... saw the diffusion of culture as the key to the transformation—and modernization—of society," Helen Graham and Jo Labanyi note.[61]

The college's aim, furthermore, was to inspire a "vanguard—believers and battlers—who believe in a lofty future mission of the Spanish spirit" and in "the New Spain."[62] It had a Spanish-English Committee, which worked to "promote stronger intellectual, artistic, and scientific relations between England and Spain and to foster friendship and sympathy between natives of both countries."[63] With funds from a joint venture between the Duke of Alba and Sir Esme William Howard, the school imported English culture through language and literature classes, arts and musical programs, even field hockey and rugby. Juan Ramón Jiménez, a champion of Anglophone literature and a future Nobel laureate, lived on campus, and Ortega sat on the board of the school. For years, Ortega also lectured and led symposia there, and his *Meditations on Quixote* was published by the school's press in its inaugural year. A great number of the leaders of the Second Republic and the artists of Spain's Generation of '27 attended the school, as did Dalí and Buñuel. In addition, the college not only attracted a number of foreign students (many of them from England and the United States) to study in Spain, but also brought its students into conversation with famous British and European writers, artists, speakers, and Hispanists. By the time of the outbreak of the civil war, the Resi had hosted on its campus H. G. Wells, G. K. Chesterton,

J. M. Keynes, J. B. Trend, Walter Starkie, Maurice Ravel, Igor Stravinsky, Leo Frobenius, Henri Bergson, Paul Valéry, Max Jacob, Louis Aragon, Le Corbusier, Walter Gropius, Marie Curie, and Albert Einstein (for whom Ortega served as interpreter). The personal associations and cooperations that began in the Resi emerged in periodicals, collections of poetry or essays, and a number of critical projects.

The most crucial intermediary among the Spanish, British, and European modernist cultures featured in this book, and one who was in part a product of the Resi, is Antonio Marichalar (1893–1973). A writer for both Ortega's and Eliot's reviews and a fabulously connected figure throughout the interwar European republic of letters, Marichalar carried out paradigmatic work of modernist internationalism. He believed that the critic must perform an act of "re-creation [*recreación*]," he must "re-create . . . the artist;" and he published in Spain the first commentaries on most every major figure of Anglophone modernism, then translated texts by Joyce, Strachey, Woolf, and Faulkner into Spanish.[64] Though among the finest literary critics, essayists, and biographers of the period, Marichalar has been "unjustly forgotten" in contemporary Spanish literary history, Francisco Javier Díez de Revenga notes, due to his turn to the political right in the late 1930s.[65] His *Criterion* colleague Charles K. Colhoun called his work "trans-Pyrenean," and those contemporary critics who have begun to recover Marichalar's work have seen him as a "double-agent between Spain and Europe" and the "European ambassador of his Generation of '27 colleagues."[66] Marichalar became the internal historian and spokesman of '27—a "Consul of the most harmonious literary republics" [*Cónsul de las más entonadas Repúblicas literarias*], as a colleague called him, who helped make modernism global.[67]

The interwar projects treated in this book stretch across four decades of volatility in Spain, which included bloody clashes in the provinces and between rising leftist and rightist movements, a constantly teetering economy, General Miguel Primo de Rivera's intensely Nationalist, Catholic, and proto-fascist military dictatorship (1923–1930), a botched neo-imperial conquest, the declining grip of a powerful church, the arrival of a post-dictatorial and post-monarchic liberal democracy (the Second Republic, 1931–1939), a civil war with grand international stakes, and in 1939, the beginning of the Franco regime, which jailed or exiled many leading writers. These projects are punctuated by failures that accompanied their moments of success; there are ruins on either side of this study, with a trail of hopeful yet unfulfilled formulations of "the new" and "the reconstructed" between them. In fact, Ortega's grand hopes for Spain's European renaissance were dimmed just two issues into his new *Revista de Occidente* when Primo de Rivera staged his coup.⁶⁸ My engagements with Spanish political history are meant to provide a background to the gaps in Anglo-Spanish literary and cultural relations that persisted through the period of Francoist autarky and into the present—a present that has seen Spain, in 2007, pass a law of historical memory of Franco's crimes. The transnational spaces that Eliot, Ortega, their peers, and their intermediaries created between the wars were contested from all sides, domestically and abroad, in pointed cultural conflicts. The possibility of these spaces as new cultural maps of the continent finally collapsed under the pressure of civil war and another World War, and the Europe that these writers imagined would not exist in most of their lifetimes. In fact, Eliot, writing in 1939, looked back on the immediate post–Great War moment with none of the optimism he previously held, calling the 1920s "a period of illusions[,] . . . the last efforts of an old world, [rather] than the first struggles of a new."⁶⁹

A political-economic version of a supranational Europe has come into being only recently with the contemporary and still evolving European Union. Gerard Delanty and Chris Rumford note that when Spain joined its predecessor, the EEC, in 1986, "in a similar way [to the case of Ireland] the Spanish Prime Minister, Felipe González, declared on the occasion of the fiftieth anniversary of the beginning of the Spanish Civil War that the civil war was history and Spain had become 'European.'"⁷⁰ That such a transition was finally valorized in Spain reflects not only a reshaping of Spanish sensibilities, but also a reshaping of twentieth-century cultural memory, by which Spain became included within Europe rather than viewed as an exception to it. As I detail in my conclusion, María Zambrano's "requiem" for the Second Republic, *Delirium and Destiny*, composed over the course of four decades, was honored in a European writing competition because it told a story of Europe in the twentieth century that was deemed "universal." The interwar dialogues analyzed in this book return to a transitional moment in Spain's European path, one in which Woolf's Bloomsbury colleague Gerald Brenan could write that "Spain is a miniature Europe," in which W. H. Auden could write human history into the country in his "Spain," and in which Trend could declare that "what was lost in the [civil] war was not merely a government, but a whole modern culture."⁷¹ Yet at the same time, this was a moment in which the inherited European universalisms of the modernist moment persisted alongside their revisions, and inconsistencies, contradictions, and disagreements over notions of Spanish modernity were plentiful among my subjects. "My country's destiny was . . . an enigma," Ortega wrote with resignation, "perhaps the most puzzling one in European history."⁷²

Organization and Argument

Because the Spanish writers and contexts I treat are no doubt less familiar to Anglophone scholars, *Modernism and the New Spain* has a bibliographical and topographical quality, and a number of the texts under consideration happen to be available in English translation for interested scholars who do not read Spanish. The first two chapters of this book deal with plans for a New Spain, the third with its possible constitution (and a generation's disillusion with it) in Spain's long-awaited liberal state, and the fourth and fifth with the Republic's war and defeat. Chapter 1, "An Anglo-Spanish Vanguard: The *Criterion*, the *Revista de Occidente*, and the Periodical Project of the New Europe," details the collaborations between these two reviews that eventually led to their joining a pan-European writing contest in 1929 within a network of modernist periodicals. The story of how Eliot's and Ortega's reviews came to align with one another originates in both editors' desire to unite an elite international vanguard of disinterested writers and thinkers. I analyze the ways in which the *Criterion* and the *Revista de Occidente* promoted often unpopular Europeanizing cultural politics in England and in Spain, and did so in part by crafting their critical voices around one another and around the writers and histories of the other's nation. Largely outside the expertise of either editor, these Anglo-Spanish journalistic relations were created by the translators and correspondents they employed: Marichalar, Curtius, Trend, Flint, Larbaud, Baeza, and others. The cosmopolitan attachments to Spanish literature and culture in the *Criterion* and to British modernism in the *Revista de Occidente* proved key to both reviews as they disseminated their own marginal continental visions and combated fatalistic arguments about Europe and the West. In fact, against the history of Spain's characterization by northern Europe—Kant in particular—the new cultural expressions of Spain's "Moorish" blood were actually invoked in *defense* of these redefinitions of Europe.

For both periodicals, James Joyce was a paradigmatic writer of the new Europe, and both treated him at length. In my second chapter, "Joyce and the Spanish *Ulysses*," I incorporate insights from Anglophone and Spanish criticism on *Ulysses* (1922) since the 1920s as a means to analyze the affinities that Joyce posits between the marginal states of Ireland and Spain, both of which were in upheaval at the moment the novel was published. These narratives in *Ulysses*, in turn, model the very symbiotic regeneration of Ireland and Spain that Joyce's first Spanish critics imagined. *Ulysses* also greatly influenced a contemporaneous generation of writers who, under dictatorship, were searching for non-statist forms through which they might express a new, more cosmopolitan Hispanicity. In the context of Spanish *regeneracionismo*, their cultural politics also highlight the critical narratives embedded in Joyce's novel about Ireland and Spain's shared histories and futures. These include the decline and suffering of both countries at the hands of the British empire, their being seen as Africanized and barbaric by Europeans, and their belonging to Joyce's sketch of a post-imperial Europe. The rising scholar Marichalar's brilliant essay/biography/translation "James Joyce in His Labyrinth" (*Revista de Occidente*, 1924) was an important document in interwar Spanish modernism and is a central text for this chapter (reprinted in the Appendix). Marichalar not only creates a vast, cosmopolitan genealogy of Joyce's interior monologues, but also makes Molly speak Spanish in short fragments, in an adaptation that predates and contrasts Jorge Luis Borges's better-known effort. By integrating Joyce's cosmopolitanism with Ortega's, Marichalar positions the exilic Joyce, who was initially condemned by Galician nationalists for being insufficiently "Irish," as a liberal-humanist Catholic member of a new "minor" European avant-garde that Ortega was forming. These alliances are captured novelistically, I contend, when Joyce places Leopold and Molly Bloom—the latter was born in Gibraltar to a Spanish mother—alongside one another as prototypes of a renewed European subjectivity.

My third chapter, "Lytton Strachey and *La nueva biografía* in Spain: Avant-garde Literature, the New Liberalism, and the Ruins of the Nineteenth Century," considers one of the greatest successes of the cross-cultural dialogues I treat: the interwar wave of the New Biography, which emerged in Spain as *la nueva biografía* during the country's liberal moment. In the years of *la nueva biografía* (1928–1934), a fantastic array of Spanish authors, both famous and undiscovered, produced what have been called "vanguard biographies" in experimental, impressionistic styles inspired both by Strachey's *Eminent Victorians* and by revolutions in interwar Spanish fiction. The *Revista de Occidente* and its book press were the primary media for theorizing and publishing these texts. I read Marichalar's remarkable, entertaining biography, *The Perils and Fortune of the Duke of Osuna* (1930), as a reworking of Strachey's critiques of nineteenth-century imperialism and hypocritical liberalism. Further enacting the modernist break with the previous century, Marichalar, after translating Strachey, builds in his own work an irony-laden portrait of Spain's historical failures around his demystifying account of the life of a notorious aristocrat who ruined the wealth and the name of one of Spain's most famous families. *Osuna* was published, too, during the final days of Spain's period of dictatorship and monarchy, stretching through the founding of the pro-European Spanish Second Republic in 1931. At this moment, when Ortega encouraged his compatriots to "vomit entirely Spanish history" since the collapsed First Republic and to "reconstruct" their state, Republican reformers looked both within and beyond Spain in their attempt to establish Europe's most progressive democracy.[73] Avant-garde authors who were part of this "new liberalism," as it was called, adapted the cosmopolitan genre of the New Biography in order to remake a state seen by the continent as hopelessly feudalistic. This concatenation of forces that produced *Osuna* registers a turning point in the commingled literary, cultural, and political histories of Britain and Spain.

Ortega's personal presence in this study fades in the 1930s, and his cosmopolitan vision of Europe moves outside Spain in chapter 4, in which I map a feminist geography grounded in the collaborations between Victoria Ocampo and Virginia Woolf. "Virginia Woolf and the Spanish Civil War: *Three Guineas*, Victoria Ocampo, and International Feminism" takes as its point of departure Woolf's plan to "fight . . . English tyranny" in response to the death of her beloved nephew Julian Bell in the Spanish war. She attempts to illuminate in *Three Guineas* the connections between fighting Spanish fascism and dismantling the English patriarchal system. I outline the ways in which Woolf, within an acrimonious and politicized British literary culture in the 1930s, comes to envision an intellectual space for cosmopolitan feminism and to attach it to Spain's war. In doing so, she models the literary-political critiques and activism of her colleague Ocampo, the *gran dama* of Argentine letters with whom she conversed about fascism and masculinity as she composed *Three Guineas*, and an overlooked feminist editor and financier of modernism. Ocampo first read Woolf's works in the *Revista de Occidente*, then extended both Ortega's Europeanism and Woolf's feminism when she founded her review *Sur* in Buenos Aires in 1931. She continually reconsidered Woolf's work and employed the form of the public epistle, marshaling her English colleague's feminism to fight battles far beyond those that Woolf conceived in her essay-letters. I follow Ocampo's work through Argentina's "Infamous Decade," through her work with the North American writer Waldo Frank, a friend of Ortega, through her series of autobiographical *Testimonios* (1935–1977), and finally through her dissidence and imprisonment during Juan Perón's regime. Ocampo's work, I argue, in turn illuminates further the stakes of Woolf's claim that "as a woman my country is the whole world."[74] Ocampo animated the cosmopolitan feminism that Woolf articulated, and their common ideals and common organicist metaphors were staked in the 1930s to the survival of the Spanish Republic—the last, endangered hope for a European New Spain and its women.

My final chapter, "Spain in Translation and Revision: Spender, Altolaguirre, and Lorca in British Literary Culture," examines the efforts of Stephen Spender, Manuel Altolaguirre, and their associates to create a European anti-fascist poetic community for which the bonds between the Auden Generation and the Spanish

Generation of '27 would be central. The frames for this work are the claims by Ortega, in several articles in English, and Altolaguirre, in his journal *1616: English and Spanish Poetry*, that England and Spain shared a unique history that compelled cooperation; the attempts, led primarily by Spender, to channel Spanish voices of the conflict through British literary culture; and the battles over the political and cultural significance of Lorca's assassination. Misunderstandings across cultures were plentiful: Ortega's plans for the New Spain did not align with the realities of the Republic, yet the *Times* deemed him "the oracle of the Republic." Lorca refused to join the Communist Party, yet some in Britain read him as a martyr for the international communist cause. In fact, Spender, one of Lorca's earliest translators, found himself defending his view of the Spaniard's mutable, populist figure against its misappropriation. With the aid of two Spanish collaborators, Spender influentially characterized him instead as an apolitical Spanish-European poet, and with John Lehmann, he edited the volume *Poems for Spain*, which intercalated British and Spanish voices on the war. At the same time, while *Poems for Spain* evinces the mutual influences of two literary generations, its publication in March 1939, when Franco's victory was ensured, made it an elegy for the lost Republic. The awkward and ultimately failed literary endeavors taken up in this chapter underwent significant revisions—from Spender's alterations to his poem "To Manuel Altolaguirre" and his re-editions of Lorca's *Poems* to the fascist poet Roy Campbell's re-readings of Lorca's figure in his own translations—that highlight the transformations in understandings of Spain that, in actuality, spanned the interwar era and beyond.

I extend the trajectory of this final chapter in a brief conclusion that considers two cases—one journalistic, one lived—of the consequences for my narrative of Franco's victory and the outbreak of another World War. After this stark disruption, Cyril Connolly in his journal *Horizon* (1940–1949) and Ortega's student María Zambrano in her *Delirium and Destiny* reflect on the unfinished international literary work that their modernist forebears began. As they pick up the themes of displacement and historical memory from two converging perspectives, one in London and one in Latin American exile, both see Spain as a synecdoche for the failure of European writers and intellectuals to prevent another war. My history of the formative, mutual influences of British and Spanish literatures ends with the shadow cast by World War II over the optimistic cosmopolitanism of the post–Great War moment that the figures in this study finally could not sustain—indeed, that was faltering and under attack from all sides from the start.

1. An Anglo-Spanish Vanguard
The Criterion, *the* Revista de Occidente, *and the Periodical Project of the New Europe*

> The Spaniards of to-day have done a real service to Europe. By remaining neutral they have not only saved their country, but they have preserved more of the European spirit . . . than any other of the belligerent peoples. . . . The European view of life and its values . . . is more alive to-day in Spain than in most other countries.
>
> —J. B. Trend, *A Picture of Modern Spain* (1921)[1]

> The Russian Revolution has made men conscious of the position of Western Europe as (in Valéry's words) a small and isolated cape on the western side of the Asiatic Continent. And this awareness seems to be giving rise to a new European consciousness . . . [and] reaffirmation of the European tradition.
>
> —T. S. Eliot, "A Commentary," The *Criterion* (1927)[2]

In 1929, T. S. Eliot's *Criterion* and José Ortega y Gasset's *Revista de Occidente* embarked enthusiastically on a shared circulation scheme built around a new international literary competition. E. R. Curtius devised this plan, in which one piece of short fiction would be selected by a jury to be translated and published simultaneously in five different reviews, each from a different nation and language, across Europe: the *Criterion* (England), the *Revista de Occidente* (Spain), the *Nouvelle Revue Française* (France), the *Nuova Antologia* (Italy), and the *Europäische Revue* (Germany). When describing the contest in the *Revista*, Ortega writes that entries both "must be deeply rooted in the author's native land" and "must have a European scope. . . . Preference will be given to works that . . . manifest the profound tendencies of our epoch." His phrase, "las tendencias profundas de nuestra época," echoes the "estado de espíritu característico de nuestra época" with which he introduced the aims of the *Revista* in its "Propósitos." He stresses, furthermore, that the judges will "underscore and ensure the European character of this experiment."[3]

In January 1930, Eliot announced to *Criterion* readers the first winner, Ernst Wiechert's "The Centurion," by commenting:

> we take particular pleasure in the inception of this form of international activity.... We remark upon it still more as visible evidence of a community of interest, and a desire for co-operation, between literary and general reviews of different nations, which has been growing steadily since 1918, and which is now much more pronounced than at any time before the war as to be almost a new phenomenon.

For Eliot, the "phenomenon" of this periodical project promises to cohere a new "community" of post-war writers, thinkers, and critics invested in rebuilding Europe's culture amid the still-visible devastation of the Great War. He continues by claiming optimistically that "perhaps the most significant thing about the War is its *insignificance*." What follows are some of Eliot's most sweeping and intriguing comments of the interwar era on the possibility of a post-nationalist Europe:

> All of these [five] periodicals, and others, have endeavoured to keep the intellectual blood of Europe circulating through the whole of Europe; and perhaps at no time during the nineteenth century was this circulation as healthy as it is now. It is of vital importance that the best thought and feeling of each country of high civilization should be contributed to the others while it is still fresh. Only so can there be any direction towards that higher community which existed in some ways throughout the middle ages, which persisted into the eighteenth century, and which was only dissolved finally after the Napoleonic wars. And without such intellectual community and co-operation of different organs in one body all peace pacts, world congresses, disarmament discussions, and reform leagues appear merely to be concerned with the body and not with the soul.[4]

Eliot places immense faith in the power of exchanges among Europeanist periodicals that represent their nations to reconstitute the multifarious "circulation" of the continent's "higher community." Ortega shared this faith wholeheartedly, seeing this moment as the best opportunity for Spain's reemergence as the "country of high civilization" that Eliot mentions. The work of creating this imagined "Europe" after the nationalisms born of Napoleon's era prospered during the 1920s in a host of periodical transactions, debates, and extensive polylogic forums among sympathetic foreign voices, and it would ideally culminate in this competition.

To understand fully what such a competition signified to Eliot, Ortega, and their colleagues—why it held such promise at this moment—is to understand how they believed their heterogeneous and multiply-authored modernist periodicals could inscribe their nations into a European culture that many English and Spanish writers had resisted.[5] But a study of this topic leads very quickly onto others that highlight several blank spaces in existing literary histories of interwar modernism. The archive of the *Criterion*'s and the *Revista de Occidente*'s near-simultaneous origins, rises, and convergence, and their dialogues, which crossed various discursive spaces—essays, translations, chronicles, letters, columns, reviews, and institutional archives in Madrid—remains largely neglected by scholars.[6] Through these periodicals, both Eliot and Ortega engaged in open-ended projects that were bigger than themselves, their own respective Francophilic or Germanophilic ideas of "Europe," or even the pages of their journals alone. These projects required extensive domestic and foreign collaborations to create a material base for an intellectual community, an interconnected public sphere for which London and Madrid were critical nodes. Here, Eliot and Ortega were key architects, publishers, moderators, and occasional interveners. They provided schematic vocabularies and compatible, intersecting cosmopolitan sensibilities; their own positions were influential, not definitive—and at times, were contradicted by their personal retreats into conservatism. The effect of their reviews' interactions was to ally with one another in order to reclaim the power of cosmopolitan thought and to foster the creation of a new trans-European generation of vanguard writers and intellectuals.

I present here a chapter in Anglo-Spanish literary history, one in which dynamic, shifting, and complex reformulations of interwar English, Spanish, and European cultures were proposed to provocative ends. The interchanges here were enabled by a cooperative European project that, within the vast and highly competitive landscapes of interwar print cultures, is only legible through certain periodical media. My account proceeds in two parts: the first details the ways in which the *Criterion* and the *Revista de Occidente* authorized their marginal Europeanisms around one another, as they worked to revise the reigning taxonomies and divides that classified national literatures. They did so by drawing reciprocally and surprisingly on one another's cultural politics, on England's and Spain's historical relationships with the continent, and, most important, on the works of English and Spanish writers whom they saw as writing new supranational, European fiction. The *Criterion* invested its sense of a cosmopolitan Europe in Ortega's New Spain and its literature as signals of the future direction of the "older European nations."

The *Revista de Occidente*, meanwhile, used the modernist movement to which Eliot's journal was central as a means of attaching its own vanguard writings to those of the reformed continent. For both periodicals, the duality and tension between national and continental projects, whether literary or periodical, is precisely what made one another matter. Both argued, that is, that reformed national literary histories must be developed—can *only* be developed—in cooperative, anti-nationalist continental contexts. In the latter half of this chapter, I analyze across both reviews the capacious set of conversations on the modernist project of refashioning Europe and the West around revisionary views of Spain and, later, England. These conversations proceeded by asserting the rebirth of Spain in Europe by way of excavating its past, analyzing its present (particularly as the *Revista* revealed it), and then recasting Europe through Spain's exceptionality. Spain's "Moorish" past both complicated these efforts and confounded the easy slips between "Europe" and "the West" that both editors make.[7] Yet, by the late 1920s, Spain's historical syncretism, its contact with Islam, and its marginal geography—the very elements that disqualified its Europeanness for Kant—were invoked in both the *Criterion* and the *Revista* in *defense* of their redefinitions of future continental and Western cultures. As this periodical "Europe" expanded around Spain, the questions of where the post-war continent would be made and who would make it motivated the shared task that these reviews engaged. But like the fiction competition, which dissolved after the prize was awarded only once, this task was unevenly successful and remained ultimately unfinished.

An "Unborn Quarterly of Unknown Qualities": The *Criterion*'s Europe

With rising domestic influence and international profiles in the early 1920s, both Eliot and Ortega believed that the post-war moment was what the former called "a hopeful period in the world of letters" for remaking the continent's culture, and it was this wide-ranging project that led them to one another's periodicals.[8] The bold plans with which Eliot launched his review give fuller context to his retrospective comment that 1922 was "the beginning of [his] adult life," marked by three interrelated events: not only the publication of *The Waste Land* and the foundation of the *Criterion*, but also "the development of relations with men of letters in the several countries of Europe."[9] These "men of letters" came to include Ortega not because Spain was Eliot's central focus in Europe. Eliot needed the help of others, both in England and abroad, to ensure that the *Criterion* would embody a "mind of Europe" that went beyond the collage of European traditions gathered at the end of *The Waste Land*. The roots of this undertaking ultimately lie in his migration to England in the mid-1910s and the readings of national and continental cultures that he offered there. When the American-born poet arrived on London's literary-journalistic scene, he established himself as a provocateur on a quest to "disturb and alarm the public" by praising continental writers such as Baudelaire and Laforgue over Kipling and Bennett.[10] (Ezra Pound's *Catholic Anthology* [1915], which included Eliot's "The Love Song of J. Alfred Prufrock," caused the critic Arthur Waugh to fear that these upstart Yankees were "bent on destroying English tradition."[11]) London's insularity and its resistance to non-native literatures at the time are well-known;[12] Eliot accused "literary London" of "cowardice, . . . a lack of ambition, laziness, and refusal to recognize foreign competition," and he found no literature "worthy of mention" there.[13] Proudly viewing London as culturally distant from Europe, the reigning critics such as J. C. Squire (of the *London Mercury*) and Edward Marsh (the leading voice of the Georgian school) thus balked at Eliot's audacious insistence that England, as he would explain, was not merely a "Saxon" or "Teuton" country, but also "a 'Latin' country"—and that "*all* European civilisations are equally dependent upon Greece and Rome—so far as they are civilisations at all."[14]

Eliot famously adumbrated the view of literary history and contemporary craft that would provide a structure for the *Criterion* in "Tradition and the Individual Talent" (1919). His syntax elaborates this vision when he emplaces England in a European context: he imagines his ideal poet as having an "idea of order, of the form of European, of English literature," and of writing "with a feeling that the whole of the literature of Europe from Homer and within it the whole of the literature of his country has a simultaneous existence and composes a simultaneous order."[15] But England could overcome its prevailing provincialism by awakening to its European roots only if Europe realized its English heritage, too, he believed. Such a cultural synthesis could create in London the cosmopolitan environment that he imagined inhabiting when he called himself a *metic*, by which he meant "a foreigner" who is at home as a "resident alien."[16] Calling to mind Ortega's grappling with his feeling of racial difference during his German studies, the term *metic* underscores Eliot's work through the *Criterion* to develop locally a culture in which a figure from the former colonial periphery might feel nourished by the expansive (and still expanding) European literature that he traced back through Dante to Virgil and Homer. A writer thus might find his "final perfection" and "consummation" by becoming "a European—something which no born European, no person of any European nationality can become."[17] It was ultimately "immaterial" for Eliot "whether English literature be written in London, in New

York, in Dublin, in Indianapolis, or in Trieste," so long as it was not bounded by the nation.[18]

Eliot, who by the early 1920s had held positions at leading periodicals, increasingly believed that these media would be ideal for creating a two-way channel between "the most enlightened part of the British public" and the writers of Europe's "higher community." He wrote to Valery Larbaud of his disappointment that London had "no literary periodical of cosmopolitan tendencies and international standards."[19] Thus, when avant-garde journals including the *Egoist*, *Art and Letters*, and *Coterie* folded, the anxious first-time founder/editor planned his "unborn quarterly of unknown qualities" for an October 1922 debut.[20] Pound, who had spent several years trying to transform England's literary culture, had just given up and left for Europe. "I cant see that England deserves a good review," he wrote to Eliot upon learning of his plan to found one.[21] Undaunted, Eliot sketched out his new *Criterion* as a review that would feature writers from across the continent who had not yet been published in English, but whose work, he claimed in an Arnoldian spirit, "ought to be known in England."[22] (He later boasted that "Marcel Proust, Paul Valéry, Jacques Rivière, Ramon Fernandez, Jacques Maritain, Charles Maurras, Henri Massis, Wilhelm Worringer, Max Scheler, E. R. Curtius, and more" appeared for the first time in English in his journal.[23]) At the same time, the *Criterion* would export the newest, best, and most innovative works from England with the aim, as Ronald Bush writes, of "affect[ing] the course of European sensibility."[24] All the while, Eliot was wary of importing literature that might incite nationalist and imperialist sentiments among domestic readers. Europe had been fractured, he wrote, by the belligerent and "artificial nationalities" of his era, along with "mistaken and artificial internationalism," "socialist internationals," and "capitalist cosmopolitans." These categories of collectivity—and for Eliot, literary history—must be replaced now by cooperative and "complement[ary]" national voices, ones that allowed for the expression of national particularity in a way that abutted one another in their work to reconstruct a European cultural identity that was a "harmony of different functions."[25] As he claimed in somewhat utopian terms when advertising the *Criterion*, the "intellectual life of Europe, like its economic life, depends upon communication and exchange."[26]

Eliot outlined the *Criterion* as a periodical with an austere, reserved design, no opening manifesto, very few advertisements, no graphics, long pieces of criticism and fiction, and minimal editorial apparatus to aid readers in understanding its difficult material—all in service of speaking to a highbrow audience. It would also include extensive reviews of contemporary literature, drama, speculative pieces or meditations on culture, religious (mostly Christian) essays, experimental and neoclassical poetics, translations, and other works mostly on the arts and humanities of Europe's past and present. The *Nouvelle Revue Française*, which had been the paradigm for European reviews since its founding in 1908, was his model here (as is apparent even in their similar covers), more than any existing English publication.[27] Allowing for a greater continental span and contemporaneity of topics were features such as the *chroniques*, much like Eliot's own "Lettres d'Angleterre" for the *NRF* in 1922–1923, which would inscribe new hotbeds of literary and intellectual activity into the *Criterion*'s cultural map. Convinced that "the hope of perpetuating the culture of any country lies in communication with others,"[28] Eliot wanted reports on the most important "literary and other artistic events from various foreign capitals: Paris, Berlin, Rome, Madrid, New York . . . [from] someone who is on the spot and active in [the city's] life"—preferably a native.[29] He had some initial success in finding such figures, though this work was incomplete: French, German, Italian, and American contributors were readily available, but Madrid's inclusion in his list (and others, like Amsterdam and Zürich, which came later) presented more of a challenge. Similarly, Eliot sought to establish review exchanges with other leading and sympathetic journals across Europe and the Americas.[30] He wrote proudly to several continental counterparts that "the *Criterion* is the only English literary review which pays serious attention to foreign periodicals," and he asked collaborators such as Richard Aldington and F. S. Flint for the names of potential magazines to include in the journal's *revue des revues* feature.[31] The Foreign Reviews section at the end of every issue began in the *Criterion*'s third number, with notes on French, German, and American magazines; Danish, Spanish, Dutch, and Italian titles soon began appearing regularly. These foreign reviews and their editors would cooperate, too, to secure wider distribution of the *Criterion*.

Rediscovering Spain

To amplify and distinguish his review's broad-minded continentalism—its power to redefine Europe from the English margin—Eliot commenced an aggressive effort to find collaborators beyond the Franco-German core of Europe. Aware of his own "gallophil[ia]," he was "*not* anxious to get many French people for the *first two* numbers, more anxious to get other (foreign) nationalities" such as Norwegian and Dutch letters, in order to "check the French hegemony of Europe," he wrote.[32] From the start, he looked to attend to sites in which Europe's insular, overlooked, or traditionally minor cultures were being refashioned with a cosmopolitan spirit—made into heretofore neglected gems that he could present to English readers. This would furthermore validate the model of national-continental revival that he had proposed, showing it to be a portable, interdependent blueprint that other nations could follow. Spain was constantly in this vision, even though Eliot, who had read of Spain's European literary past in Pound's *Spirit of Romance* (1910) and had studied the sixteenth-century mystic St. John of the Cross, the Baroque poet Luis de Góngora, and *Don Quixote*, had very little knowledge of contemporary Spanish literature. Even so, while he was not alone among English periodical editors or readers in looking to Spain, few had gone before him. What coverage of Spain did precede that of the *Criterion* was sporadic and often dismissed Spain as far removed from its "great literary past . . . when she set the fashion and the pace for the rest of Europe," claimed that Spanish intellectuals "have one grave defect . . . [t]hey are not intellectual at all," or stated bluntly that "Spain is not European."[33] Eliot's web of contacts led him instead to a renovated, Europeanizing Spain that the *Criterion* would represent.

When assembling the journal's domestic vanguard, known as the "Phalanx," Eliot looked for figures who could continue to expand the *Criterion*'s Europe. These writers mostly had robust, cosmopolitan sensibilities, and included Pound, Aldington, Wyndham Lewis, Harold Monro, Bonamy Dobrée, Herbert Read, Frank Morley, Orlo Williams, Alec Randall, and later Montgomery Belgion and Michael Roberts. Eliot was also "anxious . . . to find reliable and not too expensive translators for various languages . . . [such as] French, German and Spanish, . . . Italian and Scandinavian as well."[34] Aldington, for instance, put him in touch with F. S. Flint, an Imagist poet and polylingual translator, who would review Spanish, German, Norwegian, and Dutch periodicals.[35] Then, Eliot enlisted the versatile Hispanist and musicologist J. B. Trend, who had written for the *Athenaeum* and the *TLS*, for his new staff. Trend brought to the *Criterion* a belief similar to Eliot's that national artistic traditions thrive only symbiotically with others across Europe. He was known for engaging with "some of the most progressive minds in Spain," and the *Criterion* itself would claim fairly that he "has no equal in England . . . as a guide to Spain."[36] He spent years in Madrid and at the Residencia de Estudiantes, and was convinced that the best new thought, literature, and arts were coming from Spain and merited sustained attention in England. As would his columns for the *Criterion*, Trend's successful *Picture of Modern Spain* (1921) introduced many Britons to the leading cultural figures of Spain well before they were known beyond Iberia. (Ortega, for one, is described as a writer "whose thought is perhaps more modern, more sympathetic, and more representative of Spain at its best" than any other philosopher's.[37]) He believed, too, that Spaniards now had the potential to lead Europe by virtue of their absence from the continent's war.

Eliot's many foreign contributors, too, would be a measuring stick of the *Criterion*'s capacities as well as evidence of its membership in the European periodical community, he felt. For this element, he located two more valuable figures who circulated fluidly among British and Spanish cultures. First, he turned to a colleague, Valery Larbaud, a native Frenchman who was near-equally fluent in Anglo- and Hispanophone letters. Larbaud, who had worked as a translator in Spain and maintained many contacts there, gave him the name of Antonio Marichalar as a potential contributor of *chroniques* from Spain. The young Madrileño's criticism immediately impressed Eliot (see chapter 2 of this volume). Eliot wrote to Marichalar of his plans "to channel [*canaliser*] through London the deepest foreign currents of thought ... [of Europe and to] develop a rapport with the writers and editors of the most prestigious foreign journals" such as Juan Ramón Jiménez's *Índice* [*Sign*; literally, "Index"], which had printed Marichalar's work.[38] Marichalar was eager to offer English readers a panoramic view of Spanish literary culture, and signed on for a role in the *Criterion* that he would fill through 1938. He shared with Eliot a neoclassical view of European culture, finding commonalities between Eliot's view of Donne and his own of Góngora.

Marichalar's role at the *Criterion* and his cultural politics, like those of Flint, Trend, and Larbaud, should not be taken as arbitrary: a writer like the Anglo-Spaniard Ramiro de Maeztu, who had lived in London and already had published regularly in English periodicals, easily could have offered a portrait of a pan-Hispanic Catholic Spain that would have contrasted dramatically with the characterizations that the *Criterion* printed. The presence of Flint, Trend, Larbaud, and Marichalar when Eliot debuted the *Criterion* already ensured that the "Europe" that the review outlined had a noticeable Spanish element, but Eliot added one more salient Spanish figure for his launch: Ramón Gómez de la Serna, who was advertised alongside Marichalar on Eliot's circular for the forthcoming review. Larbaud had suggested that Eliot publish the successful avant-garde writer Ramón (as he is known) after having translated some of his work himself. Larbaud claimed in his lecture on *Ulysses* in the *Criterion*'s first issue that Ramón had done for contemporary Spain what James Joyce did when he "gave to young Ireland ... an artistic countenance, an intellectual identity" in European letters.[39] Eliot knew nothing of the Spaniard but loved the idea, especially because Ramón had "the additional interest of being quite unknown in this country."[40] In fact, he wanted his experimental short stories to appear in the first issue, which contained *The Waste Land*, and Ramón offered him the choice of several of his unpublished works; Flint ultimately translated four of them, "If 'They' Remained," "The Electric Cat," "Through the Screen," and "The Switchboard of the Skies." They were delayed until the second issue, but their publication alongside the other names that appear in the *Criterion*'s early numbers—and immediately next to Eliot's own essay on Marie Lloyd—signaled a priority rarely given to a Spanish writer in a British review at the time. The first two issues of the *Criterion*, that is, contain works by or extensive treatments of the luminaries of European literature, including Flaubert, Balzac, Mallarmé, Pirandello, and a fragment of Dostoevsky translated by S. S. Koteliansky and Virginia Woolf, and contributions from Pound, Curtius, Larbaud, and Roger Fry. Literature from Spain, the juxtapositions of tradition and vanguardism in these first issues imply, is now claiming its place alongside the great works of Europe's cultural past and present.

Windows onto the New Spain: Marichalar and Trend

From this springboard, the *Criterion* expanded its attention to the contemporary cultural life of Spain—and then to the country's historical complexity—through the cooperation of its Spanish experts. In the following (third) issue, Eliot gave some 6,000 words of space (about 15% of the pages) to Marichalar's first chronicle, "Contemporary Spanish Literature." The essay came on the heels of Hermann Hesse's German chronicle for the *Criterion*'s inaugural issue, which proclaimed bleakly, "I do not believe in a rapid recovery of German poetry" or in the country's young poets' turning away from the "East," toward the western European tradition.[41] The contrast between an increasingly Eastern and declining Germany and a Europeanizing, flourishing Spain could not be clearer: Marichalar's sweeping analysis of literary life in the New Spain has an optimistic tone that heralded the arrival of a renewed continental literary tradition. The Spaniard provides a genealogy of new writing in his country of which the *telos* is European recognition. He begins by paying an ambivalent homage to the preceding Generation of '98's writers, who responded to "the disaster that swept our country owing to its artistic, social, and political decay" by, among other things, "bringing [Spaniards] into touch with modern European thinkers" such as Nietzsche and Tolstoy. He adds, however, that they "consider their mission finished," and today's "Young Masters" are for Marichalar "the most representative of the modern movement effected in our country, parallel with others." These figures, who are leading this "parallel" European movement, include the poets Juan Ramón Jiménez, who translated Anglophone poetry, and Antonio Machado, whose work bears "traces of foreign influences."

Marichalar then singles out as Spain's exemplary talent the "intensely modern" and influential Ramón, who has "especially . . . contributed in Spain to the acceptance of modern art and helped to extend the new spirit of the time." Marichalar turns to Valery Larbaud's article in the first issue of the *Criterion* to assert, as his French colleague did, that Ramón and Gabriel Miró "have impressed the Spanish language and literature to the extent that J[ames] Joyce has the Irish"—they have brought it up to the European bar that Ortega also employs. They are peers with writers in England and across the continent who are working to rebuild Europe's shattered culture, and a leader among them is Ortega, who "represents the ideal type of the clever lecturer, facile and charming," who is "not only a thinker, but more especially an orator, in his relation to public life."[42] Ortega receives a relatively short treatment at this point, though over time he will become the most discussed Spaniard in the review. In particular, Marichalar will point to Ortega's work to revise the ingrained stereotype of Don Juan—a figure who was the subject of intense national debate in the 1920s—into a symbol of a new cosmopolitan Spanish culture.[43]

Since almost none of the figures Marichalar discusses had yet been translated into English, such a column on this unchartered literary and cultural territory was essential to bringing the thought and ideals of Spanish modernists to British literary circles. (It also sparked the interest of Curtius, a *Criterion* reader in Germany, in Spain's new writers.) Eliot appreciated Marichalar's willingness to "sacrifice himself" by writing criticism "in the interest of his colleagues[, . . . though] I have no doubt that the English public will be keen to know you better[, and your article] push[es] me to take up the study of Spanish again."[44] Intrigued further by Spain and unsatisfied with having printed Ramón alone among creative writers, Eliot wrote to Trend, "[I am] counting on you, if on anyone, to report to me some treasure from Spain which might be exploited by the *Criterion*. Unless Spain is absolutely barren," which Marichalar's essay indicated was not the case.[45] Eliot's interest in Spain grew for non-literary reasons, too, when just after Primo de Rivera's coup in October 1923, he wrote in the *Lloyds Bank Monthly* of his worries about the destabilizing effects of the new regime both for Spain and for the continent. Many possibilities circulated for new Spanish authors to represent this changing locale: Eliot first liked Trend's idea to print something by Azorín, then later endorsed Eugenio D'Ors or Juan Ramón Jiménez, and he recommended that Trend acquire an essay by the Andalusian composer Manuel de Falla. None of these Spaniards ever published in the journal, though. Nor did Eliot's plans to publish something by Pedro Salinas or José Bergamín, which he discussed with Marichalar, ever materialize.[46] In fact, no other contemporary Spanish writer's creative work appeared in the *Criterion*; Góngora would become, years later, the only other Spanish author published in the review. The effect of this exclusion, which might have stemmed from an argument between Eliot and Ramón, was not a silence, but rather an accentuation of the authority of the journal's other spaces that interpreted Spanish culture, as Eliot still desired.[47]

The most important such spaces for extending and diversifying historically Marichalar's account of Spanish letters belonged to Trend. Over the course of a decade, Trend contributed over 30 music columns, essays, periodical and book reviews, chronicles, and translations, mostly on Spanish topics. And like Marichalar, he wrote on both sides by contributing essays on English music to the *Residencia*, the journal of his host college in Madrid, and by having both his Spanish and English journalistic colleagues send him one another's reviews and new titles for him to circulate and review.[48] Eliot wanted Trend to publish something in the *Criterion* on his discovery of early modern English music in the Escorial, in hopes of highlighting the history of cultural sympathy between England and Spain (which Trend would do later). But first, Trend wrote for the sixth *Criterion* a lengthy historical study, "The Moors in Spanish Music." The essay proposes a controversial reading of the origins of Spanish national culture—a topic that would preoccupy the *Revista de Occidente* for years. Trend characterizes the Andalusian *cante jondo* ("deep song," a traditional Flamenco vocal style) by its "deliberate use of intervals unknown to modern Western music," yet which are not "oriental" either. He traces the various gypsy, Arabic, Berber, and European influences that have created contemporary Spanish music and concludes that "so long a stay of an Eastern race [the Moors] in a Western country, so many generations of warfare and intermarriage, of commercial and cultural relations, cannot but have left their mark (it is said) on the music of the original inhabitants of the country." Embracing the "Eastern" and "oriental" character of Spain, yet still considering the country assimilated to the West, Trend reads Córdoba in Andalusia as a former "centre of culture to which students came from all parts of the world," when "Moorish Spain became for a time the most civilised country in Europe." (Indeed, Córdoba was the largest and arguably the most prosperous city in the continent in the tenth century.) This process of influence, he adds, was unevenly reciprocal, as "Moorish music was more influenced by Spain than Spain by Moorish music," making both cultures hybrid in their musical constitutions.[49] Trend stretches both "Europe" and the "West" as conceived in the journal. In doing so, he marks one of the first visible fault lines between Eliot's personal ideals and those he published, and also one of the new understandings of Spain's ability to redraw the boundaries of European culture beyond northern paradigms.

Furthermore, influenced by his long friendship with Falla, Trend argued that the contemporary Spanish artists who embrace Andalusia's gypsy and "Moorish" past are producing the most progressive works of the new Europe. In a Hispanized version of the Italian thinker Michele Amari's radical claim that the roots of European modernity lay in medieval Muslim Sicily, Trend claims that Europe must be seen now not simply from Spain, but from the south of Spain. He casts Falla and Federico García Lorca, who helped organize the first modern festival of the *cante jondo* in Granada in 1922, as the greatest living innovators of Spanish arts by virtue of their incorporations of putatively impure, foreign, or degraded forms. Their music and poetry, in fact, blur the boundaries between East and West that have been used to analyze (and provincialize) modern European arts. Indeed, while Spaniards' "tendency to profuse ornamentation . . . [in] every form of art" does derive from "Muslim influence," Trend asserts again and again in his writings that the syncretism of Spanish music and national character cannot be explained through Orientalisms alone.[50] Rather, Spain represents the deeply multicultural history of Europe that the Iberian Peninsula has best preserved to the present. This history is now bursting forth in creative works that are redefining European arts, but the "Spanish idiom" in music is still dismissed by English and European audiences. Trend's time in Spain has shown him that the English must maintain a "strict neutrality" and appreciate the variety of styles in Spain; against the banal "Armistice style" of French and German music, for instance, the compositions of Manuel de Falla "might almost be said to have saved the situation in Western European [music]."[51] He criticizes both England and the continent for continuing to ignore, with brazen insularity, aesthetic movements in states such as Spain and its counterpart on Europe's eastern border, Hungary, home of Béla Bartók. Spanish arts are, for Trend, signposts of Europe's heterogeneous future, to which England must awaken.

As the phrase "Armistice style" suggests, Trend often reads music and international politics and diplomacy together, inscribing Spain into Europe as he did in his book. In his dispatches for the *Criterion* from various European international music festivals, Trend discusses the proceedings of the International Society for Contemporary Music. The Society's mission, he writes, is not "to 'represent' the music of any country as a national entity. It is by no means an international musical Wembley where each dominion has its more or less grotesque pavilion in competition with all the others." Its ideal is that "musical relations" might translate into better geopolitical relations—an ideal much in keeping with Eliot's own for periodical cooperation. The Society hopes that "differences of musical idiom as well as of spoken language fade away." But this "League of Musical Nations," he adds, "is no more free from the attacks of nationalistic mischief-makers than the other League of Nations at Geneva," for which Eliot and Ortega both had contempt, too. The kind of cross-cultural work in which he and his peers engaged, Trend suggests, held greater promise for European unity.[52]

An "Older European Nation" and its New *Revista de Occidente*

These characterizations of Spain laid the groundwork for the *Criterion*'s alliance with the *Revista de Occidente*'s own Europeanizing project. Marichalar, Trend, and Larbaud all pointed Eliot continually to Ortega, who had barely been mentioned in print in English at the time, as the motivating force behind the country's new zeitgeist. Though in the 1950s, he would speak of Ortega's "remarkable book" *The Revolt of the Masses* as "worth rereading now," Eliot himself likely had read only one piece of Ortega's work by the time of the *Revista de Occidente*'s debut in July 1923, a French essay that he published in the *NRF* in memory of Proust in January of that year.[53] When Ortega's new journal appeared just nine months after the first *Criterion*, Marichalar sent the first issue to Eliot, who called it "vraiment une belle production," and passed it to Flint to review.[54] Eliot saw an opportunity to use Ortega's editorial practices, along with the national vision that his periodical offered, as evidence that would solidify explicitly the bonds between the two reviews, their editors, and their collaborators. Flint writes in the Foreign Reviews section that

> we must accept [the *Revista de Occidente*] as significant of the present direction or tendency of intelligence in the older European nations, [which is] ... much the same as ... the *Criterion*['s], and there is no doubt that its editor, José Ortega y Gasset, would subscribe to [Eliot's] "The Function of a Literary Review" and [Aldington's] "Literature and the 'Honnête Homme'" that appeared in our last number.... It appeals to the "happy few" ... [and] will be cosmopolitan in the sense that it does not consider wisdom to have national boundaries, and, for this reason, its pages will be open to foreign writers on an equal footing with those of Spain.[55]

Flint points to the *Revista* as a representation of the regeneration of an "older" nation in a reformed European sphere, and he makes Ortega and Eliot partners in this project. His language here echoes Eliot's own about his ambitions for the *Criterion*, and the developing sympathy between the two journals also contrasted the rift that was growing between Eliot and the *NRF*. Flint praises the review for understanding that "wisdom" is inherently international—detached from nationalist projects and from party politics—and for inviting, as the *Criterion* did, "foreign writers on an equal footing" in its pages. And by 1924, Curtius had written in the *Neue Rundschau* that Ortega's journal had "rapidly gained a place for itself among the liveliest and most intelligent periodicals in Europe."[56]

After seeing a few more issues of the *Revista*, an excited Eliot wrote to Trend about the possibility of hiring Ortega to contribute regularly to the *Criterion*: "Do you think that Ortega y Gasset would be a good man for Spain, and do you think that he would be inclined to do it? I only know that you and others have spoken highly of him to me and that he is the Editor of a review which I find sympathetic and with which I should like to be on closer terms." Trend responded positively, adding that the *Criterion* "was one of the few reviews" that the discerning Ortega "really like[s]."[57] Eliot then wrote to Ortega, requesting that he "become one of our contributors" in hopes that "in this way [our] two reviews may become more closely associated." Eliot tells the philosopher that he has "formed a very high opinion indeed of [the *Revista*]" and that he appreciates their journals' notes on one another. Ortega would best represent Madrid, he writes, for the *Criterion*'s plan to have "Literary Letter[s] . . . by one of the most distinguished and authoritative men of letters in each capital," and such a column would "assist the interest in and knowledge of Spanish letters of today, in England."[58] Regular contributions from him would have claimed Spain definitively for the *Criterion*, but Ortega declined for several reasons: because his close colleague Marichalar was already filling such a role at the *Criterion*; because he did not feel comfortable composing in English; and because he had just sent such a letter (using a translator) to be published in the *Dial*. The *Dial* had beaten the *Criterion* to this "treasure" by only three months. But while Ortega's Spanish letter for the American review traces a moment in "the evolution of the European mind" and the "European soul" through the Golden Age and the decline of "the Spanish character, the hidden spring that has gushed forth the history of the most abnormal nation of Europe," it does not treat current Spanish culture or life in Madrid.[59] Ortega and the *Revista de Occidente* had made an impression on two prominent Anglophone reviews—and the *Dial* had celebrated the philosopher's "very liberal spirit, hospitable to every talent of the globe"—but there was more work to be done.[60] It was clear that the *Criterion* was not finding a forgotten treasure in Spain, but rather, was responding to and circulating abroad a community of writers who were energetically reforming Spain.

Translation, Not "Treasure"

At almost the same moment, the *Revista de Occidente* began its own path along a similar trajectory as Eliot's review, casting ever wider nets in order to foster "the widespread germination of life" and to "reveal the plane of a new architecture on which Western life is being reconstructed" in Spain—in Madrid, not the emblem of the dying West but the site of its rebirth.⁶¹ This entailed historicizing Spain's diminution over the previous three centuries, then laying out what the shape of the New Spain would be in light of the country's past. For this task, Ortega sought to make his collaborators and readers members of the same international generation of European intellectuals that Eliot envisioned. The *Revista*'s methods and stakes were essentially inverse, however: where the *Criterion* sought to Europeanize England by importing "novel" continental works and to remake Europe from a position of relative power, Ortega's review first had to find a way to circulate beyond its own national and linguistic borders in order to affect Europe.

When he looked to found the *Revista* in 1923, Ortega saw that no existing title in Spain had the range of texts or ideas that his would present, nor the heterogeneity of fields and genres that it would include. Fashioned along the lines of the *Criterion* and the *NRF*, the monthly review would establish a new channel between Spain and the continent. Ortega's periodical agenda required an extensive staff of collaborators with diverse skills that reached beyond his own philosophies and the German philosophy that he translated, both of which the *Revista* would feature. A collective of translators and specialists, many drawn from the Residencia de Estudiantes, would broaden the review's "Europe" and its "West." They came from all over Spain and Spanish America, extending already Ortega's Castilian elitist sensibilities. Fernando Vela, José Bergamín, Benjamín Jarnés, and Antonio Espina would be the review's local fixtures, and Antonio Marichalar was one of the most frequently published figures in the review. Strengthening the journal's coverage of British literature were a number of young writers and scholars with strong ties to Anglophone cultures: Claudio de la Torre, Luis Cernuda, Pedro Salinas, Manuel Altolaguirre, Ramón Pérez de Ayala, Melchor Fernández Almagro, Ángel Sánchez Rivero, Lino Novás Calvo, Jaime Torres Bodet, and Alfonso Reyes. Finally, Ortega enlisted two more veteran and established critic-translators who amplified the journal's Anglophone capacities (and those of the new Revista de Occidente publishing house), Ricardo Baeza and Enrique Díez-Canedo.⁶²

While there was greater interest in contemporary British literature across the Spanish literary landscape than vice versa in the first part of the twentieth century, English-language texts remained relatively distant commodities for Spanish readers. Ortega desired to be the first to import them en masse. Translation and criticism, which often overlapped, were the *Revista*'s means of operation—translation on a scale that the country had not seen since the Golden Age, Ortega believed. But the cultural capital gained by bringing major literatures (European and British) to a minor language (Spanish) brought with it accusations that Ortega was inviting hegemony into an already marginalized country. The cultural politics of translation—especially from English-language texts—had been at the center of these arguments. Translation had been growing in popularity in the early twentieth century, but remained diffuse in practice.[63] With his colleagues and a rotating cast of other contributors, Ortega could use his new journal to revise the primarily Gallophilic spirit of translation of the Spanish avant-gardes and to turn it into a "critical system" for reading foreign traditions into national tastes, Miguel Gallego Roca argues.[64] Ortega and his new staff sought to overshadow their peers, and they increased the value of their "fidelity" by translating directly from original language sources rather than, as was common, from preexisting French translations. The number of translated works and commentaries on them soon spiked in Spain, and the *Revista de Occidente* both led this charge and consolidated much of the work that came before it. In an essay that captures the essence of the *Revista*'s ethos of translation, Ricardo Baeza reflected on "The Spirit of Internationalism and Translation" (1928) that one of the most hopeful movements in the contemporary West [*occidente*] was the growing practice of translation carried out with internationalist ideals. Before the Great War, he writes, the English and the French had built "nationalist . . . dams" around their own cultural productions in the hope of keeping out foreign influence, and Spaniards translated very few works of European origin, leaving them out of touch with "European life" and its "spiritual civilization." But since the war, a cosmopolitan mode of translation "has been gaining ground and diminishing borders," and Spain has actually led this charge among European literatures. "Spanish letters," he writes, "now have their European bearings."[65]

Ortega's savvy and his finances in the periodical, daily, and book presses helped to transform Spanish print culture. And his timing for the *Revista* was expert, history shows. The primary magazines of Ultraism and Creationism, two of the most prominent avant-garde movements in Spain, had folded between 1916–1922; the late-*modernista* review *Cosmópolis* (founded 1919) had folded in 1922; and the new reviews of the burgeoning Generation of '27 would not appear until the mid-1920s. Of the titles that did survive in Spain, few had any continental profile, and most were content with a national audience alone. Ortega's review quickly became a premier journal of international culture. Contemporary German, British, and French texts filled its pages, alongside works by most every prominent Spanish author of the period: Ramón and Jiménez (together in the second issue), Machado, Pérez de Ayala, Eugenio d'Ors, Pío Baroja, Azorín, Corpus Barga, and many more made early contributions. Spanish writers were thus placed side by side with their British and continental peers, suggesting the polyglot dialogue across all of their works that the journal would host.

British Writing and Ortega's New Europe

In his effort to supply a Europeanist schematics and vocabulary that his collaborators at the *Revista* adapted to a host of critiques, Ortega—at the same moment in the mid-1920s that British modernism flourished in his journal—rethought his Berlin-centered conception of "Europe" and turned increasingly to Britain. Though the philosopher had insulted the English as boorish and lazy in *The Modern Theme* and had offered a skeptical review of Bertrand Russell's pamphlet *The Problem of China* (1923), he now left behind his previous criticisms of Englishmen and began to see them as valuable allies in cooperating, in proximity or from afar, to rebuild Europe. Ortega's vision of a European political order also evolved over the next two decades into one of parliamentary government very similar to the English model—one with personal, political, and expressive freedoms seen only for brief moments in Spanish history. Not by coincidence, two important strands of Ortega's thought developed at this time: his redefinition of intellectual cosmopolitanism across the continent and his famous theory of dehumanized art in Europe. For the first of these, Ortega, who had refrained from publishing explicitly political articles out of caution in the early months of Primo de Rivera's rule, broadened his journal's cultural critique. He began this project with a pair of articles, "Cosmopolitismo" (1924) and "Reforma de la inteligencia" (1926), which he simultaneously published in the *Revista* and in translation abroad, from Germany to Argentina. Building on the "cosmopolitanism of today" described in his "Propósitos," he writes in the first essay that in the post-war environment, many authors and intellectuals feel themselves more akin to their peers in other countries than they do to their compatriots. He calls for unity among "the best of the current generation" across Europe, a "select minority" who today "comprise the advanced creative front . . . [that will combat] the nationalist dissociation of the intelligentsia."[66]

This declaration of international solidarity, at a time when intellectuals and writers in Spain, Russia, and Italy were being persecuted by the state, proved central to Ortega's cultural politics, as well as those of the review. Intellectuals, he argues in "Reforma," became involved in imperialist projects in the nineteenth century and served as mouthpieces for belligerent nationalist movements in the early twentieth century, but England might offer a solution. Now praising English intellectualism, Ortega writes that the best relationship between his cultural elite and the nation-state can be found in London, where the intelligentsia expect to be greeted with skepticism and opposition by the nation—and they become better, more influential thinkers for it. These circumstances "give English thought, despite some native limitations, a serenity so pure and so true that, at least, it avoids the great errors committed, for example, by French literature and German philosophy."[67] Ortega's plea for a disinterested learned class that would cultivate its ideas independent of the church, party politics, or capitalist enterprises resonated with such calls by Eliot and by Julien Benda, among others. This task of nonpartisan reflection and intervention that Ortega advocated was a revolt against the "treason of the intellectuals" that Benda would describe only a few years later.

For his closely intertwined aesthetic theory, Ortega posited in *The Dehumanization of Art* (serialized 1924–1925) a sociological theory of contemporary cultural productions that argues—with neither praise nor condemnation—that viewers' responses to anti-mimetic works of art separate them into two camps, the enlightened elite (who understand the art) and the masses (who do not). Ortega posits that "the most alert young people of two successive generations" across the continent have created it in cities such as "Berlin, Paris, London, New York, Rome, Madrid." Placing Madrid alongside the major metropolises of Europe and one in the United States (though final among them), he lays out a sense of pan-European and Western aesthetics that looks forward to the fiction competition that his review soon engaged. His influential theory also set an internationalist standard for many writers of the Generation of '27. Ortega cites Joyce, Proust, Pirandello, and Ramón as his literary examples, and Expressionism and Cubism as his examples from the visual arts. Furthermore, tying this essay to thought from England, Ortega's argument for ending the artificial separation of reason and culture that characterizes modern life bears distinct similarities to Eliot's notion of the "dissociation of sensibility." Though scholars have not pointed out this connection, Ortega clearly had read Eliot's works by the early 1920s, for he writes that "in the mind of the [modern] artist a sort of chemical reaction is set going by the clash between his individual sensibility and already existing art. He does not find himself all alone with the world before him; in his relations with the world there always intervenes, like an interpreter, the artistic tradition."[68] Ortega almost certainly has in mind here Eliot's famous metaphor for "depersonaliz[ed]" poetics—the filament of platinum in the presence of oxygen and sulfur dioxide—in "Tradition and the Individual Talent," when he explains the poet's relationship to the literary past.

The Young Generation/*La generación joven*: British Modernism in the *Revista de Occidente*'s Spain

The *Revista de Occidente*'s engagements and exchanges with British modernism and with the *Criterion*, which went well beyond Ortega's writings, provided a crucial medium through which the journal projected Spain's attachments to Europe.[69]

Having succeeded in bringing English-language works in translation to Spain, the journal now positioned itself as the most significant critical voice on new British letters. As Ortega put it, in order to integrate his Spanish cosmopolitan minority with others across the continent, his journal must join current conversations on texts such as *Ulysses* or *À la recherche du temps perdu*—European sensations that demanded the newest reading techniques and analytic vocabularies. The *Revista de Occidente* would circulate these techniques and vocabularies in an idiom that characterized its Spanish-European vanguardism as the work of cooperative peers, not minor imitators. Animating an exciting, creative period of inquiry and debate that began in the *Revista*'s early years, British writers came to hold a privileged position as like-minded voices of the new cosmopolitanism that the journal articulated, trailing only German philosophers in foreign contributions. The *Revista* soon became the first journal to publish in Spanish works by Joyce, Virginia Woolf, and Lytton Strachey, all of which will be treated over the course of this book. By 1936, lengthy essays (often accompanied by translations) on Marichalar's *Criterion* colleagues Eliot, Lewis, and Dobrée, along with George Bernard Shaw, Aldous Huxley, Liam O'Flaherty, Katherine Mansfield, James Stephens, and Americans Eugene O'Neill, Waldo Frank, William Faulkner, Hart Crane, Langston Hughes, Jean Toomer, and several others would all appear in its pages. And they appeared not in less prominent discursive channels such as the foreign chronicles and *revue des revues* of the *Criterion*, but in headlining articles and translations. They were juxtaposed not only with the names of Spain's leading writers, but also with the figures of its literary past—Cervantes, Quevedo, Lope de Vega—and of Europe's present, from Kafka to Pirandello.

Marichalar's parallel work between Eliot's and Ortega's journals was the primary force in bridging the gap between the two editors' Europeanisms. He heralded the task of framing and disseminating the *Revista*'s view of British modernism by interpreting Joseph Conrad's journey to "Englishness" from the East and through Europe. Marichalar reads Conrad's peripatetic life, which began on the opposite margins of Europe, as a path—also an intellectual path—out of the "old continent" and into an influential cultural position in England. He writes in a memorial piece after Conrad's death in 1924 that this "old expatriate Pole . . . contributed to English literature an exotic element of inestimable value" in his "Slavic" blend of psychological and stylistic narrative complexities. Marichalar, in other words, sees in Conrad's integration in English society and literature a turn away from the East and toward the West, and thus an analogue for Spain's potential Europeanism.[70] Marichalar's essay appears, moreover, among a long appreciation of Proust, poetry by the Uruguayan-Frenchman Jules Supervielle, an essay by Bertrand Russell, and a philosophical article by Ortega, thus placing his estimate of Conrad in one of the *Revista*'s multinational and multilingual contexts. Translations of Conrad's "An Outpost of Progress," "The Brute," and "Gaspar Ruiz" soon followed, and also in 1924, Marichalar profiled "el español-inglés," Madrid-born philosopher George Santayana.

Throughout his *Revista* contributions, Marichalar positions Joyce, Woolf, D. H. Lawrence, Huxley, and several Bloomsbury figures as a vanguard of introspective writers who are creating the new Europe—the same vanguard in which he included his compatriots in his *chroniques* for the *Criterion*. Marichalar writes that they, like the "Young Masters" of Spain whom he described, represent a "young generation" of an "epoch—our own epoch—of 'transition,'" with shared intellectual and literary pursuits.[71] He uses this same phrase, *generación joven*, to refer to his Generation of '27 colleagues in his publications in Spanish. (One of the major journals of these Spanish poets, *Verso y Prosa* [*Verse and Prose*], would be subtitled *Boletín de la joven literatura* [*Bulletin of the Young Literature*].) Marichalar sees his Anglophone peers as "a fully attentive generation, . . . watchful, wide-awake. . . . The English intellectuals . . . find only one remedy" to save art's efficacy: "the regeneration of the individual."[72] These writers not only flout tradition and the conventions of representing time and space in the novel, but also have supranational sensibilities, like Joyce's creation of an Irish style that exceeds the boundaries of his birth nation. Joyce's work, he adds, "both separates and links two literary generations; among the younger, he is 'the greatest.'"[73] Marichalar finds Britain's literary responses to the "state of curiosity and discomfort provoked by the consequences of the Great War" to be more "creative" and more potent than those of French decadent authors in the project to reunite European culture. Drawing lines of continuity across disciplines, he writes—in the same issue in which Shaw, Barga, and Georg Simmel appear in proximity—that the new formulations of subjectivity and psychology "taking place in French science have already taken place in English literature," in the works of Joyce, Lawrence, Mansfield, and Dorothy Richardson.[74] Such work as Marichalar's in the *Revista de Occidente* influenced the Generation of '27 to take as their poetic forebears Eliot and Paul Valéry, for instance, as much as their recent national predecessors such as Machado and Jiménez. (Marichalar's colleague Dámaso Alonso was the first to translate *A Portrait of the Artist as a Young Man* into Spanish in 1926, and another colleague, Ángel Flores, published the first Spanish translation of *The Waste Land* in 1930.)

Marichalar, as he moved between two cultures in his columns for both the *Criterion* and the *Revista*, began translating the same conversations taking place in Britain and in Spain for both reviews, as his comment on the "young generation" indicates. Echoing his first *Criterion* column, he wrote, for instance, that Ramón "has produced in Spain—simultaneously, intuitively—similar works as the Italian Futurists, the German Expressionists, and the French Cubists," but has remained as recognizably Spanish as Quevedo.[75] As he worked to convey in his *chroniques* "what is talked about in the select circles that an English reader of the *New Criterion* would frequent in Spain," Marichalar pointed his Anglophone readers to more of his poet-colleagues, especially Rafael Alberti and Gerardo Diego, who had synthesized the literary forms of the Spanish rural and folkloric traditions with the new Anglo-European modernist and vanguard practices. He adds that Dámaso Alonso, Jorge Guillén, Pedro Salinas, Juan Chabás, Lorca, and *Revista de Occidente* stalwarts José Bergamín and Antonio Espina belong to this same group, stars of the "age of the lyric" of the Generation of '27.[76] Marichalar circulated these portraits of internationalist Spanish writing to new audiences when he co-edited with Larbaud a special double issue of the French review *Intentions* titled "La jeune littérature espagnole" ["The Young Spanish Literature"] in 1924. In his introductory essay, he alerts French readers to the "new spectacle" represented by his Generation of '27 compatriots, for whom he provides short sketches. Guillén, Marichalar writes in mode of comparison, "could be the Spanish Valéry."[77] In a transcultural idiom much like Marichalar's, Ricardo Baeza provided a comparative study of Shaw and Gerhart Hauptmann for the *Revista de Occidente*, then a long portrait of Samuel Butler that gauged him against his Spanish peers. Despite his having been a Georgian, Butler is "very contemporary, very *novecentista*," Baeza writes, referring to the Catalan avant-garde of the early twentieth century—a "complete representative of the modern artist."[78]

Following the *Revista*'s introductions and its notes on the *Criterion* (and often the *Dial*) in its brief "Mementos de revistas" beginning in 1926, coverage of these and other British writers surged in Spain through the 1920s and 1930s. The publishing house Oriente also began issuing translations of Anglophone modernists in 1928.[79] At the same time, reviews and newspapers from *La Gaceta Literaria* to *El Sol* featured notices on the *Criterion*, the *Dial*, and *Poetry*, as the loose network of media connecting Anglophone and Spanish modernisms became more visible. Eliot enlisted Spaniards, including Guillermo de Torre, to send him copies of Spanish media that mentioned the *Criterion*.[80] Marichalar praised the *Criterion* to his Spanish colleagues as "the most purely intellectual journal that exists," and he called Eliot the ideal modern poet, an expatriate unafraid to look beyond his national precursors, to the "Latin literatures" of Dante and Lucretius, for inspiration.[81] A newspaper interview that he gave encapsulates his own transnational sensibilities: Marichalar simply placed before the reporter the *Revista* and the *Criterion* next to one another and noted their similarities; the reporter was convinced of their translatability.[82] Both featured pieces by or about authors including Ramón, Joyce, Proust, Valéry, Pirandello,

Max Scheler, and others at virtually the same moment—and in many cases, in other European journals, too—and criticized common targets such as the German Count Keyserling, the Frenchman Romain Rolland, and other "mystics" in similar terms. Jorge Guillén later called these two periodicals and the *NRF* "the holy trinity of European reviews" of the interwar era.[83] Ortega's *Revista*, it seems, was taking its place alongside its English and French peers in the European republic of letters.

The *Revista de Occidente* found success when it created a forum for Spanish-European writing that catalyzed interest abroad, especially among Anglophone reviews. This was evident, for instance, when the new English-language Parisian journal *transition*, best known for serializing Joyce's *Work in Progress* (*Finnegans Wake*), lauded the *Revista* at the head of its "Current Reviews" section in its second number (May 1927).[84] *transition* then echoed Marichalar's language two months later: it devoted a section to a "series of translations... of modern Spanish poets and prose-writers... [whose works] give essentially the specific national character of the newer literature[,]... the young Spanish literature."[85] Poems by Giménez Caballero, Salinas, Alberti, and Espina—several leading figures of the Generation of '27, all of whom published in the *Revista de Occidente*—appear in this issue. And A. R. Pastor, in his often-reprinted 1927 lectures on Spanish literature at King's College, followed Marichalar's lead and cited the *Revista* and the Generation of '27 as exemplars of the country's new literature.[86] Two middlebrow transatlantic reviews, the American *Bookman* and *Littell's Living Age*, also took notice of the literature of the New Spain. The former described in 1924 the "magnificent rebirth [of Spanish literature], of which Larbaud, Supervielle, Casson, and Marichalar are the heralds in France, and the names of Gabriel Miró, José Guillén, Ramón Gómez de la Serna, [Ramón Pérez de] Ayala, etc. are soon to be given their *European* importance."[87] The *Living Age* began reprinting articles in translation from the *Revista de Occidente* regularly beginning in 1926. Between 1925 and 1926, Ortega was also profiled in several new English-language works on contemporary Spanish writing, and was treated at length by his friend, the Hispanist Walter Starkie, in the popular *Contemporary Review* as a "Philosopher of Modern Spain."

The Margins of the Occident, Spanish Exceptionalism, and the Future of Europe

As the *Revista de Occidente* expanded its international ties, it continually took up Ortega's challenge to circulate throughout Europe renovated articulations of Spain, particularly its Moorish-Islamic past. The "Spain" that the journal presented to both domestic and foreign readers was not simply European, nor could it be integrated with the continent as easily as Eliot's collaborators might have wished. Rather, it forced a reconception of "Europe" from the continent's origins through the present. Always looking both backward and forward, outward (onto the West) and inward (to Spain's past), the *Revista* resituated Spain as an exceptional limit-case of both Europe and the West. The questions of how and why Spain earned this role motivated one of the review's main projects: the excavation of Europe's and Spain's palimpsestic heritage, a project that brought forth revolutionary visions of both places and elicited difficult tests of Ortega's own historical theories. Across its entire run, the journal traced conceptions of the West through a wealth of sources in Arabic, Islamic, African, Jewish, and "Oriental" thought, then recast them through a modern lens.

The language throughout the first issues initiated this dialogue across a variety of genres and fields: from the philosopher Manuel García Morente's outline of Oswald Spengler's arguments, with references to the translation that he and Ortega had just prepared, to the writer Corpus Barga's "Viaje Occidental" ["Western Journey"], a meditation on the contrasting "occidentality" of the Americas. From other disciplines, the German archaeologist Adolf Schulten presented in the inaugural issue his findings from excavations in Tartessos, "the oldest city in the Occident" at the "extreme of the Western world" in present-day Andalusia, just beyond the ancient Pillars of Hercules. There were also articles by Schulten on Maináke, an ancient Greek city near present-day Málaga on the "edge of the West," colonized by the Foceans.[88] Another archaeologist, Pedro Bosch Gimpera, wrote of the early presence of the Ligures, a people whom "Hesiod placed at the extreme of the Occident" in northwestern Italy, even further west in Spain.[89] The implications of these contributors' works are that Spain was the West's margin long before Europe came into being. In a later piece, "Oriente y Occidente: El eterno problema" ["East and West: The Eternal Problem"], Emilio García Gómez, whose translations of Spanish-Arabic poetry for the *Revista* inspired his Generation of '27 peers, discusses the ways in which Spain has been excluded from the West because of its Islamic past, while in reality, ancient Greece was already more "orientalized" than scholars are willing to admit. Greece, in fact, was at once home to the early West and to a "great *Eastern* religious creation: Christianity," and Europeans ignore this fact—and the East itself—"with a naïve faith in Westernization [*occidentalizatión*]."[90]

García Gómez encapsulates a topic that, in various forms, preoccupied a good deal of the journal's thought when he argues that Spain, Europe, and the West are differently composed than most contemporary writers allowed. The cultural politics of the moment were such that one's reading of Spain's Arabic-Islamic past, in essence, indicated one's political and literary sensibilities and one's attitudes toward the nation's relationship to Europe. While most contributors shared Ortega's portrait of the state as a "mixture of races and of tongues," "the superation of all natural society, . . . cross-bred and multilingual," some read Spain's Moorish era as essential to its composition, while Ortega himself rejected or ignored this element (*RM* 154). He argued, rather, that "Europe" did not exist until it was forced to define itself and move northward in response to the Muslim invasions, and thus Spain was European by virtue of containing Germanic and Mediterranean elements that united *against* the Moors. The *Revista*, on the other hand, offered a more complex, commingled portrait of the country's Moorish heritage, and of what the consequences of recognizing that history might be for theories of Spain's Europeanness. Many pages were devoted to debating exactly what "Spain" had assimilated and synthesized in its blend of religions and cultures over time: what "bloods" did Spaniards embody, and did their hybridity mark them as partially non-European, as Kant had it? Or did it embody a more robust but less acknowledged Europe?

The most influential answers to these questions came from three of Spain's leading minds—the renowned philologist Ramón Menéndez Pidal and two of his former students, Américo Castro and Claudio Sánchez-Albornoz—whose debates are still alive in Hispanic studies today.[91] Menéndez Pidal published sections of his monumental study of the national legend of El Cid (Rodrigo Díaz de Vivar), the eleventh-century military leader in the Moorish wars, in an effort to explain Spain's "extra-European historical course." He writes that after the Visigoths "collected the furthest province of the West" in Roman Hispania, and after the Moors proceeded to invade them, Iberia's cultural mixing was amplified, yet that fact does not denigrate Spaniards with the stain of Moorish blood. Rather, the fact of "having been conquered by a superior Eastern culture [the Moors]" decoupled Spain's fate from that of France—and for the better.[92] Menéndez Pidal in fact reads the Spanish middle ages as "essentially a Latin-Arabic epoch" and chastises medievalists for "ignoring the importance of the contact" between Christianity and Islam. "Ancient Spain," he writes, must be "regard[ed] as being, not tangent to, but inscribed in the circle of the Western world of history; for Spain lived within that world and, indeed, linked it to Islam."[93] The story of *El Cid* was not one of purging Islam, but of assimilating and Hispanizing it. All of this adds up, for Menéndez Pidal, to an argument for Spain's exceptional modernity through its syncretic Western-Eastern past—its status as the heir of a revised Europe that the post-war continent must recognize and revive.

With what José-Carlos Mainer calls a Madrid-centered "nationalist liberalism" expressed through his reading of *El Cid*, Menéndez Pidal believed that it took the unifying historical force (and violence, which he rarely mentions) of Castile to make an empire and a nation out of Spain—to bring together the hybridized Islam of Andalusia and the "pure" Catholicism of Asturias—and thus that Castile held the key to reunifying contemporary Spain's provinces.[94] The Brazilian-born Américo Castro, an intellectual whom Ortega knew from his League of Political Education and his journal *España,* disagreed and instead proposed a theory of *convivencia* ["cohabitation," or "living together"], which he elaborated in the journal around his readings of *Don Quixote. Convivencia* argued that the modern Spanish character was the product of a unique admixture of the traditions and ethnicities of Christianity, Islam, and Judaism that accrued in the peninsula. The intolerant exclusivity of the *Reconquista* and the Inquisition, therefore, did not restore an "authentic" Hispanicity, but rather damaged it, made Spain less European ("Europe" understood as heterogeneous and multicultural) and more provincially Catholic, Castilian, and homogeneous, especially under Ferdinand and Isabella. "What we forget," Castro asserted, "is that the Spaniards were—and are—Islamic-Hebraic-Asiatic as much as they were—and are—Christian-European."[95]

Castro's literary and cultural approach to Spain's possible path to Europeanism, however, contrasted that of Claudio Sánchez-Albornoz, who claimed that there were Spanish cultural and economic structures originating after the Roman empire's fall and the Visigoths' conversion to Christianity, before the Moorish invasions began in 711. These structures, he writes, were preserved in Asturias (the region in Spain's extreme north that was never conquered by the Moors) during the Moorish occupation. Having been "situated in the Western-most corner of Europe" and having served as the "bridge that unites Europe and Africa" for centuries, Spain indeed has experienced a mingling and many battles among "Oriental and Occidental" cultures in Spain, Sánchez-Albornoz asserts. But Hispanicity was, for Sánchez-Albornoz, a transhistorical racial character that was enriched by its direct confrontations with Islam. Spain's medieval era, Sánchez-Albornoz further argued, was one in which "a river of untold splendor ... flowed through Córdoba and toward the rest of Europe," carrying in it the "richest civilization that the West would know for centuries. . . . Never as then was Spain such a torch of Europe." Spain's difference from its "Western brothers" such as "France, Germany, Italy and England" is due to its having played the roles of "sacrificer and vigil, sentinel and instructor" for Europe—a multifaceted and centuries-long guard against the Islamic threat. Spain has no "originary defect," nor is it an "Africanized country, sick with an Eastern virus" of Islam, he believes; "it is a vital and able nation, . . . a Western *pueblo*" that expressed its Europeanness again brilliantly during the Golden Age. It must not be forgotten that the authentic soul of "Spain" has been "yoked definitively to Europe" since the

Middle Ages. For Sánchez-Albornoz, Spain preserved a Christian Europe, and it would reemerge in the twentieth century as the continent's new soul.[96]

Moving beyond Spanish voices alone, the *Revista* both expanded and critiqued the positions of Menéndez Pidal, Castro, and Sánchez-Albornoz, among others, by treating or publishing figures who, as Spengler and Russell had, simultaneously attracted and infuriated Ortega himself.[97] He believed that the increasing contemporary interest in Eastern thought among Western thinkers promised both new views of Spain and dangerous dismissals of Europe. The provocative works of Waldo Frank and of Count Keyserling were crucial here: both writers were staunch critics of Europe in the wake of the Great War, and for that reason, the review published plenty of their works. However, both also turned to non-European (sometimes Eastern, sometimes "global") sources of quasi-mystical enlightenment and spiritual rejuvenation. Frank, for instance, presented a "spiritual" reading of Spaniards' "will" and "energies," which he argues are "not decadent" or "weak," but rather have been overspent and are in need of replenishment and redirection.[98] Keyserling, for his part, argued that, in truth, "Spain belongs to Africa. Whoever goes from France across the Pyrenees passes from a land of gardens to the desert." Its culture has much in common with "expressions of pre-Egyptian African civilizations"—expressions seen in Arab and Berber cultures. In fact, the Basque country in Spain retains this "primitive" character. However, *because* of this history, Spaniards can be "not only good Europeans, but ideal Europeans." While Russia and America separate themselves further from cultures of the continent, Spain can represent what Keyserling calls the "cosmic primitive" in the new Europe. It has "a new future in Europe as substance made into being." If "the European of the future is to reach his perfection," he proposes, he must look to Spain and its multicultural past, for it is "clearly ascending now" and will become the new "European synthesis."[99] For these contributors, the new Europe must embrace its African, Semitic, and non-Western roots and its mystical Eastern affinities in order to become a diverse union reborn around Spain. Ortega considered these competing, controversial accounts of Spain's history and its place in Europe to be part of reshaping the public sphere throughout the country—and by doing so, opening its mental borders to foreign influence.

Indeed, the force of these debates was not contained to Spanish matters: evincing its belief that "wisdom [does not] have national boundaries," as Flint wrote of it, the *Revista* took up a polyvocal defense of Miguel Asín Palacios, a Catholic priest and a famous Arabist who had published a radical thesis on the Islamic and Arabic origins of Dante's *Divine Comedy*. One of Asín's disciples, Ángel González Palencia, noted that Asín now enjoys the support of leading Arabists and non-Italian Danteists, but that Italian Danteists have yet to overcome their "nationalist prejudices or Dantephilia." This is keeping them from seeing the veracity of Asín's research, which the "immense cosmopolitan majority of Arabists and Romanists" have recognized already.[100] In other words, Italian Danteists have hewed stubbornly to politicized nationalist pronouncements on Dante's exclusively local, Catholic roots in the face of evidence to the contrary. Shortly thereafter, this conversion migrated northward: with English interest both in Asín's and Menéndez Pidal's works rising, the Duke of Alba (a primary sponsor of the Residencia de Estudiantes) funded translations of their works.

Spain and the Constitution of the West in the *Criterion*

Spain's complex, paradoxical role in the history of Europe surfaced most fully in the *Criterion* in the mid-to late 1920s, when it provided the topic for the most substantial intertexual conversations between Eliot's and Ortega's periodicals. Eliot had wished since the *Criterion*'s first numbers to give a "scholarly presentation of the Eastern world to occidental Europe which knows so little about it," with the goal of better understanding the "occidentality" of Europe.[101] Having briefly considered launching another journal devoted to the debate of European topics from multiple perspectives in 1925, Eliot instead relaunched his existing *Criterion* by adding "*New*" to its title and nearly doubling its size in January 1926. Eliot announced to his readers that he planned to hold a pan-European dialogue on "The Defence of the Occident"—a dialogue which, he hoped, would enliven the Anglo-European public sphere that the *Criterion* had been carving out domestically and would gather the criss-crossing trajectories of international thought in the field of literary periodicals in Europe. (This dialogue, as I have been suggesting, already reached across the two journals beyond Eliot's knowledge, as when the Spaniard Luis de Zulueta's "The Enigma of Russia" appeared in the *Revista de Occidente* in 1925, declaring that the Russian Revolution "was not, in its roots, a European revolution, but rather a mysticist Eastern one."[102]) Eliot sought a range of contributions: "in England, in Germany, in Italy or Spain, the problem [of defining Europe and 'the West'] may appear under a different light," he suggests, due to the uneven relationships across Europe among intellectuals, the state, and the imagined culture of the continent. And once again, he unsuccessfully sought a contribution from Ortega, perhaps addressing Primo de Rivera's banishment of Miguel de Unamuno, which Eliot had just discussed in his *Criterion* "Commentary."[103]

Eliot's forum, however, looked very different from what he had envisioned—"Spain" worked both for and against his positions—and it included some of the most impassioned writing to appear in the *Criterion*'s history. It began with an angry polemic: Henri Massis's *Defence of the West*. Massis, a far-right French nationalist, yet a thinker with whom Eliot, despite his distaste for nationalism, had some sympathy, argues that "the future of western civilisation, indeed the future of mankind, is to-day in jeopardy," threatened by "the awakening of the nations of Asia and Africa, united by Bolshevism." He aims, using a Spenglerian metaphor, to revive the "mangled body of Europe . . . [whose] unity . . . was physically broken in 1914." Massis cites the shift of Germany and Russia from their "Greco-Latin" roots toward "Asiatic destinies" as causes of the dismemberment of the European body.[104] Kenneth Codrington followed by attacking Massis's *Defence* as a symptom of a post-war "febrile brand of Nationalism, which, like most national anthems, is too sentimental to be convincing."[105] Other contributors continued to approach this topic from non-Western perspectives, a rare occurrence in the *Criterion*'s history. Sirdar Ikbal Ali Shah's "The Meeting of the East and West" quotes numerous Orientalist moments in Western literature in which poets and authors draw upon the East to articulate their visions of the West. Vasudeo B. Metta also defends the East against Massis's aspersions and reveals the historical permeation of the East within the West, from Egyptian and Assyrian influences on Greco-Roman sculpture to the "Oriental" elements of Christianity and of Jesus's philosophies. In the end, Eliot found little support for his own cultural politics—especially his growing anti-liberalism—among his contributors, and he printed more assaults on Massis's positions than confirmations of them, despite his own view of the *Criterion* as an English supporter of another reactionary Frenchman, Charles Maurras. Spengler, too, was often a target for criticism.[106]

Eliot's primary intermediaries between Britain and Spain then used contemporary Spain and the *Revista de Occidente* in particular as counterexamples against the intellectual trends that Massis and Spengler represented. J. B. Trend, for instance, argues that the contents of the *Revista* cross national and linguistic borders in a manner that right-wing formulations of "Europe" cannot make cohere. He points to publications such as Miguel Asín's work on Dante and a debate between Ángel Sánchez Rivero and Américo Castro on Spanish history as evidence of this. Trend also singles out one of his *Criterion* colleagues for his dissemination of British modernism in Spain, praising not only Marichalar's "understanding . . . of English things," but also "the conviction he brings that, of all foreign minds, none can appreciate the peculiarly English attitude more acutely than the mind which has had its origin in Spain." (Yet, "English critics are not very ready to admit that Spain, as a country of the mind, has any real existence," he laments in a review of Castro's work.[107] When he was named the first chair in Spanish at Cambridge, he wrote to Ortega that it was "a recognition of *your* Spain, and the Spain of all my friends."[108]) Trend continues, while celebrating Ortega's translations of Hegel's works into a Latin language for the first time, that

> this review continues to justify its reputation as one of the most broadminded in Europe. It is by no means confined to that "Near West" defended by M. Massis, nor yet to that *mundo latino* exalted by certain Spanish journalists[. . . . Through cooperation with such reviews,] we must form a united European front in which all the great powers of our culture can share.

Trend reads Eliot's and Ortega's journals together through their shared belief in Curtius's ideal—which he is quoting—of "a united European front" that would counter nationalist intellectualism. The Foreign Reviews section also featured similarly positive notes on the new magazines for which the Generation of '27 would become famous, such as *Carmen*, *Lola*, and *Litoral* [*Coastal*], as makers of a hybrid Spanish-European aesthetics.

Trend implies, moreover, that Manuel de Falla's ballets exhibit the very complexity that makes the French and Spanish reactionary positions toward the continent's culture seem hollow: "Where is . . . the 'defence of the west,' or, for that matter, Europe itself! If de Falla is Latin in this, he is like a Latin writer—Apuleius, for instance—using the Latin language to describe utterly un-Latin things."[109] Through his studies of Falla and Bartók, Trend consistently worked to decenter and reorient the poles around which European music was understood in this era, writing that these composers "combine an oriental feeling for rhythm with a sense of form which is definitely European."[110] The music of Hungary, Czechoslovakia, Russia, and Spain, Trend claims, remains "fear[ed . . . as] 'barbarian'" in the heart of Europe.[111] Only several years later does Trend believe that "we are beginning, in fact, to listen to music in a way which, for over a thousand years, has been Oriental rather than European"—liberated from the provincial and national categories that had prevailed too long on the continent, a critique that Kant had influentially voiced.[112] The Orientalist scholar Stanley Rice, another friend of Eliot's, concludes in the journal that "it is difficult to resist the conclusion that the music of Europe is looking towards the East through the eyes of a people that is more than half Asiatic."[113]

Flint, in his estimations of the *Revista de Occidente*, made Ortega's journal a paradigm of cosmopolitan journalism. Writing in the issue that followed his translation of Massis's *Defence*, Flint says that for three years now, the *Revista* has been "the most alertly intelligent of all the foreign reviews that reach me: intelligent in the sense that its eyes are open on the world, the whole world; they are not directed solely to the doings of a particular clique or coterie or even nation." Flint adds that "there is too much in these [most recent] six numbers to review in a short note[,] . . . but it will be quite clear that the *Revista de Occidente* is both catholic in its choice of subjects and international in its choice of writers."[114] The *Criterion*, in other words, which had first looked to the *Revista* as evidence of the new European spirit in Spain, now uses the *Revista* to argue, in the columns of Eliot's collaborators, that the ideals of Europe that their editor himself insisted on publishing in the *Criterion's* forum were proven false by the journal's own Spanish counterpart and its cultural milieu.

European Writing, War, and Demise: Revaluating England and the British Empire

The *Revista de Occidente*, meanwhile, continued to meditate on the same topics through foreign perspectives by printing translations of famous statements on Europe such as Paul Valéry's "Notes on the Greatness and Decline of Europe." Sounding much like the *Criterion*, a review of Valery Larbaud's work concurs with the Frenchman's belief that "in London, Madrid, and all of our Western capitals, . . . [indeed] throughout the world, there is a great intellectual family that is distinguishing itself from people of narrow and provincial spirits—a family in which all the creative and vital forces of all nations are brought together; in France it is called *l'élite*, and in his time, Shakespeare called it *the happy few*."[115] From these cross-cultural dialogues, the *Criterion* and the *Revista* finally formed a version of the Anglo- and Hispano-European components of the continental vanguard that Eliot and Ortega respectively foresaw, just before the short-lived fiction competition was launched. Eliot reasserted his belief that such work in these reviews had given new life to

> the European Idea. It is remarkable because of the variety of its appearances; it may take the form of a meditation on the decay of European civilization by Paul Valéry, or of a philosophy of history such as that of Oswald Spengler, or it may appear allied with an intense nationalism as in the work of Henri Massis. . . . It has no obligation to the thought of Romain Rolland, to nineteenth-century socialism, or to the humanitarian sentiments out of which the League of Nations arose; and it has as yet no direct connection with the League and no perceptible influence upon it.[116]

Linking his editors' thought through their shared antipathy to the League of Nations, Marichalar added in his chronicles that Ortega's work was "diametrically opposed" to the League's brand of internationalism, which does nothing to confront the threats of China and Islam.[117] When Ortega contrasts the "intellectual cosmopolitanism" of his vision of culture with the failed "political internationalism" of the League of Nations, Marichalar writes, he argues that, at best, the League preserved a form of nineteenth-century nationalism.

Curtius, a mutual friend of Eliot and Ortega, offered a sense of cooperation that exemplified the various arguments that both editors' journals had engaged; Eliot believed that "no name is more representatively that of the *European* man of letters" than his.[118] The *Criterion* and the *Revista de Occidente* published translations of Curtius's "Restoration of the Reason" (1927) almost simultaneously, and the essay appeared in the *Neue Schweizer Rundschau*, all at the same moment of the idealistic pan-Europeanisms of Aristide Briand and of Count Coudenhove-Kalergi. Curtius wrote that Spain, England, France, and Italy all had the "same historical structure," for they were all "constituted from three elements: the native stock, the Roman cultural heritage, and the Germanic invasions."[119] After seeing Europe "dismembered into geographical fragments" by "national myths and ideologies" during the Great War, Curtius worked to foster his ideal of unifying a new generation of writers as the continent's redeemers. The essay calls for a generation of "architects[,] . . . measuring, calculating, organizing master-builders of Europe. In other words, specialists with a universal attitude and orientation . . . [for on] their shoulders rests the responsibility for the preservation, the recovery and the renovation of Europe." This vanguard of "people with a synthetic consciousness" was needed to "reconstruct . . . the European man" in the face of threats by nationalist, communist, and fascist movements.[120] Curtius believed especially in "a new and productive function" for criticism within literary journals to animate continually "the intellectual energies of our age . . . [and] its emerging ecumenical, cosmopolitan culture" in which one might move freely across Europe's national boundaries.[121]

Eliot used Curtius's work, he wrote, to revaluate further his adoptive country. He is optimistic that "nine years after the end of the War we are only beginning to distinguish between the characteristics of our own time and those inherited from the previous epoch. One of the latter was Nationalism." He imagines that an intellectual minority is now uniting itself against the "aged idea" of nationalism in order "to harmonize first the ideas, of the civilized countries of Western Europe . . . [and to] reaffirm . . . the European tradition." For Eliot, this means that the continent needs Britain more than ever, and that "it is for us to see that in this reorganization of the ideas of Europe [that Curtius has proposed], the ideas of Britain and the British Empire have their place."[122] Britain is, for Eliot, the *via media*:

> To our mind, the peculiar position of Britain is this: that she is on the one hand a part of Europe. But not only a part, she is a mediating part: for Britain is the bridge between Latin and Germanic culture in both of which she shares. But Britain is not only the bridge, the middle way, between two parts of western Europe; she is, or should be, by virtue of the fact that she is the only member of the European community that has established a genuine empire—that is to say, a world-wide empire as was the Roman empire—not only European but the connection between Europe and the rest of the world.[123]

Inscribing Britain within "the European community" and envisioning its imperial power as a capacity to "connect" Europe culturally to "the rest of the world," Eliot now reads Britain—which he had criticized in the 1910s for its provinciality—as a bridge across the traditional boundaries of Europe. Flint, Trend, and others concurred with his case for *British* exceptionalism, too, with Trend referring to his countrymen as "born Teuton and bred Latin."[124] J. G. Fletcher chastised England by adding that, unlike Russia or the United States, "the power of the British Empire [is . . .] neither Eastern nor Western," and that, despite its potential to unite Europe, "England turns her back upon European problems and strives to create sovereignty out of insularity."[125] "We must not forget," Eliot believed, "amongst these glorious public meetings, proposals and resolutions, that real *intellectual* co-operation is . . . strongly conscious of a national and an imperial tradition, and at the same time of a European tradition."[126] His ideal of this balance between the local and continental was Dante, whom he called in in his 1929 study "the most *universal* of poets in the modern languages," one who was able to be both "an Italian and a patriot [. . .] not of one European country but of Europe." The Great War, for Eliot, in fact had been the "culminat[ion of] . . . the process of disintegration . . . [that] began soon enough after Dante's time."[127] The hybrid national-Europeanism that Eliot envisions—vaguely and sometimes with contradiction—as superseding the era of nationalism existed in the network of dialogues and "circulation" that he praised in his comments on European reviews.

In this moment, Eliot's vision of English and British history in Europe aligns most closely with Ortega's view of a Latin-Germanic Spain, and with Curtius's universalist reading of Europe's mingled character. But just as these editorial visions seemed to be uniting, the bonds among Europeanist periodicals quickly disappeared. The fiction competition that would crystallize the *Criterion*'s and the *Revista*'s cooperation faltered in the 1930s. The new, often openly partisan journals soon began supplanting both the *Criterion* and the *Revista de Occidente*, and the former's reviews of the latter even began to turn dismissive and sometimes negative. As if he internalized Pound's needling—"Chrissssttttt cant you see that *you are* the Criterion[?]"—Eliot read his review's failure as his own.[128] In *Four Quartets* (1943), he writes "So here I am, in the middle way, having had twenty years— /Twenty years largely wasted, the years of *l'entre deux guerres*."[129] Echoing his description of Britain as "the bridge, *the middle way*, between two parts of western Europe," Eliot's introspection couples his own unsuccessful ambitions to shape politics through culture with Britain's geopolitical failures to prevent another war.

The ramifications of unfinished periodical work will resurface throughout this book. Jason Harding shares Peter Ackroyd's estimation of Eliot's ideals, concluding that Eliot's plan to "mobilize a cohort of European periodicals in the defence of a Virgilian *penates*, for all the heroic grandeur attached to such a project, seems a curiously misguided undertaking."[130] Eliot could only blame, in uncertain terms, a "closing of mental frontiers" across the continent that led to the demise of both reviews.[131] He revises retroactively his optimism of the late 1920s and early 1930s when he explains in the *Criterion*'s final issue in 1939 that "gradually communications became more difficult, contributions more uncertain, and new and important foreign contributors more difficult to discover. The 'European mind,' which one had mistakenly thought might be renewed and fortified, disappeared from view" after 1929. He now looks back on the immediate post–Great War moment not as "a hopeful period in the world of letters," but as

> a period of illusions. Only from about the year 1926 did the features of the post-war world begin clearly to emerge.... From about that date one began slowly to realize that the intellectual and artistic output of the previous seven years had been rather the last efforts of an old world, than the first struggles of a new.[132]

Eliot dismisses these efforts in a manner that retroactively foresees the decline and eventual ends of both the *Revista de Occidente* and the *Criterion*—punctuated as they were by new wars, in 1936 and 1939, respectively.

Eliot and Marichalar's relationship and occasional meetings, like those among several other intermediaries in this chapter, would prosper through most of the interwar era, but would dissolve after 1936.[133] Ortega, for his part, was silent on the *Revista* during his exile and lost most communications with figures such as Eliot. And though he later would recall fondly his relations with foreign editors, Eliot's final judgment of his review is difficult to discern. Writing in the 1950s, he idealized their interchanges, writing that among himself, Larbaud, Curtius, Ortega, Charles Du Bos, and the editors of sympathetic continental reviews, "No ideological differences poisoned our intercourse; no political oppression limited freedom of communication," much as Curtius had claimed that a "Europe of the mind—above politics, in spite of all politics—was very much alive" between the wars.[134] Perhaps, though, the spirit of cooperation that seemed so evident in the post–Great War moment was already laden with "poison[s]" and internal contradictions. Curtius admitted that he largely lost his sympathy for Eliot when the latter converted and became a British citizen. When Eliot published Massis and Maurras, whom the *NRF* considered enemies, the *NRF* completely ignored Eliot's poetry.[135] Also undermining these efforts were Trend's comments on Waldo Frank in a letter to Ortega in 1925. Frank, whom Ortega was publishing at the time in the *Revista de Occidente* (see chapter 3), represented for Trend the "new America" that was, in fact, a "Jew America" that is wholly "un-European."[136] Furthermore, Trend, who had celebrated in the *Criterion* the role of Jewish forms in European musical history, becomes angrier the following year, telling Ortega that Frank, who had Sephardic ancestors, is a "negroid Jew" who has no place in the project of remaking Europe.[137] Given his vital position between them (and the controversies over Eliot's and Ortega's own racist moments), Trend compromises Eliot's and Ortega's shared cosmopolitanism with his anti-Semitism. The ability of collaboration to expand a periodical beyond an editor's purview was, in the end, a double-edged sword.

2. Joyce and the Spanish *Ulysses*

> Antonio Marichalar... asked me for something for [Juan Ramón Jiménez's review] *Índice*, and I suggested my article [on *Ulysses*], freely and out of the love of making Joyce known to the people of the land of María Santísima. (Molly Bloom in Gibraltar, reading about herself in a Madrid review.)
>
> —Valery Larbaud to Adrienne Monnier, 24 March 1922[1]

Valery Larbaud's parenthetical comment in the epigraph above conjures a fascinating scenario that connects the world evoked by a fictional text to a critical world in which it circulated: James Joyce's Spanish-Irish heroine Molly Bloom reads an analysis of herself (as depicted by an expatriate Irish author) in an actual Spanish periodical in the 1920s. Even if it would require Molly to return to the disputed territory of Gibraltar of her youth and to remaster the "little Spanish" she has mostly "forgotten" (*U* 4.60–61), Larbaud's vision of her reading his own influential article in translation raises several intriguing questions: How did Silver Age Spanish critics initially receive *Ulysses* and interpret Molly's character and avant-garde monologue, in contexts that dramatically contrasted those of their Anglophone and continental counterparts? What political critiques did they see entwined in Molly's Hispanicity and in the Spanish and Irish affinities staged throughout the novel? As writers and intellectuals in Spain searched for new, foreign literary forms that would regenerate the culture of their marginalized "land of María Santísima," what kind of map did they see in Joyce's postcolonial Ireland integrated within an imagined *post-imperial* Europe? That is to say, when Stephen Dedalus overhears the claim by the Irish man of letters Dr. George Sigerson that

Ireland has no "Don Quixote and Sancho Panza" and that its "national epic has yet to be written," Joyce points unawares to a challenge that many Spaniards saw for a country whose national epic from its Golden Age had become outdated, if not altogether irrelevant (*U* 9.308–309). How does all of this bear on present readings of Joyce, his complex cosmopolitanism, and the politics of *Ulysses*, tied as they were to a country where civil war broke out in 1922?

To answer these questions about the reciprocity between the "Spain" within *Ulysses* and *Ulysses* in Spain, this chapter begins with a close reading, rooted in Anglo- and Hispanophone literary-critical history, of the embedded and multilayered political narratives in *Ulysses*. Widely circulated throughout Europe but largely unavailable in the emerging Irish Free State, *Ulysses* spoke to a generation of Spaniards living under dictatorship who modified Joyce's sketch of the future continent. This work was both inaugurated and, in many ways, crystallized by Antonio Marichalar, the first critic to use *Ulysses* as a means of linking specifically Ireland, Spain, and Europe, and the first to translate portions of *Ulysses* into Spanish. Marichalar did not translate Larbaud's piece for *Índice*, as suggested in the letter above. Instead, he published his own groundbreaking work, "James Joyce in His Labyrinth" ["James Joyce en su laberinto"], in the *Revista de Occidente* in 1924. It became one of the most important pieces of interwar Spanish-language literary criticism and a broadly disseminated touchstone for the Spanish-European modernism that this book treats. It also launched Marichalar's career along paths that led to Sylvia Beach and briefly to Joyce himself. A review in the *Criterion* proclaimed rightly that Marichalar's essay was

> not only the best that could be imagined for readers in Catholic countries, it also—and the two things are not unconnected—has claims to being the best estimate of the intellectual significance of Joyce that has appeared in any language so far.[2]

The Spanish-Irish alliance posited in this powerful note is one that Marichalar explores in his portrait of the "Spanish Joyce" and that I trace further through *Ulysses*. Furthermore, Marichalar, against some of his contemporaries, reads and extends *Ulysses* as a transnational epic, as Joyce hoped his "class . . . of foreignborn admirers" would do.[3] This epic crossed numerous historical and fictional borders to become a template of Europeanist, post-imperial writing in the New Spain, where Joyce's influence was arguably greater than in Ireland. Marichalar's unique translation of Molly's speech, which differs in telling ways from Jorge Luis Borges's better-known version, combines with his cosmopolitan genealogy of Joyce's interior monologue to demonstrate a critical-creative (or "re-creative") adaptation of Joyce's "international" style for his own Generation of '27 colleagues. His work also offers a heuristic model for closing some of the gaps that persist between current English- and Spanish-language critical narratives about Joyce and *Ulysses* in his reading of Joyce's international "Dublin" and its connections to a cosmopolitan "Madrid."

In the interconnected fields of Joyce's work and contemporaneous Spanish cultural politics lie symbiotic modernist movements forging ambitious efforts to reform Europe from marginal states in transition: from Europe's internal colony (Ireland) and its internal Other (Spain). Joyce innovatively converts Ireland and Spain—countries that shared ingrained tropes of impurity, dehumanized Africanism, retrogressive Catholicism, and cultural decline—not into a single religious or ethnic community, but into the two paradigmatic countries that had been disconnected from Europe by British imperialism and that would emerge as shared redeemers of the continent. These affinities prefigure postcolonial critical understandings of Ireland's and Spain's capacities to trouble Eurocentric center/periphery or metropole/colony models of modernisms. José Ortega y Gasset and Marichalar viewed their own compatriots as "the most belated race in Europe," as Joyce wrote of the Irish, and were eager to see that Spain no longer remained Europe's emblem of defeat, imperial loss, and decadence—characterizations attached to Hispanicity, usually via Molly, throughout much of *Ulysses*.[4] By enlisting *Ulysses* in the project of Spanish modernism, Marichalar fuses Joyce's continentalist cosmopolitanism with that of Ortega, demonstrating that cosmopolitan sensibilities were enmeshed in a set of practices that both Joyce and his critics drew upon in order to ally themselves with the broader project of a new hyphenated European aesthetics. Joyce's new Ireland and Ortega's New Spain meet here, and toward the end of this chapter I return to the novel through an Anglo-Spanish lens to interpret fully the payoff of this intersection. Across a century of literature, history, criticism, and politics, the project of Spanish-Irish cultural rejuvenation that Molly eventually represents, when animated by the historical convergence of rising British and falling Spanish imperial forces that "produced" her, takes up from minor perspectives the post-war task of envisioning the new Europe, its literary cultures, and its prototypical subjects, as Joyce imagines them through the Blooms.

Molly's "Spanish Type" and Cultural Decadence

Throughout the course of *Ulysses*, Joyce circulates through multiple characters and voices a pastiche of these same tropes of Hispanicity and its implications of decline that Ortega and his circle continually confronted. They are scattered and they resist taxonomy, but their fixation on Molly and their connections to Joyce's depictions of Irishness illuminate several crosscurrents in the novel. Molly's "Spanish type" has multiple sources that Joyce weaves into the novel, one of which is the author's impression of Mamie (or Mamy) Dillon, the daughter of a family friend, whom he recalled as a "cigarette smoker and Spanish type."[5] But the Spanish-Irish thematics of *Ulysses* derive more historically from the Spanish past of Galway, hometown of his wife Nora Barnacle. He elaborates on this in his short travel pieces written for the Triestine paper *Il Piccolo della Sera* in 1912, just after he and Nora had visited Galway and the Aran Islands. Joyce writes of the Spanish King Philip II's ill-fated attempt to invade England:

> Under the waters and along the coast of this gulf [in Galway] lies the wreckage of a fleet of ships from the rather unfortunate Spanish Armada. After their defeat in the [English] Channel, the ships set sail northwards where they were scattered by squalls and ocean storms. The peasants of County Galway, recalling the long friendship between Spain and Ireland, hid the fugitives from the revenge of the English garrison and gave holy burial to the shipwrecked dead.[6]

The victories of the British empire leave behind in Ireland the still-visible wreckage of the Spanish empire and, through the position of Molly's father Brian Tweedy in the British military, make possible Molly's Spanish-Irish origins in Gibraltar. Joyce also describes the recognizable but fading Spanish presence in Ireland:

> The lazy Dubliner who does not travel much and knows his country only by hearsay thinks that the inhabitants of Galway are of Spanish stock, . . . a true Spanish type with olive features and crow-black hair. The Dubliner is both wrong and right. Nowadays, at least, dark hair and eyes are rare in Galway . . . [and the] old Spanish houses are in ruins. . . . However, it is enough to close one's eyes against this unsettling modernity just for a moment, and the "Spanish City" can be seen in the shadows of history. . . . The signs on the street corners recall the connections of the city with Latin Europe: Madeira Street, Merchant Street, Spaniards Walk.[7]

Joyce identifies in the "unsettling modernity" of Galway several elements that he fashions throughout *Ulysses* into a microcosm of Spain's decline—its fading into the "shadows of history," as did "Latin Europe."

When he transfers this Spanish-Irish hybridity to Gibraltar, a site with which Galway shared geographical and cultural features, he adds to it Molly's account of the local population: "the Greeks and the jews and the Arabs and the devil knows who else from all ends of Europe."[8] Gibraltar becomes a gathering point for the cast-offs of Europe and more that Molly will embody. In keeping with such associations, Bloom, in his own Hispanist fantasies, imagines Molly as such an amalgamation of nationalities and races from the heterogeneous world to Ireland's south and east that begot Molly: "Coming all that way: Spain, Gibraltar, Mediterranean, the Levant."[9] Molly's origins remain in a distant world that is unknowable and inaccessible to him; he can only remember her "thinking of Spain. Before Rudy was born" (U 8.24–25). Instead, he relies on stereotypes and cultural associations. Bloom adds to his portrait of Molly the "Moorish" qualities that recall her inclusion of "Arabs" in Gibraltar, where she used to look across the strait at Morocco, and where she kissed Mulvey under the Moorish Wall. For him, Molly's physical traits and her sensuality; her *Peau d'Espagne* perfume ("that cheap peau dEspagne that faded and left a stink on you more than anything else," Molly says); her "form . . . [and] figure[,] . . . blood of the south. Moorish"; her "passionate temperament" and "impetuous[ness]"; and the "darkness of her eyes. Looking at me, the sheet up to her eyes, Spanish" (later "Spanishy eyes," elsewhere "Moorish eyes") all lead him to conclude that "she has the Spanish type. Quite dark, regular brunette, black."[10] He sexualizes these traits and believes "certainly . . . [that] climate accounts for character" (U 16.880). Molly's Spanish qualities and her "blood of the sun" are to blame in part for her decadence in his mind—and therefore her adultery (U 16.889). When Bloom fantasizes himself witnessing her illicit lovemaking with Blazes Boylan in "Circe," Molly calls Boylan "Raoul darling," referring to the Don Juan figure of the erotic novel *Sweets of Sin* that Bloom purchased (U 15.3770). (Both Bloom and Molly, in fact, dream about living in Spain and speaking Spanish at different points in the novel.) Even the very minor character Mrs. Miriam Dandrade, a "divorced Spanish American," is mentioned first in "Lestrygonians" as an unblushing woman whose "old wraps and black underclothes" Bloom once bought (U 8.350–351). When Bello subjugates a feminine Bloom in "Circe," she taunts him for cross-dressing and lying "across the bed as Mrs Dandrade about to be violated" by a list of men; he is pursued later in this episode by a gang of characters brought up in the rear by "Mrs Dandrade and all her lovers" (U 15.3000, 15.4360–4361).

Stephen and Bloom's erroneous conjecture in "Eumaeus" that the famous adulteress Kitty O'Shea (who was actually Irish) was "Spanish or half so," a "type . . . that wouldn't do things by halves, passionate abandon of the south, casting every shred of decency to the winds," perpetuates these imaginings (U 16.1409–1410).[11] The comment leads Bloom's mind immediately to the copy of *Sweets of Sin* in his pocket. Bloom then produces from his pocketbook the photograph of Molly in a sensual "evening dress cut ostentatiously low for the occasion to give a liberal display of bosom."¹² In the picture, she stands beside a piano on which rests the sheet music of the ballad *In Old Madrid*; Bloom asks Stephen, "Do you consider... that a Spanish type?" (*U* 16.1425–1426). The Hispanist typology culminates in "Ithaca" with the "2 erotic photocards" from Spain that Bloom owns, one "showing: a) buccal coition between nude señorita... and nude torero," the other showing two religious figures in a sexual position (*U* 17.1809–1812). Molly internalizes these portraits, calling herself "a little like that dirty bitch in that Spanish photo he has" and noting that the permissive Andalusian girls, with whom she identified in her youth, tended to wear nothing under their dresses (*U* 18.563–564, 18.440). Appropriately, Stephen bundles—or rather, is reported by the imprecise narrator of "Eumaeus" to bundle—several assorted references to Spain and Hispanicity from throughout the novel when he rambles a response to the comment about Kitty O'Shea: "The king of Spain's daughter, Stephen answered, adding something or other rather muddled about farewell and adieu to you Spanish onions."¹³

Some historical context helps explain these references and some obscure but important details that Joyce embeds in *Ulysses*. Many of these notions of Hispanicity, especially in the British imaginary, date back to contradictions and extremes familiar from the Black Legend: oppressive Catholicism and corrupt licentiousness, nobility and treachery, Europeanism and Africanism. Tom Buchanan writes that since the eighteenth century (if not earlier), Britons, who knew Spain mostly from vacations and rest cures, became "fascinated with Spain's decline, especially at a time when Britain was forging its own empire." In the early twentieth century, Spain "remained a symbol for international failure and decline."¹⁴ "Decline" and "decay" became bywords for Spain when the nation was mentioned in the British press, associations that were further ingrained by the historian Martin Hume's popular study *Spain: Its Greatness and Decay (1479–1788)* (1898). Hume claims that by understanding the history of Spain, "the ordinary observer may see the working of the process by which nations are ruined."¹⁵ Also in 1898, when Prime Minister Lord Salisbury included Spain in the group of "dying nations" that stood in contrast to "living nations" such as England, France, and the United States, his characterizations quickly made their way to the front pages of popular Spanish newspapers such as *El Imparcial* and *La Época*.¹⁶

Spain's fallen blood and fallen empire, however, provide Joyce an entrée to explore the history of Spain's marginalization from Europe; through that history, he elucidates its connections to Ireland, home to "the last European port," Galway. Spain and Ireland, he suggests, crossed paths through the former's imperial ventures. The first allusion to Spain in *Ulysses*, in fact, is to the shipwreck of that "unfortunate Spanish Armada." While walking on Sandymount Strand, Stephen, self-described servant of the "imperial British state" that ascended to global preeminence with its victory in 1588, sees the ruins of Spain's navy, and ponders the "wood sieved by the shipworm, lost Armada" (*U* 3.149). That is, evidence of Spain's decay—which occurred *after* its expulsion of Jews, Bloom will note—lies in the Irish sand. Joyce's characters also suggest that Ireland and Spain, both victims of the "revenge of the English garrison," share a commonality in their detachment from Europe at the hands of an un-European empire. In "Cyclops," the citizen revisits Ireland's many continental affiliations of the past, including Galway's prosperous wine trade with Spain and "king Philip of Spain['s]" offer to pay to fish in Irish waters (*U* 12.1310). He recalls the migrations of the ancient Milesians, Gaelic Celts who came through Galicia to Ireland; Milly Bloom's name alludes to this race ("Return, return, Clan Milly: forget me not, O Milesian" [*U* 14.371–72]). He also waxes nostalgic on the same "long friendship between Spain and Ireland" that Joyce described in his journalism. The citizen scoffs at the French, "Firebrands of Europe" who were "never worth a roasted fart to Ireland," but not at the Spanish, who were not complicit in the "entente cordiale . . . with perfidious Albion" (*U* 12.1386–1388).

John Wyse Nolan later echoes the citizen's claims: "We gave our best blood to France and Spain, the wild geese[,] . . . O'Donnell, the duke of Tetuan in Spain" (*U* 12.1382–1383). The final reference here is to Leopold O'Donnell, or Leopoldo O'Donnell y Jorris, the Spanish duke of Irish (and also wild goose) descent whose first name also fits Joyce's designs for the novel.¹⁷ At the same time, this invocation of O'Donnell deepens the "Moorish" and African associations with Spain: as Tetuan (now Tétouan, Morocco) was only "in Spain" and O'Donnell only its duke by virtue of his having led a Spanish invasion into North Africa in 1860. Joyce pointed to these Irish-Spanish bonds at least as early as "Ireland, Isle of Saints and Sages" (1907), which outlines some of the means by which the Irish "spread [their] culture and stimulating energy through the continent" (*OCPW* 108). He writes of the Irish priest Sedulius the younger, who was rebuffed by the local clergy when he arrived to settle quarrels in Spain, but was accepted upon announcing that "as he was Irish and of the old Milesian race, he was, in fact, of Spanish origin" (*OCPW* 112). When Joyce notes that in "Ireland we can see how the Danes, the Firbolgs, the Milesians from Spain, the Norman invaders, the Anglo-Saxon colonists and the Huguenots came together to form a new entity, under the influence of a local god, one might say," he not only looks forward to the Ireland of *Finnegans Wake* (including its "Hiberio-Miletians"), but also grounds a reading of his country's syncretism through the same kinds of European connections that the citizen voices, then ultimately suppresses in favor of his nativism.¹⁸

The "European Family" and the End of Empires

The sources of the shared histories and hybridities of Spain and Ireland become clearer in the context of *Ulysses*'s intersecting narratives about the British empire. Britain's leaders, Buchanan explains, saw Spain's decline from imperial supremacy as a "warning" to protect their own overseas assets.[19] Stephen sees the armada's debris shortly after his conversation with Mr. Deasy, who asserted that "England is in the hands of the jews. In all the highest places: her finance, her press. And they are signs of a nation's decay.... Old England is dying" (*U* 2.346–351). Within Joyce's wider schema of civilizational *ricorso* adapted from Vico, the collapse of Spain's empire functions as an analogue for the well-known critiques of British imperialism and Anglo-Irish politics that he articulates through his characters' pronouncements and prophecies.[20] Joyce himself had witnessed the Austro-Hungarian empire's power crumbling in Pola and, while composing *Ulysses*, had watched with great interest a strong anti-monarchical and anti-imperial irredentist movement swelling in the polyglot and cosmopolitan Trieste, the "small European melting pot" that was called the "city of many nations."[21] In "Eumaeus," Bloom indirectly corrects both Mr. Deasy—and Haines, who fears "German jews" in England—when he argues that

> jews ... are accused of ruining [empires].... History, would you be surprised to learn, proves up to the hilt Spain decayed when the Inquisition hounded the jews out and England prospered when Cromwell ... imported them.... Spain again, you saw in the war, compared with goahead America. Turks. (*U* 16.1119–1128)

Invoking the failing Ottoman empire here, too, Bloom attempts to explain Spain's decline through social and military history, while dubbing the upstart American empire the heir to Britain's own declining power.

Britain's rotting imperial "syphilisation," the citizen declares, has corrupted the "European family" with its "great empire ... of drudges and whipped serfs" (*U* 12.1197, 12.1202, 12.1349–1350). Skin-the-Goat predicts "a day of reckoning ... in store for mighty England, despite her power of pelf on account of her crimes. There would be a fall and the greatest fall in history. The Germans and the Japs were going to have their little lookin[.] ... The Boers were the beginning of their end ... and her downfall would be Ireland, her Achilles heel" (*U* 16.997–1003). He also rejects Murphy's comment that the "Irish catholic peasant ... [is] the backbone of our empire," for Skin-the-Goat "cared nothing for any empire, ours or his, and considered no Irishman worthy of his salt that served it" (*U* 16.1021–1025.) The novel is replete with such claims, beginning in moments like Stephen's classroom lesson on Pyrrhus, which is an implicit commentary on Britain's conquest of Ireland ("*Another victory like that and we are done for,*" his student Cochrane recites [*U* 2.14; italics in original]). They continue through the many references and parallels in "Aeolus," insisting that the British "follow in . . . [the] footsteps" of the collapsing Roman empire (*U* 7.492). (Joyce "hated," Andrew Gibson notes, his own brief stay in "the most ancient and enduring of all imperial capitals, Rome."[22]) These assertions also offer a range of answers to Stephen's question to Buck Mulligan about how much longer Haines, the British occupier, will remain in the Martello tower.

The lesson is not that Spain's decline is unique, nor is it intrinsic to the "Spanish type," but rather that imperialism—especially British imperialism—has fractured the "European family" and *created* the continent's national margins. The citizen insists further that the British are "not European[.] . . . I was in Europe. . . . You wouldn't see a trace of them or their language anywhere in Europe except in a *cabinet d'aisance*" (*U* 12.1203–1205). Lenehan warns the citizen—and by extension, the Irish state coming into being—that "Europe has its eyes on you," and throughout the conversation, J. J. (O'Molloy), by way of his initials, adds a Joycean presence who constantly points his countrymen toward the "European family" (*U* 12.1265). (In fact, Stephen was present in the pub in the early drafts of *Ulysses* and was mocked for his Europeanism.[23] The young Stephen's cosmology in *Portrait* already linked Ireland to Europe by notably skipping the "United Kingdom": "Stephen Dedalus / Class of Elements /Clongowes Wood College /Sallins /County Kildare /Ireland / Europe /The World /The Universe."[24]) The citizen responds to him, "And our eyes are on Europe," tempering his politics with Europeanism even as he believes that "our greater Ireland beyond the sea" will "put force against force" (*U* 12.1296, 12.1364–1365). Regarding Ireland's relationship to Europe, in "Aeolus" Professor MacHugh maintains that the Irish are "liege subjects of the catholic chivalry of Europe that foundered at Trafalgar," a Greek spirit that has been dominated by the materialistically driven "*imperium*" of the British (*U* 7.565–567). Myles Crawford also tells Stephen that he, the colonized, can recover this spirit, for he has the power to "paralyse Europe" (*U* 7.628–629). Crawford reappears in "Circe," "*dangl[ing] a hank of Spanish onions in one hand,*" now calling on Bloom to "paralyse Europe" (*U* 15.807–12; italics in original). In such moments, in allusions, in arguments, in obliquity and irony, and in hallucinatory visions, Joyce's ideal of a European Ireland—never sketched out in clear, utopian terms—begins to take shape.

Joyce, Ortega, and the Cultural Politics of Gibraltar

The intersections of both Joyce's and Ortega's projects and their contexts become more visible through a deeper understanding of the cultural politics that centered on Gibraltar. The Rock is at once a concentrated emblem of Spanish decline and British imperial triumph and a nexus around which Joyce, his characters, his sources, and his Spanish peers fixed their readings of empires and national histories. Against the British and Anglo-Irish colonialism represented by Haines and Mr. Deasy, respectively, the citizen, Bloom, Molly, and Mrs. Rubio (Molly's childhood maid) all offer often contradicting commentaries on the Rock's history and symbolism. The citizen, with his hostility to British colonialism and his fervent Catholic nationalism, embodies another, less noticed connection between Ireland and Spain that is located by Gibraltar, which he notes was "grabbed by the foe of mankind" (U 12.1249). He is mirrored by Mrs. Rubio, another "Spanish type" in *Ulysses*—one who, given that she owns "a black blessed virgin," may be of African descent (her last name, ironically, means "blonde" or "fair-haired," and Molly notes that she wears "a switch of false hair") (U 18.759, 18.752). Molly recalls her maid's anger over Spain's loss of Gibraltar to Britain:

> vain about her appearance ugly as she was near 80 or a 100 her face a mass of wrinkles with all her religion domineering because she never could get over the Atlantic fleet coming in half the ships of the world and the Union Jack flying with all her carabineros because 4 drunken English sailors took all the rock from them and because I didnt run into mass often enough in Santa Maria to please her.... (U 18.752–758)

Here, Molly resists a more stereotypical version of Hispanicity, just as she resisted Mrs. Rubio's attempts to have her read the novels of Spain's beloved realist Juan Valera. Under occupation in two of Britain's key overseas garrisons, the angry citizen and the "vain," "ugly," and "cantankerous" Mrs. Rubio voice the political histories symbolized not only by Gibraltar, but also by the monuments to which Joyce connects it—the Martello tower, Nelson's Pillar, London's Trafalgar Square—through the Napoleonic Wars (U 18.752, 18.1474).[25]

A body of largely Anglophone postcolonial criticism has concentrated, however, primarily on the Irish connections to Gibraltar, seeing that Joyce uses the Rock to "(1) synecdochically represent British imperialism, (2) project colonialism in its contemporary, international guise in his study of the displaced and dispossessed, and (3) associate the theme of colonialism and its implications with his female persona . . . [at an] imperial crossroad[s]," Susan Bazargan summarizes.[26]

But Gibraltar also provides an axis on which to turn toward accessing the Spanish voices that it contains—narratives by Spaniards about their own purported decline, for instance, that were debated in the early twentieth century. In fact, Spanish sentiments toward the Rock were familiar even to the nineteenth-century travel-writers whose works Joyce used to construct his fictional Gibraltar. The American Henry Field registers in his guidebook *Gibraltar* (1888), for instance, that "the retention of Gibraltar is to England a matter of pride" and is a "constant irritation" to Spaniards, who lost the Rock by "folly." He hails the English "masters of Gibraltar" who "hold . . . Gibraltar, I will not say in an enemy's country, but certainly in a foreign country. . . . [T]he English are here, not by right of birth, but of conquest. Gibraltar is not a part of England: it is a part of Spain."[27] Briton Richard Ford's jingoistic *Hand-book for Travellers in Spain* (1845), another of Joyce's sources, portrays the Rock as a "motley masquerade" where "civilization and barbarism clash":

> The barren, cinder-looking, sunburnt mass [of the 'neutral ground' separating Gibraltar and Spain] is no unfit sample of tawny Spain, while the rope of sand connection is a symbol of the disunion, long the inherent weakness of the unamalgamating component items of Iberia. . . . Cross that strip, however, and all is changed, as by magic, into the order, preparation, organization, discipline, wealth, *honour*, and *power* of the *United* Kingdom.[28]

These Anglophone portraits bespeak the political currency of a symbolically "disuni[ted]," "weak," and "unamalgamating" Spain—all notions common in Hispanist fantasies and juxtaposed with an "order[ly]," "*power*[ful]," "*United* Kingdom"— put into circulation through Gibraltar. "Mammon is the god of Gib., as the name is vulgarized," Ford adds; nevertheless, the hellish Rock "is now a bright pearl in the Ocean Queen's crown."[29] When Bloom comments to Stephen that "my wife is, so to speak, Spanish, half, that is. Point of fact she could actually claim Spanish nationality if she wanted, having been born in (technically) Spain, i.e. Gibraltar," he calls forth the centuries of disputes over Gibraltar's sovereignty and the abiding Spanish claims to the Rock that Field and Ford noted (*U* 16.876–879). After its capture by Moorish soldiers in 711, Gibraltar was taken by the Spaniards in 1462, just as they were embarking on their own colonial epoch. They held it until the British invasion of 1704, making 1904 the bicentennial of Gibraltar's occupation by the empire. The Rock became a geopolitical cynosure of what Buchanan characterizes as the "changing balance of power between [Britain and Spain]," which was solidified after 1588 by "the British seizure [and] . . . dogged defence of the Rock . . ., and its development as a strategic imperial base."[30] As a geographical intersection of the Spanish mainland and Britain's empire, the "stone in Spain's shoe," as it was known, constantly reminded Spaniards of this shift in geopolitical standing. Britain's militaristic arrogance throughout the nineteenth century, during which they fortified their docks at Gibraltar and threatened to press Spaniards into their armed forces, offended many Spaniards and often prompted fears of British designs on conquering southwestern Spain.[31]

Just as the British empire arguably reached its zenith, Spain suffered its "Disaster" in 1898. The Spanish, Sebastian Balfour writes, "channelled [through Gibraltar their] resentment against the British government whom they suspected, with justification, of favouring the United States in the [Spanish-American War]."[32] The war cost Spain its last remaining New World colonies, leaving only its protectorate in Morocco and scattered holdings in Africa from its once vast empire. In response, competing strategies of *regeneracionismo* flourished across the country, prescribing everything from technocratic authoritarianism to anarchism to neo-imperialism. In fact, just before the 1898 war, Ángel Ganivet, a diplomat and writer from the Generation of '98, had already voiced this final call. As had the novelist Pedro Antonio de Alarcón before him, Ganivet argued in his *Idearium Español* (1897) that Spain could counter perceptions of its decay by taking on England:

> The history of England ... is one of long aggression. ... The restoration of Gibraltar should be a task essentially and exclusively Spanish. ... Gibraltar is a source of strength for England as long as Spain remains weak; if Spain were strong it would become a weak point for England and lose its *raison d'être*. ... Gibraltar is a standing offence. ... [Spain, a] founder-nation of numerous other nations, after a long period of decadence, [must attempt] to reconstitute itself as a political force animated by new sentiments of expansion.[33]

Ganivet speaks of an aggressive expansionism to restore Spain's autonomy and global eminence. Spain had been all but absent from the Scramble for Africa, and Gibraltar seemed—to a strong right-wing and military contingent—more feasible to regain, after which Spain would likely invade North Africa again.

Ortega and his colleagues generally rejected the politics of Ganivet, along with the monarchical Carlism of Juan Vázquez de Mella and the nativism of Miguel de Unamuno, among others. After the Great War, Ortega, who was emerging as the bridge between the end of the Generation of '98's influence and the rise of the Generation of '27, began to suffuse his work with a sense that Europe's imperial age had finally ended, as Spain's virtually had in 1898. But in 1921, at the moment when the Irish Free State was on the verge of establishment, Spaniards were exasperated anew by the "Disaster at Annual," another surprising and embarrassing defeat by rebels in the breakaway Rif region of Morocco. Alfonso XIII, the "infant king of Spain" whom Molly mentions, was popularly blamed for this second "Disaster" and was nicknamed "El Africano" (*U* 18.781). The popular socialist Indalecio Prieto then declared in the Congress of Deputies, "we are at the most acute period of Spanish decadence."[34] In this climate, Ortega's critiques of decline and decadence, which he always coupled with pronouncements about Spain's European renaissance, gained further traction. Joyce's role in this project was facilitated by Marichalar's sudden rise to critical prominence in the early 1920s.

Marichalar's Spanish Joyce

When Ortega launched the *Revista de Occidente*, Marichalar had barely finished his studies and begun writing criticism. The young critic's socially connected father, who was a patron of the arts, sent samples of his son's work to some leading figures across Spain, from the director of Madrid's Prado Museum to Miguel de Unamuno.[35] José Ortega Munilla, father of José Ortega y Gasset and a powerful publisher, was impressed and desired to see more. He wrote that the younger Marichalar's work had "the mark of a fertile and elegant ingenuity" that could promote successfully the rising generation of authors in Spain. He cautioned, though, that the precocious scholar who loved foreign literatures should study the Spanish classics and spend more time interpreting the works of his own national literature.[36] Marichalar's reviews and columns on both literary traditions began appearing regularly in *Los Lunes de El Imparcial*, Madrid's weekly arts supplement, in 1920. This brought him into contact first with Ortega, whose *Meditations on Quixote* had opened many critical paths for him, and then with Valery Larbaud, who encouraged him to write on Joyce.

Larbaud, who is also familiar to Joyce scholars for his help in translating and lecturing on *Ulysses* in Paris, was more broadly a prominent and versatile "introducer and intermediary" among the "cosmopolitan clergy" across the "intellectual map" of Europe. As a leading "foreign exchange broker . . . [in] the world of letters," he foresaw from Paris "the advent of a small, cosmopolitan, enlightened society that would silence national prejudices by recognizing and promoting the free circulation of great works of avant-garde literature from all over the world," explains Pascale Casanova.[37] He envisaged a continent-wide "aristocracy open to all . . . [across] a country of Europe" centered in Paris, as Victor Hugo had seen it before him.³⁸ This utopian ideal led Larbaud to Spain, where he translated into French and championed tirelessly the works of Ramón, Gabriel Miró, and others, and where he befriended Ortega, Marichalar, Alfonso Reyes, and their circle, all in hopes of increasing the "collaboration al 'intelligence reciproque' entre l'Espagne et la France."³⁹ European letters, he believed, would be rebuilt on new axes: Ireland, Spain, and France.⁴⁰ When Marichalar sent him several numbers of *Índice*, the Frenchman felt that they were further evidence of the emerging "grande renaissance des lettres espagnoles."⁴¹ Just after learning that his lecture on *Ulysses* would appear in the first issue of the *Criterion*, Larbaud wrote Marichalar and pressed him to join the international critical dialogue on Joyce. Marichalar, still in his twenties, suddenly found himself thrust into a dynamic world of literary commentary, translation, and scholarship centered in Paris around Europe's most celebrated author. As studies such as Patrick O'Neill's *Polyglot Joyce* and the essays in Karen R. Lawrence's *Transcultural Joyce* have shown, Joyce's work provided a common text of supranational literary practices that figures like Marichalar could engage productively with their counterparts across the continent. Joyce's postcolonial Irish-Europeanism also held a privileged place among the Spanish-European critics in Ortega's circle.

Where Joyce connects Ireland and Spain primarily through their shared history of disconnection from European culture at the hands of the British empire, though, Marichalar binds two strands of modernist thought and writing from Europe's margins by seeing a shared obligation among the Irish and the Spanish to overhaul their national cultures in the post-war moment. In Joyce, Marichalar found an adaptable Irish paragon for Ortega's Spanish vision: he noticed a homology between Larbaud's claims about what *Ulysses* did for Ireland's Europeanness and Ortega's minor-European cultural politics. Joyce's success as a writer who came from the continent's sidelines to revise both Irish and European literatures was promising. His iconoclasm and his sense that "nationality" had been a "useful fiction" associated with the bourgeois sensibilities of nineteenth-century realist literature also resonated among a generation of Spanish writers searching for models of art that departed from inherited national forms (*OCPW* 118). Like Eliot at the *Criterion*, Ortega was eager to capitalize on the currency of Joyce's name as a means to extend his program of cultural politics through a critical enterprise. But because of the climate of Primo de Rivera's rule after September 1923, importing Joyce's work, which had been denounced in England, Ireland, and America as blasphemous and pornographic, was a serious risk. Joyce's work did not immediately receive the level of commentary in Spain that it did in much of western Europe, as Spanish Joyce scholars have documented.⁴² A Catalan journal called *La*

Revista (unconnected to Ortega's) featured short notices on Joyce, Ezra Pound had mentioned him in *Hermes* in 1920, and Douglas Goldring had related his style to that of Picasso and of Aleksandr Archipenko in 1921–1922.[43] Marichalar himself had briefly discussed Joyce's works in a profile of Larbaud and in a piece on Proust (both in 1922). In *España* in 1923, Enrique Díez-Canedo wrote that among contemporary Irish writers, Yeats and Shaw represent the best current talent and Joyce the talent of the future; together they pose "a delicate question: whether it is possible to develop a national literature without their own language."[44] But the publication of Marichalar's "James Joyce in His Labyrinth," as a sustained engagement with Joyce, was a watershed moment in the arrival of Spanish critical thought in the post-war European republic of letters. The critic believed, one must infer, that he could craft the proper idiom and maintain the correct detachment for receiving Joyce's work while avoiding dictatorial censors. The essay promoted Joyce—cautiously—as an author who shunned the aesthetic boundaries of national paradigms without making overtly institutional or religious critiques.

"James Joyce in His Labyrinth" headlines an issue of the *Revista de Occidente* that includes articles on Cervantes, Quevedo, and Azorín, creating material juxtapositions that situate Spanish writers, past and present, within Joyce's European context, and vice versa. The essay takes as its point of departure an impressionistic scene in Paris in which a sleek Rolls Royce pulls up to the front of Sylvia Beach's rue de l'Odéon bookstore on a still night. A glamorous woman—"the most elegant duchess in Paris"—has arrived under the cover of darkness and haze in order to secure a copy of the notorious, contraband novel on whose cover the "prestigious [initials] J. J. . . . correspond exactly to the R. R. that flaunts on the sparkling grille of the hawklike car. James Joyce: Rolls Royce." Marichalar continues by relating legends of lords who, like modern-day Don Quixotes, sold their lands in order to buy copies of *Ulysses*, or of students who spent four days in bed without food to save money for it.[45] Capturing the senses of excitement and intimidation, rarity and exclusivity that surrounded the novel in its early days, Marichalar notes that such scenes as these are products of our own time, not of fables. "Scandal, Style, and Criticism" all converge around the name of Joyce—"Irish author, our contemporary"—who belongs in a chain of "supreme literary beacons" of Europe that begins with a Spaniard (surprisingly, not Cervantes): "Calderón, Shakespeare, Dante, Goethe, and Joyce" (appendix, page 210).

We must clarify the "cloudy legend" of scandal and infamy attached to Joyce's name, Marichalar adds. After a brief biography of the author, he turns first to an account of Joyce's battle with royal censors over "Ivy Day in the Committee Room," concluding that the "unknown buyer" who confiscated and burned the entire first printing (save one copy) of *Dubliners* was motivated by a "sovereign impulse." By the same token, he documents the "relentless persecut[ion]" of Joyce's work in the *Little Review* by "American puritanism" and the banning and seizure of copies of the novel in Ireland, England, and the United States (appendix, pages 211, 212). "What is it," Marichalar asks, "that causes Joyce's works to be persecuted with such bitter determination? Of course it is neither lewdness nor excessive liberties. Such things are absent in his books, and one would be mistaken to search through them for cheap, sinful thrills." In fact, that which Joyce treats in an allegedly "scandalous" manner is treated "without shame" in a medical text because it is oriented toward a scientific end. Marichalar concludes that the "rawness of expression and the desire to transcribe reality with absolute truthfulness occasioned these persecutions of Joyce"—and, even worse, caused critics to mistake him for an epigonic realist rather than an inventive vanguardist (212).

Marichalar characterizes Joyce, accordingly, as a model of the unpopular avant-gardist that Ortega described contemporaneously in *The Dehumanization of Art*. His writing "doesn't simply conform to the passing predilections of a fickle, snobbish public," but rather belongs alongside that of the circle of writers gathered around the *Revista de Occidente* and of the broader supranational vanguard in which they participated (210). Marichalar suggests that Joyce's decision to become a voluntary exile, much like Ortega's travels to Germany for his philosophical *Bildung*, lays out a road map for the intellectual bonds that Spain must make with the new Europe. He moves back and forth between author and creation to see Joyce's alter-ego Stephen Dedalus, "monster of his own labyrinth" (a play on the Spanish *monstruo*, "monster," "giant," or "freakish genius"), as a figure for Ireland's European formation (219). Drawn by the "spell of Europe," Stephen-Joyce transcends the limits of "his birth, his education, his nationality" when following his "true calling: expatriotism," yet he retains "constitutive elements" of his homeland as he forges "the uncreated conscience of his race" (213). That is, he never abandons his Irishness fully, but rather integrates it with his Europeanism.

While following Joyce's peregrinations through the continent, Marichalar speculates—wishfully but wrongly—that the author had spent time in Madrid.[46] Turning to *Ulysses*, he groups Joyce's novel alongside works by Dostoevsky, Proust, Goncharov, Waldo Frank, and Dominique Braga, all of whom he portrays as critics of decadence and creators of the "psychological novel" (214). Their stylistic slowness rewrites notions of literary time and kinesis, and, Marichalar claims, Joyce's in particular presents an intense "documentary value that modern sensibility requires" because it takes the same amount of time to read as the action described would occupy in reality. Concomitant with such claims about the "scientific" nature of *Ulysses*, Marichalar asserts throughout his essay that Joyce is a faithful Catholic misunderstood, for while he was "denounced by the moralizing societies of North America," his works "received intelligent accolades from some representatives of the Catholic orthodoxy in his country." Indeed, the best critical article on *A Portrait of the Artist as a Young Man*, he writes, appeared in the *Dublin Review*, published by the Irish clergy. Furthermore, "despite a recalcitrant puritanism's branding Joyce a pornographic writer, his colleagues have seen him as a 'Jesuit'" (212). Through this multifaceted trope of "persecution," Marichalar writes Joyce, Jesuit-educated like Ortega, into a literary-philosophical tradition of thinkers that encompasses two controversial Spanish Jesuit casuists specifically: Tomás Sánchez, the sixteenth-century author of works on marriage and lying, and Antonio Escobar y Mendoza, the seventeenth-century author of treatises on morality that were condemned by Pascal, among others. Marichalar later relates Joyce's radical religious temperament to that of the Jesuit Padre Francisco Suárez of Granada, a sixteenth-century Thomist mentioned in *Portrait*. The force of these invocations becomes apparent when Marichalar suggests that a deep-seated anti-Catholicism in Protestant countries is to blame for the persecutions of Joyce, rather than the author's "heresies." Marichalar's sympathy for Joyce's temperament was likely not personal—he was a devout Catholic himself—but rather was an aesthetic principle that he felt negotiated the line between exploiting artistic freedom and provoking censorship, under which many contemporary writers were working.

He finally sees the gargoyles of a Gothic cathedral as ideal emblems of Joyce's Catholicism: revolting yet sacred. "With its audacities, with its crudeness," he writes, "Joyce's work presents to us man, abandoned and frozen stiff, because it is a work essentially Christian in its roots. . . . [It] encompasses a world both exalted and grotesque." And although "long years of persecution and of obscurity give way today to moments of unprecedented esteem," Joyce remains, like the English Catholic poet Francis Thompson, "hounded first by his persecutors, later by his enthusiasts, and by Grace always" and much like the "cornered poet" in Thompson's "The Hound of Heaven" (220). That is to say, a constant tension, grounded in both Joyce's fiction and his identity, exists between the notoriety and persecution that have followed the Irish-Catholic Joyce in his European-American fame. These Catholic affinities are not only ones to which Marichalar returned when he revised "James Joyce in His Labyrinth," but also ones that strengthen the through-lines between Spain and Ireland that he highlights throughout his essay.

Translating Joyce and Hispanophone Vanguardism

Having defended both Joyce's style and his sensibilities, Marichalar offers his most original contribution to early writings on Joyce when he translates three excerpts that he takes to represent *Ulysses*'s breakthroughs in prose. Two are from "Ithaca": the set of permutations on the relative ages of Stephen and Bloom (*U* 17.447–461) and the word-game on the name "Sinbad the Sailor" (*U* 17. 2322–2326). The former is a straightforward translation: "16 años antes, en el año 1888, cuando Bloom tenía la edad actual de Stephen, éste tenía 6 años. 16 años después, en 1920, cuando Stephen tuviese la edad actual de Bloom, éste tendría 54 años...." In the latter, on the other hand, Marichalar creates new puns on Spanish words, even while claiming that Joyce's "originalities... and very complicated word-games are untranslatable on the whole." He writes: "Simbad el Marino y Timbad el Tarino y Yimbad el Yarino y Whinbad el Wharino y Nimbad el Narino y Fimbad el Farino y Bimbad el Barino y Pimbad el Parino y Mimbad el Malino y Uinbad el Uarino y Rimbad el Rarino y Dimbad el Karino y Kimbad el Carino y Cimbad el Jarino y Ximbad el Sarino." Marichalar reads Joyce's original as a series of graphic and musical inventions emerging from the play with "Sailor"/"Marino." He thus creates oblique or quasi-words such as "Tarino" (*taurino*, "bullfighting"), "Narino" (*nariz*, "nose"), "Farino" (*faro*, "lighthouse," or *faraón*, "pharoah"), "Barino" (*barrio*, "neighborhood"), "Parino" (*padrino*, "godfather"), "Rarino" (*raro*, "rare, strange"), and "Carino" (*cariño*, "darling")—others still are possible. Joyce's word-games, he insists, succeed where the jarring but senseless provocations of the Surrealists and Dadaists do not, and they perpetuate themselves into further verbal originalities in translation (see appendix, page 218).

Marichalar then begins his vast, international genealogy of Joyce's version of the interior monologue and his idiosyncratic translation of fragments of "Penelope." He marshals an immense array of literary and philosophical resources for this project. He traces what he characterizes as Joyce's most significant achievement through French literature—Montaigne, Flaubert, Dujardin, and Proust—then through poets including Poe and Browning, through Russian and German expressionist traditions, and finally through the English ballad "Turpin Hero" that Stephen cites toward the end of *Portrait* (216). He attempts to explain the artifice of the interior monologue, writing that

> in the rich realm of the interior monologue, we see its components parade rhythmically, blooming forth from consciousness, and we discern the most unexpected formation of pristine, natural thought. To watch this unguarded

sleep is to settle oneself in the deepest and most remote fountains, then to marvel at their spontaneous integration into unified flow. . . . The difficulty is in aesthetically evaluating these genuine, completely wild materials. When looking at them, we tend to stumble over a preliterary crudeness because the poet (maker) [*el poeta (hacedor)*] does not make but simply feels by instinct. In such moments we tread along the boundaries between science and art. Proust's *My Wakings* [*Mes Reveils*, 1922], for example, delves into the confines of wakefulness and sleep, and, by transcribing the results of his analysis, he brings forth a document of dual interest: scientific and literary. (216)

While highlighting again the "scientific" origins and value of Joyce's stylistics, Marichalar also points to the eclectic cosmopolitan heritage (extending through Europe to Russia and the United States) within which he and his peers must understand themselves as working. His theory that the critic—and by implication, the translator—must recover the "wildness" and the "preliterary," "instinctive" material of the interior monologue is also his reading of Joyce's modernist praxis: not simply anti-ornamental, but pre-ornamental.

Marichalar next makes Molly speak Spanish, and more than the handful of words and phrases that Joyce intersperses in her soliloquy, at least. Using translation as a testing ground for the experimental Spanish-European aesthetics that he wants to demonstrate and diffuse among his own Generation of '27 peers, he renders the end of "Penelope" by fusing together words and phrases to replicate Joyce's depiction of Molly's speech.[47] The passage appears on the page as follows: " . . . en China peinan sus coletas para todoel día bueno pronto oiremosa las hermanas tocar elángelus no tienenadie que vengaperturbar susueño si no esun curaodós para su oficio nocturno el despertar dela gente deaquialado con su cacareo . . . " (216). Since Marichalar cannot reproduce Joyce's incidental wordplay like "cant" for "can't," "hell" for "he'll," or "Ill" for "I'll" because Spanish has no contractions, he instead joins articles, verbs, and nouns to recreate this effect.[48] Thus, Molly's "coming in to spoil their sleep" thus becomes *vengapertubar susueño* (literally, "hemaycometodisturb theirsleep"), and "accompany him and" becomes *acompañarley*, which creates the Spanish word *ley* ("law") after the infinitive *acompañar*. Her "howling for the priest" becomes *curagritos* (literally, "priestshouts," which also plays on the earlier *curaodós* for "priest or two"), and "the day we were lying" (among the rhododendrons) becomes *eldiaquél questábamos echados* ("thatday thatwewere lying").

The provocative neologisms and portmanteaux that Marichalar creates extend in translation and in new directions Joyce's experiments with the English language.

No other Spanish translator, to my knowledge, has rendered "Penelope" in such a manner. At the same time, he provides fertile grounds for contemporary critics to understand the challenges encountered in the moment by Joyce's translators who sought to recreate the innovations of "Penelope." Two months after Marichalar's article appeared, in January 1925, Jorge Luis Borges would famously yet erroneously proclaim himself "the first Hispanic adventurer [*aventurero*] to have arrived at Joyce's [*Ulysses*]" when he published his celebrated translation of the novel's final page in the Argentine journal *Proa* [*Prow*].⁴⁹ Borges's version employs the Rioplatense *voseo* form, an Argentine dialect, for the second-person singular (Marichalar uses the generic Castilian-Spanish familiar *tú*) and, as Sergio Waisman explains, a distinctly Argentine idiom that downplays or sometimes omits Molly's references to Gibraltar and Ireland.⁵⁰ The critical focus on Borges's translation, though, has obscured Marichalar's attempt to account for the vanguardism that Joyce embeds in Molly's monologue and the readings of *Ulysses* that the contrasts between the decisions of Joyce's early Spanish translators evince. Marichalar does not seek to capture or reproduce, that is, something dialectal or colloquial in Joyce's interior monologue, but rather something pre-conscious and therefore purer in the aesthetic realm. His view of this mode of writing, colored heavily by his readings of Proust and of early psychoanalytic texts in the 1910s and 1920s, is an argument for his own reading of Joyce's modernism.⁵¹

Marichalar continues by contextualizing "Penelope" within the "oneiric" styles of German writers Jean Paul and Friedrich Hebbel; by comparing *Ulysses* to the "psychological writings" of Apollinaire, Valéry, and Freud; and by linking the novel to the poetics advocated by his own colleague Juan Ramón Jiménez (217). He sees Molly's speech as an avant-garde articulation of Spanish-Irish subjectivity, nourished by the same continental forms and influences that Marichalar and Ortega circulated in the *Revista de Occidente*. Molly's monologue spans centuries to revise the cultural heritage of "Europe" from its geopolitical, cultural, and gendered margins.⁵² Marichalar's own critical and translational style in turn emphasizes the multiple perspectives, contexts, and literary-historical juxtapositions necessary to read *Ulysses* as an ur-text and a model of transnational European writing—as the "indubitable representative of our epoch in the History of World Literature," he writes (211). In *Ulysses* and in the cultural politics of Marichalar's importing the "cloudy legend" of Joyce, there is a symmetry between postcolonial Ireland and post-imperial Spain that depends on various ideals of the end of imperial Europe. Studies of the novel's dissemination have shown that for writers all across Europe's margins, and Marichalar in particular, *Ulysses*—a portable allegory of the "arrival" of a minor nation in the new Europe—signaled great possibilities for a bourgeoning generation of vanguard writers in Spain.

Joyce's Cosmopolitanism in Anglo- and Hispanophone Literary-Critical History

Throughout "James Joyce in His Labyrinth," Marichalar incorporates and quotes claims about *Ulysses* by Larbaud, Eliot, Pound, Middleton Murry, and Havelock Ellis, entering a pervasive, pan-European debate among Joyce's early readers. Traditionally, Joyce's readers have been characterized as emphasizing either the Catholic-Irish or the secular cosmopolitan-European elements of his figure and his aesthetics—categories and terms that were very much in circulation among the debates over Spanish regeneration. Dissatisfied with an audience of the "English reading public" alone, Joyce portrayed himself as a mutable figure of multiple cultural identities and shrewdly marketed *Ulysses* as an "epic of two races (Israelite-Irish)" rooted in a universalist desire to "transpose the myth [of Ulysses] *sub specie temporis nostri*."[53] The polymorphous character of Ulysses was, for Joyce, as he told Frank Budgen, "the first gentleman in Europe."[54] In his correspondence, in his own criticism, and in the paratextual documents concerning *Ulysses* that he created, Joyce expanded his own heritage, fashioning a genealogy of his vanguardism as an embrace of European writing—Ibsen, Dujardin, Flaubert—even on the level of typography, with his disdain for "perverted commas" in dialogue.[55] His identification with Ibsen, "a spokesman of the European avant-garde" from a minor country, as Casanova writes, also dovetails with his creation of Dublin as an "international literary space," and thus his redefinition of Irishness, by way of *Ulysses*'s stylistics.[56] From "Trieste-Zürich-Paris," Joyce, the cosmopolitan ethnographer, conceived of Dublin as "contain[ing] the universal"—"a capital for thousands of years, . . . the 'second' city of the British Empire," and a "European capital," albeit one cut off from the continent by British imperialism, paralyzed by parochialisms that cloud its cosmopolitan history.[57]

Recently, scholars have revaluated and historicized Joyce's cosmopolitanism, understanding it as fluid both during Joyce's lifetime and in critical history since the second half of the twentieth century. It maintained in its stylistics abiding elements of liberalism and anti-colonialism; its orientation toward the middlebrow Irish reader as well as the elite European audience has played a part in leaving unsettled debates over the author's positions and over the effects of his critiques in *Ulysses*.[58] Aware that literary fame lay increasingly in the hands of critics, Joyce was complicit in downplaying his Irishness when it fit certain purposes and in highlighting it at other moments in his career. He generally cast his lot with Larbaud, Eliot, and Pound, who were, despite some disagreements among them, the principal figures in promulgating the cosmopolitan-European Joyce in the interwar era. Larbaud praised Joyce for having done "as much as did all the heroes of Irish nationalism to attract the respect of intellectuals of every other country toward Ireland." He continues, Joyce's work

> did for Ireland what Ibsen's work did in his time for Norway, what Strindberg did for Sweden, what Nietzsche did for Germany at the end of the nineteenth century, and what the books of Gabriel Miró and Ramón Gómez [de la Serna] have just done for contemporary Spain. . . . English is the language of modern Ireland[,] . . . which shows how little nationalistic a literary language can be. . . . [With *Ulysses*,] Ireland is making a sensational re-entrance into the first rank of European literature.[59]

Reading *Ulysses* as a national epic in non-nationalistic language, Larbaud sees Joyce's achievement—raising a minor nation to the "first rank of European literature"—to be transferable. Larbaud cites the authors whom he had recently translated as already having done similar work for Spain as Joyce had in making Dublin European. His claims about Joyce and *Ulysses* led to the French scholar's famous battle with the Irish critic Ernest Boyd, who accused him of ignoring the author's native cultural heritage. But as Geert Lernout notes, Boyd was actually a cosmopolitan figure himself, a translator of French literature, and a critic with whom Joyce sympathized to a degree. It is inaccurate, Lernout writes, to see this tension merely as "a quarrel between a cosmopolitan Frenchman and a provincial Irishman."[60] In other words, the earliest responses to *Ulysses* illustrate precisely how much nuance can be lost when contemporary scholars read Joyce as a purely postcolonial or purely European figure. The proximity and occasional symbiosis of such understandings of Joyce's politics continue to inform, in what Sean Latham has called a "valuable and creative dialectic," contemporary portraits of Joyce as sympathetic to both Irish nationalism and European secularism.[61]

Further accentuating Joyce's European credentials were Eliot and Pound, each with his own critical agenda. Eliot emphasized Joyce's reliance on "myth" and "tradition," claiming that Joyce had developed "a way of controlling, of ordering, of giving a shape and a significance to the immense panorama of futility and anarchy which is contemporary history. . . . [*Ulysses*] is, I seriously believe, a step towards making the modern world possible for art."[62] Joyce represented, for Eliot, the "future" of literature, and he was the first Irish writer since Swift "to possess absolute

European significance" because he has "used what is racial and national and transmuted it into something of international value ... for a European public."[63] Pound, meanwhile, read Joyce as the greatest contemporary heir to Flaubert's realism and couched his accounts of Joyce within the arguments about modernity and contemporary arts that Pound himself was circulating journalistically. Since *Portrait*, he had emphasized the portability of Joyce's visions: "perhaps the best criticism" of Joyce's first novel, he wrote, "has come from a Belgian who said, 'All this is as true of my country as of Ireland.'"[64] Pound read Joyce's portraits of Dublin in his short stories, with some hyperbole, as images of "Ireland under British domination[.] . . . By extension he has presented the whole occident under the domination of capital."[65] He claimed that Joyce "writes as a European, not as a provincial," and that "it is surprising that Mr Joyce is Irish. . . . He accepts an international standard of prose writing and lives up to it[;] . . . [he] writes as a contemporary of continental writers."[66]

Marichalar attempts to have it several ways at once: he offers a moderate, cosmopolitan understanding of Joyce, his Catholicism, his Irishness, and his Europeanness that, in its wide-ranging genealogy of the author and his innovations, aligns with Joyce's own syncretic and multiethnic figurations of Ireland. Marichalar's Irish-European Joyce is attached to both his homeland and to Paris and is more conservative, more affiliated with Spain than the writer would likely have seen himself. By making Joyce and his work more palatable to Spanish interdictions, Marichalar crafts the author into a humanistic Catholic voice (much like Marichalar himself) *against* modern devolution, rather than the emblem of it that Anglophone censors had made the Irishman. This Joyce for the New Spain—"our contemporary" for Spanish readers—is most similar to Pound's, and Marichalar also cites Flaubert on several occasions, though he works toward different ends than Pound does. Marichalar in fact quotes Pound's "James Joyce and Pécuchet" (1922), which Joseph Brooker notes made *Ulysses* "a critique of modernity: an 'inferno,' not an encomium, a satire of degradation, not a capitulation to it."[67] More important, Marichalar continually imports Joyce's modes of national critique, minor Europeanism, and readings of imperialism in order to revise them for another "impure" state on Europe's margins, in a manner that is neither purely nativist nor Europeanist. In the wake of "James Joyce en su laberinto," other literary-cultural groups in Spain offered differing visions of Joyce. Against Marichalar's emphasis on Joyce's Irish-Europeanness stands the greeting that *Ulysses* received among the writers of the Galician *Xeración Nós* (Generation Ourselves, an allusion to "Sinn Féin"). In their review *Nós*, the primary medium of their project of imagining an autonomous Galician nation bound to its "Atlantic" sister Ireland through Celtic history, Vicente Risco and Ramón Otero Pedrayo read Joyce as "a writer of universal stature who belonged to 'la hermana Ireland' [... and] represented the success of the Celtic spirit in the world."[68] But Risco also construed Joyce as, in the words of Alberto Lázaro, "demonic, difficult, weird, and anti-Irish," making his reception in Galicia cooler and more distanced.[69] Eventually Joyce was embraced as an "example. . . . of Celtic genius," Risco published a rich part-fiction part-criticism "Dédalus en Compostela" (1929), and "the successes of [Joyce's] works in Spain signified the triumph of the *Atlantista* movement" that *Nós* had championed.[70] Blunting the Galicians' initial reactions, however, Marichalar writes that "from a certain perspective, Joyce's case could be reduced to the drama of an Irishman insistent on not being one," but that such a reading is overly simplistic (see appendix, page 220). Some of Joyce's early Catalan critics, on the other hand, had no time for his elaborate aesthetics because of their own felt "urgency to consolidate a Catalan audience" in a moment in which their linguistic tradition was in danger.[71] Thus, they greeted Joyce's poetry and short stories well, but the literary and moral provocations of *Ulysses* were treated cautiously and suspiciously for over a decade. The prevailing celebrations of Joyce's cosmopolitanism in contemporary criticism, that is to say, have a history of contestation in several languages—a history that elucidates key parts of the shifting cultural politics of Spain's Silver Age.

"Joyce est un peu espagnol—pas?": Re-reading *Ulysses* and the Afterlife of Marichalar's Joyce

"James Joyce in His Labyrinth" earned Marichalar relative fame as Joyce's unofficial Spanish interpreter and secured the place of the *Revista de Occidente*, which would print more pieces on Joyce in the following years, as the premier medium of commentary on and translation of his works in Spain. As Carlos G. Santa Cecilia writes, "Ortega himself completed this first period" of Joyce's reception in Spain by citing Joyce's work, alongside Proust's and Ramón's, in *The Dehumanization of Art*.[72] Marichalar would capitalize on his own growing name and its attachment to figures like Joyce by publishing widely in media from Argentina, Cuba, France, Germany, and England in the following years. The life of this essay and its author's career, however, extend well beyond Ortega and the *Revista*, to paths that lead back to the novel through the contemporary "Spanish Joyce." Just before he published "James Joyce in His Labyrinth" in the *Revista de Occidente*, Marichalar forwarded a copy of his article and a letter to Joyce through their mutual friend Sylvia Beach. Joyce knew little of the culture of Spain's Silver Age, especially in comparison to his fluency in

French traditions, and Pound's few Spanish contacts did not do much to disseminate Joyce's work locally. Nevertheless, always eager to spread his fame among his "class... of foreignborn admirers," Joyce responded to a letter from Marichalar by noting that he had read his "gracious article, which [he] was able to decipher pretty well, thanks to [his] knowledge of Italian."[73] He also offered to send more biographical details to Marichalar, who informed him that a revised version of "James Joyce in His Labyrinth" would serve as preface to Dámaso Alonso's popular pseudonymous translation of *Portrait* (1926), which further catalyzed Spanish writers' interest in Joyce. Marichalar also set a precedent for a Spanish-European reading of Joyce that ensuing articles in the Madrileño press about the author would follow throughout the 1920s, often citing Marichalar's article.[74] Marichalar continued to spread Joyce's influence among the Generation of '27—which included Alonso, who exchanged letters with Joyce—widely and effectively, as Marisol Morales Ladrón has documented.[75] This influence also grew as the *Revista de Occidente*'s circulation grew, and peers of Ortega, such as Ramón Pérez de Ayala, were reached as well. A remark by the '27 novelist Rosa Chacel captures the sensation that many writers of this moment felt: "discovering Joyce gave me certainty that in the novel, anything could be incorporated: poetry, beauty, thought, horror, ugliness, blasphemy, pertinacity of faith."[76] These qualities were blended with Ortega's demand, Chacel recalls, that young writers and artists create new works "without a trace of typism, localism, provincialism."[77]

Marichalar expanded his article once again for his own collection of essays, *Mentira Desnuda (Hitos)* [*The Lie Undressed (Milestones)*, or *The Naked Lie (Milestones)*] (1933). This time he added sections from his other articles on British modernism and the English-language novel that he had published, clarified some facts about Joyce's life, and widened the European scope of his contextualization of Joyce's achievements. Marichalar now writes that "Circe," in fact, is the best and most original chapter of *Ulysses*; that Joyce's aesthetics resemble those of Picasso as much as those of Proust; and that the imprints of Nietzsche and Paul Morand on Joyce's work should be acknowledged and studied, too. Ibsen and Strindberg were Joyce's dramatic forebears, he writes, while Goethe was both a novelistic and dramatic one because "Circe" draws on the *Walpurgisnacht* episode of *Faust*. Virginia Woolf, D. H. Lawrence, Dorothy Richardson, William Carlos Williams, and Frank Swinnerton all find their way into the essay, too. Marichalar's meditations on Joyce's work—his revisions of his own readings of *Ulysses*—culminate in his revaluation of Joyce as the iconic figure of a transhistorical version of modernism. He imagines the novel in the hands of Friar Juan de Santo Tomás, or John of St. Thomas (1589–1644), the Portuguese-born confessor to King Philip II. The Dominican

Friar was the most esteemed theologian in early seventeenth-century Spain, and Marichalar believes he "would not have been greatly surprised by the enormity ... of the immeasurable [*Ulysses*]." Rather, he has the Friar welcome the novel by ventriloquizing, in effect, the arguments about modern art that Marichalar made in his lectures and writings:

> Art proceeds always by its own certain and determined ways or rules; the debt art owes us need not be repaid with an artist's straightforward intentions or with work done for honesty's sake itself. . . . The artist is only worthy of reprehension if he sins by ignorance of his art, but not if he sins against the knowledge and awareness [*ciencia y conciencia*] of exactly what he has made. . . . A perfect work of art may be created even when the will of the artist is perverse.

This defense of the autonomous art-object of modernism, an object whose very reality defends it and disallows censorship, is Marichalar's forward-looking claim about the legacy of Joyce's writing, projected back through Spanish cultural history. This legacy exists outside the formulations of didactic or moralizing art. The lasting image of the author that he gives is one in which Joyce "has an indubitable aspect at once peevish and luciferian" and a "circumflex smile" as he hides from his persecutors.[78]

Joking to Sylvia Beach that "Joyce est un peu espagnol—pas?" because of his and his colleagues' attention to the writer, Marichalar, in subsequent articles, used Joyce's works to frame his discussions of other modernist figures.[79] He grouped Joyce with Ramón as originators of modern poetic prose; he called Woolf's *Mrs. Dalloway* a scientific artifact of consciousness, like *Ulysses*; he characterized O'Flaherty's experiences in the Great War as a version of Joyce's continental flight from Ireland; he read Faulkner's Mississippi as an incarnation of Joyce's Dublin; he presented Katherine Mansfield and Clemence Dane as engaged, with Joyce, in the project of bringing psychoanalysis to bear on literature; and he introduced Spanish-language readers to the early published sections of *Finnegans Wake* as Joyce's re-invention of the same craft of fiction that he had reinvented in *Ulysses*. Marichalar also discussed with Beach the unrealized project that Victoria Ocampo had envisioned in 1931: a full translation of *Ulysses* into Spanish.[80]

Marichalar initiated around Joyce's work a critical mode of cosmopolitan Spanish-European modernism that was interrupted by the Francoist autarky imposed in 1939. Alberto Lázaro has documented the obstacles that, despite some surprising moments of isolated success among the Spanish reading public, Joyce's works encountered at the hands of censors under Franco.[81] Unlike the attention to

Borges's long and evolving relationship throughout his career with Joyce's fiction, however, the lives of Joyce's works in Spain have primarily been the subject of more recent titles in the thriving industry of Joyce studies in Spain, including: *Joyce en España I* and *II* (1994 and 1997, respectively); *La recepción de James Joyce en la prensa española* [*The Reception of James Joyce in the Spanish Press*] (1997); *James Joyce in Spain: A Critical Bibliography (1972–2002)* (2002); *Silverpowdered Olive-trees: Reading Joyce in Spain* (2003); and several chapters in *The Reception of James Joyce in Europe* (2004). Among these texts, and among an array of articles and bibliographies, are a host of notes on Marichalar's role in launching the circulation of Joyce's works in Spain. With translations or reissues of many of Joyce's works in every major peninsular language since the 1970s, Spanish scholars have extended in new directions Marichalar's originary work; the appearance in 2010 of Enrique Vila-Matas's much-anticipated novel *Dublinesca* [*Dublinesque*] further diversified this body of work and thought.[82]

In contrast to Anglophone scholarship on *Ulysses*, Hispanophone (especially Spanish) criticism generally has been oriented more by studies of reception and has focused more acutely, but less politically, on *Ulysses*'s figurations of Hispanicity and Spanish-Irish relations. Francisco García Tortosa, for instance, demonstrates in "España y su función simbólica en la narrativa de *Ulysses*" that certain allusions to Spain such as "The Rose of Castile" joke, Molly's recollection of Málaga raisins, and the persecution of Jews during the Inquisition, tie together themes in the novel such as Bloom's preoccupation with ethnic origins or Molly's infidelity, developing "our ever-expanding vision of Leopold and Molly."[83] In a similar vein, José M. Ruiz catalogues "the Hispanic component" of Joyce's work in great detail in order to trace the ways in which "Joyce connects Hispanicity with Mediterranean cultures: Arabic, Jewish, and Hellenic. The three cultures came to Europe and finally to Ireland—in Stephen's opinion—through Spain."[84] And while some recent collections of essays have brought together scholars from both Hispano- and Anglophone traditions, on the whole, a perceptible distance remains between the approaches and arguments of the two.[85]

A return to *Ulysses* with an eye to these topics and to the contexts detailed above helps to shorten the gap: the Spanish response *around* the text (from the 1920s to the present), that is, can illuminate further a topic such as the postcolonial politics of Spanish-Irish relations *within* the text. In the *nostos* of *Ulysses*, Bloom, who has previously seen his wife through the tropes of retrogression and imperial decline emblematized by Spain, ultimately points out that Molly does not "claim Spanish nationality" (*U* 16.879). Instead, her marriage to Bloom, rather than concentrating a set of tropes of Otherness familiar to Irish, Spanish, and Jewish peoples, extends the Spanish-Irish union that she already represents. Joyce thus symbolizes the Blooms in "Ithaca" with "two onions, one, the larger, Spanish, entire, the other, smaller, Irish, bisected with augmented surface and more redolent" in their kitchen (*U* 17.309–311). That is, Molly's Hispanicity, formerly a pastiche of tropes of decadence, now connects along Europe's margins to Joyce's new Ireland, where Leopold is Everyman; he is "the basis of democracy," Pound writes.[86] Reversing the symbolics, the Spanish onion is now whole and robust, representing a vitality rather than decay that it might impart to the pungent and divided Irish one, and representing, together with the Irish one, a potent alliance on Europe's formerly fallen margins. Nor does the Blooms' union simply perpetuate or militate against imperialisms; rather, it maps a cooperation that the project of the "Spanish Joyce" enacted.

Molly's character also rejuvenates stagnant "Spanish types" in a manner that complements the literary-aesthetic work that Marichalar sees her monologue as modeling for his colleagues. Through her, Joyce recreates Gibraltar as a microcosm of his Europe: a site not of violent battles nor Spanish decline and British triumph, but of multiethnic, multilingual subject formation portable to his European Dublin—and to a European Madrid, as the circulation of his novel attests. Coalescing around multivoiced readings of the end of European empires and exclusionary notions of national belonging, Joyce's two subjects of the new Ireland and their implied models in the New Spain are adaptable as prototypical subjects who unite spatial and racial peripheries from Hungary to Israel to become models of a hybrid, cosmopolitan Europeanism. Joyce inscribes a post-imperial sensibility onto late colonial Dublin to achieve what Mark Wollaeger identifies on the novelistic, rhetorical, and theoretical levels as "a major aim of [his] project: the invention of a cosmopolitan subject that incorporates without fully assimilating" the various interconnected subject-positions of Irish citizens in 1904.[87] The living product of the Blooms' marriage, Milly, is one manifestation of such a subject projected into the European future of Ireland. Bloom's vision of a humanist democracy in the "new Bloomusalem in the Nova Hibernia of the future" also grants a rough sketch of the political underpinnings of the "Europe" that the novel thematizes (*U* 15.1543–1544). The transcultural process of adapting and revising this vision around Joyce's figure enabled a vital element of Spanish-European modernism to emerge in a symbiotic dynamic with its better-known modernist counterparts.

Though the two never met, Ortega and Joyce shared interests, sensibilities, and a number of mutual friends. Both criticized—out of concern, they noted, even as they drew the ire of their peers—their nations as paralyzed, infirm, and in devolving states of provincialism, as in the "figure of this bewildered old man, left over from a culture which is not ours, deaf-mute before his judge" with which Joyce described the Irish (*OCPW* 146). They also shared strident critiques of insular cultures and shared a goal with sympathetic figures across the continent of renovating the category of "Europe" not by submitting to its hegemony but by infusing it with their locally grounded cosmopolitanisms. Joyce's recasting, through Gibraltar, Europe's "motley" cultural heritage parallels Ortega's determination to "combine all [Spain's] ancestral heritage in one firm integration" in his syncretic thought.[88] Ortega's interest in the state of the European novel in *Notes on the Novel* (the companion to *The Dehumanization of Art*), along with his homage to/analysis of Proust in 1923, coincided not by accident with the blossoming of Marichalar's critical voice and the *Revista de Occidente*'s treatment of British modernism.

Meanwhile, Marichalar's relationship with Joyce continued, primarily through Sylvia Beach. In 1927, when Beach was gathering signatures from international figures in protest of Samuel Roth's piracy of *Ulysses* in the United States, she turned to Marichalar to collect them from Spain's writers and thinkers.[89] The petition amassed over 150 signatures, including those of Marichalar, Ortega, Unamuno, Azorín, Ramón, Jacinto Benavente, and Juan Ramón Jiménez. With a number of Spanish names alongside figures ranging from Einstein to E. R. Curtius to Julien Benda in defense of a cosmopolitan Irish writer, the petition (which originated in Paris) resembles a document of the Orteguian ideal of a European intellectual community. But when Ortega and Marichalar met in refuge just across the French border during the Spanish Civil War, with the *Revista de Occidente* having suspended publication in 1936, their vision of a Spanish vanguard that would lead forward a cultural reformation into Ortega's United States of Europe seemed an impossible dream. In a series of letters to Ortega, Marichalar describes the massive confusion and disillusion that had overtaken intellectuals such as himself during the war. Perhaps when Joyce inserts Bloom's flatulence among phrases from the nationalist martyr Robert Emmet's speech—"When my country takes her place among the nations of the earth, then and not till then let my epitaph be written. I have done"—this disruption of this ideal coherence "among the nations of the earth" is also transferable to interwar Spain (*U* 11.1284–1294). This critique, as a recognition of the failure of a hope for European unity, was one that these modernist critical projects theorized from without, from Europe's allied geographical and cultural margins.

3. Lytton Strachey and *La nueva biografía* in Spain
Avant-garde Literature, the New Liberalism, and the Ruins of the Nineteenth Century

> Crossing through literary space now are . . . an Italian Christ and a German Napoleon, a Voltaire of English craftsmanship and a Disraeli 'made in France.'
>
> —Antonio Marichalar, "'Lives' and Lytton Strachey" (1928)[1]

> The Young Literature came to the Republic of Letters with the greatest of riches. . . . Now we witness their conquest of the reading public without compromising their art. . . . [Marichalar's book offers] to our provincial, backward cultural sphere the insertion of Spain in the European spirit, . . . giving our country a new air of culture . . . from one of the most learned and European spirits of our intellectual world.
>
> —Luis Valdeavellano, review of Marichalar, *Riesgo y ventura del duque de Osuna* (1930)[2]

The vitality of Lytton Strachey's iconoclastic *Eminent Victorians* (1918), the touchstone of modernist biography, unfortunately has been lost to many contemporary readers. Cyril Connolly famously called it "the work of a great anarch, a revolutionary text-book on bourgeois society," and, despite its publication date, "the first book of the twenties."[3] Strachey, celebrated as "a destroyer of illusions and a liberator of forms" who made biography an art and a space for critique, initiated a burst of creativity across Europe known as the "New Biography," which had particular appeal to a younger British and European left.[4] The Anglophilic Frenchman André Maurois, the Austrian-Jewish Stefan Zweig, and the German Emil Ludwig, among

95

many others, found great success during this renaissance of the genre. The critic George Alexander Johnston claimed in 1929 that "no feature of the literary history of Europe in the last few years is more remarkable than the simultaneous appearance in Germany, France, and England of a new conception of biography."[5] Yet this international modernist movement remains on the periphery of most contemporary Anglophone and European literary histories of the era, and it appears that Spain was once again absent from an interwar cultural phenomenon occurring in the London-Paris-Berlin nexus.

An overlooked synthesis of politics and literature, however, brought Spanish writing—albeit briefly—into the European "literary space" that Antonio Marichalar mentions in the epigraph above, and did so by way of its interpenetration with British literature. In January 1930, just days after the dictator Miguel Primo de Rivera relinquished his rule and fled Spain, a new journal appeared in Madrid called *Nueva España*. Its editors were Antonio Espina, Adolfo Salazar, and José Díaz Fernández (the first two were regulars at the *Revista de Occidente*), and they evoked José Ortega y Gasset's plans for a New Spain both in the review's title and in columns such as "Vieja y nueva liberalismo" ["Old and New Liberalism"], which recalls Ortega's "Vieja y nueva política" ["Old and New Politics," 1914]. Throughout the first issue, there are reports on progressive movements among European and Latin American youth who are clamoring for democracy, for new governments, for a "future politics" of "the New Liberalism" embodied by a reformist state that intervened to create a "social organism."[6] Featured prominently in this first issue, too, is a large advertisement for a book published that same month, Marichalar's biography *Riesgo y ventura del duque de Osuna (ensayo biográfico)* [*The Perils and Fortune of the Duke of Osuna*, 1930]. The second issue contains a review of the text that calls it "marvelous" and "magnificently written" and that calls Marichalar "deserving of prestige" among contemporary writers.[7]

The story of why a biography of an infamously profligate nineteenth-century Spanish aristocrat became inscribed in the project of a journal of Spain's New Liberalism is but one part of the expansive and fascinating history that this chapter analyzes. This history traverses both biographies such as those by Strachey and Marichalar and their reception, domestically and internationally. In these texts, the practices of the New Biography were tied to the rise of the Spanish Second Republic in April 1931, and to the efforts of figures like those at *Nueva España* who saw art as a key medium for the dissemination of the Republic's new social order. Against the general disdain for biography on the left, the Spanish new liberals treated here believed that biography would play a literary and cultural role in helping to attach their country to Europe. In a test of how much a genre could affect the course of a nation, they believed that the New Biography could help make the country's first post-monarchic government—the "New Spain," as the Second Republic was called at its birth—the most culturally and socially progressive state on the continent.

Fundamental to the new liberalism that emerged in Spain was a critique of the nineteenth-century imperial state, its hypocrisies and self-destructive ruin, and its *anti*-liberalism—a critique that Marichalar saw clearly in Strachey's *Eminent Victorians*. Where Strachey captured the zeitgeist of the generation of the Great War, Marichalar believed that his mode of biography could be adapted for the liberal moment in Spain. When Ortega, the country's leading spokesman for liberal causes and Europeanism, became convinced that Spain should join in the New Biography, the *Revista de Occidente* and his book publishing ventures were soon at the center of what became *la nueva biografía* (1928–1936). Within this dynamic and widely popular movement, an array of Spanish writers produced experimental biographies of figures ranging from a controversial nun, a famous boxer, and a famous robber; to Goya, Cervantes, and Isabella II; even to Mikhail Bakunin and Greta Garbo—and Marichalar's *Osuna* is considered the finest of the "vanguard biograph[ies]."[8] *La nueva biografía* was an effort to invigorate Spanish culture with cosmopolitanism, much as Strachey sought to do for England when he renovated the genre, and to bring about the country's overdue, modernized Enlightenment. This vision is central to Marichalar's dismantling of nineteenth-century Spanish decadence and the country's failed First Republic of 1873–1874, and to his literary aim of demystifying and democratizing elite national culture with his *Osuna*.

In this chapter, I propose an intertextual, comparative reading of Strachey's *Eminent Victorians* and Marichalar's *Osuna*, which is a more traditional case of foreign influence beyond the major author's (Strachey's) purview than the previous chapters have studied. The similar hypocrisies of the British and Spanish states in the nineteenth century, however, provide the common text for both writers. But I also focus on the literary techniques such as irony, satire, comedy, and impressionistic speculation that Marichalar, Strachey's first Spanish critic and translator, takes in new directions that exceed the influence of his adoptive partner. Production and reception, originals and translations, primary and adapted arguments all worked together to extend *la nueva biografía*'s potential. My recovery of the sociology of this Anglo-Spanish component of the New Biography seeks not only to account for a neglected site of the vast geography of the biography genre in the interwar period, but also to chart the propitious coincidence of personal, political, and literary histories that enabled this development of modernist internationalism. These histories formed the contexts necessary for understanding

Marichalar's minor masterpiece in twentieth-century Spanish letters. They also elucidate the text's afterlives in a rare English translation and Marichalar's ambivalent retractions once he realized his disillusion with the Republican experiment to—as Ortega charged them—"reconstruct" their state and revise the European republic of letters.[9]

Modernist Critique and Strachey's New Biography

Anglophone modernist variations on biography and autobiography, while impressive in their breadth and diversity, have been notoriously difficult to classify in literary history. What common thread exists among Gertrude Stein's *The Autobiography of Alice B. Toklas* and *Everybody's Autobiography*, Ezra Pound's *Gaudier-Brzeska: A Memoir* and *Hugh Selwyn Mauberley*, James Joyce's *Giacomo Joyce*, E. M. Forster's *Maurice*, and Virginia Woolf's *Orlando*, *Flush*, and *Roger Fry*? Furthermore, the successes in this genre were often qualified, and the failures were many. The "newness of the New Biography," which Laura Marcus has attempted to recuperate, centered loosely around a "new level of critical self-awareness" by the biographer of her involvement in producing the subject.[10] As a "quintessentially Victorian genre," biography had been done in service of men of "genius," many modernists felt, written as hero-worship, with a "belief in personal creativity, autonomy, and freedom for the future."[11] Strachey's centrality to creating a visible, if not audacious break with their Victorian predecessors—including Woolf's father, Sir Leslie Stephen, first editor of the *Dictionary of National Biography* (*DNB*)—is difficult to overstate. Strachey articulated a lack of faith in the ideals embodied by Victorian biography and shifted the genre toward a leftist politics. Though now familiar from postcolonial critiques of empire, European liberalism, and notions of "civilization," his arguments about the Victorian era were groundbreaking, especially for the semi-sacred genre in which he lodged them. He accepted that the late Victorian works of Samuel Butler, Charles Whibley, and Edmund Gosse had begun to reform biography, yet he felt that the genre had been overtaken by insularity, misplaced certitude, and unnecessary length. In a letter to Woolf, Strachey called the Victorians "a set of mouthing bungling hypocrites," and, believing that their approach to biography epitomized their era, he stages a symbolic funeral for the genre in the famous preface to *Eminent Victorians*.[12]

Strachey believed that the biographer must not paper over inconsistencies, irrationality, contradictions, and unflattering or taboo moments in the lives of his subjects. When such things might cause shock or controversy that would increase his book's sales, he was only more eager to include them. With an impressionism indebted to Walter Pater and a sense of the hypocrisy of "progress" inherited from Joseph Conrad, Strachey argues in his manifesto-like preface that the biographer must also "row out over that great ocean of material, and lower down into it, here and there, a little bucket, which will bring up to the light of day some characteristic specimen, from those far depths, to be examined with a careful curiosity" (*EV* vii). He proceeds in search of "certain fragments of the truth which took [his] fancy," animated by "motives of convenience and of art" rather than by a quest for objective knowledge (*EV* viii). Strachey's critique of a Victorian belief in the transparency of the medium and invisibility of the biographer comes to life in his statements of a preference for metaphor over fact, personal impression over material fidelity. He wrote as he responded to his subjects' lives, not as a scrupulous documentarian would; he wrote with irony and aloof detachment, not with personal investment in validating or upholding their reputations; and he wrote with satire, subtle mockery, free indirect discourse, symbols and motifs rather than "whole" accounts of persons—even with "camp" styles and intentionally "banal bad prose," critics have noted. And thus, Strachey alternately has been praised or dismissed for overestimating and misjudging his project—and for being a "contemptible sniggerer."[13]

At the same time, Strachey sought to internationalize English literature through his project. In his preface, he distances himself from his national predecessors and binds his new style to a foreign model: "the art of biography seems to have fallen on evil times in England. We have had, it is true, a few masterpieces, but we have never had, like the French, a great biographical tradition."[14] Born into a lineage whose wealth and standing were built on the British empire's dominance in India, Strachey owed much of his cosmopolitanism to the spoils of privilege. He traveled often while young, including plenty of trips to Europe and a stay in Egypt. After becoming enamored of France, he published *Landmarks of French Literature* (1912), and by the time of the outbreak of the Great War, he wrote to his brother James, "I don't care much about England's being victorious (apart from personal questions)—but I should object to France being crushed," because France was "civilized," not "barbari[c]." As he styled his own writing after that of his foreign forebears—primarily Voltaire and Racine, but also Dostoevsky—he developed a skepticism that had been incubating at least since he was 18, when he wrote in a diary that "my character . . . is not crystalized [*sic*]. So there will be little recorded here that is not transitory, and there will be much here that is quite untrue."[15]

"I have attempted," Strachey states in his own preemptive defense, "through the medium of biography, to present some Victorian visions to the modern eye," with "modern" serving as his byword for "international" (*EV* vii). He chooses as his subjects Cardinal Manning, Florence Nightingale, Thomas Arnold, and General Gordon, who respectively represent Victorian evangelism, humanitarian sympathy, liberalism and reform, and imperialism. All four fail, by Strachey's account, to follow through on the "visions" that they imagined as their missions. The gap between the popular portraits of these figures' achievements and what Strachey rewrites as their actual legacies motivates and sustains *Eminent Victorians*. Strachey writes, for instance, that Florence Nightingale

> was heroic; and these were the humble tributes paid by those of grosser mould to that high quality. Certainly, she was heroic. Yet her heroism was not of that simple sort so dear to the readers of novels and the compilers of hagiologies—the romantic sentimental heroism with which mankind loves to invest its chosen darlings: it was made of sterner stuff. (*EV* 155)

Instead, Strachey insists, she was bitter, angry, "mad," and "ruthless," for a "Demon possessed" this apparently saintly woman whose tyrannical personality contributes to the early death of Sidney Herbert (*EV* 165, 166, 135). Similarly, his criticism of Cardinal Manning, which appears to the "modern eye" by way of "the light which his career throws upon the spirit of his age, and the psychological problems suggested by his inner history," is that

> growing up in the very seed-time of modern progress, coming to maturity with the first onrush of Liberalism, and living long enough to witness the victories of Science and Democracy, he yet, by a strange concatenation of circumstances, seemed almost to revive in his own person that long line of diplomatic and administrative clerics which, one would have thought, had come to an end for ever with Cardinal Wolsey. (*EV* 3)

Strachey traces the resistance to liberal and democratic reforms throughout parts of English ecclesiastical and secular history alike, and he often judges the Church and the State to have led the opposition to these movements. He asks tongue in cheek whether "the Nineteenth Century [was], after all, not so hostile? Was there something in it, scientific and progressive as it was, which went out to welcome the representative of ancient tradition and uncompromising faith? Had it perhaps, a place in its heart for such as Manning—a soft place, one might almost say?" (*EV* 3–4).

Even while declaring that he will not treat "human beings . . . as mere symptoms of the past," Strachey focuses on the power-hungry motives of his subjects as embodiments of their era's faults (*EV* viii). He writes that when Manning was appointed to the See of Westminster, power had come to him at last; and he seized it with all the avidity of a born autocrat, whose appetite for supreme dominion had been whetted by long years of enforced abstinence and the hated simulations of submission. He was the ruler of Roman Catholic England, and he would rule. (*EV* 86)

Noting the "despotic zeal" with which Manning "rule[d]," Strachey traces also the Church's reluctance to recognize the social work of Manning's adversary, Cardinal Newman, even once "liberalism had become the order of the day" (*EV* 114, 118). In the short third essay, "Dr. Arnold," Strachey claims that this figure, too, failed to join in the reformatory spirit of his day: "reform was in the air—political, social, religious; there was even a feeling abroad that our great public schools were not quite all that they should be, and that some change or other . . . was highly desirable," but Arnold's actual reforms were "tentative and few" (*EV* 207, 218). Strachey's cynical manner of pointing up the omissions, hypocrisies, and faults of his subjects translated well when his Spanish contemporaries took aim at the same century in their national past.

Power and "Inevitable Destruction" in "The End of General Gordon"

The anti-democratic and brutally authoritarian strains of Victorian liberalism that Strachey sees as still present in the Great War are explored most fully in "The End of General Gordon," his great and daring final chapter. "Gordon" was written while Strachey, as he wrote to Forster, was "still about to be examined by military doctors, still wondering about the nature of conscience, still appearing before 'Tribunals.'"[16] Quentin Bell believed that "Strachey altered his original concept of the book [because of the war] so that its theme became the ironic sifting of those Victorian pretensions that seemed to have led civilizations into a holocaust of unparalleled magnitude," while David Garnett concluded that Strachey's "essays were designed to undermine the foundations on which the age that brought war about had been built."[17] The martial metaphor for the biographer's task that Strachey employs in his preface calls for a "subtler strategy" than the "direct method of a scrupulous narration": "he will attack his subject in unexpected places; he will fall upon the flank, or the rear; he will shoot a sudden, revealing searchlight into obscure recesses, hitherto undivined" (*EV* vii). This "strategy" and its politics were developed with the aid of his Bloomsbury associates, who believed that they were, as Leonard Woolf recalled, "living in the springtime of a conscious revolt against the social, political, religious, moral, intellectual and artistic institutions, beliefs and standards of our fathers and grandfathers."[18] Strachey wrote political reviews for Leonard Woolf's journal *War and Peace*, campaigned vociferously against conscription during the war, and supported Bertrand Russell in his trial. His associates pushed him to renovate biography through contemporary pacifist, leftist polemics against the British liberal-imperial state.

The war exacerbated these polemics and Strachey's anger at the government of his "wretched country."[19] In August 1914, just after the war began, he describes the geopolitical scene as "a puppet-show, with all the poor little official dolls dancing and squeaking their official phrases."[20] This disgust and this vision of the ruin at the heart of British domestic and imperial politics would permeate his revisions of *Eminent Victorians* before it was finally published in May 1918, when the war still raged. Gordon, the once-successful general who met a tragic end, becomes his ideal emblem: he is a confident hero who is also merely one of the "creatures in a puppet show to a predestined catastrophe," Strachey writes in similar language. Far from autonomous or destined, Gordon's "fate," Strachey writes, was actually "mingled with the frenzies of Empire and the doom of peoples. And it was not in peace and rest, but in ruin and horror, that he reached his end" (*EV* 246).

"The End of General Gordon" is a study of "curiously English" and "strange characters, moved by mysterious impulses" toward ruin on multiple levels: the style and the arc of Strachey's narrative expose how the internal mechanisms of the governmental "imperialist wave" conspired with Gordon's own blind hubris to create the general's "end"—that is, both his death and his purpose (*EV* 246, 303). Gordon indeed becomes a synecdoche for the self-destructive imperial ventures of European powers writ large, with his first formative experience abroad being his arrival in Peking just in time to "witness the destruction of the Summer Palace at Peking—the act by which Lord Elgin, in the name of European civilisation, took vengeance upon the barbarism of the East" (*EV* 248). While undermining ironically the notion of "European civilisation," Strachey portrays Gordon, whom he characterizes in the first line of the essay as a "solitary English gentleman . . . wandering . . . in the neighbourhood of Jerusalem," as out of place, not belonging, and likely not wanted (*EV* 245). Similarly, an illusion of his greatness and his status as a "demi-God" in China come to Gordon by circumstance, not by merit, Strachey writes, thus undermining Europe's implicit claims of universal authority. And when he gains power as the leader of the Ever Victorious Army, Gordon rules like a brutal despot. He "drill[s his troops] with rigid severity," and though he pays them and provides them sanitary supplies, "there were some terrible scenes, in which the General, alone, faced the whole furious army, and quelled it: scenes of rage, desperation, towering courage, and summary execution. Eventually he attained to an almost magical prestige" (*EV* 252). For his ability to subdue the Chinese, rather than to spread "civilisation," Gordon was given by the "English authorities ... the reward usually reserved for industrious clerks"—which is to say, he had become an ideal bureaucratic instrument of empire (*EV* 256).

Ambition and a thirst for pure power ultimately drove Gordon more than his desire to glorify the British empire, for the

> grosser temptations of the world—money and the vulgar attributes of power—had, indeed, no charms for him; ... ambition was, in reality, the essential motive in his life: ambition, neither for wealth nor titles, but for fame and influence, for the swaying of multitudes, and for that kind of enlarged and intensified existence "where breath breathes most even in the mouths of men." Was it so? In the depths of Gordon's soul there were intertwining contradictions. (*EV* 260)

Like Strachey's other subjects, Gordon desires a vain glory in power that leads him to foolhardy decisions, such as accepting a post in "the unexplored and pestilential region of Equatoria" in southern Sudan, where "the savage inhabitants were to become acquainted with freedom, justice, and prosperity" and where, Strachey notes cynically, "incidentally, a government monopoly in ivory was to be established" (*EV* 261, 262). Gordon abuses his subordinates, and Strachey suggests that the General's "passions" are in fact the "ungovernable" force: "the gentle soldier of God ... would slap the face of his Arab aide-de-camp in a sudden access of fury" (*EV* 265). As Gordon gains authority and prestige, his appetite for more only grows, for he "confessed ... [t]hat the world was not big enough for him, that there was 'no king or country big enough'" (*EV* 269). But it is the effect of "Gordon's administration" that "by its very vigour, [it] only helped to precipitate the inevitable disaster" that would befall him (*EV* 271). By Strachey's account, Gordon's misrule in the Sudan creates his foil, the Mahdi, the man whose army will eventually kill him—and the leader with whom he shares qualities such as visions of grandiosity and defiant, draconian sensibilities.

When Gordon, back in England, presumably retired, and in his fifties, was still, Strachey writes, "by the world's measurements, an unimportant man[,] ... unrecognised and almost unemployed," he then believed himself to be "chosen" for a new "mission" to return to the Sudan and find there "not only a boundless popularity but an immortal fame" (*EV* 283). Through free indirect discourse, Strachey cites an air of public opinion—not any identifiable sources—in which he incorporates imagined quotations from the press about Gordon's high public standing and the gravity of his mission, all of which lead to the conclusion that "General Gordon must go to Khartoum" again (*EV* 285). Strachey intervenes to note that the "whole history of [Gordon's] life, the whole bent of his character, seemed to disqualify him for the task for which he had been chosen[:] . . . to carry out a policy laid down from above" of evacuating from Khartoum in 1884 (*EV* 289). Gordon rebuffs the empire's Egyptian administration and declares that he will bring the whole of the Sudan "under civilised rule" (*EV* 290). In the process, he becomes at once the Governor-General and the puppet for the government that opposes and controls him (*EV* 292).

In his account of the government's and Gordon's machinations, Strachey alternates between speculation—based on "our present information" about closed-door meetings or private thoughts—and "the solidity of fact" that he emphasizes at times (*EV* 294, 295). Little of either one squares with Gordon's belief that he was "already famous; he would soon be glorious" (*EV* 298). Gordon instead rides "the imperialist wave" to becoming the hypocritical "Christian hero" who, for instance, "had spent so many years of his life suppressing slavery [in Sudan, but] was now suddenly found to be using his high powers to set it up again" (*EV* 303, 300). Now he makes the headstrong and ill-fated decision to—in a phrase Strachey repeats a number of times—"smash up the Mahdi" (*EV* 302). Moving back and forth between domestic and international politics, Strachey adds that Prime Minister Gladstone, "champion of militant democracy," thwarts his plans, though Gordon "never understood the part that Mr. Gladstone was playing in his destiny" (*EV* 307, 312). Instead, Gordon fixated upon Sir Evelyn Baring, who represented for him "the embodiment of the English official classes, of English diplomacy, of the English Government with its hesitations, its insincerities, its double-faced schemes. Sir Evelyn Baring, he almost came to think at moments, was the prime mover, the sole contriver, of the whole Sudan imbroglio" (*EV* 313).

Gordon is a victim both of his own rule and of his government's failure. He sits at his desk and writes letters and a diary "with ruin closing round him" and only grows more adamant in his refusal to obey his government and evacuate (*EV* 328, 331). By the time the long-delayed British arrive in Khartoum, his fate is already sealed and the "signs of ruin and destruction on every hand showed clearly enough that the town had fallen." Strachey writes that the details of exactly what happened are "unknown to us," so he works instead from "glimpses" and hearsay (*EV* 343). His depiction of Gordon's death is paradigmatically inconclusive:

> Another spear transfixed him; he fell, and the swords of the three other Dervishes instantly hacked him to death. Thus, if we are to believe the official chroniclers, in the dignity of unresisting disdain, General Gordon met

his end. But it is only fitting that the last moments of one whose whole life was passed in contradiction should be involved in mystery and doubt. Other witnesses told a very different story. The man whom they saw die was not a saint but a warrior. With intrepidity, with skill, with desperation, he flew at his enemies. When his pistol was exhausted, he fought on with his sword; he forced his way almost to the bottom of the staircase; and, among a heap of corpses, only succumbed at length to the sheer weight of the multitudes against him. (*EV* 347)

Strachey's speculative portrait of the scene of Gordon's death—one already ingrained in his audience's minds by George William Joy's famous mythical painting *General Gordon's Last Stand* (1885)—leaves his subject, in the final of the possible scenarios, crushed under the mass of those he tried to oppress.

In Strachey's own bitterly ironic final lines come his most severe criticisms of the empire: "General Gordon had always been a contradictious person—even a little off his head, perhaps, though a hero[.] . . . At any rate, it had all ended very happily—in a glorious slaughter of 20,000 Arabs, a vast addition to the British Empire, and a step in the Peerage for Sir Evelyn Baring" (*EV* 350). In a section in which he has alluded scandalously to Gordon's possible homosexuality and has impugned him as "a disciple of Baudelaire" because he was perpetually drunk, Strachey reserves his greatest contempt for the empire that capitalized upon Gordon's death by "slaughter[ing] . . . 20,000 Arabs" and taking their lands (*EV* 298). His inclusion of Baring's rise toward peerage lays guilt on an antiquated order of nobility, too. Strachey extended these attacks three years later with *Queen Victoria* (1921), a text in which he treats the queen herself with some sympathy, but dissects the internal logic of imperialism further—specifically in English cultural history. The misbegotten fervor of empire both "mysti[fied]" and corrupted the Victorians, from the average citizen to the Queen, Strachey suggests.[21]

Strachey's "Lives," Vanguard Writing, and *La nueva biografía* in Spain

If the course of the New Biography in Anglophone modernism proved blurry, especially once Strachey's style fell out of favor, in Spain, on the other hand—and especially in the *Revista de Occidente*—the cross-cultural dialogue with Strachey's work is quite visible, pronounced, and provocative.[22] This occurred during a period of political upheaval in which battling literary camps were forging new aesthetics. In particular, the Spanish avant-garde novel, the genre that most influenced and overlapped with *la nueva biografía*, took dramatic new turns beginning in the mid-1920s.[23] The Revista de Occidente press's "Nova novorum" series showcased the metafiction, thick metaphorics, self-referentiality, and ornate stylistics that characterized these new novels, which included Benjamín Jarnés's *El profesor inútil* [*The Useless Professor*, 1926], Pedro Salinas's *Víspera del gozo* [*Prelude to Pleasure*, 1926], and Antonio Espina's *Pájaro pinto* [*Colored Bird*, 1927]. Ortega's *Dehumanization of Art* and *Notes on the Novel* (1924–1925) were key texts for both novelists and biographers, many of whom were Ortega's collaborators at the *Revista de Occidente*. Ortega's writings on the novel, which share a number of similarities with the arguments that Strachey and Woolf were making at the time, conclude that the genre had become exhausted and was dying because realists, in their attempts to bury the traces of both handiwork and medium, had made it fixed and predictable rather than flexible and adaptable. But as Nigel Dennis writes, Ortega was displeased with the direction that Spanish vanguard literature had taken since he published *Dehumanization*. He thought that "with the anchorage of a historical figure, biographers would be able to reestablish contact with the reading public by 'humanizing' their work, precisely at a time when the rarified intellectualism and self-indulgent virtuosity of avant-garde prose were being criticized."[24] Vanguard biographers, many of whom were primarily novelists, would bring their work into new terrain, while also maintaining the goal of reconciling a fidelity to facts with a commitment to iconoclasm and obliquity, as Gustavo Pérez Firmat writes.[25] They would also create a form of modernist innovation that would bring avant-garde techniques from abroad to new middle-class and popular readers in Spain. The revival of biography—even a paradoxical "dehumanized biography"—would revive other genres while also inscribing Spanish writing into a pan-European literary movement, Ortega and others believed.

Biographies of saints and conquistadors were common during Spain's Golden Age, and the Real Academia de la Historia [Royal Academy of History], since its founding in the eighteenth century, had commissioned thousands of biographies similar to those that England's *DNB* would later collect. The private series *Vidas de españoles célebres* was successful in the mid-nineteenth century, and in the 1880s and 1890s, publishers Montaner y Simón and Espasa had begun compiling what would become an expansive encyclopedia of biography. But biography as a literary practice had been nearly abandoned in Spain by the early 1900s.[26] The press of the Residencia de Estudiantes published a series of well-known biographies from other languages in 1915, including Juan Ramón Jiménez's translation of Romain Rolland's *Beethoven* and *Tolstoy* and Enrique Díez-Canedo's translation of Voltaire's *Charles XII*. In the following years, texts such as José Bergamín's short sketches

Caracteres (1927) and Ramón's *Goya* (1928) and his series of portraits of modern writers, *Efigies* (1929), moved even further toward a new form of biography. None of these more recent efforts yet had the cultural standing, though, that Ortega believed biography could—indeed must—have in Spain. The *Revista de Occidente*, which had begun looking to appeal to a broader readership in the mid- to late 1920s, had been attuned to the New Biography in small degrees from its early days.[27] By now, it regularly published extracts of biographies by German historians, then commentaries on and pieces by a host of European biographers, then the first articles on and translations of Strachey's work (for a time, the only ones), then finally pieces by Spaniards themselves.

The central pieces in the journal's coverage and dissemination of the New Biography were Marichalar's "School of Plutarchs" (1927) and "'Lives' and Lytton Strachey" (1928). In the former, he writes that "with the recent style of biography, new masters [*patrones*] of its genre have arrived: no longer is Boswell cited as the sempiternal model, but rather Maurois or Lytton Strachey is. Today, *Ariel* and *Eminent Victorians* prevail everywhere by virtue of their style and their customs." Marichalar points his compatriots to the Parisian standard, where series of biographies published by the houses Plon and Nouvelle Revue Française have been very successful in spreading the popularity of this genre (similar series are planned by Spanish publishers, he adds). Its popularity has emerged in France, Marichalar notes, despite the uneven quality of Plon's *Roman des grandes existences* series. The fault lies in the demands of editors who have hamstrung their biographers by asking them to "convert diffuse and excessive lives" into ones with "admirable courses and just dimensions." Such a task is impossible, he writes, because "these are the times of Picasso, not of Regnault." The NRF's *Vies des hommes illustres* series has shortcomings, too, Marichalar insists, and should also feature more "figures who led curious lives which, although some of them have been well recorded in history, still maintain a suggestive power for those who hope to novelize them" (he will later regret endorsing the "novelized" biography).[28] Marichalar concludes by listing some figures whom Spanish biographers should treat, almost all of them foreign: Girolamo Savonarola, Pico della Mirandola, Walter Pater, Francis Thompson, Ingres, Kierkegaard, Castiglione, Novalis, Paracelsus, Louis XV, Whistler, Blake, and Degas. Like Strachey, the Spaniard believes that in order to inaugurate a new mode of biography nationally, one must adapt foreign models, for biography cannot thrive in a national context alone.

In his longer review-essay "'Lives' and Lytton Strachey" (1928), published in the *Revista* alongside his translation of "The End of General Gordon," Marichalar develops with greater detail and complexity his theory of what has occurred and will occur in the realm of biography in England, in Europe, and soon in Spain.[29] The reasons why Strachey's pacifism and his study of a botched imperialist mission in Africa would appeal to readers of the *Revista* at this point are plain enough. But since Strachey himself had virtually no interest in Spain and or in the dissemination of his work there, Marichalar became his primary interpreter and spokesman. To excavate what he sees as the power of Strachey's cultural politics and to adapt them to Spain, Marichalar traces in his article the roots of the "new era of biography" through the history of English biography generally, then turns to the recent influence of Anglo-American criticism on psychoanalysis and behaviorism on thought about biography.[30] The English, mostly through the *DNB*, created an ideal of "homage to the hero" that has become pervasive. What Marichalar calls its "cult of heroism" is found "everywhere, . . . even the unknown masses have their hero, raised suddenly on the anonymous shoulders of the rest." Like Johnson and Boswell, Strachey, the era's most influential contemporary biographer, "had to be English," for the English have been its foremost innovators, he writes. But thanks to the portability and translatability of Strachey's work, biography now crosses national and linguistic boundaries in modern "literary spaces." Thus we have an "Italian Christ and a German Napoleon, a Voltaire of English craftsmanship and a Disraeli 'made in France'" ("LLS" 131).

Strachey has overhauled biography much like Joyce, Woolf, and T. S. Eliot have fiction and poetry, and Strachey's work bespeaks the angst and despair that permeates the current European generation of "transition," Marichalar writes ("LLS" 132). He is now the unquestioned "renovator of the genre" and its "supreme authority," having "rehabilitat[ed]" it and made it an artistic and critical enterprise ("LLS" 130–131). Marichalar reads the Englishman as a type of psychologist; as one who speculates rather than argues or demonstrates; as one who gives "opportune" and "characteristic," not "irrefutable" facts; and as one who turns his subjects into literary figures who transcend their works ("LLS" 133). In "our epoch in search of personalities," a modern epoch with a "Freudian distrust" of itself, the concept of "personality" has been reassembled and re-presented to us in disfigured yet beautiful form by Baudelaire, Flaubert, Proust, Joyce, and now Strachey ("LLS" 129). Strachey's critique operates by a process of expressive "mirroring," revealing that "Victorian complacency" was supported by blind and vain belief in its self-sufficiency—and he does so in a manner that makes the hypocritical "epoch itself" its own skeptic. Marichalar believes that Strachey has forced a "country sure of itself," a country of "blind smugness," to confront its "vain national spirit." England thus appears "excessively self-assured, having complete faith in all that enabled its imperial project" to a grave fault. This confidence, "resting under the British flag, took no notice that underneath its majestic folds, a humble and quiet enemy had slipped in. The Pharisee paid no attention to the tax collector" ("LLS" 134). Like Maurois, Marichalar most admires "The End of General Gordon" for its exposition of the ways in which Gordon was "abandoned" by his country, which "believed itself invulnerable until the last soldier." He was also the victim of the "fearless government" and its belief in the "indubitable power of the country" ("LLS" 135). Strachey recuperates a voice for Gordon, Marichalar argues, through irony and cold sarcasm. Like Woolf, who coined the term "New Biography" in a contemporaneous discussion of Strachey in 1927, Marichalar sees liberatory politics in Eminent Victorians: the biographer "no longer . . . toil[s] . . . slavishly in the footsteps of his hero. Whether friend or enemy, admiring or critical, he is an equal," Woolf writes. The New Biographer "preserves his freedom and his right to independent judgment," for being "raised upon a little *eminence* which his independence has made for him, he has become an artist," she notes with a subtle nod to Strachey.[31]

After the *Revista* captured the phenomenon of the New Biography in Europe, a spate of biographies by familiar authors quickly appeared in translation in Spain, and *la nueva biografía* found firm footing. In 1928, *Revista de Occidente* collaborator Juan Chabás noted that "store windows are full of 'lives'" from France, England, Italy, and Germany.[32] Between 1928 and 1929 alone, Maurois's *Ariel: The Life of Shelley* and *Disraeli*, Ludwig's *Kaiser Wilhelm II* and *Napoleon*, and Zweig's *Three Masters: Balzac, Dickens, Dostoevsky* were all published with great success locally. Thus, in his study of this literary flowering that is marginalized in most Hispanophone treatments of this era, Enrique Serrano Asenjo dates the beginning of *la nueva biografía* to 1928. In this year, the Madrid daily *El Sol* also created a review section dedicated to biographies, for which Ricardo Baeza was the chief critic. Baeza, who had published some of his ideas in his article for the *Revista* on Samuel Butler, also traces the modern biography form back to England, and he speculates that Spaniards have not had the same concern about "distant lives" that their English peers have had. He celebrates the current "catholicity" of biography and informs Spanish readers that it now flourishes among a "broad radius" of nationalities—that in fact it has made inroads with readers who normally bought only novels.[33] In 1929, Ortega capitalized upon this rising interest in biography in Spain and solidified the arrival of *la nueva biografía* by launching through the Espasa-Calpe press the series *Vidas españolas del siglo XIX* [*Spanish Lives of the Nineteenth Century*], the first dedicated specifically to biography.[34] Modeling his plans on those of houses such as Plon and the NRF, Ortega gathered his young periodical collaborators and, in a scene memorably and humorously recounted by Rosa Chacel, began pointing his finger and assigning them figures for research. His choice of the nineteenth century as the limitation of figures to be treated in experimental new modes of writing evinces both his sympathy for Strachey's work and his own broad-ranging assault on this era of Spain's past.

The rate of production was impressively swift: by 1936, the collection had accumulated over 50 titles and had proven commercially successful. The end of the censorship laws of the Primo de Rivera regime enabled both this production and translations of foreign biographies to grow in the early 1930s.[35] Not only young writers, but also more established figures contributed biographies in a range of vanguard styles—"oblique lives," as some were called.[36] Benjamín Jarnés was the most prolific biographer, and novelists Pío Baroja, Antonio Espina, the Count of Romanones, Juan Chabás, and Ramón Gómez de la Serna all published in the series. The figures treated included the best-known names of nineteenth-century Spanish history (Isabella II, Carlos VII, Cánovas, Zumalacárregui, Maragall), a romanticized small-time bandit known for his "bloodless robberies" in Espina's *Luis Candelas* (1929), and the ruined aristocrat of Marichalar's *Osuna*. Ortega put Melchor Fernández Almagro in charge of this series, then had Marichalar direct a smaller offshoot, *Vidas extraordinarias*, founded in 1932. The titles in the latter collection featured more works in translation—many of them even more experimental than *Vidas españolas* titles—that treated figures from across history and the globe, most famously Ludwig Pfandl's *Juana la loca* (1932).[37] In a moment when many new publishing houses were appearing, other Madrileño publishers such as Ediciones La Nave and Ulises issued biographies by prominent writers as well, including César Arconada (author of *Vida de Greta Garbo* [1929]), José María Salaverría, and Ángel Flores. As *la nueva biografía* grew in popularity, the biography review section of *El Sol*, Dennis writes, reviewed over 300 biographies—more than half of them of Spanish origin—between 1929 and 1936.[38] By 1932, a critic noted in the same paper the "irrefutable evidence" of the popularity of biography in the new Spanish Republic: the people "cry for it, on every street corner, in every shop's window, catalogs, advertisements, shelves, and libraries all proclaim it. The voracious appetite for reading in our time can only be sated with the flesh of life—that is, with biography, with stories."[39]

Reform, Reconstruction, and the Liberal Project in Spain

The political contexts of the rise of *la nueva biografía* help to clarify the cultural work of these diverse texts, especially Marichalar's *Osuna*, and their stunning popularity in the new Second Republic. By the late 1920s, Primo de Rivera and his royal backers were losing their handle on the Spanish populace, and the dictator's purges of universities and intellectual salons were infuriating Ortega and his circle.[40] Cries for autonomy in the provinces grew louder and strikes became more common. The urgent desire for a new liberal-democratic state was palpable, especially among the young, educated class. These Spaniards had attended schools such as the Institución Libre de Enseñanza and the Residencia de Estudiantes, and they had moved leftward in reaction to Primo de Rivera's rule. The Federación Universitaria Escolar [Federation of University Students], an alliance of young scholars, intellectuals, and militants, was formed in 1927 in order to speak nationally for this growing group.

For many of this generation, Ortega embodied in his cosmopolitan Europeanism and his steadfast liberal anti-monarchism the various calls for reform.[41] The philosopher's proclamations in *El Sol*—"¡Delenda est monarchia!"—and an exhortation to his compatriots to "reconstruct" their state struck a chord for such groups across the country. In 1928, Ortega also reissued a pamphlet of his influential lecture "Old and New Politics," reiterating its call for a "New Spain." His treatise *Misión de la universidad* [*Mission of the University*, 1930] summarized his calls for reforming Spain's schools into centers for liberal education and enlightenment. Ortega remained closer to the political center than did his younger associates, but they shared a vision of an intellectual vanguard who would serve as cultural guides for the country.[42] In 1929, a group of 25 writers sent him a petition asking for him to lead a national group to represent the new liberalism in Spain. The writers, who claim to represent "all of the 'new' men of Spain whose liberal sensibilities are in tune with our own, ... a group of ... resolute liberalism," see themselves as "bound intellectually" to Ortega and his plan to "make a new State" with the Spanish youth.[43] These causes all fit neatly together at the moment; Shlomo Ben-Ami notes of Spain's "Europeaniz[ing]" movement in the late 1920s that the "demand for the abolition of the Monarchy was inextricably bound up with a quest for human emancipation, civil rights, and an end to clericalism."[44]

In this propitious moment for Ortega, his philosophies and his readings of Spain's history of anti-liberalism merged. In fact, this intersection is clearest in some of his earlier works—in particular, his often-reproduced essay "Nada 'moderno' y 'muy siglo XX'" ["Not at all 'modern' and 'very twentieth-century,'" 1916], which characterizes the nineteenth century as responsible for the death of Spanish liberalism. Here, Ortega spells out his "certain hostility" to the nineteenth century and especially to a version of Romanticism born of an "obligation to shake out of our consciousness the dust of old ideas." Using the same dichotomy of "old" and "new" eras of Spanish history that he employed in "Old and New Politics," Ortega positions contemporary Spaniards on the precipice between "the old" and "the new" [*lo viejo* and *lo nuevo*] in "the battle of a nascent century against the one that preceded it." The previous century, he writes, claimed in a deceptive self-prophecy to be "the century of progress! The century of modernity!" However, "modernity" and "progress," while "very pretty and enticing" words, contain little substance, and Spain's youth are enchanted "prisoners of the modern—that is to say, of the nineteenth century."[45] "Modern" and "modernity" were, in part, contaminated words for Ortega because they had been appropriated in the nineteenth century; thus he grounded his philosophies of "circumstance" and his politics squarely in the twentieth century, which for him would be Spain's true moment of modernity.

The anger among Spain's youth and its rising left was directed not only at the present dictator, but also at the failures of the nineteenth century to which Ortega alludes. Spain's constitution of 1812—one of the earliest and most progressive expressions of liberalism of its day—hardly had a chance to be enacted before it was abolished in 1814. The next brief, chaotic attempt at establishing liberal parliamentarianism came during the Third Carlist War, when the First Republic lasted only from February 1873 until the restoration of Bourbon monarchism in December 1874. From the Restoration until Primo de Rivera's coup, the Cortes remained stiffly and fraudulently controlled by an antiquated alliance of oligarchs, while the prime minister was appointed by the king. The experiments in democracy that generations of Spaniards believed they had witnessed their European neighbors undertake had but flickered domestically; a brief push for liberal reforms in the early 1910s, for instance, resulted in the assassination of Prime Minister José Canalejas. Now, an Orteguian New Spain seemed on the brink of existence to many both within and beyond Spain, and the *Revista de Occidente*'s collective saw the coming Second Republic as a manifestation of their cultural aims—albeit a revised one, since Ortega's ideal of an intellectual aristocracy and the journal's elitism would have to be transformed into a more populist shape. But Spain, as Rosa Chacel wrote, "knew nothing of living in a democratic era," and its entrenched social divisions and corresponding ideologies had to be reformed quickly.[46] Therefore, just before the Second Republic came to power, Ortega spearheaded the founding of a new national Agrupación al Servicio de la República [Group in Service of the Republic], which looked both to prepare Spaniards for liberalism and to disseminate elite culture among everyday Spaniards.

When elections ushered the Republicans' leftist coalition into power in April 1931, King Alfonso XIII fled the country, as had Primo de Rivera. Stanley Payne calls the early success of the Second Republic the "most unusual, and probably the most positive, political event in Europe during the first years of the Great Depression," when much of Europe was, at that moment, heading toward anti-democracy.[47] The Republicans, in contrast to Primo de Rivera, were pronounced internationalists and supporters of the League of Nations. They welcomed most intellectual cultures except those of the right, and they introduced massive land reforms that reshaped class relations across the country. New aesthetic movements and programs flourished, especially those linked to continental avant-gardes and to Soviet movements that had been repressed under the dictatorship, as the cultural landscape was altered in the Republic's early years. The unprecedented levels of involvement in and support from the state that intellectuals and writers enjoyed led historian Manuel Tuñón de Lara to call it "la República de intelectuales."[48]

Behind this work was the force of Spain's pro-European and secular Krausists, whose founder Francisco Giner de los Ríos had been dismissed from a Spanish university under the First Republic. He and his colleagues now continued—in spaces such as the Residencia de Estudiantes—the interrupted work of the liberal, popular, and democratizing mandates that the previous republic had never delivered. They sought further to inculcate an overdue Enlightenment in Spain through educational programs that the Republicans carried to the country's most remote and impoverished villages in the early 1930s. Giner himself boasted that no such venture of this cultural magnitude had been attempted in the history of Europe.

Aristocracy and the Self-destruction of "the Greatest Fortune in Spain": Marichalar's *Osuna*

When Marichalar seized the opportunity to reform biography in his own country, he did so at a nexus of intellectual trends formed by his readings of Strachey and other New Biographers and the contexts of this liberal moment in Spain. Both in form and in topic, Marichalar's *Duke of Osuna* participates in this process of cultural renovation that took place during the late 1920s and early 1930s in Spain. After appearing in part in the *Revista* in 1929, it caused a minor sensation when it was published in January 1930. Marichalar's conservative sensibilities moved to the left with his peers in the late 1920s, when he distanced himself from his aristocratic origins and joined his colleagues in supporting the reforms that led to the Republic— and initially, in supporting the Republic itself. He was already known in Spain for having "cultivat[ed] a new prose [style] . . . that, like that of his contemporaries, rebels against the academic prose of the past," but he had written mostly criticism to date.[49] His subject, the Twelfth Duke of Osuna, was loathed and ridiculed in popular memory, a symbol of the reckless, wasteful, and domineering aristocracy that had kept ordinary Spaniards in grinding poverty for centuries. Taking a cue from Ortega's conviction that "true patriotism is the criticism of the land of one's fathers and the construction of the land of one's children," Marichalar created in his *Osuna*—his first attempt at biography—a critical allegory of aristocratic decadence in an avant-garde style that he would help popularize.[50]

Britain was, for Marichalar and his colleagues, "the most aristocratic country in the new Europe," one whose empire was admired more than Mussolini's was by José Antonio Primo de Rivera, son of the dictator and founder of the fascist Falange in 1933.[51] Marichalar transfers from Strachey's critiques a demystifying tone and an irreverent, sometimes mocking disposition toward the "eminent" figures of one's national past. His style, however, is more satirical and his prose more expressive than Strachey's. He also jumps back and forth in time, has intense moments of self-reflexive speculation, builds in semi-fictional scenes, and intersperses lines of poetry and epigraphs from a range of authors, many of them French or British—Baudelaire, Shakespeare, Apollinaire, Blake, Valéry, Cocteau, Chesterton—alongside excerpts from Spanish classics. He draws on the styles of the Spanish avant-garde novelists that surrounded him, too, as he fashions the Duke into his emblem of nineteenth-century Spain's self-destruction. Marichalar explained that he researched the Duke mostly so that he could "lay a historical foundation, then make the leap toward fantasy" in the book. "In my biography," he adds in a kind of wit that Strachey would have appreciated, "everything is true except the Duke of Osuna."[52]

Strachey and Marichalar share more in common than a primary role in shaping the New Biography as an international movement. Both came from elite families with which they were at times uncomfortable, but which they did not fully reject.[53] Marichalar, a marquis himself, came from a line of liberal aristocrats who sided against the monarchists during the Carlist Wars; given his personal history, one can infer why the Twelfth Duke of Osuna, Don Mariano Téllez-Girón y Beaufort (1814–1882) had considerable interest to him at this moment. The Duke came from a prominent and powerful Andalusian family with a history of governmental and military figures dating back at least to the sixteenth century. The catastrophic Twelfth Duke Mariano, however, was a notorious gambler and ostentatious spender who disgraced his family's name and left many of its assets in the hands of creditors at his death. He was most famous, in fact, for having inherited an annual income of five million pesetas and having left a debt of 44 million pesetas, leaving himself on the "margins of history, playing out his own farce, once and for all" (*O* 17). His ruin itself already gathered the elements of Spain's decline and historical failures that were the objects of critique for the young Republicans-to-be.

Marichalar's *Osuna*, which contains an epigraph from French writer Joseph Joubert on the title page reading "Quand je luis, je me consume" ["When I shine, I consume myself"] next to the Duke's portrait, was the fifth in the *Vidas españolas* series. The biography is told through 50 short vignettes, some episodic, some impressionistic, some factual to the point of hilarity. In a short overview that comprises the first, Marichalar begins his biography in mid-nineteenth-century Spain, when "Osuna" is "the first name in Spain," when this name "is the one jewel in the rubbish heap. Spain is crumbling to pieces at this time . . . [and its] people [*pueblo*] seek a patron saint that shall incarnate its own generosity and nobility."[54] Casting his subject's ancestors *against* the Spanish decline for which the Duke will become a synecdoche, Marichalar traces the "build[ing] up [of] a legend" around the name "Osuna" as it becomes embodied by Don Mariano Girón, the Twelfth Duke. The Duke is "the offspring of a race [*raza*] which contemplates its own image in him, and satisfies through him its own stifled longings" (*O* 16). Marichalar also begins here a game of wordplay that he will carry throughout the biography, stemming from the etymology of the name of the "Girón" family (a *jirón* is a "shred") from which Osuna's ancestors emerged. He has the Twelfth Duke appear first in "the capricious image of a dashing aristocrat, his breast a 'tatter [*jirón*] of blood and gold'" (*O* 16). He elaborates the pun by describing Osuna upon his horse as "tearing [*jironando*] to tatters once and for all the fabric his progenitors had alternately woven and rent," and he returns to variations on *jirón* at least ten times in the text, eventually explaining how the family acquired the name (*O* 17). This Duke, an epigonic Byron, "never spends merely to be spending; he spends because he feels that he is the cynosure of attention," because he is obliged by his people to do so. "He burns bridges and returns to the arms of his people [*pueblo*]," Marichalar writes of Spain's emblematic prodigal son (*O* 17). From such behavior, which had been attacked by the novelist Juan Valera during the Duke's lifetime, originated the phrase that still echoed in Madrid in Marichalar's day, usually in reference to gratuitous, irresponsible spending, "¡Ni que fuera Osuna!" (loosely, "Not even Osuna would!").

In language that recalls Strachey's preface to *Eminent Victorians*, Marichalar admits that "it is not easy to get to Osuna. Embattled behind his shield he always interposes between himself and the public's curiosity, on palaces, carriages and liveries, his coat-of-arms, made up of a motley assemblage of the most aristocratic devices" (*O* 21). His long ekphrasis of the originating Girón family's coat-of-arms borders on the absurd in its detail. Marichalar lists the shield's attributes in a mock-heroic fashion reminiscent of Joyce's style in "Cyclops," or as Woolf will read the decorated soldier as a ridiculous spectacle in *Three Guineas*. Osuna inherits "the greatest fortune in Spain in the nineteenth century" [*la primera fortuna de España*, a phrase repeated throughout the biography, with "fortuna" also meaning "luck"], but leads it into a "bottomless pit, the house of Girón, an abyss . . . [,] a trapdoor down which so much was thrown, and where everything would go, today, with the male line of the Giróns extinct." Of its "glory," much like Spain's past glory, "there remains nothing but a solitary echo" (*O* 23–24). Marichalar begins his account of the Osuna line, which absorbed the Giróns, with similar nihilism and with more self-reflexivity as biographer: "Nothing remains of Osuna; neither the name, nor the race, nor the fortune, nor its history, hardly a paper or a record. . . . Osuna always took care to efface his every vestige" (*O* 25). Marichalar portrays the Osunas as a line of characters in a historical caricature "played out for all time," one in which 14 grandees (some of them respectable), "fifty-two titles, four princedoms and the greatest fortune in Spain" are reduced to "a huge funeral pyre with which [a Téllez-Girón] dazzled his contemporaries" (*O* 29). He traces the oddities and abnormalities through the history of the family, too—its characteristic fops, its history of "*dandismo*" ["dandyism"], the "pretentious court circles" it frequented: "they were cultured, exacting, insolent, overbearing, dissatisfied, and voluble, and the slightest offence to their self-esteem flicked them on the raw" (*O* 31). "Better to Fly" was the motto of this family—"to fly, to reach the sun, to be suns themselves was the consuming passion of this proud, presumptuous lineage" before it was "consumed in the insatiable fire of its own passions" (*O* 28). As was the case with Gordon, Marichalar's subject is predestined to ruin himself, and his excesses are symbols not of glory but of futile gain and, ultimately, his own disaster. The overly symbolic garb of the Duke is matched by the overdone, humorous catalogues that the biographer gives.

A segment called "The Interlude of Don Pedro the Wasted" [*el malogrado*, also "the Frustrated"] throws into relief the Duke's character by way of his brother, the Eleventh Duke of Osuna, who was "the embodiment of the Romanticism of the epoch": a wise, dashing bachelor who served admirably in the legislature and army (*O* 44). The Eleventh Duke ("the legitimate Osuna"), however, never marries and dies broken-hearted and misanthropic; his death fully converts Mariano into a figure who,

> in his own eyes, is the embodiment of everything desirable on earth. Upon his brow descended the Osuna coronet, with all its honours, privileges, rights, entailments, all as a natural, logical occurrence. . . . And yet, let us for a moment imagine a man who were suddenly to put upon his forehead an ornate gold circlet, teeming with figures and battle-cries, in a mass of confusion and

uproar; and were to secure it there with the solemn gravity of one who fulfils a duty and exercises a right.... This man would be demented, or on the point of becoming so—but perhaps not: this man is simply a true aristocrat. (*O* 141–142; translation modified)

Marichalar proceeds to dissect the aristocracy into two types—the proud, rebellious knight and the dutifully servile courtier—only to claim that Osuna belongs to a "third degree of nobility which combines both tendencies: the aristocrat of the highest rank [*el prócer*]. For he is his own servant, the slave of his own name.... He is the despot of an imaginary kingdom [*imperio verbal*]. Unlike a real king he has no responsibility, no liability" (*O* 143). This last category explains "the fatuousness of a man like Osuna who suddenly feels upon his thick, yet empty head a crown as rich in glitter as it is poor in responsibilities" (*O* 144). The nobility, Marichalar suggests, derive their power and standing from their own ridiculous imaginations, and their power is never democratic, but makes even themselves into "slave[s]." The Duke is a deluded figure who was, "as [Jean] Cocteau would say, a madman who believed himself Osuna. He was a man possessed, possessed of himself, who ended in total dementia, in absolute derangement" (*O* 145).

Jumping back and forth in time, Marichalar writes that "lonely solitude[,] ... in the last analysis, was the only companion of [the younger Duke Mariano, who had] ... the intimate psychology of the disinherited, and perhaps this was why he fulfilled the destiny of ruining himself" (*O* 82–83). Moving seamlessly from the bare facts of Mariano's birth to speculation on his "psychology" and "destiny" in the matter of only a few lines, Marichalar describes his subject, as Strachey did several of his, as having a "feeble constitution," as being prone to "madness and delirium." "I imagine him as a young child wandering about the Alameda [his family's estate]," Marichalar writes, interposing himself into the narrative, "and I see him change from timorous to rash" (*O* 87). Worldly ambitions and the desire for control rule Mariano, for, as was the case with Gordon, "power was a magnificent vision which he must keep ever present, but which fled from him as he pursued the steps of the first-born." Osuna came of age, he asserts, in a moment in which Spain's era of "romantic idealism" is "imminently crumbling," for the "nineteenth century is moving forward like a broken-down wagon, wobbling through over dusty trails ... [amid] ... the vulgarity of a decaying age which is taking complete possession of it" (*O* 92–93; translation modified). His language here echoes, nearly verbatim, Ortega's description of the "old" nineteenth century in "Nada 'moderno.'"

Marichalar later scripts "scenes" of Osuna's life as if they were plays, imagining the "characters," "secondary figures," and "musical selections" that would accompany the Duke's bitter youth, and creates fictional characters who converse about Mariano's failures (*O* 94). The Duke suddenly sniffs the "scent of combat from afar," and "true gentleman" that he was [*Caballero de raza*], he is off to war (*O* 103). And like Gordon, Osuna is not fully in control of his military career. He is patriotic to a fault, loves battle and never accepts a salary; but even the war between monarchists and republicans for control of Spain does not satisfy his urges. "The solidarity of the army was broken, and Mariano, moving from place to place, lonely and discouraged, felt himself once more a puppet, a spectre, a glittering, hag-ridden shadow," he adds (*O* 115). He is awarded the scarlet cross and the cross of St. Ferdinand, he fights "like a Trojan" and is "worthy of his name," Marichalar concedes. But the author again echoes Strachey's descriptions of Gordon when he writes of Mariano's service on Isabella's liberal side in the First Carlist War (1833–1839): "Little is known of him [when he crossed into France in battle]. As a matter of fact, little is ever known of anybody at this age, when all that is not action is still a mystery. Mariano Osuna was unknown and he was himself his only companion" (*O* 122–123).

Not Don Juan, but Don Quixote—The Dandy

As a younger brother who believed that he would never inherit the dukedom, Osuna went directly from the military to "expatriating himself" in a restless mission to "achieve ... a transcendent act of dandyism" (*O* 124). In his search for "life outside of Spain," a country he has convinced himself is his *patria ingrata*, he attends the coronation of Queen Victoria in 1838, where he finds that "British society was entering upon the grey, stolid, bourgeois, comfortable Victorian doldrums" (*O* 124–125). He refashions himself in this climate as the dandy of all dandies—or so he thinks: he is, in actuality, still an unthinking product of his moment, Marichalar argues, and an indiscriminate one, for the "purpose blindly assigned him by his epoch is to triumph, and triumph he would, let it cost what it would" (*O* 127). He frequents the Parisian courts and casinos, falls in unrequited love with many women, and when he returns to Spain, feels "weary of crosses and uniforms" and "attract[ed] ... by what he had glimpsed in his time abroad, a dominion [*imperio*] ... that certain men held over their fellow beings, tyrannizing their peers with only the magic art of properly handling a cane, a silk hat, and a pair of gloves" (*O* 131). Thus, Marichalar writes, he believes that fashion can symbolize power, but in the "long run it was calamities rather than triumphs this dandy reaped, for he resembled not Don Juan, but Don Quixote. And like that knight he persisted unmoved in his pursuit of new failures" (*O* 133). This nineteenth-century Don Quixote, an absurd avatar of Spain's national legend, will fail in his quest to become a Baudelairean dandy—and will become a ludicrous failure for all Europe to observe. The Duke's problem is that he cannot put on decadence as a dandy must; he *is* decadence personified.

Suggesting deep roots for this problem, Marichalar traces the name "Osuna" back to the Latin *ursus* ["bear"] and notes that the Duke, when in Russia, shot a white bear—a miniature allegory for his ruining the family's name. At the close of Romantic-era Spain, "a period that was dying away," Marichalar writes, Osuna is a perfect emblem of the ways in which "things become hollow, pompous parodies of themselves," "the genuine is falsified" (*O* 58, 163–164). He attempts to serve in public office, but even here, he cannot reconcile the conservative interests of the aristocracy with his instinctive rebelliousness, so he quickly abandons the project. He goes to join other Spanish expatriates in Paris, where he becomes a balding, nearsighted and inferior copy of the French dandy, then returns to Spain to waste money by betting on horse races. Through the Duke, Marichalar rewrites the disintegration of Spanish culture and its desperate, failed attempts to imitate Paris (even when Marichalar himself often sees Paris as a cultural capital of the present). Marichalar continually plots Osuna's life against the eclipse of the nineteenth century, when "the aristocrats displayed the arms and costumes of the illustrious ancestors," while the newspapers read "'Yesterday, at the customary hour, there were put to death,' etc." (*O* 190).

Disappointed at the lack of romantic adventure in his life, the impetuous Duke concludes that "there's no future for a person in this country," and thus he

> look[s once again] beyond the Pyrenees. . . . His prow was headed toward Europe, and soon he was to embark, in his magnificent galleon, with all sails set, on the perils of the European seas, leaving behind him shabby, poverty-stricken Spain, where the royal frigate was foundering, while the Queen danced polkas and mazurkas. (*O* 200)

Marichalar's condemnation of Spain's decadent national past is perhaps clearest here, and like Strachey, he notes that what happened to Osuna abroad is a matter of conjecture, rumor, hearsay, and speculation. In fact, he writes, "although many of the things told about [Osuna] are not true, they are authentic, for they engender a myth. . . . His true figure is disfigured and forged into a type and a legend: an eternal figure" (*O* 201). The peripatetic life of this foolhardy knight-errant has its "culmination" in Russia, where the Duke serves as an ineffective ambassador who "make[s] a spectacle of himself" (*O* 147).

Marichalar calls Russia the "empire of the superlative, the kingdom of the unbounded," and asks, "where could Osuna have found a better stage than this, for his pompous, vain realities . . . [and his] delirium of grandeur[?]" (*O* 236, 147). In Russia, he was "a romantic, a lost star [*estrellado*, also 'ruined']. He squandered and spent, left and right, but without any purpose, for he was the purpose" (*O* 242). The self-destructive Duke kneels before the Czar and admires the despot's power, but he fumbles in diplomacy, and as stories of his exploits "reached Madrid in different versions, sometimes contradictory, others incomplete, and the popular echoes assemble them into his legend. There in distant Russia the sturdy house of Girón was crumbling to pieces" (*O* 250). After another comical episode of the Duke's failed pursuit of a woman, Marichalar writes, with a rhetorical flourish linking back to his recurring wordplay and his titular phrase ("perils and fortune"), that when the Duke received for his service the Grand Cross of Carlos III, he had little more than "another shell to hang from the tattered pilgrim's garb [*jironado ropón de peregrino*; *peregrino* also connotes 'outlandish'] he wore on that foolish journey in which he risked his name and fortune through the perils and fortune [*riesgo y ventura*] of sea and sky."[55] Equally lengthy *ad absurdum* are the lists of possessions, from art treasures to palaces, of this "nihilistic prince of the house of Osuna" (*O* 160).

Juxtaposed with this section is Marichalar's implicit critique of the Duke's—and Spain's—failed liberal reforms. By the late 1850s, Osuna was known across Europe; but as an ambassador of Spain, actually and figuratively, he was an international embarrassment. Marichalar emphasizes that Osuna was "alone, always alone" throughout his life; he finally marries a demanding princess while "refus[ing] to see his ruin; strictly speaking, his dandy's code prevented him from seeing it" (*O* 276). For this reason, Marichalar titles the final section of the biography *Humos de Osuna*, a play on the double sense of *humos* as "smoke" and "airs of rank or nobility." As he aged, the Duke became neurasthenic and suffered from gout; he was grossly overweight and deaf late in life, and he appeared to the average Spaniard a "remote, fabulous, legendary figure" of little significance (*O* 276, 281). In a vain effort to restore his national image, he was coerced into politics again in 1873, at the birth at the First Spanish Republic. Two later chapters of the biography are entitled "Al servicio de la República" and "Grandeza y decadencia," respectively. By this juxtaposition, Marichalar means to suggest that Osuna was at best a failed and halfhearted democrat who fought on the liberal side of the Carlist Wars and lived through the First Republic, but ultimately did nothing to put Spain on the path toward the liberal modernity toward which it was still struggling. He "served the Republic" mostly because it served him, and despite his aristocratic origins, "he served the ideals of democracy, for deep in his soul he carried the hidden instincts of a destructive leveller" (*O* 280). Marichalar speculates that, in the end, Osuna supported the Republic not out of principles or even opportunism, but because he felt that he had a "buried popularity" among the Spanish people (O 281).

As he approached death, Osuna had no heirs, no titles, no money, no more creditors willing to extend him loans: "the circle is complete. Now he is devouring himself; now he is eternal" (O 283). Marichalar uses his final years as a means to recast his own task as biographer, for the Duke "had little use for history" and "left no biographers," only a "disfigure[d]" record of himself taken down by uninterested historians or antagonists (O 283). He dies miserably and without note, unable to be buried alongside his ancestors because he left no money for that purpose, and the newspapers carry an announcement that his creditors will begin auctioning his assets to pay down his 44 million pesetas of debt. "The novel of the count of Monte Cristo," Marichalar writes, "is less improbable than the history of the last Duke of Osuna" (O 288). Coming back to his original wordplay, Marichalar writes that the Duke leaves his wife "a tattered patrimony" [*un patrimonio jironado*], then quotes several accounts of the Duke's death such as "Today the official gazette exhibits the last tatter [*el último jirón*] of the opulent and powerful Giróns" (O 295). He closes his biography with a mock-prayer:

> God save the Duke of Osuna, the Duke of perils, the valiant Duke[,] . . . a life went up in a holocaust to itself . . . and from the sparks of a puppet, emerged the rigid structure of a soul. Ours is this edifying ruin whereby a man fulfilled his destiny. "There are triumphant defeats that are the envy of victories," was Montaigne's appropriate line. (O 299–300; translation modified)[56]

Decline, Disillusion, and the Fate of *La nueva biografía*

Marichalar demonstrated that the new liberals' critique of the historical Spanish state could be animated by a treatment of a universally known figure in an avant-garde style. The biographer's irony and satire become tools of cultural pedagogy, offering both implicit and explicit lessons on the state's and the aristocracy's failures. *Osuna*'s international circulation bears out the effects of what Serrano Asenjo calls Marichalar's "pedagogical disposition."[57] The book was very well-received across Spain, in elite and popular media alike. In the definitive review-essay in the *Revista de Occidente* on *la nueva biografía*, Jaime Torres Bodet welcomes the effect of the New Biography as a "corrective" to the Spanish tendency toward reverent exaggerations of the greatness of past figures. It comes at the end of Primo de

Rivera's rule, "in a moment of national revaluation, [as] . . . a generation of biographers doesn't simply adapt its conventional tone from worldly tastes, but rather, it responds to our country's internal necessities . . . [with a] mature critical consciousness." He sees in Strachey's work "a complete renovation" of nineteenth-century biography that has made it an "artistic genre" that has burst from its previous frames and found unexpected new riches. Among the five biographies published so far in the *Vidas españolas* series, Torres Bodet reserves his highest praise for Marichalar's, appreciating his use of "the fragmentary sense, the 'precious,' which characterizes a large part of contemporary Spanish prose" in a manner that "suits well the superficial life of a dummy covered in ornate golden braids and titles," this "life of a superfluous man." He finds *Osuna*'s "poetic" quality appealing and the outlook for Spanish biography positive, seeing that the genre now can shape national politics.[58]

Not only was *Osuna* a success in Spain, with its third edition printed in 1933, but also word spread to publishers abroad, and Marichalar soon had the book translated into French (1931) and English (1932); a Catalan edition followed in 1933.[59] *Osuna* is one of very few (if not the only) titles from the *Vidas españolas* series to appear in English, and it was praised in the *Criterion* by Marichalar's associate Charles K. Colhoun. Colhoun lauds Marichalar for not "concerning himself overmuch with the roots and first shoots of the [Osuna] family tree" who figured prominently in the *Reconquista* and in a famous work by Quevedo. Instead, Marichalar "reserv[es] his researching energies for the nineteenth century, where he can rummage in peace among the welter of crosses, garters, stars, dukedoms, count-dukedoms, palaces and castles[,] . . . all the pompous glitter and magnificence that has collected in the form of a solid protective carapace" around the Eleventh and Twelfth Dukes, and for documenting the means by which the Twelfth Duke "became obsessed with pride of position and fortune" as he "absorbed title after title."[60] In the *TLS*, J. B. Trend was optimistic that "the translation [of *Osuna*] may do something to make up for the neglect of nineteenth-century Spanish biography in foreign countries."[61] American reviews were enthusiastic, too, calling Marichalar's writing "brilliant." "He writes an exciting prose," one reviewer claims, that treats his "colossally unimportant" subject with the "the context and texture of the Goya *Caprichos*," referring to the controversial series of caustic prints with which the artist condemned the myths and superstitions of his compatriots.[62]

After the early success of the *Vidas españolas* series, the *Revista de Occidente* increased its publication and coverage of biography, following Marichalar's translation of "The End of General Gordon" with Strachey's "Madame de Lieven" (1921) in 1931 and the Osuna-like self-destructive "Lady Hester Stanhope" (1922) in 1933. Continuing the liberal pedagogy, Ortega also issued, through his Revista de Occidente press, two new political education series in June and October of 1931, *Libros de política* and *Cuadernos de política*. The journal, at the same time, began a new section, "Visto y oído" ["Seen and heard"], initially written by Marichalar.[63] Topics ranging from student rallies to agrarian reforms to parliamentary elections were discussed here in a manner that mostly had been absent from Ortega's apolitical journal, and many of Ortega's pupils at the review became high-profile figures in the Republic's cultural arms. The writers of '27 saw their debates as not "merely aesthetic," writes Rafael Osuna, but charged with politicized visions of a "a new conception of literature and of the role of the learned, and of the dynamic between them in the social sphere."[64] During his brief period of sympathy with the Republic, Marichalar became involved with several new periodicals. In 1932, he joined the editorial board of *Arte*, the journal of the Society of Iberian Artists, and he helped found the short-lived *Cuatro Vientos [Four Winds]* the following year.[65] Also in 1933, Marichalar translated fragments of letters and lectures by Cardinal Newman for the first issue of José Bergamín's *Cruz y Raya*, a review that attempted to reconcile Catholicism and communism.

But around the same time, just as it seemed that Spanish arts and the Spanish state were entering the idealized European sphere that Ortega had envisaged, he, Marichalar, and many others became fully disenchanted with the Republic. The government had allowed atrocities against priests and nuns and the rampant persecution of the right, and it suffered crippling losses in the elections of 1933. Marichalar turned his disappointed eye toward *la nueva biografía* and revised his position (poor sales of the translations of Osuna had disheartened him as well).[66] He abandoned his second project, a biography of Savonarola that he had promised to Ortega, never to finish it. When his new edition of *Osuna* was finally published in 1945, he revealed a profound ambivalence about his work. In a foreword, he writes bluntly, "I abhor 'novelized' biographies," and he says that his account contains a "considerable dose of lyric irony" that readers should not enjoy too greatly. He worries that he had taken on in his prose the bombast and braggadocio of his subject, but more important, he feels that *la nueva biografía* had become irresponsible by straying too far into the territory of fiction. Marichalar now regrets parts of his biography and is more sympathetic to Osuna, seeing him as a figure who genuinely sought fame in the terms through which it was accessible, but who did not have "the soul of the powerful." Osuna, despite his clumsy boastfulness, "imposed on the world a reputation of Spanish grandeur," Marichalar concludes; though with a final note of irony, he adds, "it is the duty of Spaniards to preserve the memory of one who sacrifices his estate to the name of Spain."[67]

The genre's promise and fall, to Marichalar's mind, tracked that of the government. His devout Catholicism put him at odds with the Republic and, along with family connections, eventually allowed him to return to Franco's Spain after fleeing during the war. He held a position in the Royal Academy of History and returned to biography, now writing on the legendary sixteenth-century soldier Julián Romero. He did not return to producing or to writing at length on vanguard literary trends under Franco, but he tacitly accepted these limitations in exchange for not drawing the attention of censors. In retrospect, Osuna's failed politics and the failure of the First Republic look something like the failures of the writers of '27 and the Second Republic. Serrano Asenjo sees a parallel between the Duke, a "man essentially outside of his century, a nobleman in a time of the bourgeoisie," and Marichalar's own internal conflict as an "aristocrat-intellectual" swept up in a movement of popular anti-nobility.[68] Chacel's account of Ortega's assigning figures for their biographies may not tell the full story. Marichalar, an aristocrat, chose an aristocrat; Jarnés, a soldier and almost a priest, chose a soldier and a priest; and so on.[69] (In fact, Marichalar said in an interview that he wrote the book in place of keeping a diary while recovering from an illness.)[70] Others, such as Count Rodezno's biography of Carlos VII and César Silió's of Antonio Maura, were written with no ironic detachment, but by believers in the causes of their subjects. The results of the fruitful but incomplete cross-cultural work that *la nueva biografía* began—and that Marichalar's *Osuna* epitomized—must be traced through other, sometimes more diffuse literary transactions that would span the rest of the 1930s.

4. Virginia Woolf and the Spanish Civil War
Three Guineas, *Victoria Ocampo,* and International Feminism

> If, as you hope, Virginia, all [feminist] efforts might... converge to give birth to a new form of expression that still has not found a climate proper for its flourishing, may my efforts join with others by all women, unknown or famous, as they have worked throughout the world.
>
> —Victoria Ocampo, "Letter to Virginia Woolf" (1934)[1]
>
> I have never known anyone of my generation to have that feeling about a war [the Spanish Civil War].... My natural reaction is to fight intellectually: if I were any use, I should write against it: I should evolve some plan for fighting English tyranny.
>
> —Virginia Woolf, "Memoir of Julian Bell" (1937)[2]

In her response to the death of her beloved nephew Julian Bell in the Spanish Civil War, Virginia Woolf remained unable to understand his decision to join the Republican effort. Her "natural reaction," however, makes what might seem a puzzling logical leap: she plans to combat fascism in *Spain* with an intellectual assault on *English* tyranny. Woolf's radical and still-controversial *Three Guineas* (1938), an epistolary polemic against the fascist tendencies of her native culture, attempts to make this connection—and to link it to patriarchal repression around the world. In it, a set of unseen photographs of "dead bodies and ruined houses" from the Spanish war to which Woolf refers constantly becomes her representation in miniature of "the whole iniquity of dictatorship, whether in Oxford or Cambridge, in Whitehall or Downing Street, against Jews or against women, in England, or in Germany, in Italy or in Spain."[3] The Spanish photographs, together with the five photographs of English men in ceremonial garb that Woolf actually includes in *Three Guineas*, have played a significant role in prompting a renewed critical attention to Woolf's cosmopolitan alliance of the fight for women's rights in England with the battle against fascism, from the time of Creon through Napoleon, to the misogyny and tyrannies of her moment. As her text evolved over at least six years of research and revision, Woolf turned the arguments and realities that the Spanish photographs encapsulated for her into essential elements of her rejection of the English nation-state and her vision of a cosmopolitan feminism, which culminates in the often-cited outsider's claim that the "law of England denies us, and let us hope will continue to deny us, the full stigma of nationality.... As a woman, I have no country. As a woman I want no country. As a woman my country is the whole world" (*TG* 109).

This chapter takes a wide-ranging approach to analyzing the innovative visual-textual strategies that Woolf employs around the photographs and to recovering the sources of *Three Guineas*'s language and the dialogic development of Woolf's transnational arguments. The pictures, I argue, are first a broad, polyvalent index of the Hispanic conjunctures of her personal and political life, from some of her obscure early writings through her activism on behalf of Spanish refugees. At the same time, they represent causes brought together not only by Woolf, but also by her colleagues and readers in the "whole world" to which she connected herself—most notably, by her primary Hispanic interlocutor, translator, and publisher, Victoria Ocampo, the famous writer and editor of the journal *Sur* [*South*, 1931–1966] in Buenos Aires. The personal relationship between Woolf and Ocampo has been documented, and I do treat the means by which their feminist anti-fascisms drew on one another's works. But more important to this chapter, the English-Spanish affinities that Woolf posits were carried further, revised, and then marshaled for battles beyond both countries that were distant—yet, following Woolf's own logic, inextricably tied to her own. "By defending your causes, I defend my own, too," Ocampo claims in her public "Letter to Virginia Woolf," written just weeks after she had met Mussolini and Woolf in quick succession.[4]

This chapter moves back and forth across three continents in order to re-create these battles by gathering arguments, activist positions, periodical initiatives, and translations, all held together by the mutually influential relationships among four figures—Woolf, Ocampo, José Ortega y Gasset, and Waldo Frank—to one another and to the cultural history of Spain's ties to Europe and the New World. The numerous international implications of the outbreak of the Spanish Civil War in 1936 concentrated the collective work that these figures undertook. The war displaced the *Revista de Occidente*'s circulation of British modernism into the hands of Ocampo and threatened Ortega's Europeanist agenda; it endangered women's social gains under the Second Republic; it created acrimonious political divisions among British writers; it emboldened fascist regimes in Europe and their sympathizers in the New World; and, by Woolf's account, it exposed both the tyranny at the heart of English masculine society and the danger of foreign attacks on English liberal democracy. When the expanded histories of the composition, arguments, and dissemination of *Three Guineas* are seen in these lights, the ways in which "Spain" opens into Woolf's "whole world" comprise a vital movement in the history of interwar feminisms and modernisms.

Ocampo's work in particular demonstrates that the cosmopolitan feminist community that Woolf articulates in *Three Guineas* as necessary to fight tyrannies was being animated throughout the 1930s by a sympathetic foreign colleague and reader who, though a minor figure in Woolf's life, merits sustained attention alongside her English peer. She was a powerful female editor, not unlike her better-known Anglophone peers such as Margaret Anderson or Harriet Monroe, and her vision of global modernist production frames the feminist geography that this chapter delineates.[5] For both writers, the Republic comes to stand for women's rights globally, and in the fate of Spain—to which Ocampo felt tied by familial and cultural bonds, in addition to her feminism—lies the fate of England, of Europe, and of Argentina. Woolf captures for Ocampo the ruined status of women's bodies and their intellectual "hunger" created by the masculine public sphere that has violently excluded them. She intervenes in this sphere with the public epistle, which converges with *Three Guineas* not only formally, but also topically, as both attempt to carve out and revise a public sphere for women around the world in which they could assert themselves democratically as equals to men. Ocampo, in her groundbreaking collaborations with Woolf and meditations on her cultural legacy, also created both the material and the intellectual connections among Woolf's London-based cosmopolitanism, Ortega's Madrid-based Europeanism, and her own and Frank's shared New World Europeanism that were central to this movement. From the geographical, cultural, and gendered margins of Europe and the Americas, she offers a synthetic route into Anglo- and Euro-American modernisms as they were reformulated in the Spanish New World and highlights the necessary place of Latin America in Ortega's Spanish-Europeanism. In the process, she begins to historicize and to trouble concretized notions of "Latin America" in a manner that postcolonial scholars of the region have pursued much further. The interchanges within this vanguard network of thought and writing form a diverse and tightly interlocking literary history that crosses national, continental, and linguistic boundaries and that clarifies the causes to which Woolf and Ocampo attached their work and the ideals that undergirded them.

Woolf's "Innumerable, Indescribable, Unthinkable" Spain

Woolf's writing placed her at the forefront of some of the most salient and progressive sociopolitical thought of her day. But as Ocampo herself noted, Woolf's ideas of South America, which were derived from her notions of Spain and Hispanicity, did not change much between *The Voyage Out* (1915) and her meeting Ocampo in 1934.[6] How do we reconcile Woolf's abiding, unflattering, and exoticized Hispanisms with her sympathy for the Spanish Republic? Woolf's "Spain" of the early 1930s—before the civil war—was a combination of legends and personal impressions, simultaneously romanticized and revolting. Her three decades of habits of thought on Spain, its people, and its language, originated in her tourism, beginning with an Iberian journey with her younger brother Adrian Stephen in April 1905. Prior to the trip, she attempted to learn Spanish but quickly abandoned the project. Virginia (Stephen) nevertheless carried with her a "Spanish grammar," a Baedeker guide, and two of George Borrow's popular travel-histories, *The Bible in Spain* (1843) and *The Zincali, or Account of the Gipsies in Spain* (1841).[7] Borrow presented her a stereotypically Victorian updating of the Black Legend, much like what James Joyce saw in Richard Ford: Spain is a "land of wonder and mystery ... [where] amongst much that is lamentable and reprehensible, I have found much that is noble and to be admired; much stern heroic virtue; much savage and horrible crime." "Spain never changes," he asserts, and "atrocious projects of power" from its past linger in the present.[8] Woolf records in her diary, with similar language, her visions of the "romantic, heroic" shoreline, the "wilder and more interesting country[side]," the exotic "Moorish" character of Spanish architectural styles and of the Alhambra, and the "elephantine beauty" of the Seville Cathedral.[9]

The trip yielded her early short story "An Andalusian Inn" (1905), which she alternately called her "Spanish Sketch" and her "Spanish rubbish."[10] The story details a humorous gap in communication and translation as the English narrator and her party search for a hotel. Woolf mixes Borrow's language with her diaristic reflections when she notes the "noble virtue" among innkeepers in Spain and in England and points to the "Moorish castle[s]" and the "Spanish desert." Notably, the story includes some reflections on the Spanish language, which she had failed to master: "Scraps of vehement Spanish penetrated the canvas partition [in a cottage], and somehow seemed to be concerned with us. Spanish is a fierce and bloodthirsty language when heard under these conditions." The story ends when the traveling party is awakened by an "assault on the door" that turns out to be only a "peasant woman with a basin of goat's milk in her hands."[11] Upon her return to England, Virginia was also asked to write a review of two travelogues on Spain for the *TLS*; "you will be surprised to hear that I am an authority upon Spain," she wrote to Violet Dickinson, "but so it is."[12] In actuality, Woolf's "Spain" remained an amalgamation of her own impressions and recycled tropes from England's cultural imagination.

Woolf returned to Spain in 1912 as part of her honeymoon tour of the continent with Leonard, who learned some Spanish before the trip. In her letters from this journey, she begins to articulate her own sense of Spain's character. She writes to Duncan Grant that "Madrid is without exception the beastliest place I have ever seen." Leonard has an attack of malaria in the "blazing sun" there, yet Virginia asserts that "we have had a most splendid time however in every way, and happily there's still a good deal to come. Spain is far [*sic*] the most magnificent country I have ever seen." Furthermore,

> we are the only two people approximating to British blood in the whole of Spain. . . . It's on a much larger scale than Italy, and the colour[,] . . . you begin with sand colour, go on with—however, when I come to describe I can't even name the colours right. . . . The Cathedral [in Madrid] is the best thing we've seen.

Woolf also comments again on the Spanish women, who are "voluptuous. . . . The middle class women grow to an immense size . . . [and the] poor women are sometimes most lovely; they have such good shaped heads, and beautiful clothes." At times enchanted, at times repulsed by "beastl[y]" yet "magnificent" Spain, Woolf finds herself in awe of parts of Spain, but disgusted by the "droppings of Christian, Jew, Latin, and Saxon" in a toilet at their hotel.[13] She speaks of the Spanish women, this time in greater detail and variety, and continues with her imagery of heat, blood, and fevers. Woolf would recast some of these exotic and colorful Iberian landscapes as South American in *The Voyage Out*, which she was then composing. In it, Mr. and Mrs. Dalloway have traveled to Spain and "mounted mules, for they wished to understand how the peasants live. Are they ripe for rebellion, for example?," while Mrs. Ambrose echoes Woolf's diary when describing South America's "amazing colours of sea and earth. The earth, instead of being brown, was red, purple, green. . . . [T]here is no colour like it in England."[14]

With these impressions still in mind a decade later, Woolf wrote to Gerald Brenan that "my eyes are entirely grey with England—nothing but England for 10 years; and you can't imagine how much of a physical desire it becomes to feed them on colour and crags—something violent and broken and dry—not perpetually sloping and sloppy like the country here."[15] Spain provided this contrast when the Woolfs, who had not traveled abroad since their honeymoon, returned to Spain for the final time in early 1923 to visit Brenan, a Bloomsbury associate who had relocated after the Great War to a small village near Granada. Upon seeing "violent and broken and dry" Spain this time, along with all the "colour" and "congeniality of temper" on the continent, Virginia wrote to her sister Vanessa, "I am determined never to live long in England again" and called herself, in an expression of her developing cosmopolitanism, "a confirmed continentalist."[16] She also describes a more typological "religious festival at Madrid, [with] stuffed images of great beauty (emotional, not aesthetic) . . . parading; and Christ . . . showered under with confetti."[17]

The literary fruit of this trip was her essay "To Spain" (1923), in which Woolf compares post-war British and continental civilizations: "You, who cross the Channel yearly, probably no longer see the house at Dieppe [a French port on the English Channel], no longer feel, as the train moves slowly down the street, one civilisation fall, another rise—from the ruin and chaos of British stucco this incredible pink and blue phoenix four stories high. . . ." The essay, narrated from the perspective of an English passenger on a train on the continent, is as much about France as it is about Spain—and about the weary, routinized, and generally drab life of London. Woolf describes a woman on the train "so pale, so plump, so compact, . . . riding life over ditches and boundaries smoothed out by the genius of the Latin race," and contrasts her with an imagined average Englishwoman sitting next to a cow, "unmoved, incurious, monumental." Finally reaching Spain, she relates the same scene of "a child in Madrid throwing confetti effusively upon the figure of Christ." Spain, with its colorful, irrational religious passions, is "innumerable, indescribable, unthinkable" for Woolf: "It is hot; the old man; the frying-pan; it is hot; the image of the Virgin; the bottle of wine; it is time for lunch; it is only half-past twelve; it is hot." Her style attempts to mimic a repetitive, immobile culture in which "the mind's contents break into short sentences." "Listen," she writes,

> and as one listens this random life begins to be issued from the heart of a village which has faced the African coast with a timeless and aristocratic endurance for a thousand years. But how say this (as one descends from the blaze) to the Spanish peasant woman who bids one enter her room, with its

lilies and its washing, and smiles and looks out of the window as if she too had looked for a thousand years?

Woolf invokes around this "peasant woman" the familiar stereotypes of Spain's immutability and its associations with Africa. After describing fictionally the journey on mules that she and Leonard took in the Sierra Nevada mountains, she imagines toward the end of the essay a group of riders on the backs of "beasts" and ponders "how strangely it seems as if they were riding in England, a long day's journey, hundreds of years ago," transferring figuratively this "timeless" foreign civilization onto English soil.[18]

Woolf never returned to Spain, but she meditates, in a different register, on notions of Spain's putative wildness in *Flush* (1933), her mock-biography of the Brownings' spaniel. With tongue in cheek, she opens the text with an etymology of "Spaniel" and its derivation from "Spain":

> The origin of the name ["Spain"] itself is lost in obscurity. Many million years ago the country which is now called Spain seethed uneasily in the ferment of creation. . . . Some historians say that when the Carthaginians landed in Spain the common soldiers shouted with one accord "Span! Span!"— . . . *Span* in the Carthaginian tongue signifies Rabbit. . . .
>
> [But] the word Hispania, . . . [other] scholars say, has nothing whatever to do with the Carthaginian word *span*. Hispania derives from the Basque word *españa*, signifying an edge or boundary. . . . [And still other] antiquaries . . . maintain that just as a lover calls his mistress monster or monkey, so the Spaniards called their favourite dogs crooked or cragged (the word *españa* can be made to take these meanings).[19]

These notions of an uncivilized, primitive Spain, an "edge or boundary" of Europe with a "vehement" tongue, frozen and timeless, "violent" and "broken" and "crooked" yet colorful, mention nothing of contemporary politics. The country did not inspire the fear and dread in Woolf that her visits to fascist regimes in Italy and Germany would; it is static, a nation with no state, and it would mostly remain that way until its model leftist government was attacked by fascists.

Spain's Woolf

Meanwhile, in Spain in the early 1930s, Woolf's work was being interpreted and translated amid a national culture undergoing enormous transformations. In 1927, Woolf was dubbed "the English Proust" in an article in *La Gaceta Literaria*.[20] She received substantial treatment in a series of articles that Dora Russell (the second wife of the philosopher Bertrand Russell) published in *El Sol*. Russell writes that Woolf's "feminine literature" not only surpasses the "masculine literature" such as the novels of Hemingway and Lawrence that had been resurgent since the end of the Great War, but also does so in a manner that makes the categories of "masculine" and "feminine" literature seem inadequate and antiquated.[21] The critic Eugenio Montes also discussed "the art of killing time" in Woolf's work, and he traced her manipulation of time through a host of philosophical lineages and through the work of Proust and Kafka.[22] Montes also suggests that the future decline of Britain's empire is apparent in the style of Woolf's novel-writing. Not surprisingly, Antonio Marichalar was a primary voice in the dissemination in Spain of Woolf's poetics and works. As he had in Joyce, Marichalar found in Woolf an author with literary sensibilities that he could inscribe into Ortega's vanguard project at the *Revista*. In 1928 he related her work to Joyce's by noting the similarities between *Ulysses* and *Mrs. Dalloway*, for instance, and then grouped her with Lytton Strachey as renovators of the English biographical tradition begun by Leslie Stephen. Returning to her work in 1931, Marichalar admires her "endtime poetics," her "fine impressionist pointillism," and the "wholly feminine" quality of her work. Woolf, he writes, fashions a fictional world out of objects that disappear, evade conscious perception, and effervesce. Through the blurry windows and evanescent scenes that she paints with immaculate detail, Woolf links herself not only to Tolstoy, Marichalar asserts, but also to her Spanish contemporary Gabriel Miró.[23] Several years later, he calls her a feminine Proust and praises, with language reminiscent of the opening scene of his "James Joyce in His Labyrinth," her "Proustian monadism."[24]

Woolf's works, along with those of her Bloomsbury colleagues Strachey, David Garnett, and Aldous Huxley, provided an exemplary literary dimension to the *Revista de Occidente*'s revaluation of Spanish writing in the 1930s that was discussed in chapter 3. Laura María Lojo Rodríguez notes that Spanish writers looked extensively to Woolf's novels "in their attempt to give a new turn to the decaying Spanish novel" that Ortega described contemporaneously in *Notes on the Novel*.[25] The *Revista de Occidente* published the first translation of a part of Woolf's work into Castilian—"Time Passes," the middle section of *To the Lighthouse*—in March 1931.[26] Shortly thereafter, Marichalar juxtaposed Ortega and Woolf in his "Spanish Chronicle" for the *Criterion*. He claims, in his own Woolfian language, that in her work, "forms, colours, approach one another and recede in the atmosphere; they fly or fall upon us, dusting all around us with the rapid gleams and glimmers of a butterfly." He also furthers his earlier analogy: "Virginia Woolf is to Gabriel Miró as Seurat is to Velázquez."²⁷ Like Ortega, Marichalar views Bloomsbury mostly in aesthetic and cultural, not political, terms. When the Spanish Civil War interrupted this blossoming of Woolf criticism in Spain, that project moved to Argentina, where it was immensely amplified, diversified, and politicized by Victoria Ocampo in her work within a network of Anglo- and Hispanophone periodical exchanges.

Ocampo, Frank, and "Our America"

Ocampo, who discovered Woolf's work through the *Revista de Occidente* just before Sylvia Beach gave her a copy of *A Room of One's Own* (1929), came to her future colleague's work with cultural sensibilities that were irrevocably influenced by Ortega (who was one of her first publishers) and by the American writer Waldo Frank.²⁸ She initially modeled her writing on the French literature that she had appreciated because of her family's strong aristocratic European ties. French was her first language—Ocampo was actually more comfortable in English than in Spanish at the time—and her parents allowed her in her youth to quietly audit courses at the Sorbonne and Bergson's lectures at the Collège de France. Soon, her study on Dante, "De Francesca a Beatrice," translated from French to Spanish by Ricardo Baeza, appeared in the Revista de Occidente's press in 1924, accompanied by an epilogue from Ortega. In this first major publication, Ocampo intervened boldly in a masculine world of literary criticism and offered a democratic reading of *The Divine Comedy*, arguing that one need not have an elite education to grasp the work. Ortega also pushed Ocampo to compose in Spanish, which she began to do. Two years later, she found herself and her countryman Jorge Luis Borges published alongside their French and British modernist peers when her play *La laguna de los nenúfares* [*The Pool of the Water-Lilies*] appeared in the *Revista de Occidente*.

Ocampo had felt these supranational bonds since a young age. She wrote when she was 18, "I'd like to go to Europe. To get away from here. I have to get away. I have to. To anywhere. Or I'll die."²⁹ Instead, she was forced, as she would discuss with Woolf, into an unhappy marriage largely arranged by her parents, one that would effectively end (after Ocampo had several affairs) in estrangement and separation in 1920. As she became increasingly independent and outspoken through the 1920s, her cultural politics and her periodical work, as she often stated, brought her into a close, reciprocally formative relationship with Waldo Frank, who shared her burgeoning pan-Americanism and hybrid Europeanism. Though a minor figure in English- and Spanish-language criticism today, Frank was a prominent interwar writer with eclectic interests and transnational ideals that found their first expression in the short-lived journal of Greenwich Village radicalism, *Seven Arts* (1916–1917). Here, Frank collaborated with Van Wyck Brooks, Randolph Bourne, James Oppenheim, and others of the Lyrical Left to found an "organ" for native artists that would disseminate to American and European readers alike the newest and best "expression[s] of our American life" in the country's "renascent period."[30] Asserting the arguments in Bourne's pioneering piece of cultural criticism "Trans-National America" (1916), Frank and his colleagues argued that while Europe had fallen into internecine warfare, the United States finally might forge the "cultural wreckage" of a "transplanted Europe" into the model of a "cosmopolitan federation of national colonies, of foreign cultures, ... the world-federation in miniature," as Bourne put it.[31] "America," Bourne argues, "is coming to be, not a nationality but a transnationality" whose pluralism could "save this Western world of ours from suicide." But the premature collapse of *Seven Arts* in 1917 and the premature death of Bourne in 1918 left no certain answer to Bourne's question, "What shall we do with our America?"

The nativist tendencies of *Seven Arts* always had been paired with Frank's desire to circulate its innovative and regenerative American "spirit" in Europe by enacting the Euro-American "dual citizenship" that Bourne had discussed.[32] Indeed, the centerpiece of the first number (and the only article advertised on its cover) was the Frenchman Romain Rolland's "America and the Arts." Frank continued this element of the group's work with his widely successful study *Our America* (1919), which he called a "book for France about my country" that was also written "*for* my country ... *to* my country." That is, his dual gaze looked always at his native country and at perceptions of it abroad, just as *Seven Arts* had. In France, he saw such journals as the *NRF* and its publishing house as a "flexible, rather sharply integrated organism since it includes creators so varied in mood and outlook [as Gide, Claudel, Copeau, and others]. . . . [It] is an organism that justly stands for a great portion of Young France."[33] (He later reflected on *Seven Arts* as an "embryo[nic]" and "growing organism" whose development remained incomplete.[34]) In language to which Ocampo returns when she launches *Sur*, Frank, who became a correspondent for the *NRF*, hopes to give "Young America . . . [a] voice in Paris" by inviting his French colleagues to join him in "discovering America together"—to embark as "spiritual pioneers" who will lead an overly mechanized America out of its present "inchoate state." Our "task," he declares optimistically, is to "begin to generate within ourselves the energy [to create]. . . . And in a dying world, creation is revolution."[35]

Constantly reformulating his cultural histories of the New World, Frank pursued America's Hispanic roots and decided that Spain provided the basis for synthesizing the European history, imperialism, and modern pan-Americanism that formed the basis for "our America." After reading Ortega's works, he wrote to the philosopher, calling him "a great Critic, perhaps the greatest literary critic" of the moment, above the "arid stretches of contemporary critic[s]" in England and France, and telling him of Frank's maternal ancestors' Sephardic roots in Spain. Frank argued that, contrary to popular imagery, "great things have happened in your land [Spain] since 1898 . . . since the war that gave birth to a new spirit in Spain, and to Imperialism in the United States"—two movements whose historical and current dynamics he wanted to capture.[36] In the early 1920s, he traveled twice to Spain, where he was praised by the writer Luis Araquistáin for combating Spenglerian thought, and where he became engaged in public debates through the Spanish press with some of the country's preeminent literary figures. He sparred first with Ramón Pérez de Ayala on the inaccuracies of H. G. Wells's *The Future of America* (1906), then took Ramiro de Maeztu to task for his reductive and anti-Semitic readings of American culture.[37] Through these arguments, Frank not only promulgated in Spain the cultural agendas of his generation of American writers, but also came into contact with such renowned Spaniards as Azorín, Pío Baroja, Juan Ramón Jiménez, Federico García Lorca, and, most consequentially for him, Ortega. Frank made a literary impression in Ortega's circle similar to the one he had made in Paris, where he had met with Joyce; both his novel *Rahab* (1922) and his collection of stories *City Block* (1922) were greeted by a number of Europeans as paragons of new American writing. Marichalar's "James Joyce in His Labyrinth" in fact relates the stylistics of *Ulysses* to those of Proust, Dostoevsky, and—in the same breath—Frank (see appendix, page 214). Ortega began publishing translations of Frank's work, both in the *Revista de Occidente* and in its press in 1925. Frank's next major project, the successful historical-cultural study *Virgin Spain* (1926), was serialized in both English and Spanish in the *Revista*, the *Dial*, and several other periodicals on either side of the Atlantic. It was compared favorably to Ortega's own work, and Miguel de Unamuno himself translated its conclusion for an Argentine paper.

In *Virgin Spain*, Frank expands his growing pan-Americanism *through* his understanding of Spain, taking the advice of his colleague Alfonso Reyes: "do not forget that Spain is the path to our America."[38] Frank dedicates the book to "those brother Americans /whose tongues are Spanish and Portuguese /whose homes are between the Rio Grande /and Tierra del Fuego /but whose America /like mine / stretches from the Arctic to the Horn." Embracing the Black Legend when reading

Spain as at once "more African in nature than European; more aboriginally close to Semite than to German," Frank posits a theory of New World hybridity rooted in the Iberian Peninsula's history.[39] *Virgin Spain* dissects the European "Organism" from the medieval era to the present as it has been torn apart and reanimated, leading finally to the origins of what Frank soon calls "America Hispana," where "Berber Phoenician, Arabic, Jewish, Moorish elements... [mixed] with Germanic and... Celtic strains... created in Spain... and in Portugal too."[40] Frank's European pan-Americanism, which culminates in an imaginary dialogue between Cervantes and Christopher Columbus, extends both Bourne's and Ortega's thought through the New World, converting Spain from the symbol of European decline to the cauldron for the regeneration of both Europe and "America Hispana" in its new arts.

Sur, the Intersection of Europe and the Americas

Frank's manner of straddling the Old and New Worlds eventually led him to Ocampo, with whom he shared an investment in Anglo-American-Spanish ideals of interwar Europe's regeneration. In his next study, *The Re-discovery of America* (1929), serialized simultaneously in the *New Republic* and the *Revista de Occidente*, Frank envisions the Americas as the lively "organism" that will rejuvenate the "decomposi[ng]" body of Europe.[41] As he gained a level of fame in Latin America rare for an author from the United States, Frank saw his Hispanophilic notion of "Our America" read by the Mexican poet José Juan Tablada as a signal of a new pro-Mexican and anti-imperialist attitude among writers to the north. ("Our America" was a translation of the phrase "Nuestra América," coined by Cuban revolutionary writer José Martí in 1891.) Frank's Argentine admirers soon arranged for him to make a lecture tour of Latin America in 1929. He spoke to hundreds of intellectuals and thousands of students in Mexico and Argentina, giving a "First Message to America Hispana" that circulated in the *Revista de Occidente* and a number of Latin American magazines. In his collected lectures and writings from the tour, which came at a time when both academic Latin American studies and economic interests in South America were forming in the United States, Frank outlines his America Hispana as two "American Half-Worlds," a masculine Anglo North and a feminine Hispanic South, united at the Panama Canal and, recalling Ortega, "vertebrated" into an "active, universal Body," an "organic whole" tied vitally to Europe. For Frank, this feminine South was embodied in Buenos Aires by Ocampo, whom he met during his lecture tour. Frank recalled that at the author's family estate, Villa Ocampo, one wall of the library contained a symbolic "painted map... [of] the Americas and Europe [with] a sun-blue sea between them," while *objets d'art* from all corners of the world filled the house. He emphasizes that "all these details have been transfigured and composed by an Argentinean—an American will."[42]

At the same time, Ocampo was accruing prestige through her writing and the new contacts she made during her regular trips to Europe and New York, where she met Valéry, Cocteau, Shaw, Wells, Ramón Gómez de la Serna, Jacques Lacan, and Sergei Eisenstein. As she was contemplating the relationship between the cultures of Europe and the Americas, Ocampo read a fresh American perspective on the Old World in the work of Frank. She planned a review, published with her own funds, that would correlate Argentina's national culture with those represented by the *Revista de Occidente* and the *NRF*. For his part, Frank believed that Ocampo could "prophesy" a new Argentina, and he hoped that her journal would be printed in both Spanish and English—perhaps titled *Nuestra América*. Instead, in 1931, Ocampo founded the Spanish-language *Sur* [*South*], the name suggested by Ortega, and the periodical became central to South American literary production and the primary bridge among the cultures of the Americas and the project of the New Spain. It spoke to a cultural elite at a moment when little magazines of vanguard arts, such as *Proa*, *Prisma*, and *Martín Fierro*, were thriving in Argentina. *Sur* distinguished itself as a luxurious and expensive periodical of some two hundred pages, noted for its colored image of an arrow pointing south on its cover (also a directional twist on Ortega's review). One of its main purposes, Berete E. Strong writes, was to "present... Argentina to its own people through the filter of the European gaze" with the Orteguian hope of "sav[ing] the West from Spenglerian decline... [with a] humanistic light."[43] For this task, Ocampo assembled an impressive international board for the journal: Frank, Ortega, Reyes, Pierre Drieu La Rochelle, and Jules Supervielle, among others. (Reyes, one of the most prominent voices against Spengler's influence in Latin America, wrote to her upon seeing the first issue that "*Sur* is going to be like our own country. And you will see what an active citizen I shall be."[44]) Guillermo de Torre, María Rosa Oliver, Eduardo Mallea, and Borges would join several others as local editors; both groups would contribute frequently to the journal, as would Ocampo's sister Silvina Ocampo and Silvina's husband, Adolfo Bioy Casares.

Ortega immediately used this opportunity to extend further his vanguard and his own influence in Latin America, where his aesthetic philosophies were alternately inspiring new arts, or being rejected loudly by "rehumanizing" aesthetics, among leading vanguardists.[45] (Buenos Aires, after all, already had a greater population and per capita income than Madrid.) John King notes that he idealized Ocampo as "the Mona Lisa of the Pampas" and "the fusion of the body of America and the spirit of Europe" who might help revitalize both civilizations.[46] Ortega wrote to her in 1928 that "the whole world" was now convinced of "two propositions: Europe is in decline [*decadencia*]—America is peaking"; but these propositions told an incomplete story, he added, since both civilizations needed one another in order to flourish.[47] In his *Revolt of the Masses* (1930), Ortega asks,

> Is it as certain as people say that Europe is in decadence; that it is resigning its command; abdicating? May not this apparent decadence be a beneficial crisis which will enable Europe to be really, literally Europe. The evident decadence of the *nations* of Europe, was not this *a priori* necessary if there was to be one day a possible United States of Europe, the plurality of Europe substituted by its formal unity?

A disintegrated Europe, Ortega suggests, is in danger of being upstaged globally by the rising powers to its east and west, Russia and the United States. But Americans, he claim, are a "primitive people" masked by a hyper-technicized society who do not have the cultural and historical foundation to inherit Europe's global supremacy (*RM* 139). Ortega envisioned, in any case, a cooperative relationship between the Old and New Worlds, though Europe was to retain the upper hand. Ocampo was sympathetic but not convinced; the mysticist and Orientalist critiques of Europe that Keyserling and Gurdjieff had offered still had some appeal to her.

Like the cultural work that Ortega's *Revista de Occidente* performed for Spain in the 1920s, *Sur* brought from this nexus of thought the works of a diverse range of writers and critics—including Ramón, Joyce, Keyserling, Jarnés, Malraux, Rabindranath Tagore, Martin Heidegger, Jean-Paul Sartre, André Breton, Walter Gropius, Thomas Mann, Aldous Huxley, D. H. Lawrence, and Woolf, and many others—to Argentina in the 1930s. Ocampo's friendships with Ortega and with French editors ensured European circulation for *Sur*. And as Ortega and Eliot had, Ocampo encountered local resistance; the review, as King shows, was "condemned as *extranjerizante*," or "foreignizing."[48] *Sur* had arrived in the wake of General José Félix Uriburu's military coup in Buenos Aires in 1930, in which intellectuals were persecuted and those with cosmopolitan tastes were viewed with great suspicion. These conditions were not unlike the Spanish 1920s, and they would not end soon. Ocampo thus felt fully at home in neither the New World nor the Old—a "soul without a passport," as she put it.[49]

Ocampo resolves in her review's opening manifesto of sorts, "Letter to Waldo Frank," that she will not "turn her back on Europe." Rather, she will cultivate a "vital" sentiment in "our continent" by re-reading "all America" from an integrated pan-European, pan-Hispanic, and pan-American perspective, one that remains constantly critical of Europe's past in the Americas.[50] Ocampo writes that *Sur* was born of her anguish—a bodily illness that overcame her because of the realization that her native Argentina was culturally remote from both Europe and North America. With language that recalls Frank's studies, she embarks on her "search for America," for its "hidden treasure," accompanied by Frank from New York and with the help of Ortega from Madrid. She and Frank are "in love with America," she writes, "your America and mine—let us write it more simply as 'our America,'" one that must be revealed not only to its inhabitants but also to their European colleagues.[51] Frank's physiographic account of Brazil, "La Selva," headlines this first issue, along with an address to South Americans by Drieu La Rochelle. The second number follows with a piece on South America by Keyserling; more important, it includes a bilingual edition of Borges's translations of several Langston Hughes poems. In the first of these, "I, Too," the opening and closing lines—"I, too, sing America" and "I, too, am America"—gain a new pan-American resonance in this journalistic adaptation. *Sur* would develop Ocampo's synthesis of Frank's and Ortega's influences with her own feminist, psychoanalytic, and liberal-humanist ideals in the 1930s. It was published without major interruptions until the late 1960s, even when Ocampo had to sell properties to sustain it during Juan Perón's rule, and boasted a greater circulation in the 1930s than the *Revista de Occidente* would see. The review's press published books that Ocampo desired to see in Argentina, even when she thought she would lose money on them, thus bringing the works of Lorca, Huxley, Jung, Lawrence, Sartre, Camus, Orwell, and Graham Greene, all of them unproven in local markets, to South American readers for the first time.

"Living History": Woolf, Ocampo, Misogyny, and Fascism

With these foundations and contacts in place, Ocampo increasingly concentrated on international feminism in the 1930s, seeing it as the bridge across the various cultures that she wanted to meld. She came to view Woolf as an ideal woman writer and public intellectual who had achieved fame beyond her own country and language. Ocampo sought a meeting with Woolf during a trip to England in 1934 in which she stayed with Aldous Huxley and his wife. Woolf records in her diary her impressions of their first encounter, at a show of Man Ray's photographs:

So we go, & find Aldous, . . . & a South American [R]asta—was that what Roger [Fry] called these opulent millionaires from Buenos Aires? Anyhow she was very ripe & rich; with pearls at her ears, as if a large moth had laid clusters of eggs; the colour of an apricot under glass; eyes I think brightened by some cosmetic; but there we stood & talked, in French, & English, about the Estancia, the great white rooms, the cactuses, the gardenias, the wealth & opulence of South America; so to Rome & Mussolini, whom she's just seen. He was simple & kind—on purpose. She sat & forgot to call him Excellency. . . . [They also] spoke of women: how no great man—Bismarck, Napoleon, Caesar, needed them: how Beatrice was only Florence. And how we all make mistakes: hers had been that she made an unhappy marriage. "But now go & have a child" he told her.[52]

Woolf refers to the fact that while in Italy on an invited lecture tour just two months earlier, Ocampo, who had impressed many locals with her bold ideas and fluent Italian, was invited to meet Mussolini in Rome. She was not a fascist sympathizer—in fact, she had initially declined to lecture in Italy in the first place; her justification for accepting Il Duce's offer was simply, "I like living history." Ocampo wrote in her memoir of the meeting, "Living History" (1935) that she

> asked Il Duce several questions about women, about their roles in the fascist state and about his opinion of their abilities. His responses were launched at me as if by a catapult. . . . He left . . . no place for misunderstanding, no doubts: . . . Fascist Italy . . . thinks that the first duty of women is to bear children for the State. . . . They should not collaborate with men in any other manner. . . . "Do you think that Julius Caesar, Napoleon, Bismarck needed any of this sort of collaboration?" he asked.[53]

Ocampo explains that Mussolini elaborated that women cannot participate in politics because they do not understand it, nor do they understand philosophy, music, or architecture; they should only leave their husbands' homes to work as nurses or governesses. Upon hearing Ocampo's account, Woolf simply commented, "the brute."[54] Woolf had made one of her recent attacks on Il Duce in *A Room of One's Own* for his insisting, with Napoleon, "so emphatically upon the inferiority of women," and for abolishing women's suffrage.[55] Ocampo and Woolf thus enjoyed belittling Il Duce's apparently fragile ego together.

"Fascist Italy appears to a foreign traveler to be a country for men, a country in which the accent falls on unmitigated masculinity," Ocampo writes, a country in which the leaders appear to take their signals from grammar, in which "'State'

[*Estado*] belongs to the masculine gender."⁵⁶ The men—and she singles out F. T. Marinetti—celebrate heroism through war, and they expect women to produce a boundless supply of soldiers for them. The associations among masculinist warmaking, fascist states, misogynistic cultures, and women's "duties" that Woolf explores centrally in *Three Guineas* are articulated in a similar critique by Ocampo. This moment also foreshadows the reference in Woolf's text to Lysistrata's archetypal refusal to produce children for war (*TG* 147n10). Ocampo's firsthand report of a fascist leader's "categorical way of limiting women by the north and the south, by the east and the west of their humanity," excluding them from the public sphere, no doubt colored and solidified Woolf's image of Mussolini, even if Ocampo herself felt somewhat persuaded by his charm at one point in their conversation.⁵⁷

In Madrid, days after meeting Woolf, Ocampo wrote her appreciative "Letter to Virginia Woolf," then published it in the *Revista de Occidente*. Her cross-cultural declaration of loyalty to Woolf's British feminism parallels her hemispheric declaration of affiliation with Waldo Frank in the public epistle that opened *Sur*. It also contributes the missing perspective of international feminism to the *Revista*'s reception of Woolf's work. Ocampo's formal corollary to *Three Guineas* speaks indirectly to Ortega, who had told Ocampo that women write letters because they are addressed to only one person: they are private, while men speak publicly. Ocampo replied that the "epistolary genre . . . is then only nominally private," in reality no less private than works such as the "poems of Anna de Noailles or the novels of Virginia Woolf."⁵⁸ In her letter to Woolf, which is also an essay and memoir, Ocampo initiates her literary dialogue with her British peer in the feminine sphere of the drawing room of Woolf's Tavistock Square home, its walls full of "panels painted by a woman" (Vanessa Bell), where women converse about women. She pictures herself in the third person speaking to Woolf; Woolf is "curious," Ocampo is "enchanted." Each of them holds inside something "exotic" and racially different that the other desires: "two women, born in very different circumstances and climates, one English, the other Latin and American, one within a formidable tradition, the other in a vacuum." Switching to a direct address of "Virginia," Ocampo insists that she will leave the encounter the richer, for she finds herself both "authentically American" and yet more fulfilled in Europe. She finds herself, in a metaphor that she will employ frequently, less "hungry" in Europe.⁵⁹

Ocampo quotes and then revises Woolf's line from *A Room* that "[l]ike most uneducated Englishwomen, I like reading": "I would like to confess publicly, Virginia, . . . that like most uneducated South American women, I like writing." Here, she makes her most ambitious move in the letter by inscribing herself into the lineage of British female writers that Woolf champions—Jane Austen, the

Brontës, and later George Eliot and Elizabeth Barrett Browning. For centuries, male writers have either ignored or failed to capture feminine psychology, thus Ocampo's "only ambition is to find my way to writing one day ... *as a woman*" who can "translate her thought, her feelings, her vision" successfully into prose. Presently she feels like she's writing with a "false national pride," like the ostentatious patriotism of a recent immigrant, declaring herself a feminine writer all the time, unable simply to let that quality manifest itself in her prose. But she will now work with Woolf within a new global tradition with "all women"—she will "finally begin to write and to live; similarly, but worse than you, Virginia."[60]

Ocampo was deeply invested in these worldwide efforts; she wrote to Woolf soon after their meeting that "what frightens me in Europe (France, Spain, Italy) is a kind of failing appetite in people. Where I'm from, there is the appetite ... but nourishment is still lacking. And so we come here, famished."[61] In Woolf's work, Ocampo saw a spirit that could inculcate women's intellectual freedom further in Argentina: the spirit that the defense of one woman's cause is the defense of all women's causes. This includes the cause of Shakespeare's sister, as Woolf imagined her; Ocampo believes she lives in all contemporary women writers and someday herself "will be reborn and will write." Ocampo sees her own and her colleague's advocacy work as apiece with one another, across borders, in a manner that prefigures the logic of *Three Guineas*. Throughout the letter, too, Ocampo writes for the word "us" the Spanish "nosot*ras*" rather than the generic (but implicitly masculine) "nosot*ros*" to emphasize the gendered dimension of their encounter and this shared language. She hopes to create between herself and Woolf, and among all women writers, a "bridge of words."[62] Her "Letter to Virginia Woolf" in fact initiated her "series of testimonies of my hunger"; it opens the first volume of *Testimonios*, her ten-part collection of personal reflections, public letters, and literary and cultural criticism that spans over four decades.[63]

Woolf found in Ocampo a new interlocutor as she was gathering material for *Three Guineas*, and the two outsiders continued their conversations at Woolf's home. Ocampo was initially starstruck by Woolf; she sent orchids to her in gratitude and in hopes of continuing their friendship. In their interactions, Woolf reworked her imaginings of Spain and Hispanic peoples as she conjured Argentina as a wild, exotic, utterly foreign and butterfly-filled landscape of women like Ocampo with mercurial "Latin blood."[64] She imagined Ocampo "among the butterflies," in "a million acres of pampas grass," or "playing tennis on board ship with a dark gentleman something like the King of Spain."[65] She referred to Ocampo as "the Sybil (Colefax) of Argentina," and she declared later to Vita Sackville-West that "I am in love with Victoria Okampo [*sic*]."[66] As a failed student of Spanish,

Woolf confessed to Ocampo, "How interested I am in your language, which has a gaping mouth but no words—a very different thing from English."⁶⁷ Ocampo's overtures continued through the mid-1930s, punctuated by a case of butterflies she sent Woolf from South America. Woolf often received Ocampo's lavish gifts reluctantly, but wrote that she thinks of Ocampo often: "every time I go out of my door" over which the case of butterflies hangs, "I make up another picture of South America."⁶⁸

The butterflies, however, reminded Woolf of "the difference between two worlds" (hers and Ocampo's), a difference that Ocampo's stereotypical gifts did not help to bridge.⁶⁹ This "difference" is evident in Woolf's repeated Hispanisms, however informal these epistolary references might have been. Woolf was writing from a center of imperial power, albeit one whose power she disowned. The gap between her imaginings and Ocampo's reading of the liberatory power of Woolf's writing produces a quandary similar to that of the famous "very fine negress" passage in *A Room of One's Own*. In a dialectical tension common to the modernists' European and global visions, that passage has been read by postcolonial writers and critics as patronizing and racist, yet also as promising and emancipatory. Ocampo tolerated Woolf's remarks as simple curiosities; revising Woolf's Eurocentrism, she transmitted her colleague's cultural politics beyond the confines of her own class, nation, and *criollismo*. In letters and in infrequent reunions, Ocampo became a partner (though unequal) in intellectual dialogue, seeing, with Woolf, the threats to women's rights and women's writing that fascism posed. Woolf read some of Ocampo's work from the first volume of her *Testimonios* (probably "Aldous Huxley in Central America") and told her that "I'm so glad you write criticisms not fiction[.] . . . I still have a dream of your America. I hope you will write a whole book of criticism and send me, if you will find the time, now and then a letter."⁷⁰ Though she was personally uncomfortable with "autobiography in public," she also encouraged Ocampo to write about herself, as she would for the rest of her life.⁷¹ Ocampo invited her to address Argentina's PEN Club in 1935; Woolf was tempted but declined, "tied to England" by Hogarth Press and "by politics."⁷² In response to Ocampo's proposal to have *A Room of One's Own* translated into Spanish, Woolf was "honoured and delighted. I want to write a sequel to it," she confided, looking forward to *Three Guineas*, "denouncing Fascism."⁷³ Woolf wrote to Ocampo soon after, "I hope you are making new friends and finding new things to make hum and buzz in South America. Here we live under the shadow of disaster. I've never known such a time of foreboding."⁷⁴

Ocampo's exchanges with Woolf having directed her rebellious spirit fully toward global feminism, she brought a bold political agenda to Argentina. There, she could not celebrate, as Woolf does in *Three Guineas*, the "door of the private house" having been "thrown open" for women to enter professions, as it had in England in 1919 (*TG* 16). The movement for women's rights in Argentina had suffered a setback in 1935, when conservatives aimed to retract some of the rights that women had gained in 1926. Thus, in 1936 Ocampo co-founded with María Rosa Oliver and Susana Larguía the Unión Argentina de Mujeres [Argentine Women's Union], for which she served as president from 1936–1938. The Argentine Women's Union focused on better working conditions, civil rights, and reviving the bill for women's suffrage that had been proposed but defeated several times in the 1920s.[75] Ocampo pinpointed a strong correlation between the Union's goals and those in Woolf's work, especially in their attribution of war-making to capitalist patriarchal systems and in seeing women, as Ocampo put it, like "men's colony to exploit."[76] Ocampo writes in "La mujer, sus derechos y sus responsibilidades" ["Woman, Her Rights and Her Responsibilities," 1936] that nevertheless, "the most important . . . revolution of all . . . is taking place today around the world—that of women." She continues by noting that this revolution, which she traces across a number of countries, will "finally stop men from invading the territory of women," and it is being carried out without violence or brutality. It is liberating women not to declare war against men, but finally to become citizens equal to men, united with them in their social roles and work: "the emancipation of women, as I conceive it, attacks the same roots of the ills that afflict all women [*humanidad femenina*] and, in turn, all men [*humanidad masculina*]. One is inseparable from the other."[77] Throughout Argentina's Infamous Decade, a period of grinding poverty and depression, social unrest, and power struggles among corrupt bodies, Ocampo and her review offered a contested medium for internationalist thought and literature that tied the work of Frank, Ortega, and sympathetic liberal figures into an antifascist, universalist appeal for women's rights.

The Republic at War, British Literary Politics, and the Contexts of Woolf's Activism

In the 1930s, Woolf's activism and political sympathies, meanwhile, increasingly came to focus on Spain. For Woolf and many of her colleagues, the rise of the Spanish Second Republic was a model liberal-democratic and non-military antidote to the spread of fascism. The Republic was idealized by leftists and intellectuals around the world for displacing both a monarchy and a proto-fascist dictatorship. The members of Bloomsbury, who were well-known continentalists, and their colleagues among the British left were frustrated by their own government's impotence against continental fascism. Those who looked to Spain believed that the Republican workers' nation-state was also a paradigm for instituting pacifist progressive reforms across the continent. W. H. Auden captured such dreams in a dispatch from Spain during the war: "a revolution is really taking place [in Spain], not an odd shuffle or two in cabinet appointments. In the last six months these people have been learning what it is to inherit their own country, and once a man has tasted freedom he will not lightly give it up."[78] Furthermore, the Republic gave women the rights to vote and to hold office, to divorce, and to keep custody of their children, and it supported them in higher education. All of this was well-known to Ocampo, who spent time there and was impressed by the new status afforded to women.

From afar, the Republic's political freedoms also manifested many of the principles of Leonard and Virginia Woolf's long-standing anti-imperialist leftism. Their Hogarth Press published numerous tracts and Day-to-Day Pamphlet series on pacifism, the League, socialism, communism, fascism, and colonialism, with regular commentaries on Spain. In particular, two publications appeared in illustrative juxtaposition in 1933: the Hispanist H. R. G. Greaves's explication and analysis of the new *Spanish Constitution* and Jane Soames's translation of Mussolini's anti-socialist, anti-pacifist polemic *The Political and Social Doctrine of Fascism*. Greaves's narrative, which commends the work of Spaniards such as Ortega, Salvador de Madariaga, and Francisco Giner de los Ríos, includes the bold claim that "to the Spanish liberal the events of 1931 represent the final achievement in a long battle for freedom; to the socialist they are but a beginning." It also praises the constitution's "dynamic and evolutionary rather than a static and ultimate view of rights."[79] Leonard and Virginia Woolf also worked with a number of activist and intellectual groups, the Labour Party, and the League of Nations in publicizing the Republic's causes through political education programs in England.[80] For his part, Leonard edited a set of essays called *The Intelligent Man's Way to Prevent War* (1933), and traced in *Quack, Quack!* (1935) the "primitive" elements of Europe's descent toward barbarism. He accentuates his case in the latter text, however, with a crudely racist device: he juxtaposes photographs of an effigy of the Hawaiian war god Kukailimoku with pictures of Mussolini and Hitler. Leonard wrote in *Barbarians Within and Without* (1939) of his repulsion at the "atrocities" in Spain, the danger of German and Italian involvement there, and the British government's indefensibly having "connived at the destruction of the Republican Government in Spain."[81] Elements of all of these texts will appear in *Three Guineas*, though Woolf's peers in Bloomsbury will respond unevenly to her radical feminist case.

Affirmation of Woolf's sense of a "time of foreboding" that she mentioned to Ocampo came when the Spanish Civil War erupted in July 1936. Leonard and Virginia Woolf were among the first prominent intellectuals to defend the Second Republic in the press. Shortly after the war began, the Woolfs, E. M. Forster, G. E. Moore, H. G. Wells, Julian Huxley, J. B. S. Haldane, and over 20 other intellectuals signed a letter to the *Times* called "The Vortex in Spain." The letter lauds England's historical defense of constitutional governments in Europe against centuries of invasions by anti-democratic forces and regimes in Spain, France, and elsewhere. Now, they claim, a sovereign Spain is under attack by a "junta of generals" and "Moorish troops" under the banner of fascism. The letter emphasizes that the Second Republic is a "liberal democracy" with no communist or "Bolshevik" commitments, and it calls for the British government to express solidarity with the defenders of the Republic. Revising some Hispanisms, it recalls the Moorish invasions of Europe through Spain hundreds of years ago, and the letter's defense of "British freedoms" is juxtaposed with its language of an "invasion of Spain by an African army." Framing the battle as one of European civilization against Africanized barbarism, this letter still maintains the persistent associations of Spain with a denigrated Africanism surface, even in sympathetic discourses—yet now, applied only to one side of the combatants in a civil war (the rebels), not all Spaniards. Though the letter hints that Hitler's and Mussolini's fascist expansionism could soon reach England, the actual consequences of the mostly pacifist signatories' call for "sympathetic benevolence" with the Republic remain uncertain; they stop short of any explicit call for armed intervention.[82]

The embattled Republic's cause nevertheless quickly became the "first and last crusade of the British left-wing intellectual."[83] Gerald Brenan, who fled to England when the war began, came to the conclusion in his landmark study *The Spanish Labyrinth* (1943) that "no one who cares for European culture can close his eyes" to the significance of the war.[84] But the war polarized the British literary community at large: while nearly all of the younger writers were united in supporting the Republic, those high modernists still living were far from unanimous, especially in the strong anti-communist climate of the culture at large. Joyce had almost nothing to say about the conflict, for instance, while Eliot was lambasted for his silence at the *Criterion* (his French colleagues Henri Massis and Charles Maurras, however, both spoke publicly in favor of Franco). Pound, from Italy, offered only a few oblique comments. Wyndham Lewis, on the other hand, was stridently anti-Republican and mocked the government's British sympathizers in several works, most famously *Revenge for Love* (1937). Many other opinions are recorded in *Authors Take Sides on the Spanish War* (1937), a pamphlet of responses to a questionnaire solicited by Nancy Cunard for the *Left Review*. The pamphlet reveals not only generational divisions, but also the pressures to make public pronouncements that Woolf addresses in her works of the moment. Of the 148 writers featured, nearly all (127) support the Spanish Republic, as did Cunard and her fellow editors.[85]

Despite her disgust with her pro-fascist peers, Woolf abstained from comment in the pamphlet, as did E. M. Forster and Bertrand Russell; their pacifist commitments outweighed taking sides in a war, as the ambivalence in "The Vortex in Spain" indicated. Evincing divisions that permeated Bloomsbury, however, Leonard Woolf, Aldous Huxley, and David Garnett all register their support for the Republic in Cunard's survey, while Vita Sackville-West is "Neutral" (and angry at the bias of the survey). Virginia, meanwhile, noted her frustrations and her plans in her diary: "So we shant let arms through: we shall sit on the fence: & the fighting will go on—But I am not a politician: obviously. Can only rethink politics very slowly into my own tongue."[86] She wrote to Margaret Llewellyn Davies that she "felt it great impertinence to come out with my views on such a subject [in *Three Guineas*]; . . . to sit silent and acquiesce in all this idiotic letter signing and vocal pacifism when there's such an obvious horror in our midst—such tyranny, such Pecksniffism—finally made my blood boil into the usual ink-spray."[87] Her frustration with the pressure to "sign a manifesto [and] pledg[e] 'to protect culture and intellectual liberty'" that Woolf voices in *Three Guineas*—and which she voiced in her essay "Why Art To-day Follows Politics," her only published work of 1936—fed the creative anger of her treatise throughout its composition (*TG* 85).

Woolf's political "rethink[ing]" was a combination of writing and activism that manifests what Christine Froula calls "Bloomsbury's vanguard spirit," which "affirms the principle that to fight one form of tyranny is to fight them all."[88] Seeing the survival of Spain as essential to the survival of England, Woolf, who was already involved with a variety of feminist causes, began participating more visibly in relief efforts and anti-fascist intellectual groups that advocated for the Republic and its refugees.[89] She recalled in her diary having seen "a long trail of fugitives—like a caravan in a desert—c[ome] through [Tavistock] square: Spaniards flying from Bilbao, which has fallen, I suppose. Somehow brought tears to my eyes, tho' no one seemed surprised." Thus, she saw the refugees, "impelled by machine-guns in Spanish fields to trudge through Tavisock Square," bringing the Spanish war's effects to her own doorstep; she attended a relief rally for Basque refugee children and mourned the fate of refugees from Barcelona, too.[90] She then sat on the platform at a relief program entitled "Spain and Culture" at the Albert Hall on 24 June 1937, and was one of 170 signatories on a telegram to Prime

Minister Neville Chamberlain that read "PROFOUNDLY DEPLORE RAPPROCHEMENT MUSSOLINI BEFORE HIS TROOPS LEAVE SPAIN."[91] Woolf was among the sponsors of a showing of Pablo Picasso's *Guernica* at the Burlington Gallery in 1938, and in February 1939 she worked with the Artists Committee for the Spanish Relief.[92] Woolf signed a manifesto of support of Spanish and Austrian refugees issued by the International Bureau for the Right to Asylum and Aid to Political Refugees in Paris in 1939, contributing the note that "like all other civilised people I have the greatest sympathy with the refugees and all victims of the present political persecution."[93] From the early days of the war, she traced in her diary the destruction in Spain with a conviction that the war was headed inevitably toward England: "Madrid not fallen. Chaos. Slaughter. War surrounding our island."[94]

The Meaning of Death in Spain

Through all of these works and ideals, Woolf read the Anglo-European anti-fascist cause and the emerging worldwide feminist cause directly onto the war in Spain. Her aid work and humanitarian pronouncements stood in deliberate contrast to the ideal of "commitment" espoused by Julian Bell, who wanted to fight in Spain. In fact, over a year before the war, she had already half-consciously foreshadowed his decision and evoked their generational differences in her diary:

> J[ulian] says all the young men are communists in order to gratify their desire to do things together & in order to have some danger; which will only last a few months. . . . But this was not the 1914 emotion. Lust & danger. . . . I say many people have found life exciting without war and bull fighting.[95]

Bell's fixation on the war further steered Woolf's focus toward it as well. He became an imagined interlocutor as Woolf composed *Three Guineas*: though she had meditated on the central issues for years, she "wrote it as an argument with him," she would note a month after his death.[96] (Indeed, her well-known line, "What can I do but Write?," comes from an earlier letter to him.[97]) Lines such as "You, of course, could once more take up arms—in Spain, as before in France—in defence of peace" and "In the first place, what reason is there to think that a university education makes the educated against war?" seem directed at him specifically (*TG* 12, 31). She corresponded with him often, attaching the questions of war and masculinity to him and exploring his psychology as paradigmatically English. Woolf wrote to him with resignation days after the war began that "in a moment I shall turn on the wireless and listen to the latest massacres in Spain."[98] Five months later, as Julian's desire to fight in Spain intensified, Woolf wrote him another letter that, in retrospect, proves telling:

> My dearest Julian,
> ... I have seen the young poets—Spender and [William] Plomer, and been induced to subscribe to the young poets paper, The Left review. That shows you that politics are still raging faster and fiercer. I've even had to write an article for the Daily Worker on the Artist and politics.... When it comes to making a practical suggestion, which will convince Mr Gillies, Berties [Bertrand Russell's] book [*Which Way to Peace?*, 1936] is not much use. However, I leave this out of my letters—that and Spain, which is now the most flaming of all the problems.... Quentin told me you mean to stand for Parliament. I dont see how any one can keep out of it as things are. Except Nessa and Duncan all our friends are in it—even Adrian, who deprecates it, but still marched all through the East end the other day with Karin in the anti-fascist procession.... Charles [Mauron] ... says for Gods sake don't leave China and come to fight in France—in which I think he is right; but no doubt he has said so already. So I wont go on.... Lord Cecil is coming to tea, to talk about Spain I think. He too is a nice man—there are many nice men; why are men in the mass so detestable? This morning I got a packet of photographs from Spain all of dead children, killed by bombs—a cheerful present.[99]

At once, Woolf's letter brings together her thoughts on domestic politics, on her colleagues' anti-fascist work, on "men in the mass," and on the Spanish photographs that she will discuss in *Three Guineas*. She writes again in her diary three months later that "Lord & Lady Cecil rang up to ask us to lunch to meet the Spanish Ambassador. (I am making up 3 Guineas)."[100]

While Virginia urged Bell not to fight, Leonard kept him abreast of the fascists' advances in Spain. Leonard also worked to find Julian a non-combat role in the Republic's defense. His letters capture the fear felt by Bloomsbury and the British left that Spain would be the first European state to fall into fascist hands by war:

> The difficulty is that by the time you get this some new horror will have started up in Poland or Czechoslovakia or Iceland or even Paris or London, and the ruins and corpses of Madrid will no longer be even of 'interest.' At the moment for the first time for two years it looks as if there is a faint, faint chance

of a Fascist [Franco] being beaten. . . . [But t]he Labour Party has cut a poor figure once more. . . . The League [of Nations] is dead; collective security is dead and rotten. . . . Spain was the first test case of the new dispensation of a world without the League. The corollary of isolation was non-intervention; the corollary of alliance was to support the Spanish Government.[101]

Leonard's "ruins and corpses of Madrid" look forward to the "dead bodies and ruined houses" in the photographs from Spain that Virginia will discuss in *Three Guineas*, and his reference to London as a possible site of "some new horror" bears the same logic as Virginia's polemic. He paints for Julian a dire scene of Britain and Europe in crisis; Spain is the frontline in the fight against fascism, in which national and international organizations are proving impotent. But while such visions influenced Virginia Woolf's interest in Spain in *Three Guineas*, Leonard's analysis—and the work of Labour and the League—lacked the radical feminist critique that Virginia understood as essential.

With the flow of British writers and artists into Spain to attend the Second International Congress of Writers for the Defense of Culture in Valencia and Madrid in July 1937 and to join the International Brigades in defense of the Republic, Spain became the cause célèbre for which a new generation of writers would risk their lives romantically. Woolf resisted the pressure from colleagues to attend the Congress, while Bell remained determined to fight in Spain. His decision defied and shocked his mother, Woolf, and the "Old Bloomsbury" generation. After arguing with him and his colleagues about the proper "duty" for British intellectuals regarding the Spanish war, Woolf only became more frustrated: "I felt flame up in me 3 Gs," she writes, and she poured her anger at Julian's decision into her treatise on intellectual duty.[102] She continued writing amid her anger and anxiety, "in full flood every morning with 3Gs," as Julian left for Madrid in early June 1937.[103] As a concession to his family, he agreed to go as a non-combatant. On 18 July came the news that he was killed while driving an ambulance for the Spanish Medical Aid Organization at Villanueva de la Cañada on the Brunete front. As Quentin Bell writes, "public tragedy was merged with private tragedy" for Woolf: Julian's death united for her the issues that *Three Guineas* engages, and she turned her anger at him into her argument with the English patriarchal order that produced his mentality.[104] What discomfited Woolf was not only the myth of masculinity that drew Julian to Spain, but also the question of how virtually the same English culture made her, a generation before him, a staunch feminist and pacifist. Julian was raised by Bloomsbury pacifists, yet he "had to be killed in Spain—an odd comment upon his education & our teaching," Woolf felt.[105]

Woolf wrote to Ocampo that she was "furious at the waste of [Julian's] life."[106] His death at age 29 felt to Woolf like a "complete break; almost a blank; like a blow on the head: a shrivelling up."[107] She put down *Three Guineas* and attempted to understand him in a memoir written almost two weeks after his death, asking "without finding an answer, what did he feel about Spain? What made him feel it necessary [to go]?" She continues, "I suppose it's a fever in the blood of the younger generation which we cant possibly understand. . . . We were all C.O.'s [Conscientious Objectors] in the Great war. The moment force is used, it becomes meaningless & unreal to me."[108]

With Julian gone, Franco became for Woolf a persisting emblem of her nephew's death and the tyrannies (plural) against which she would "fight intellectually." "The Spanish war is being won yesterday today tomorrow by Franco. I dreamt of Julian," she would write.[109] Near the end of the war, she adds with resignation, "Yesterday, Franco was recognised. And Julian killed for this."[110]

"Dead Bodies and Ruined Houses": Spain, War, and Feminism

As Woolf worked to amalgamate "history, biography, and the daily paper" in a manner that exceeded both fiction and "the fashionable and hideous jargon of the moment" in *Three Guineas*, she found that at "the end of six years floundering, striving, much agony, [and] some ecstasy[, she] . . . was always thinking of Julian when [she] wrote."[111] Julian Bell was not, in fact, on Woolf's mind for the entire six years, but at the time of his death, with the foundation of her argument in *Three Guineas* in place, she saw the Spanish war as having both an international and a personal attachment to her freedoms and restrictions as an English woman. This logic is borne out in the scrapbooks of newspaper and journal clippings that she maintained, along with assorted notes, from 1932–1937. Woolf researched a range of issues that she felt defined the cultural history of the moment: from war and writers to pensions and military funding, from imperialism to coronations and regalia, from military tattoos to suffrage and sexological history. The overarching subject in the first notebook is the intersections of fascism (usually Nazism) and misogyny and the specter of another war, as exemplified by an article from C. E. M. Joad that quotes Goebbels, Goering, and Hitler on women's role in the state. Stories of women arrested by Nazis and mothers reluctant to produce babies as "cannon fodder for the next war" are among those Woolf saves, alongside a letter to her from the Six Point Group for international women's rights deploring the "degrading of women in Germany, [which] lowers the status of women all over the world, and is bound to react against a better understanding between the Nations."[112] Though she would not live long enough to know much of Franco's regime, she certainly would have been disgusted equally by his provisions that barred women from professions or property ownership, required women to gain their husbands' permission to travel, and stripped most of the suffrage rights that women had gained under the Second Republic.

Spain enters Woolf's scrapbooks toward their end. She first includes the letter that she and a number of intellectuals published on the Spanish war (above) and an article from the *Daily Telegraph* on the shelling of Almería, where British destroyers did not intervene while the German navy bombarded the Republican stronghold. The document that orients the third scrapbook, however, is French reporter Louis Delaprée's widely circulated pamphlet *The Martyrdom of Madrid*. Written in November 1936, Delaprée's account occupies some 40 pages, alongside Woolf's newspaper clippings, short quotations from books, and one-page journal articles. Delaprée calls *Martyrdom* a "simple book-keeping of horror" that focuses on the women and children of the city. He notes the "women pressing against their breasts little babies wrapped within a blanket drag behind their skirts unhappy children, with dry eyes, with trembling chins, old women carrying a canary within a cage" and declares that "I feel ashamed at being a man, when mankind proves to be capable of such massacres of innocents." He writes of numerous dead women and children, their bodies in pools of blood—in one building, "in the ground-floor, three old women kept quiet round a table. They have been crushed against the ground. Two are dead. The third one, her knees broken, has remained for seven hours by the two corpses."[113]

Early in the first letter of *Three Guineas*, Woolf offers a similar image when she points to the set of photographs that have been sent "with patient pertinacity about twice a week" by the Spanish Government. The means by which they arrived in her hands cannot be overlooked: they were sent directly by "the Spanish Government" that she had worked to support. They were not, that is, filtered through any newspaper or magazine, nor are they identified as such images as Robert Capa's ubiquitous "Falling Soldier" (1936) or the infamous dead child in "Madrid—The 'Military' Practice of the Rebels" (1937). A footnote—the lone footnote in a book with 124 endnotes—indicates that this line was "Written in the winter of 1936–7," or just when Julian Bell set his mind on going to Spain (*TG* 10). The photographs—at this moment—are meant to evoke distinctly the Republic under attack and its civilians' suffering, the "fact[icity]" she will accentuate at the end of the third essay-letter. She notes later in the text that the Spanish Government now sends them "almost weekly," and she returns to the pictures about 15 times in her three letters, citing the "dead bodies and ruined houses" in them as evidence of the urgency of the problems she addresses in *Three Guineas* (*TG* 68, 141). Among the many violent images and metaphors that Woolf employs to demonstrate "that war is barbarous, that war is inhuman . . . horrible and beastly," these photographs (which readers never see) are the most jarring; they are "actual facts" (*TG* 8, 12, 11). Her description of them centers on:

> what might be a man's body, or a woman's; it is so mutilated that it might, on the other hand, be the body of a pig. But those certainly are dead children, and that undoubtedly is the section of a house. A bomb has torn open the side; there is still a bird-cage hanging in what was presumably the sitting-room, but the rest of the house looks like nothing so much as a bunch of spilikins suspended in mid-air. (*TG* 10–11)

Her descriptions clearly recall Delaprée's accounts, including the detail about the "bird-cage." In this ekphrasis, Woolf marks the "dead bodies and ruined houses"— the reduction of humans to slaughtered animals and the literal destruction of the domestic private sphere—with a phrase that will resonate throughout the text. The "dead bodies" in Spain, of course, now included her nephew's, and the figuratively "ruined houses" included Vanessa's. But the women in the picture are far from the "Latin" women of Woolf's essays, the "Spain" invoked far from that of her travels. It seems there are two "Spains" coexisting, but only tenuously connected, in Woolf's mind: the exoticized Spain of her writings and her conversations with Ocampo, and the Spain that is home to an idealized leftist republic and to civilians under attack by fascists.

Exactly what Woolf hopes to achieve argumentatively with both the present and absent photos remains a critically debated topic. Are they a shock tactic, as Jane Marcus argues?[114] A generic condemnation of war, but a refusal to engage with Spain's political realities, as Susan Sontag suggests?[115] Should they be placed in the context of Woolf's "growing awareness that photographs of all kinds had permanently transformed the problematic of the visible . . . [and] redefine[d] the imaginary as the realm in which women might share with men collective responsibility for evil," as Emily Dalgarno asserts, or seen as registering the contrast between the "masculine, patriarchal world" and the "feminine 'affect' of the narrator's visual memories of fascist atrocities," as Maggie Humm reads them?[116] The contexts that I have outlined in this chapter show that when Woolf uses the photos to transfer the violence of war in Spain onto the encrusted traditions of patriarchal culture at home, she anchors a multifaceted bridge from England to Spain that her collaborators extend to all of

Europe (and later, "the world"). She first achieves this by syntactically aligning spaces and places from around Europe in an effort to make "the whole iniquity of dictatorship, whether in Oxford or Cambridge, in Whitehall or Downing Street, against Jews or against women, in England, or in Germany, in Italy or in Spain apparent to you"—both the addressee and the reader (*TG* 103). Woolf then attaches the Spanish photographs, as emblems of the spread of European fascism, to virtually all of the critical ideas in *Three Guineas*: Englishmen's "sartorial splendours," the desire to "protect culture and intellectual liberty," the "prostituted culture and intellectual slavery" that occludes feminist thought, and the Dictator-Creon figure. The masculinist-fascist violence that they illustrate also binds together Woolf's critiques of her colleagues' pronouncements on "duty" and the Spanish war, their "prostitution" of culture, her arguments and grief over Julian Bell's death, and the sociopolitical topics that she had been researching for six years.

Woolf uses the photographs rhetorically to position her addressee and her reader next to her, writing, "for now at last we are looking at the same picture; we are seeing with you the same dead bodies, the same ruined houses" (*TG* 11). She soon asks, returning to her linkage of English tyranny and deaths in the Spanish war, "What connection is there between the sartorial splendours of the educated men and the photograph of ruined houses and dead bodies? Obviously the connection between dress and war is not far to seek; your finest clothes are those that you wear as soldiers. . . . [The soldier] is on the contrary a ridiculous, a barbarous, a displeasing spectacle [to women]" (*TG* 21). The soldier-as-typical-male appears "daubed red and gold, decorated like a savage with feathers he goes through mystic rites and enjoys the dubious pleasures of power and dominion while we, 'his' women, are locked in the private house without share in the many societies of which his society is composed" (*TG* 105). At the same time, Woolf's insertion of the pictures of such Englishmen in their "barbarous" regalia owes something strategically to Leonard Woolf's less subtle photographs in *Quack, Quack!* and to texts like Strachey's *Eminent Victorians*, which included staid portraits of the figures he treated. *Three Guineas* differs from a host of other texts on Spain, though, by not including grisly photos of the type reproduced in some pro-Republican propaganda in Britain, or the near-prurient ones that Hemingway had accompany his essay "Dying, Well or Badly" (1938).

By transposing barbarism onto the English soldier as viewed by a woman, Woolf uses the photographs to do work that she had not seen adequately articulated in the manifestos, political societies, and aid groups familiar to her. Her repeated allusions to them culminate in the third letter, which she dates more than a year after the first (1938). She opens, "let us consider how we can help you to prevent war by protecting culture and intellectual liberty, since you assure us that there is a connection between those rather abstract words and these very positive photographs—the photographs of dead bodies and ruined houses" (*TG* 85). When she concludes with a rhetorical crescendo built around what has become a cadence in her treatise, she transposes the archetypal misogynist-tyrant of her study, Creon, onto the Spanish war:

> And Creon we read brought ruin on his house, and scattered the land with the bodies of the dead. It seems, Sir, as we listen to the voices of the past, as if we were looking at the photograph again, at the picture of dead bodies and ruined houses that the Spanish Government sends us almost weekly. Things repeat themselves it seems. Pictures and voices are the same today as they were 2,000 years ago. (*TG* 141).

She has noted already that it matters not whether "the voices of Dictators" are speaking "English or German" or any other tongue, and has asked, "are we not all agreed that the dictator when we meet him abroad is a very dangerous as well as a very ugly animal?". Transferring the animalistic imagery from the photographs onto the dictator, Woolf sees him in England as "the egg of the very same worm that we know under other names in other countries. There we have in embryo the creature, Dictator as we call him when he is Italian or German" (*TG* 53). From the sites and names she has associated with him, Woolf's Creon-dictator is clearly a pan-European creation whose history stretches through the West's past, at least to Greek antiquity. Likewise, dissident women in the present are heirs of Antigone's spirit (*TG* 81). This grounds Woolf's imperative to her colleagues: "Let us never cease from thinking—what is this 'civilization' in which we find ourselves?" (*TG* 63). Regarding this "black night that now covers Europe" in *Three Guineas*, she discusses Hitler in her diary at precisely this moment, too, as "the complete ruin ... of civilisation, in Europe."[117] European civilization, from which Spain once was removed in Woolf's imagination, is now at stake in her tract.

The equation of the ancient and the modern that Woolf makes through the Spanish pictures is not all, however; the photographs and the Spanish scenes that *Three Guineas* draws upon undergo one final transmutation. Woolf shifts our focus from the ruins of war that opened *Three Guineas* to a different photograph. Distinct from the Spanish photographs and the "horror and disgust" they evoked,

> as this letter has gone on, adding fact to fact, another picture has imposed itself upon the foreground. It is the figure of a man; some say, others deny, that he is Man himself, the quintessence of virility, the perfect type of which

all the others are imperfect adumbrations. He is a man certainly. His eyes are glazed; his eyes glare. His body, which is braced in an unnatural position, is tightly cased in a uniform. Upon the breast of that uniform are sewn several medals and other mystic symbols. His hand is upon a sword. He is called in German and Italian Führer or Duce; in our own language Tyrant or Dictator. And behind him lie ruined houses and dead bodies—men, women and children. (*TG* 142)

The clarity of the figure in this photograph ("He is a man certainly") starkly contrasts the obscurity of the Spanish photographs that opened the text, where Woolf could only point, with similar grammatical structures, to "what might be a man's body, or a woman's; it is so mutilated that it might, on the other hand, be the body of a pig." Her description of this new picture makes explicit her suggestion of the significance of the five photographs of Englishmen in "uniform," with "several medals and other mystic symbols." As she superimposes the invisible "dead bodies and ruined houses" onto the background of this new photograph, Woolf argues that they are proof "that the tyrannies and servilities of the [public] are the tyrannies and servilities of the [private;] . . . that we cannot dissociate ourselves from that figure but are ourselves that figure" (*TG* 142). In order to "change that figure" and thus preserve "ourselves," Woolf argues, women must ally themselves with men in the public sphere. Stating her case now squarely in the present, she writes that women must realize and act upon a cosmopolitan feminist conclusion that "common interest unites us; it is one world, one life. How essential it is that we should realize that unity the dead bodies, the ruined houses prove. . . . Both houses will be ruined, the public and the private, the material and the spiritual, for they are inseparably connected" (*TG* 142, 143).

Like Ocampo, Woolf makes her feminist call to arms not divisive, but rather unifying: in all of the spaces listed above, she writes, "now we are fighting together. The daughters and sons of educated men are fighting side by side. . . . Take this one guinea then and use it to assert 'the rights of all—all men and women—to the respect in their persons of the great principles of Justice and Equality and Liberty'" (*TG* 103). In her invocation of the Enlightenment, Woolf revises, as Froula has shown, the familiar terms of the French Revolution by dropping "Fraternity"/"Brotherhood" and—not replacing it with "Sorority"/"Sisterhood"—adding "Justice," a Kantian end of her project. Only moments later, Woolf revises this key term of "Justice." She imagines that her "Outsiders' Society," a group distinct from the anti-fascist committees she has joined, will work "for liberty, equality and peace" (*TG* 106). Pacifism *is* justice, the substitution implies. The Outsiders'

Society will work "with private means in private. Those experiments will not be merely critical but creative," she adds, staking out a place for the feminist artist envisioned in *Room* (*TG* 113).

Woolf's humanitarianism grows out of this cosmopolitan feminism; "What does 'our country' mean to me an outsider?," the outsider must ask her brother. Rejecting fraternity again and the nation-state, "she will do her best to make this a fact, not by forced fraternity, but by human sympathy" (*TG* 107). (In fact, as early as 1927 Woolf had declared that "nationality is over. . . . All divisions are now rubbed out, or about to be."[118]) The portability of Woolf's universalist case for the "rights of all" lies in this vision of world citizenship from London to Buenos Aires and beyond, ideally superseding the class strictures that both Woolf and Ocampo have been criticized for overlooking (*TG* 102). Rather than the poets' utopian "dream of peace, the dream of freedom" that she mentions at the end of *Three Guineas*, Woolf and her readers, she declares, will ground their conclusions in and "fix [their] eyes upon the photograph again: the fact" (*TG* 142). Ocampo takes precisely this vision of marginality—which was "meant to stir, not to charm," Woolf wrote—to her struggle against an even more recalcitrant anti-feminist culture in Argentina.[119]

Woolf's Hispanic "Outsiders"

The topics engaged in *Three Guineas*, Woolf's "war pamphlet" on "politics and people; war and peace; barbarism and civilization," surpass the lives of English women alone. Woolf invites her readers to a polylogue that traverses, as her text does, multiple genres, fields, and voices: history, sociology, politics, biography, the personal essay, the epistle, literature, feminist scholarship, economics, and the political pamphlet.[120] (One of Woolf's working titles was *Answers to Correspondents*, which was the name of a mass weekly published by Alfred Harmsworth [Viscount Northcliffe] that claimed that it would answer all questions submitted by readers.) Her vision of a supranational society of outsiders detached from the *patria*— women of "the whole world"—traveled to Argentina in Ocampo's hands during the Spanish Civil War. Ocampo had seen the state of women in Spain before the Republic: only a small, privileged minority of women had been allowed access to education, and, Shirley Mangini adds, the post–Great War economic distress had meant falling wages, rampant prostitution, and an increased "white slave traffic" in Spain.[121] Like other liberals, Ocampo also feared that a fascist victory in Spain would lead to a fascist invasion of Latin America by the continent's former colonizers, which would be yet another defeat for Argentine women. She wrote in *Sur* that she conceives of her ethical responsibilities first through her identity as a woman, then as a journal editor. "I understand nothing of politics," she says, "wars or revolutions, killings—in a word, they horrify me. . . . We women [*nosotras las mujeres*] are accustomed, whether in times of peace or of war, to risking our lives; but by giving life, and not death."¹²² Against her earlier inclination to keep her journal above politics, in 1937 Ocampo joined an international chorus and made *Sur* a vocal pro-Republican journal. In a dense issue that contains an essay of hers on Woolf, a translation of a scene from Joyce's *Exiles*, and Rafael Pividal's "Católicos fascistas y católicos personalistas," Ocampo opens with a statement, "Posición del *Sur*." Her journal has been accused by the Catholic periodical *Criterio* of being "openly leftist," she writes. Politics and literature can no longer be separated, Ocampo claims, but her review's interests are first and foremost literary, intellectual, and spiritual. She lists *Sur*'s aims in a new manifesto:

> We want to continue the rich tradition of our country, which is a democratic tradition. . . . We want a better country, a more authentic culture, and a less corrupt and more just society. . . . We . . . will fight all persecution on the grounds of race, politics, or law. . . . We want a better clergy and a reformed church. . . . We are against all dictatorships, against oppression, against all forms of ignominy exercised against humanity.¹²³

As the Spanish war continued, *Sur* increasingly published anti-fascist and pro-Republican writing, including essays by Shaw, Huxley, and Ocampo herself. The July 1938 number was a special issue devoted to the "Defense of the Intelligentsia." Ocampo also continued to take in Spanish writers who had fled or were exiled. The journal published, for instance, Marichalar's translation of "Time Passes" in 1938, which was followed by his full translation of *To the Lighthouse* through *Sur*'s press later that year.

Ocampo published in *Sur*'s press the first full-length Spanish translations of Woolf's works, beginning with *A Room of One's Own* in 1936 and *Orlando* in 1937 (both translated by Borges), followed by *Mrs. Dalloway* (1939) and *Three Guineas* (1941). The translations of Woolf's nonfiction were rare not only in Spanish letters, but also globally: *Room* was not translated into any other language again until the French edition in 1951, nor was *Three Guineas* until the Italian in 1975. These editions came to influence other leading South American writers and thus to broaden the international community of feminist writers. Gabriela Mistral, the Chilean poet who became Latin America's first Nobel laureate, wrote to her friend Ocampo that she first read *A Room* when it was serialized in *Sur* (1935–1936), and that it was "the first time that a feminist argument has *so profoundly rung true for me.*"¹²⁴ By the 1950s, Ocampo had published translations of all of Woolf's major works, and sales were high in both Argentina and Spain. After World War II, she would publish translations of works by Camus, Colette, Faulkner, Gandhi, Claudel, Graham Greene, and Jawaharlal Nehru.

Ocampo's dialogues with Woolf, both personal and literary, further shaped her politics and, even though Woolf did not address this topic, her pan-Americanism. The second volume of *Testimonios* (1941) outlines her views in great detail. This volume, written in Spanish, French, and English, includes writings on Emily Brontë, Ocampo's abiding love of English literature, letters to Lorca and Tagore, essays on war and current events, and a lecture that Ocampo gave to an English audience. She quotes in the prologue from Whitman's image of America in "Song of Myself" and declares, "America is not an abstraction. . . . America is exactly what we are," including the parts of "our beloved Europe" that journeyed with them.¹²⁵ Ocampo opens this volume with a long lecture that she gave in Argentina, "Virginia Woolf, Orlando and Company" (1937), an account and reading of Woolf's career to that point. She sees Woolf's work as a testament of all the women of the world, one that would remain as a "megalith" if the women of the world disappeared tomorrow.¹²⁶

At the center of the second series of *Testimonios* are Ocampo's three essays on women's rights, responsibilities, and forms of expression. She writes in "La mujer y su expresión" ["Woman and Her Expression," 1935], recalling the opening of her "Letter to Virginia Woolf," that the putative "dialogue" between men and women had been for centuries a monologue, spoken by a male who eternally says "don't interrupt me." Her own "interrup[tion]," which was broadcast by radio in both Argentina and Republican Spain, makes the case that Woolf, Mistral, and the Spanish educational reformer María de Maeztu have provided together a template for international feminism that is now more urgent than ever. Abutting the case for "international solidarity," she writes that

> the fate of women in China or in Germany, in Russia or in the United States (in the end, which corner of the world is not important) is an extremely serious concern for all of us [*nosotras*], for we will feel its repercussions. Thus, the fate of South American women is a vital concern to Spanish women—and to everyone around the world, in all countries. . . . I wish to see among women all over the earth a solidarity that is not only objective, but also subjective.¹²⁷

Agreeing with Woolf's logic that feminists of the past were "fighting the tyranny of the patriarchal state as you are fighting the tyranny of the Fascist state," she continually cited in her own activism the campaigns for suffrage that Emmeline Pankhurst had initiated decades before, and that Woolf had sustained (*TG* 102). Tying together her interrelated critiques of fascism, arguments for liberalism, efforts to create a feminist public sphere, and calls for Argentine attachments to European feminism, Ocampo's essay collection *Domingos en Hyde Park* [*Sundays in Hyde Park*, 1936] praised London's liberal democratic society and its tradition of free speech epitomized by Hyde Park. Ocampo felt compelled to carry forward Woolf's work after her suicide, she wrote, and this spirit animated her anti-fascism during World War II as well. Ocampo provided the funds, for instance, for Roger Caillois's anti-Nazi journal *Lettres Françaises* to be printed during the German occupation of France; at one point in 1944, the editors dropped translations of stories by Borges from the sky over Paris. Still disappointed that Europeans knew little of Latin American literature, despite the successes of Mistral and Pablo Neruda abroad, she worked with Caillois to become a leading distributor of Spanish American literature in translation in France.

Moving constantly back and forth between Argentina and the world, Ocampo took up the cause of Indian independence (she eventually met Gandhi), was present at the Nuremberg trials, and later worked with UNESCO and Julian Huxley. Her most conspicuous act locally, however, remained her use of *Sur* and the public testimonial form to position herself as an independent and a dissident. She angered the Catholic church and most every political party in Argentina. She then denounced both Juan and Evita Perón in *Sur*, which earned her harassment, intimidation, and, finally, imprisonment in April 1953. Reflecting on her English colleague once again the following year, she saw that "*A Room of One's Own* and *Three Guineas* are the true history of the Victorian struggle between the victims of the patriarchal system and the patriarchs, between the daughters and the fathers and brothers. . . . against the tyranny of the fascist, Hitlerist state" that still exists after the war.[128] Indeed, over four decades after she first read *Room*, Ocampo still referred to it as "the best book about women" that she knew.[129] When she finally became the first woman elected to the Argentine Academy of Letters in 1977, she realized a new marker of her success in usurping and revising the male public sphere that had violently excluded women.

The interpersonal relations among these figures—Woolf, Ocampo, Frank, and Ortega—were not without tension or deterioration at certain moments. Likewise, the trajectories of their shared work were interrupted and often left incomplete: Madrid and Buenos Aires, for instance, did not become the bases for the cosmopolitan projects that each writer conceived when working to adapt and reconcile foreign models with native arts. Frank was not the first to imagine the magnetic Ocampo and her works in sexualized terms, and Ocampo herself would quickly tire of being seen by male writers as a muse or object of desire rather than an intellectual peer. While Frank had imagined a metaphorical feminine "Latin body," Ortega actually made an indiscreet, unwelcome pass at Ocampo, thus souring their relationship. Despite inspiring one another from afar, the two did not communicate for several years, and Ocampo took personally Ortega's various published dismissals of women's philosophy and writing. She also challenged his readings of Bertrand Russell's works, finding greater sympathy for the Bloomsbury associate's arguments. Frank and Ortega's amiable and mutually beneficial friendship was never an easy fit, either: Frank's interest in Marxism, for instance, was at odds with Ortega's conservative European and strongly anti-Bolshevik commitments. In *The Revolt of the Masses*, in fact, Ortega specifically refutes Frank's *Re-discovery of America*, which he claims takes Spengler's analyses of Europe uncritically as truth and believes naively that America is ready for global supremacy. That is, the reaction against Spengler that Ortega and Frank shared in the early 1920s became a matter of contention between them only a few years later. Ortega, meanwhile, angered Argentines by speaking condescendingly to them and by ranking Spaniards' "blood" above those of the indigenous and creole populations.[130] Frank also antagonized some Latin Americans when he preserved a role for the continent's brutal colonizer, Spain, in the post-imperial New World. And when Frank began to turn his attention to Russia and to the communist League of American Writers, his mystical version of Marxism, which valued the spiritual and organic over the material, led to disagreements with party members in the Americas and in Europe. Frank became an emissary of the Good Neighbor policy, but in 1942, he was severely beaten by fascists in Argentina for being a "Jewish Bolshevik" after he criticized the regime of President Ramón Castillo.

Meanwhile, in her last meeting with Woolf, Ocampo all but forced herself into the writer's house, accompanied by photographer Gisèle Freund, and coaxed an angry Woolf to sit for some portraits. Woolf wrote her a terse letter and complained to Vita Sackville-West, "Dont you think it damnable?—considering how they filched and pilfered and gate crashed—the treacherous vermin."[131] Yet this incident did not dim Woolf's light in the eyes of Ocampo, who remained in contact for years with many of the Bloomsbury crowd, including Leonard Woolf, Vita Sackville-West, Harold Nicolson, and Aldous Huxley, along with Julian Huxley, Cyril Connolly, Cecil Day-Lewis, and Louis MacNeice after World War II. These relationships bespeak British modernism's broader equivocal and complex relationship with interwar Spain: Ortega, like Eliot, could not see the Second Republic as the fulfillment of Spain's project of European modernity, and Woolf's anti-fascism does not entail support for the Republic's *war* efforts. Rather, Woolf and Ocampo's exchanges offer what Mónica G. Ayuso characterizes as a marker of contemporary "transnational feminism" and its "analysis of the uneven, unequal, and complex relationships among women in places as different as England and Spanish America."[132] What bridges the imbalance between Woolf's and Ocampo's positions is their work to collapse what Woolf called the "difference between two worlds" into the "whole world" (an *entire* world and an *unfragmented* world) of the cosmopolitan feminism of *Three Guineas*, which remains the most enduring of Woolf's legacies that Ocampo brought to life both near and far in her work to "create for [Shakespeare's sister] a world in which she could find it possible to live wholly, without mutilations."[133]

5. Spain in Translation and Revision
Spender, Altolaguirre, and Lorca in British Literary Culture

[The members of the Auden Generation] cannot be considered in their island isolation; they were European writers almost as much as they were British writers, deeply influenced by events and thoughts beyond our own shores, . . . [who] became more and more closely identified [with their French and Spanish peers] during the interwar period.

—John Lehmann, *New Writing in Europe* (1940)[1]

[Communist critics in the 1930s] made . . . Dante, Shakespeare, Goethe, Balzac, [and] Blake . . . ex-officio Marxist saints, in the same way as they canonized the poet García Lorca, who had been obligingly assassinated by the Francoists, and whom they would have attacked as a Catholic reactionary, had he survived.

—Stephen Spender, *World within World* (1951)[2]

The two works about the Spanish Civil War that Anglophone readers tend to know best—George Orwell's *Homage to Catalonia* (1938) and Ernest Hemingway's *For Whom the Bell Tolls* (1940)—represent a small fraction of the literature that arose from the legendarily idealized "Poet's War," as the critic Hugh D. Ford called it. The war, which drew participants and observers from around the world, spawned a vast array of texts in a number of languages and, in Britain, it "put Spain on the publishers' map," the *TLS* noted in 1937.[3] But even among English-language publications on the war, Orwell's and Hemingway's works belong to a literary history of what Jed Esty has called, in other contexts, a late modernist "existential male antiheroism in a world of corrupt politics and culture."[4] Both authors seek to claim the mantle of the most reliable domestic voice of the conflict by depicting brutal and uncomfortable truths grounded in their own experiences. The war sparked such a competition for authority on Spain in a public sphere created in the vacuum of Britain's and America's governmental stances of non-intervention, and these two accounts earned their reputations. But relying primarily on such texts has significant limitations, for it leaves hidden other voices of the war—in particular, Spanish cultural voices, which did not interest Orwell or Hemingway greatly—that were part of this same competition. This chapter recovers several projects that aimed to "speak" for Spain throughout the 1930s, projects that claimed their own authority through channeling foreign voices, through reception, through translation, and through literary collaboration as a means of expressing privileged bonds between England and Spain. These bonds, the writers treated in this chapter believed, would best defend Europe's poetics and its political modernity against fascism.

At the center of this effort was Stephen Spender, whose shifting political commitments through the 1930s, from communism to socialist liberalism to liberal-democratic anti-fascism, form one of the primary backdrops of this chapter. His experiences with Spanish writers, I contend, in part motivated several of these shifts. When Spender joined the Communist Party of Great Britain (CPGB) in 1936, he was told by the General Secretary Harry Pollitt to fight in Spain, to "get himself killed, to give the Party its Byron."[5] He declined, and instead traveled to Spain first as a reporter, then as a delegate to a global anti-fascist congress. The result of these trips was that Spender returned to England determined to continue the poetic projects of the Spanish Generation of '27, a group of writers who were being imprisoned, exiled, or killed during Franco's rebellion. In the divided literary cultures of the 1930s, Spender's works evince a belief that the poetics of his generation, the Auden Generation, were inextricably bound to those of its Spanish peers and their fight against fascism, and that "in Spain is Europe. England also is in Spain," as Rex Warner stated. Spender's domestic claims for cultural authority eventually were attached, both implicitly and explicitly, to his readings of his contemporary Spanish colleagues' works as the artistic expressions of a cosmopolitan, European, and liberal-democratic state.

The contexts for these assertions were articulated in arguments by José Ortega y Gasset, who was Britain's best-known (but often known wrongly) figure of the Spanish Republic, and by Manuel Altolaguirre, both of whom inscribed Spanish political-cultural history into a European sphere to which England and Spain together formed a unique bond. This history, Altolaguirre further argued, extended back for centuries, as he illustrated in his journal *1616: English and Spanish Poetry*

(1934–1935). This journal, made possible by the Republic's sponsorship of Altolaguirre's work in London, initiated two key modes of collaboration between Altolaguirre and Spender: first, reinvigorating the sonnet as an internationalist form across a European republic of letters, and second, reviving the British Romantics' sympathy with Spain during Napoleon's invasion. Altolaguirre and his English colleague developed together a sense of translation as a mode of expressing cosmopolitan attachments to Spain at war—whether in the 1800s or the 1930s. Their Benjaminian notion that "a translation participates in 'afterlife' of the foreign text, enacting an interpretation that is informed by a history of reception," as Lawrence Venuti puts it, is visible in their visions of cross-cultural solidarity.[6] As editor and translator for the Anglo-Spanish collection *Poems for Spain* (1939) and as co-translator with the Spaniard J. L. Gili of the pioneering edition of Federico García Lorca's *Poems* (1939), Spender further demonstrates this conviction. With Rafael Martínez Nadal, an intimate friend of Lorca, Spender ultimately attempts to rescue in another country (and in a more widely spoken language) the works of Lorca, whom Franco's regime had executed and whose poetry and drama would be suppressed for decades in Spain. To translate Lorca is to promulgate a reading of "Spain," and thus of Britain's relationship to both, and Spender and his Spanish collaborators use not the semantics of translation, but editorial and organizational politics to make translation into a "mode of cultural politics."[7]

That the figure of Lorca was "Spanish" was never in doubt; rather, what "Spain" he and his syncretistic Andalusian identity represented—that of the gypsies, the Republic, the Moors, the anti-fascist movement, the modern European arts—and thus what his assassination meant were disputed topics. Lorca became, in the British afterlife that Spender enabled amid competing readings of him, a symbol not of the Spanish Republic alone, nor of the international communist revolution, as some on the left tried to make him, but of a cosmopolitan Spain that had become European—retroactively, after Franco's victory. The circulation of Lorca's works in British literary culture focuses the primary questions of this chapter: Who speaks for Spain, and why? What is the relationship between poetry and modern war? The answers to these questions posited by the figures in this chapter represent a convergence of the modernist movements of Britain and Spain that culminated at a moment when Spain became the object of much of Europe's consciousness. They were lodged in poems, translations, paratexts, reviews, and revised or alternate book editions, including Spender's own poem dedicated to Altolaguirre and rewritten multiple times. This archive also contains a history of misreadings, miscommunications, and poor timing that left much of the work imagined by these writers incomplete, and left the rich potential of poetic forms such as the *romance* only partially tapped.

In this rapidly changing political landscape, Spender's pro-Republicanism in *Poems for Spain* gives way to an argument for preserving the conditions of poetry throughout Europe. Finally, after the hope of saving the Spanish Republic has been extinguished, Spender joins a profound but confused clamor of voices—some still competing today—who re-read Lorca as an emblem of Spain's tragedy.

Speaking for Spain, Misreading Ortega

Through his work at the *Revista de Occidente* and his publications in foreign periodicals, Ortega enjoyed international renown in the late 1920s and emerged as the cultural ambassador of a country that began to shift from the margins of British and European thought. Gerald Heard, editor of *The Realist*, captured this sense of Ortega's role in a request for a contribution in 1929:

> Señor Antonio Marichalar has informed us that we might write to you and ask whether you could give us an article on the present state of Spain[,] . . . a survey of modern life since the Dictatorship. . . . You are no doubt aware that the English are very often far better informed about what goes on in northern and central Europe than in southern Europe. It is therefore all the more important that they should be given an insight into the developments of the Latin countries by an authority.[8]

Heard hopes that Ortega might bridge the divisions of Europe that the philosopher himself sought to overcome. The response across Europe and the Americas to Ortega's *La rebelión de la masas* [*Revolt of the Masses*, 1930] was greater than that of any Spanish writer's works in decades. In short time, this led to a series of translations of his books into English: *The Modern Theme* in 1931, *Revolt of the Masses* in 1932, *History as a System* in 1935, and *Invertebrate Spain* in 1937. Ortega became a minor sensation among English intellectuals and writers. H. G. Wells met him in 1932, then dedicated *The Shape of Things to Come* (1933)—which projects a future in which English and Spanish are interchangeable languages—to "José Ortega y Gasset /Explorador" after reading *Revolt*. The following year, Ortega was invited to give the Godkin Lectures at Harvard (he declined), to teach with Federico de Onís at Columbia (he accepted, but could not travel because of illness), and to contribute to numerous Anglophone periodicals and newspapers.[9]

The timing of this burst of popularity, however, was not necessarily fortuitous. At nearly the same moment, the election of the Second Republic in 1931 attracted international attention and commentary—positive and negative—in a host of media in England. As the only contemporary Spanish figure known to large bodies of readers outside Spain, Ortega was linked to this new government, and not entirely without reason. He was a leading intellectual in what many hoped would be the European New Spain that he had imagined, and it was rumored that he declined an offer to be the first president. Ortega agreed to serve as a delegate for León and on the government's commission on foreign relations, but as it became clear how far to the left the new workers' state would be, Ortega began withdrawing his support. Where the younger generation of leaders saw promise in anarchism and labor syndicates, Ortega saw dangerous and self-destructive alliances with "Bolshevik" power.[10]

The responses of several leading British media of different political stripes to Ortega and his Republican contexts illustrate the difficulties that they faced in understanding the "Spain" that the philosopher represented. The London *Times*, which was generally unsympathetic to the Republic, began following Ortega's political life in Spain with more interest in hopes of finding in him a more moderate and conservative Europeanist face for the Republic. The paper dubbed Ortega the "oracle of the Republic," sometimes the "Philosopher of the Republic."[11] It also quoted him more often than the other figures who were actually more integral to the ruling coalition. But as the schisms between Ortega and the Republic became apparent, even to foreign observers, beginning in 1933, the paper abandoned its awkward effort and rarely mentioned Ortega, noting only his anti-fascism and his disillusion with the government. The *English Review*—now a right-wing journal that even called for the return of Primo de Rivera as dictator—was less sympathetic and more insistent on reading Ortega onto and through the new government. It had stated its hope that the Republic would "not add to the instability of Europe, for the Spanish temperament favours short regimes and many changes of Government, not always unaccompanied by bloodshed."[12] A hostile review of Ortega's *Revolt*, which is called "very sorry stuff," followed. The critic, Charles Petrie, further recycles old tropes of Hispanicity to claim that

> Spanish genius is not fertile in the production of philosophers or political scientists of the first rank, and Señor Ortega y Gasset, who aspires to be both, is clearly not one of the exceptions to this rule.... His philosophy is typically Spanish, that is to say, it is an amalgam of the ideas of the thinkers of other nations put into rhetorical form.

Recasting Spain's hybridity as a shortcoming in original thought, he equates Ortega's faults with those of the new government when he writes that "it is to be hoped that there soon will be a revolt of the Spanish masses against the government of Señor Ortega y Gasset and his friends."[13]

Petrie's reference to *Revolt of the Masses* points to another reason that Ortega was misread in England. *La rebelión de las masas* was published serially in Spain from 1926–1929, then in book form in 1930, a year before the Second Republic came to power. However, its appearance in English in 1932 caused it to be associated with the new government, sometimes as a critique of its vision of the new leftist state, sometimes as an affirmation of the revolution. (*Revolt* sometimes continues to be misinterpreted as a text primarily concerned with the rise of mass popular cultures, rather than a critique of the philistinism of Primo de Rivera's regime and a new meditation on Ortega's supranational Europeanism.) At the center-left *New Statesman and Nation*, Sylvia Pankhurst's review of *Revolt* was the most accurate historically, noting that

> the turning point which rallied the intellectual classes of Spain to the Republican cause is held by many to have been José Ortega y Gasset's article, 'Delenda est Monarchia'. . . . Ortega has long been a [moderate among the] leader[s] of the Republican intellectuals.

Pankhurst notes, however, Ortega's "vehemence" in his "dislike of Spanish Syndicalism," which, through its "sturdy, militant growth . . . may be destined to carry the Spanish revolution many stages farther on the road to a new social order than the learned José Ortega would desire." *Revolt*, she writes, presents "Bolshevism and Fascism" as two sides of the same barbarian coin in modern Europe, and Ortega "denounces" both of them as "retrogressi[ve], typical movements of [the] massman." In the end, however, Ortega "offers us no new social order, no new idealism, no new hope," she writes, but rather "urges the unification of Europe, as a great enterprise, to inspire the European and stimulate him to control the world, . . . [to make Europe] a great national State."[14]

The most sustained and sympathetic engagement with Ortega's work in the 1930s continued to come from the *Criterion*. Antonio Marichalar, who remained the review's chief Spanish voice, wrote in the early days of the Republic that "it is hardly possible to speak of literary life in Spain during the last few months, without showing how closely it is related to the world of politics." And for Marichalar, Ortega best represents the "collective" will of Spain now. He explains why Ortega and other intellectuals have gone against their former ideals of philosophical detachment and have taken their "share[s] in politics" in support of the Republic: rather than pressing intellectuals into service as Hitler and Mussolini have done, Spain's dictator "banished Unamuno, imprisoned Marañón, and provoked the hostility of Ortega y Gasset, Menéndez Pidal, . . . and others." Ortega has therefore placed his oratorical and philosophical "weapons unreservedly at the service of the Republic," Marichalar claims with some overstatement; he is "more restless, influencing History and Politics with his new theories; his full-blooded aggressive style calls forth discussion, praise, and protest." Moreover, the Republic "has sent men of letters as ambassadors: Ramón Pérez de Ayala to London, Salvador de Madariaga to New York, Américo Castro to Berlin, . . . Ricardo Baeza to Santiago . . . [and Luis] de Zulueta [to] the Vatican."[15] Marichalar thus reconciles Ortega and the Republic by highlighting the internationalist and pro-intellectual elements of the new state.[16]

In Spain, Ortega's major initiatives, even when he tempered his Castilian centralism with arguments for provincial autonomy, fell flat under the Republic, and the government's violent anti-clericism appalled him. He resigned his deputyship, dissolved his Group in Service of the Republic, and, as Anthony Kerrigan writes, "walked away from the state he had been instrumental in creating."[17] Since 1933, he wrote, the Republic's actions had become "the gravest problem of my life, *which until now had been one with the destiny of my country*."[18] Ortega's younger associates largely remained supporters of the Republic, though Marichalar, also disenchanted with the government, briefly pressured him to join a rearguard Catholic group supporting the rebels.[19] The philosopher's despair deepened when José Antonio Primo de Rivera, son of the former dictator, claimed to draw on his "Old and New Politics" when founding Falange; when Ortega's brother Eduardo, a Republican figure, narrowly escaped an attempt by the fascist Falange to assassinate him in a bomb attack; and finally, when his sons joined the rebels once the war broke out.[20] Exile seemed the only option, and he turned down invitations to the Americas in order to stay in Europe. His peripatetic flight took him—in grave health all the while—to France, Holland, Argentina, and Portugal. Asked for his position on the civil war by a variety of European media, Ortega only stated his staunch anti-fascism while offering nominal support for the Republic. In his final contribution to the *Criterion* in 1938, Marichalar makes no allusion to the war and instead outlines a defense of the "Ideas and Beliefs of José Ortega y Gasset," declaring that his mentor remains a "champion of European civilization."[21]

Ortega finally turned his attention directly to England in the midst of Spain's war. Indeed, the philosopher added a special "Epilogue for the English" for the new edition of *Revolt of the Masses* in 1938. The English, he writes, "who make so few grave historical errors, commit the most gigantic one" in supporting their government's stance of non-intervention in Spain. Ortega has believed for some time "with robust faith in the European mission of the English people," but regrettably, they are now ensuring the "unmaking" of Europe—indeed, of the dystopian "destiny of the world." The English have been so insular, Ortega writes, that they have made the "radical decision of not wanting to hear any Spanish voice capable of clarifying matters" such as his own, or "to hear it only after deforming it."[22] Making one of the most impassioned pleas of his career, Ortega declares "above all . . . [his] earnest desire to collaborate [with the English] on the reconstitution of Europe." Reiterating the call with which he began his *Revista de Occidente*, Ortega speaks of the "cosmopolitanism" of the Enlightenment, which "is the opposite of [contemporary] 'internationalism.' It is nourished not by the exclusion of national differences, but rather, by the enthusiasm toward them—not by their cancellation, but by their integration."[23] He followed up this epilogue with a rare return to English-language periodicals with his essay "Concerning Pacifism" (1938) in the British journal *Nineteenth Century*. He restates his belief in a "community of . . . Europeans who, besides being Europeans, are also Englishmen, German, or Spaniards," and who genuinely desire the best for one another.[24] But when the possibility of the European Spain that he had envisioned for decades was eliminated by Franco's victory, British readers would look to Ortega—and to Spain—with less frequency.

An Anglo-Spanish Literary History: Altolaguirre's *1616*

Ortega was not alone in asserting that England and Spain shared a collaborative mission to redefine Europe in the 1930s. This belief was fundamental to a literary-historical project of cultural politics undertaken by the young Andalusian poet Manuel Altolaguirre, who arrived in England in 1934 with the hope of joining his British counterparts in crafting the internationalist aesthetics of the new left. This project took place in his fascinating bilingual modernist magazine *1616: English and Spanish Poetry*, which his biographer John Crispin has called "one of the most unusual journals in literary history."[25] Altolaguirre, a member of the Generation of '27 and an alumnus of the Residencia de Estudiantes, had published widely in the *Revista de Occidente* and was "drawn to the work of making generational reviews."[26] He became a regular presence in many of '27's journals, including *Verso y Prosa*, *Carmen*, *Mediodía* [*Midday*], and *Litoral* (he co-founded the final one). After visits to London, Buenos Aires, and Paris, which helped foster his cosmopolitan sensibilities, he returned to Spain to work enthusiastically for the Second Republic. With his new wife, the writer Concha Méndez, Altolaguirre started a populist review in Madrid called *Héroe (Poesía)* [*Hero (Poetry)*], and he used his own printing press to publish it and a variety of literary texts.

In 1934, Altolaguirre won a government-funded university scholarship to study printing methods and "English spiritualist poetry" (including Donne, Blake, and Thompson) in London. While in England, Altolaguirre set out to disseminate his criticism and publications on contemporary Spanish literature to a number of audiences. He was a representative of the Republic's internationalism and a spokesman for its principal poets. He lectured at King's College London, met with England's leading Hispanists, joined a BBC radio program on modern Spanish verse, and published reviews of his Spanish colleagues' works in London magazines. His apartment became a gathering place for foreign intellectuals, especially those exiled from Italy and Germany.[27] Altolaguirre's deepest interest remained the modernist periodical; he bought a new printing press in London and, with his wife, launched his ambitious attempt to integrate centuries of Anglo-Spanish literary history. His synthetic periodical had no regular form, reflecting his protean attempts to bring together the poetry of two disparate and apparently disconnected literary traditions. The title refers to the year in which Shakespeare and Cervantes both died (the title page of each number reads "1616 /saw the death of /W. S. & M. de C."), and the balance of poetry in English and Spanish across the ten issues of (appropriately enough) 16 pages each is roughly equal. Printed on fine, large paper with colorful type, the inaugural issue of *1616* (November 1934) contains no editorial statement or manifesto, but rather opens with a piece of literary diplomacy: a sonnet by Ramón Pérez de Ayala, the Republic's new ambassador to England. In a form that *1616* will employ variously throughout its run, the poem is rendered with a Spanish title in red and an English body in black. It is followed by works from Lorca, Luis Cernuda, and Percy Shelley (translated by Altolaguirre), all entirely in Spanish.[28]

The centerpiece of the first number, though, and an indicator of its cultural work, is Lord Byron's "A Very Mournful Ballad on the Siege and Conquest of Alhama" (printed in English), a poem that Byron himself translated in 1817 from the anonymous Spanish "Romance de la Perdida de Alhama"—which was, in turn, thought to be translated from an Arabic original. This publication represents Altolaguirre's first major attempt to recover texts from across English literary history that incorporated Spanish texts and themes. His interest in the Romantics was no accident, as the topic of Byron's poem suggests, and contemporary scholars have returned to these writers' momentary fixation on Spain. Wordsworth, Coleridge, and others, who had supported the French after their revolution, pivoted in their continentalism when they were repulsed by Napoleon's invasion of Spain and Portugal in 1807–1808, which began the Peninsular War.[29] The Romantics backed the Spanish insurgency against the occupation, and they registered their support for Spain in multiple ways: Wordsworth wrote a series of sonnets on Spanish topics; Southey wrote a history of the war and translated some Spanish works; Coleridge wrote a "Letter on the Spaniards" (1809); Felicia Hemans wrote *England and Spain* (1808) and translated several classics of Spanish and Portuguese poetry; Walter Savage Landor, who attempted unsuccessfully to join in the battle in Spain, based his tragedy *Count Julian* on Spanish legends; and Percy Shelley later translated Calderón. For Altolaguirre, this history of sympathy and mutual inspiration, mostly forgotten among contemporary British and Spanish readers, must be revived in the present. As for *1616*, it extends its Romantic Hispanophilia back over two more centuries when Altolaguirre publishes "Los Versos de la 'Diana' de Jorge de Montemayor, traducidos al inglés por Sir Philip Sidney, publicados en 1590" ["Verses of Jorge de Montemayor's 'Diana,' translated into English by Sir Philip Sidney, published in 1590"], known in English as Sidney's "Translated Out of the 'Diana' of Monte-maior." In a moment just after the defeat of the Spanish Armada in 1588, and during which some 5 percent of titles published in England were originally Spanish-language texts, Sidney translated Montemayor's pastoral cycle of 1559, the best-known Spanish sonnets of the era.[30] Altolaguirre reclaims, with a Spanish title and English body, the forgotten significance of Spain's Golden Age to a formative moment in the history of English literature.

Altolaguirre accentuates this point differently in another issue by weaving together several more historical documents. He writes Spain and England into a deep, hybrid literary history by printing three sonnets by Garcilaso de la Vega alongside their translations (on facing pages) by William Drummond of Hawthornden, a Scottish sonneteer from the early 1600s who, like Garcilaso, translated the sonnets of the Italian Renaissance.[31] The sonnet proved for them an adaptable, translatable, and mutable literary form for this sort of international participation, and for Altolaguirre, its brevity allowed him to effect his juxtapositions and his experimentalism and to keep down the page count (and printing costs) of *1616*. Garcilaso and Drummond thus were also two avatars, Altolaguirre suggests, of his and his '27 colleagues' own work to bring foreign sensibilities to their domestic cultures. Thus, *1616* later prints a group of nature poems by contemporary English and Spanish poets in the same alternating fashion. Altolaguirre even foregrounds his own poetry in this way by printing a series of five of his poems as a mixed set, with four in Spanish, one in English translation.

The final two numbers of *1616* continue this pattern by featuring the works of a number of young British and Spanish poets—most of them now forgotten—intercalated among one another, followed by Concha Méndez's poetry in both Spanish and English (by the hands of three different translators). Critical to Altolaguirre's vision, too, are the facing bilingual versions of contemporary poems that occupy a large section in the middle of *1616*'s run. For this project, Altolaguirre collaborated extensively with the Cambridge Hispanist Stanley Richardson and the Anglo-Colombian poet Edward Sarmiento of the University of Manchester. Richardson was a local champion of the Spanish Republic and a presence at the Anglo-Spanish League of Friendship, a London club established in 1919. He and Sarmiento both translated Spanish works and published their own poetry, along with works of their university students, in the journal. In an exemplary moment in *1616*, Méndez's "Qué angustía . . . " ["What anguish . . . "] appears alongside its translation by Sarmiento; reversing this is Richardson's "Murderer" with a translation by Altolaguirre. The translations in *1616*, for the most part, are not as interesting in themselves as the content of the poems and the editorial agenda that they manifest. Altolaguirre's commitment to the fluency of bilingual publication not only leads him to circulate Spanish poetry in a country mostly ignorant of it, but also enables him to act as a curator, a *bricoleur*, of both classical and modern English-Spanish poetry.

Creating printed and topical correlations between contemporary writers in England and in Spain, *1616* would juxtapose writers of '27, including Lorca, Cernuda, Méndez, Rafael Alberti, Jorge Guillén, and Vicente Aleixandre, with Anglophone writers including Richardson, A. E. Housman, and T. S. Eliot. The eighth number is remarkable because it includes not only Sidney's work, but also Luis Cernuda's "Gloria del Poeta" in Spanish, followed by Eliot's "Journey of the Magi" in both English and Spanish. Altolaguirre was not alone among the poets of '27 in having been influenced by Eliot's poetry, nor in capitalizing on the international prestige that Eliot's name signaled. After meeting Eliot himself in London in 1935, Altolaguirre translated this poem, then published it next to Lorca's "Omega: Poema para muertos" ["Omega: Poem for the Dead"] in Spanish and Alberti's "Myth" in English (translated by Richardson). This series itself—Eliot sandwiched among three leading poets of '27—creates an implicit declaration of loyalty to Eliot's *poetic* (and not political) influence on the part of his Spanish contemporaries. It also Hispanizes Eliot, then inscribes him into a bi-national poetic context, making translation a form of ordering that goes beyond Eliot's own understanding of the contexts of his work. Altolaguirre's translations of Housman's "As I gird on for fighting" and "In midnights of November" follow, as do his translations—in a return to the Romantics—of the first 33 stanzas of Shelley's *Adonaïs*, for the first time in Spanish. Altolaguirre casts all of these poets into a Spanish-British literary sphere that *1616* stretches from Lope de Vega and St. John of the Cross (the mystic whom Eliot published in the *Criterion*) to modern English university students. By doing so, he provides a London-based counterpart to his colleague José Bergamín's *Cruz y Raya*, which printed in translation religious meditations by British writers.

Altolaguirre and Méndez then published several collections of Spanish poems, books of verse by English poets, and anthologies of recent Spanish poetry in English translation. Altolaguirre also collaborated with Richardson on a number of translations, including some of Thomas Hardy's and G. K. Chesterton's poems.[32] Richardson publicized Altolaguirre's work in the journal *Contemporaries*, in which he profiled contemporary Spanish poetry and poets. After making cross-cultural links among works like Lorca's *Blood Wedding* and Auden's *Paid on Both Sides*, he writes that Altolaguirre "is active poetry, a 'maker' in all the best senses of the word"; he discusses *1616* (which advertised in *Contemporaries* as well); and he recommends Marichalar's "Spanish Chronicles" in the *Criterion* for interested readers.[33] Altolaguirre's work to mesh Anglo-Spanish literatures together, however, was left unfinished in the end, and he attempted to import it to Spain when he returned home. He published a poem called "Percy B. Shelley" (1936), which imagines the scene of Shelley's death at sea. Reading Shelley's defiant, wandering soul as a spirit that confronts tyranny wherever he finds it, Altolaguirre creates a vision of the freedoms for which Romantic poets stood that will be invoked only a few months later by both himself and Spender against the fascist threat in Spain.[34] Indeed, during the war, Altolaguirre published his completed version of *Adonaïs* (1938). His sense of the depth of a specifically Anglo-Spanish literary history, drawing as it does on an Eliotic ideal of the past's relation to the present, also looks forward to the claims of a privileged relationship between the two countries during the Spanish Civil War.

From Disgust to Sympathy: The Evolution of Spender's Spain

Altolaguirre's work—to show through *1616* and through his own poetry that British and Spanish writers formed a single literary generation—was continued in England by his friend Stephen Spender, who came to know Spanish poets over a series of trips to the country. Spender was in a prolonged competition for the authority to speak both *on* Spain and *for* Spain with the more famous George Orwell, much to Orwell's consternation. Both were successful authors in the Left Book Club's subscription series and both initially supported the Republic, but Orwell detested Spender. In his response to Nancy Cunard's questionnaire on Spain (see chapter 4), Orwell, who refused to be published, sent a homophobic rant to Cunard personally, writing that "I am not one of your fashionable pansies like Auden and Spender. I was six months in Spain, most of the time fighting, I have a bullet-hole in me at present, and I am not going to write blah about defending democracy."[35] The two figures' treatments of Ortega highlights their differences. Orwell panned

Invertebrate Spain, saying that there "is no use hoping that [*Invertebrate Spain*] will explain the Spanish civil war. . . . You will get a better explanation from the dullest doctrinaire Socialist, Communist, Anarchist, Fascist or Catholic."[36] (Never mind that the book was published in 1921.) Spender, on the other hand, recommended *Invertebrate Spain*, claiming that Ortega reads "Spanish character" in a manner that resolves the paradoxes of the coexistence of the modern and the ancient, the European and the African, which are at the heart of the "cultural heritage of Spain." Ortega explains the history of Spain's "disintegration," and the book is also valuable for "the light it throws on Europe," including its lessons for Germany, Russia, and England. He concludes by writing both the Spanish war and Ortega's work into the European present: "Whoever wishes to understand the background of the Spanish conflict and to enjoy one of the richest products of contemporary European literature, should read this book."[37]

Spender and Orwell eventually came to share a disillusion with the Spanish war and with factions of the international left. But Spender understood Spain through its poets and its culture, not through military service. He and his colleagues in the Auden Generation, as they have been called—Lehmann, Louis MacNeice, Cecil Day-Lewis, Christopher Isherwood, and Auden himself—generally embraced social realism and criticized the high modernist generation of writers for failing to guard against the catastrophic Great War. Scholarly accounts of this era have focused often on the debates about "committed" literature that prevailed in Britain in the 1930s, but for Spender, the Spanish war had a broader and more complicated significance. This is due in part to his changing politics throughout the decade. In a visit to Spain in 1932, Spender had seen Spaniards as disgusting and abhorrent. He recorded a shocking entry in his diary by writing of a man next to him on a bus in Málaga who "had an enormous and festering boil on the side of his face[. . . .] I indignantly detest [such people], and I wish that I were some kind of a feudal tyrant who could order them to be killed. They seem an insult to humanity."[38] Spender returned to Spain in the spring of 1936 (just before the war began) for another vacation. During this trip, however, he wrote letters to Christopher Isherwood condemning Europeans who denigrate Spaniards as "niggers" and noting that the "British [consuls] talk about the Spaniards, and particularly the Catalans, as though they were Colonists talking about the natives."[39] This dramatic shift from callous racism to anti-imperialist rhetoric that condemns his own government registers an early point at which Spender begins a sympathetic identification with the oppressed in Spain. His interest, during the second trip, in the "politics . . . and . . . artistic movements" of the country led him to Lorca's work, thanks to an introduction by the Catalan writer and translator Marià Manent. Lorca was the reigning star of this generation of Spanish poets, and Spender, his Spanish now being proficient, made his first attempts to translate him. He wrote to Isherwood, "I like what I can understand of the poems by Lorca ... [they are] really very beautiful. ... I would like to understand [them] better than I do at present."[40] He then recommended (unsuccessfully) to Eliot that Faber publish a book of Lorca's work.

Spender traveled to Spain twice during the war. First, in 1937, he was sent by the CPGB as a reporter, and he wrote somewhat propagandistic articles on the Republic's battle and its ideology. He called the Republic the product of a "social revolution," one against the "common enemy ... [of] property," and characterized the war as "class war played out on an international scale, in which the small capitalist class is backed by international imperialism against the democratic will of at least eighty percent of the Spanish people."[41] Spender then argued in *Forward from Liberalism* (1937) that "we must give our fullest support to the actions of the Spanish Popular Front without blinding ourselves to the fact that excesses in Spain are inevitable ... [in order to prevent] a similar conflict ... in England."[42] This "responsibility" means that the individualism of liberal democracy was trumped by communism, for the moment at least, because of the latter's more resolute commitment to fighting fascism. Spender's most formative trip, however, came when he returned for the final time during the war as part of a delegation that included Auden, Edgell Rickword, Ralph Bates, and others bound for the Second International Congress of Writers for the Defense of Culture in Valencia and Madrid in July 1937, over which José Bergamín presided. The conference aimed to show solidarity among writers and artists from more than 30 countries with the embattled Republic. Spender made a speech that eulogized the British writers who now lay alongside Lorca, who had been executed one month into the war: Ralph Fox, Christopher Caudwell, and John Cornford, who are his country's leaders in the "movement to support Spanish democracy." Spender also declares that English writers fighting there, such as Bates and Tom Wintringham, are "ties between ourselves and the dead" in Spain, while the Spaniard Miguel Hernández is an "international comrade," one who merits fame for being "a soldier of civilization and the moving and profound poet of this war." Spender's anti-capitalist polemic concludes that "Spain has shown the world that there is a moral way" for poets and intellectuals to fight "fascist crime."[43]

Elaborating on these cross-cultural ties, Spender reflected that the Congress "enabled writers from abroad to become acquainted with the varied, fantastic, paradoxical, subtle, and yet passionately simple Spanish poets and writers" including Alberti, Antonio Machado, José Bergamín (who was "a little like" E. M. Forster), and "perhaps most astonishing of all—the young soldier-poet of Madrid, Miguel Hernández."[44] The new relationship between poetry and politics in Republican

Spain that the Generation of '27 strove to create, through their adaptations of "pure" poetic styles from Góngora and fusions of the stylistics of the European avant-garde works with popular and folk forms, now were directed toward the fight against fascism. Poems protesting or lamenting Lorca's murder crystallized such work. At the Congress, Spender not only heard these, but also saw productions of Lorca's plays. Each delegate was given copies of over 300 *romances* written about the war by Spanish poets, collected in the *Romancero de la guerra civil* (edited by Altolaguirre).[45] The *romance*—not to be confused with its English cognate, but rather, a form of ballad in eight-syllable lines with assonant rhyming on even-numbered lines—had been revived by the poets of '27, and Lorca's *Romancero Gitano* [*Gypsy Ballads*, 1928] was at the center of this movement. Ramón Menéndez Pidal had recently and influentially claimed that *romances*, having developed out of late medieval adaptations of the epic song, were integral to the Spanish poetic tradition from the Golden Age to the Baroque Era. They became a popular form for hymns of resistance among the Republicans, who produced thousands upon thousands of them during the war.[46] In the glimpse of the poetic Spain that Spender gained at the Congress, the seeds of his *Poems for Spain* are visible: international solidarity against fascism, *romances*, Lorca's figure. His emerging anger over the politicization of Lorca's figure is visible, too, however; he makes the point that "to say that those who happen to be killed are heroes is a wicked attempt to identify the dead with the abstract ideas which have brought them to the front, thus adding prestige to those ideas, which are used to lead the living on to similar 'heroic' deaths." "Shortly before he died," Spender adds, "the poet García Lorca is reported to have said that he would write in time of war the poetry of those who hate war," not those of any partisan or ideological cause.[47]

The Congress was also where Spender first met Manuel Altolaguirre, "one of [his] best friends in Spain," who made an impression on him by presenting him, just after their first meeting, with his 11-volume set of the 1786 Shakespeare, inscribed "*A mi querido camarada Spender, con profunda gratitud por su visita a España*" ["To my dear comrade Spender, with deep gratitude for your visit to Spain"].[48] This gesture of a Spaniard giving an Englishman a valuable collection of books by the greatest English writer (with an inscription in Spanish) epitomizes Altolaguirre's cross-cultural vision of literature. Spender came to understand the domestic and cultural politics of the Spanish war more concretely through his time with Altolaguirre, who had lost two brothers already to the war. The Spanish poet had written a lament for Lorca, his friend since childhood, and as a demonstration of the persistence of poetry, he had reissued his own collection of poems *Las islas invitadas* [*The Invited Islands*, 1926] in the early days of the war. Spender enjoyed reading Altolaguirre's work, and as their friendship developed, he offered refuge at his house in England during the war to the Spaniard, who declined and fled to Mexico, then to Cuba, and tried unsuccessfully to revive *1616* in Latin America.[49] Altolaguirre helped Spender in his effort to secure the release of his former lover Tony Hyndman from a Republican jail, where he was being held for having deserted the International Brigades.

These experiences shaped the collaborative relationship between Altolaguirre and Spender. Shortly after their meeting, Altolaguirre initiated their literary transactions by publishing Spender's speech from the Congress, then translating four of his leftist poems from the early 1930s for a new journal that he helped found, *Hora de España* [*Spain's Moment*].[50] Spender returned the favor by translating several of Altolaguirre's poems for British periodicals before including them in *Poems for Spain*. Finally, Altolaguirre revisited his appreciation of the Romantics—while linking them to the Second Republic at war—when, in 1938, he published in *Hora de España* Stanley Richardson and Luis Cernuda's translations of two of Wordsworth's Spanish sonnets, "The Oak of Guernica" and "Indignation of a High-Minded Spaniard" (both 1810).[51] The former, which appeals for the defense of "Ancient Biscay's liberty" for which the famous tree stands, was apposite to the moment, as the Nationalists had just bombed Guernica in 1937, prompting Picasso's famous painting. The latter sonnet depicts Napoleon as the "Tyrant," much as Woolf did, who seeks to break the "bands" of the Spanish people, to "speak" for them, and to foster a "future day /When our enlightened minds shall bless his sway," and who was reincarnated by Franco.

New Writing and *Poems for Spain*: Translation, Sympathy, and Solidarity

Now with a solid knowledge of the Spanish language and the country's leading young writers (one of whom he now knew very well), Spender sought to enact his sense that the futures of the Auden Generation and the Generation of '27 were one and the same, and that they were under threat in Spain. Upon returning home, he noted that John Lehmann's journal *New Writing*, which had been launched in early 1936, might provide a forum for his efforts to sustain from abroad the endangered voices and cultural work of his Spanish contemporaries. Lehmann had declared in his opening manifesto that *New Writing* would not "open its pages to writers of reactionary or Fascist sentiments," but would be "independent of any political party. . . . [and would] represent the work of writers from colonial and foreign countries," including France, Russia, China, and Spain.[52] He envisioned *New Writing* as "a new life breathing through the old," simultaneously establishing both continuity and difference across literary generations.[53]

Once the Spanish war broke out, Lehmann saw that for himself and his colleagues, "all our fears, our confused hopes and beliefs, our half-formulated theories and imaginings, veered and converged toward [the war's] testing and its opportunity, like steel filings that slide towards a magnet suddenly put near them." The third issue of *New Writing*, for instance, was dedicated to Ralph Fox, a founder of the CPGB, who had been killed recently in Spain. The review had a vital cause as a journal of "a new international literature;" it would, Lehmann wrote,

> become the place where whatever imaginative writing came out of the Spanish experience should naturally be published. . . . I soon began to hear not only of what famous authors such as [Ramón] Sender, Alberti and Bergamín were writing, but also of the *Romances of the Civil War*, that extraordinary outburst of lyrics on themes of the day, which poets all over Republican Spain were writing. I wanted to get the best of these translated as soon as possible, . . . [and] almost every English writer whose sympathies were engaged on the Republican side seemed to be burning to tackle them[:] . . . V. S. Pritchett, Stephen Spender, Inez Pern, . . . Nancy Cunard, [and] A. L. Lloyd.[54]

Translations, Lehmann believed, could bring authentic voices of "the Spanish experience" to England, where few had been translated and others risked being lost in the "interval of history."[55] *New Writing* thus printed, "side by side with poems and stories . . . from [British] writers," translations of a number of works by Spanish poets, including Lorca, Alberti, Miguel Hernández, Rafael Dieste, and César Arconada.[56]

Lehmann was especially impressed by Spender's translations of those "Spanish poets who were working in the common cause." Furthermore, Lehmann saw the potential of reading Lorca as an emblem of a united Spanish Republican literary movement that the journal could transmit in its work for this "common cause." Lehmann writes that Lorca "belonged to no political party," but rather, his assassination made him "a symbol for all the other writers of Spain, and many poems were composed as laments for his death." Lehmann's distinction is critical: Lorca represents "no political party," but rather "all the other writers of Spain."[57] Thus, while the war was raging, *New Writing* claimed Lorca for its cause while presenting a stereophony of British and Spanish voices supporting the Republic. Spender shared this belief that Lorca was a popular, not an ideological, poet whose execution was a portent of fascist aggression against poetry per se. In this sense, the Republic's cause was a poetic cause, a cause to which Spender, who by now was moving further away from communism and toward liberal socialism, could stake his own poetic profile in Britain and in Spain.

When Lehmann became a partner in the Hogarth Press with Leonard Woolf in April 1938, he would use it to publish the volume *Poems for Spain* that he and Spender were now planning. The Spanish *romanceros* [collections of ballads], the American volume of poems . . . *And Spain Sings* (1937), and Nancy Cunard's pamphlets *Les poètes du monde défendent le peuple espagnol!* (printed simultaneously in English, French, and Spanish in 1937) were models for their work. . . . *And Spain Sings* presents American writers' translations of "Fifty Loyalist Ballads," drawn mostly from the journal *El Mono Azul* [*Blue Overalls*] and written by Spanish authors who saw Spain as "the defender of Western civilization."[58] But neither the *romanceros* nor . . . *And Spain Sings* did the type of cross-cultural work that both Spender and Altolaguirre valued: neither featured original poems about Spain by Anglophone poets juxtaposed with works by their Spanish peers. With this task in mind, Spender and Lehmann gathered poems by mostly British and Spanish writers from *New Writing*, the *New Statesman and Nation*, the *Left Review*, and *Volunteer for Liberty*, the magazine of the International Brigades. Spender also solicited and translated several new ones. His introduction frames *Poems for Spain* as a "document of our times" of "poems written from *inside* Spain" that presents not the best poems (which is true—the quality is uneven), but those that arise from the "experience" of the Spanish war.[59] Spender believes that in contrast to "the rest of Europe, . . . poets and poetry have played a considerable part in the Spanish War, because to many people the struggle of the Republicans has seemed a struggle for the conditions without which the writing and reading of poetry are almost impossible in modern society." "Modern society" here includes both Spain and England: any concession to fascism abroad is a concession at home, Spender believes. He asserts that this same "struggle" to "obtain freedom, education, [and] leisure" has produced poems that serve, like Wilfred Owen's did, as "a warning that it is necessary for civilization to defend and renew itself" in Spain, in England, and across Europe (*PS* 9, 7–8). Backing away from his earlier positions on the war, Spender's evolving view of the battle in Spain and his evolving political commitments lead him to recast Spain's war as one for "civilization" (an assertion that is left vague) and for the political foundations of poetics and free expression—the "future of writing," as David Callahan puts it.[60]

The "hope" that saving Spain may save European civilization, Spender claims, "has expressed itself not only in English poetry, but in poems of many languages" (*PS* 9). The Republic's cause is thus pluralistic and is taken up beyond its borders; it "represents pure tragedy," and Lorca's death was the emblem of its poetry.

Spender characterizes the Republic as democratic, too, when he writes that the "poets of the English Liberal tradition responded to Spain crushed by Napoleon as they do to contemporary Spain crushed by Fascism." He follows this statement by reprinting Wordsworth's sonnet "Indignation of a High-Minded Spaniard"—the same poem that Altolaguirre had just published in translation in *Hora de España*, and the author to whom Lehmann would compare Spender in 1940. For Spender, "public policy and poetry" merge in moments of crisis like the one that his Romantic forebears witnessed. "Auden's *Spain* is in the tradition of Wordsworth's Sonnets on Spain," he adds, a poem inspired by "fundamental, political and moral ideas of liberty, justice, [and] freedom" (*PS* 9, 10). Poetry should not *always* be political or committed, that is, but it must be when the stakes are so dramatic. He shares with Altolaguirre a goal of reviving this past era of Anglo-Spanish sympathy.

Spender widens his view when he writes of contemporary Spanish poets who have,

> with few exceptions, . . . supported the Republic, because they defend the spoken Castilian and Catalan and Basque word against the unified centralized speech or against the foreign tongue; they defend their own lives whose fate under Fascism is foretold in the murder of García Lorca; they defend a government which makes the exercise of their tradition of a popular romantic Spanish poetry possible (*PS* 13).

Spender's argument thus focuses on the autonomy of Spanish poetry and provincial languages under the Republican government, on mobilizing British poetry more than British soldiers for the cause against dictatorial appropriations of the arts. He also describes Lorca's relationship with the Republic as one in which the government facilitated his craft and he spread the cultural work of the Republic. Still hopeful about the defeat of Franco, Spender continues to internationalize the volume's themes, noting that the "long, crushing, and confused process of defeat, which the democratic principle has been undergoing, has been challenged in Spain, and this challenge has aroused hope all over the world . . . [that] . . . has expressed itself . . . [in] poetry."[61] Spender's vision of himself as a collector, translator, and disseminator of this poetry coalesces here with his vision of his and Lehmann's colleagues as poets of a new European generation.

The contents of *Poems for Spain* are heterogeneous in form, content, and politics: there are ballads, sonnets, songs, traditional quatrains, free verse, grotesque imagistic poems of death and disease, elegies for the dead (individuals and anonymous), first-person narratives and pleas for action, reconstructions of Spanish history, symbolic explorations, and Auden's distinctive "Spain," in the center of the book. The volume is not ideologically uniform either, with Cornford's dogmatic communism, Altolaguirre's populism, and Herbert Read's anarchism all represented, but the anti-fascism and pro-Republicanism of all poets are readily apparent. *Poems for Spain* is divided into six sections—Action, Death, The Map, Satire, Romances, Lorca—and represents a cross-section of British figures including Spender, Auden, Day-Lewis, MacNeice, Read, Rex Warner, Sylvia Townsend Warner, and Edgell Rickword, and Spanish writers Altolaguirre, Miguel Hernández, Antonio Agraz, Leopoldo Urrutia de Luis, José Herrera Petere, and Pedro Garfias. Stanley Richardson (from *1616*) also contributes, as do Pablo Neruda, veterans of the Spanish war Tony Hyndman and Tom Wintringham, and the Irish poet Charles Donnelly, who was killed in the war in 1937. The arrangement of the works forges an immediate connection between Britons who died in Spain (Cornford and Fox especially) and Lorca as tragic figures of the anti-fascist cause. The first juxtaposition, in fact, is a poem by Cornford with one by Hernández, "Hear This Voice" (translated by Spender and Pern). Hernández was still alive, though he had been arrested before the war broke out and was stuck hopelessly in prison, where he eventually died in 1942—as this text seems eerily to forecast.

Spender-as-translator thus places himself between a fallen compatriot of his poetic generation and an imprisoned Spanish colleague—as he will place his poetic ego between those of his British and Spanish peers throughout the volume. On two different occasions, he pairs his voice with Altolaguirre's by printing his own poems next to those of his Spanish colleague whose poems he translated, making Altolaguirre an unofficial collaborator on *Poems for Spain*. The first of these two occurs when Spender follows Altolaguirre's "I Demand the Ultimate Death" with his own "Regum Ultima Ratio" (later changed to "Ultima Ratio Regum") (*PS* 31). In addition to the philological connection between "Ultimate" and "Ultima," the two poems both make moral arguments against fascism by focusing on the death of an individual, not of masses of people. Playing on "ultimate" further, Spender writes bleakly in his first lines that "The guns spell money's ultimate reason /In letters of lead on the spring hill-side."

Romances, Lorca, and the Fall of the Republic

Calls for support and intervention, such as Auden's "Spain," fill the middle sections of *Poems for Spain*, voicing alternately optimism, despair, disgust, or propagandistic condemnation. Rex Warner's "The Tourist Looks at Spain"—the source of the pithy claim of transnational identification "In Spain is Europe. England also is in Spain"—wryly twists a slogan of the British tourism industry ("See Spain and see the world") into a claim that Spain's war represents the world's war, for "it is us too they defended who defended Madrid" (*PS* 66, 69). Building on this sentiment, the final two sections of *Poems for Spain* do the most work to authorize its representation of Spanish voices in an English-language text for mostly British readers. "Romances" gathers 17 ballads and adaptations by Spanish and British authors alike. Keeping alive this ballad form and transporting it to Britain, *Poems for Spain* first features Antonio Agraz's bucolic, populist ballad "In the Sweat of Thy Brow," which tells of a mother and son working in the fields. It is complemented by Day-Lewis's "Bombers," which includes the imperative to its reader, "Choose between your child and this fatal embryo [of the aerial bomber]. /Shall your guilt bear arms, and [your] sons . . . /haunt the houses you never built?" (*PS* 83). Spender and Altolaguirre are paired again in this section, when Spender's "Port Bou" precedes Altolaguirre's lament "My Brother Luis." (The two poems, however, do not share much in common.)

In contrast, another of Spender's loose attempts at a *romance*, "Fall of a City," pairs "FOX and LORCA claimed as history on the walls /Are now angrily deleted" (*PS* 86). Drawing on the same sense of "delet[ion]" that he employs in "At Castellón," as well as on Lehmann's fear that Spanish poetry would be lost to the "interval of history," Spender seeks to ingrain in popular and historical memory the names of a British writer and a Spanish poet who had died at the hands of Spanish fascists. Later, Altolaguirre's final contribution, "Madrid," is paired with a memorializing work by a colleague of Spender's, MacNeice's "Remembering Spain." "I can evoke nothing," writes the Spaniard in the former, "There is no absence, no legend, no hope /to calm my agony with its illusion" (*PS* 96). MacNeice's sprawling journey through Spain's geography and cultural landmarks presents the country through a Briton's eyes, ending with the narrator's heading home by boat and "forgetting Spain, not realizing /That Spain would soon denote /Our grief, our aspirations."[62] Between these two pairs, José Herrera Petere's "Against the Cold in the Mountains" (translated by A. L. Lloyd) and Pedro Garfias's "Single Front" (translated by Tom Wintringham) round out the section of *Poems for Spain* that contains the most Spanish contributors.

The final section of *Poems for Spain*, "Lorca," includes three poems dedicated to the fallen poet, whose figure already pervades the contributions from various Spanish poets throughout the collection. Geoffrey Parsons's amateurish lament "Lorca" blames fascist anti-intellectualism for Lorca's murder, then writes that the poet "merges with Spain" and embodies its people (*PS* 104). Jacob Bronowski's "The Death of García Lorca" reads Lorca through the poet's own figures—gypsies, tricksters, gunmen, picadors— and also claims him as a fallen poet of the oppressed in

Spain, arguing that Britons share in his "cause / of the grinding mill and the crowded house" (*PS* 105). Finally, Leopoldo Urrutia de Luis's "Romancero a la Muerte de García Lorca" (translated by Sylvia Townsend Warner), one of the hundreds of poems written by Spaniards in honor of the murdered poet, imagines Death stalking Lorca throughout Granada, "your old, your gipsy-coloured town" (*PS* 106). With invocations of Lorca's poetic style and repetitions of "Ay, Federico García"— recalling Lorca's signature untranslatable expression "Ay de mí"—this *romance* captures the sort of addresses to nature and to the sea that Lorca employed throughout his works. "Ay, Federico García," the poem concludes, "Death is here, is here! / All Granada has seen it.... / But Federico García / They took by a surprise" (*PS* 108). Only two months later, Spender will continue and expand this brief tribute by attaching his own poetic reputation to Lorca's.

The production and reception of *Poems for Spain*, however, left Spender's task unfinished. His and Lehmann's plans for the collection were delayed, and the two editors did not work well together. Spender, whose troubled marriage would end in the summer of 1939, was working on multiple projects at the time, and was moving away from his hope that poetry could foster social change and toward an introspective, contemplative style of writing. Furthermore, in December 1938, the British Battalion of the International Brigades returned to England, with over 500 members having died in Spain, resigned to Franco's imminent victory. Thus, what was initially conceived as a "militant volume," as John Sutherland writes, was not published until March 1939, just weeks before Franco declared victory on 1 April. (Spender's introduction, likely composed close to publication, indeed is far more "apolitical" than "militant.") Sales were poor, and a review in the *New Statesman and Nation* called it "alas, a valedictory work."[63] J. H. Willis sees the collection as "an elegy for a lost cause, a posthumous memorial volume, and not the stirring call to arms suggested by the title."[64] In retrospect, this timing seems to recast the memorials and laments in *Poems for Spain* as requiems not only for fallen brethren, but also for the Republic.

The Spanish Cause, Through Lorca

Even as it failed in its ostensible purpose, *Poems for Spain* presented a united international group of poets writing against fascism (and it did so without distorting in translation the political messages of any poems). It also focused Spender more acutely on the relationship between his own poetics and politics and those of Lorca, who remains to most Anglo- and Hispanophone readers alike the best-known cultural symbol of Republican Spain. Before his assassination, Lorca's reputation had been growing slowly but steadily in England, though he did not yet have the standing that Ortega enjoyed. Like his other Generation of '27 colleagues, he published his poetry in the *Revista de Occidente* and his *Romancero Gitano* through its press; he attended Ortega's lectures and *tertulias*; and he was influenced by writers such as Eliot. Alongside his friends from the Residencia Luis Buñuel and Salvador Dalí, Lorca gained attention in Europe and South America as a leader of Spain's new poetry. J. B. Trend was among the first to introduce his works to Anglophone audiences in the 1920s, and though the *Criterion* remained more interested in Ortega, Marichalar had discussed Lorca and their poetic colleagues for some time.[65] Several of Lorca's poems appeared in translation in British and American periodicals in the mid-1930s, and soon A. L. Lloyd called him, in a review, the leading "avant-garde poet in Spain."[66]

The necessary question for all of Lorca's translators and reviewers to answer was how to characterize his Hispanicity and, by extension, his place in European letters. The influences on his works—which ranged from *El Cid* to the *cante jondo*, Greek theater to the Baroque of Góngora, Cuban idioms to Whitman's odes—provided no simple genealogy. For Lorca, the essence of Spain lies in the syncretistic history and population of Andalusia. In other words, the local is by definition global in its composition. Lorca famously proclaimed his cosmopolitan attachments through this history by stating that "I believe that being from Granada inclines me to a sympathetic understanding of the persecuted, gypsies, Jews, blacks, . . . the Moorishness that all of us hold within."[67] He elaborated shortly before his death that "I am completely a Spaniard, and it would be impossible for me to live outside my geographical boundaries; but I hate the man who is a Spaniard only to be nothing more. I am a brother to everybody and I despise the man who sacrifices himself for an abstract nationalist idea only to love his country with a bandage over his eyes."[68] This sense of "Moorishness" also led him to experiment with a variety of poetic forms of Arabic (and sometimes Persian) origins, including the *ghazal* and the *qasida*. Most relevant to Spender's translations, though, are Lorca's *romances*, which he infused with Flamenco rhythms and Andalusian folklore and vernacular. In both cases, Lorca creates cosmopolitan identifications and literary styles at once by integrating the traditions of the marginalized.

Lorca's attempts to capture the sounds and styles of the oppressed or forgotten fit with the Second Republic's cultural programs. He co-directed the theater troupe La Barraca, funded by the new Ministry of Public Education, but his works were never partisan or dogmatic.[69] (With a sense of his own mutable figure, he claimed, "I am an anarchist, communist, libertarian, Catholic, traditionalist, and monarchist."[70])

His associations with the regime criminalized him in the eyes of the Francoists, however, and Lorca was lured out of his home and assassinated by Falangist paramilitaries in August 1936. Few could believe that such an outrageous murder had taken place, even given the Nationalists' strident opposition to the Republic's intellectual and artistic cultures, but after it was confirmed, Ian Gibson writes, "almost overnight Lorca became a Republican martyr" to leftists around the world.[71] The soldiers of the International Brigades "took Lorca into their kitbags, and thence back to Paris, Moscow, London, Boston, Havana," Robert Stradling notes; meanwhile, the Nationalists burned his books.[72] The *Times*, in a sympathetic moment, called the outrage over Lorca's death an emblem of the Spanish people's "defiance" and their desire for democracy in Spain, adding that "no modern writer better than he has been able to express the rising popular enthusiasm for liberty" there.[73]

But just as understandings of the Republic's "cause" were multiple, diverging critical and translational portraits of Lorca soon multiplied in Britain and the United States. Spender recalls in his autobiography his particular resentment toward communist critics in the 1930s who sought to make Lorca's assassination a call to arms for their revolution. This charge, in fact, is often made in accounts from this decade, and however greatly it might have existed informally and in conversation, the written record of that effort presents a complicated case. The CPGB's *Daily Worker* ran a story, "Fascists Murder Poet," which noted that "Spain's leading poet and dramatist Federico Garcia Lorka [sic]" was executed, then aligned his murder with those of a French journalist and a cartoonist from a Spanish communist paper as evidence of Fascist hatred of culture.[74] A few days later, A. L. Lloyd, a communist and a collector of folk songs, published in the *Daily Worker* "Spain's Poet Whom Fascism Killed," in which he calls Lorca's death an "immeasurable loss to the modern literature of Europe," not merely of Spain. He stresses that Lorca is "not a martyr, . . . not a Communist, not a Red," but rather a poet who was religious and was interested in folklore. He does characterize Lorca as a "comrade," a "fellow-fighter" who supported the Spanish Republic and endorsed Alberti's communist poetry, but his claims go no further.[75] Rickword's *Left Review*, which was not officially tied to the CPGB but published mostly communist critics and writers, also published a short essay by Lloyd, "Lorca: Poet of Spain." Here, Lloyd characterizes Lorca as a "lamb" murdered by wild "black pigs" and writes that "the finest and proudest poet in Spain . . . was dragged through the walled streets of Granada to face the Fascist firing squad." (Lloyd's description of the fascists as "black pigs" recalls the racist undertone of Woolf and her colleagues' public letter, "The Vortex in Spain.") Lloyd claims that Lorca is Spain's greatest poet since Góngora, and that "it is probably because Spanish poets have a vital popular tradition on which to draw, that they alone of European poets are able to write verse of a high literary quality which is, at the same time, popularly accessible, easily understood by all." But in contrast to Alberti, who is "now the foremost *revolutionary* poet" of the communist cause in Spain, Lorca was a poet of the Andalusian people and their culture:

> Small wonder that Lorca's hatred of the great landlords who kept the peasants in such want was only exceeded by his deep sympathy for the oppressed people of Spain. . . . And now Lorca, one of the greatest poets in Europe, is dead, murdered by the representatives of those same landlords and their class.[76]

Lloyd thus positions Lorca as both regional and universal, Spanish and European, and though not a communist, specifically anti-bourgeoisie.

Lorca's death prompted an almost immediate spate of translations, and here, Spender's battle for authority on Spain and on Lorca and his charges against communist critics both take shape. Lloyd was the first to publish a small collection of translations, *Lament for the Death of a Bullfighter* (1937), further circulating his vision of Lorca, which Spender would revise. The collection includes only six poems; depending on the publisher and edition, they are printed either in English only or in both English and Spanish. Its dust jacket calls Lorca "the national poet of Spain," but stresses that he was an "unpolitical person and a Catholic" who was killed by "insurgents." Lloyd writes in the preface that Lorca "will live when future generations have forgotten Franco." The volume includes a portrait of Lorca with his signature below to assert its version of authority. Lloyd's preface for the Oxford edition, an extension of his essay from the *Left Review*, depicts Lorca again as a Christ-like sacrificial "lamb" murdered by fascist "black pigs." His "murder" not only left Spanish poetry the worse, but also represented a "profound loss . . . [for] European literature."[77] In the version published that same year by Heinemann, Lloyd's preface is more polemical. Writing that Lorca's "appeal goes far beyond the frontiers of Spain and the tight little knot of modern-poetry lovers," Lloyd claims that "he was already one of the great poets of our century, and perhaps the most universal of all." And while he does not claim him for communism specifically, he now speaks of Lorca's "martyrdom" at the hands of "fascists." The poems that Lloyd translates are suggestive; he includes two, for instance, that depict the infamous Spanish Civil Guard and its reckless brutality against the rural, minority population ("Ballad of the Spanish Civil Guard" and "The Arrest of Antoñito El Camborio on the Road to Seville"). The Heinemann edition has "Ballad" lead the collection, and Lloyd's preface calls the Civil Guard the "symbol of black repressive Spain."

(In contrast, this poem is absent from Spender and Gili's volume of Lorca's poems.) Lloyd also includes a lament for a bullfighter ("Lament for Ignacio Sánchez Mejías"), and "The Martyrdom of Saint Eulalia," by which he means to comment indirectly on Lorca's murder.[78]

As the rhetorical battle over Lorca's image grew, the *Left Review*, several months after having published Lloyd's essay, posed a set of questions about how to interpret Lorca's death:

> Lorca was never a political thinker, but a poet of folk-lore and the countryside. Are not these lives too precious to be poured out so generously? . . . It may seem inhuman to [print Antonio] Machado's poem against Lorca's death, but is the reward indeed so poor when that elegy lives in the mouths of men? Is the word, the idea, 'hero,' indeed so suspect?[79]

No clear answers came. In the only *Criterion* review of Lorca's work, Edwin Muir discusses Lloyd's translations alongside new books by Pound, MacNeice, Auden, and Rex Warner, placing Lorca in the literary-political context of these Anglophone writers—the final three being part of Spender's generation. He notes that

> Lorca seems to have been the best living poet until Franco's followers executed him last year. Their reason for doing so cannot be discovered from this book, for Lorca seems to have been a traditional poet and a Catholic. Mr. Lloyd's introduction does not help us much to understand him. . . . Perhaps Franco approved of the Moorish note in practical politics, but not in literature. These poems do have something Oriental or African in their incandescent imagery.

Condemning the "act of stupid hatred" that ended Lorca's life, Muir's review typifies the centrist-conservative attempts to highlight Lorca's "traditional" poetry, his Catholicism, and his abstruse but apolitical imagism.[80]

In the other prominent review of Lloyd's translations that took up the question of Lorca's significance for contemporary Britons, V. S. Pritchett, who had met Lorca while studying at the Residencia, similarly sees Lloyd's volume as bringing out the "primitive" yet complex elements of Spanish and Andalusian culture in Lorca's poetry. Reading the war and Spanish poetry together as Spender did, he writes in the *New Statesman and Nation* that "it seems to have been no accident that the modern revival of that kind of ballad in Spain should have preceded the rising of the Spanish people against treachery above and invasion from abroad."[81] The flourishing of the Spanish arts, he suggests, was a response to a fascist invasion and a defense of autonomous traditions. Spender, in his own short review, also praised Lorca (and to a lesser degree Lloyd) for his "strong and original imagery, . . . mastery of a simple narrative style, . . . and . . . a magic which is perhaps the rarest of all qualities in lyric poetry."[82] The meaning of Lorca's death, the political and/or cultural causes of the Republic, and the relation of both to contemporary British writing, however, remained very much in the air in the politicized literary culture of the late 1930s.

The Logic of Attachment: Spender, Lorca, and Spain's European Fate

In the context of these claims, Spender and Gili's collection of Lorca's *Poems*, an unofficial companion volume to *Poems for Spain*, appeared as the most capacious publication of the poet's work to date. It appeared in May 1939, two months after *Poems for Spain* and one month after the civil war's end, making it an implicit statement of defiance against the Franco regime that had murdered the poet and would suppress his writings for decades, but not an endorsement of the now-lost Republican cause.[83] Rather, the timing further identified Lorca with Spender, whose own collection *The Still Centre*, which includes all of his contributions to *Poems for Spain* plus six others on Spain, was published that same month. As the final element of his effort to gather cultural capital domestically on "Spain" through his reporting, editing, translating, and reviewing, Spender staked his reading of the war to his representation of Lorca's figure and works.

Spender wanted his work with the Catalan translator and publisher J. L. Gili to do much more to authorize its "Lorca" across its 140 pages than Lloyd's slim volume had. Only two poems overlap between the two collections, and Spender and Gili's contains nearly 40 poems and songs from across all of Lorca's poetic and dramatic oeuvre, including his then-unpublished *Poeta en Nueva York*, whereas five of the six that Lloyd translated came from *Gypsy Ballads* alone. Spender and Gili's volume also includes a frontispiece portrait of Lorca and facsimiles of a handwritten draft of one of his poems and of his crayon sketch of Our Lady of the Seven Dolours. The first edition was also bilingual, printing the Spanish originals and English translations on facing pages, with only Spanish titles in the table of contents. Key to the volume's work, however, is the contribution of Rafael Martínez Nadal, a friend of Lorca's who selected the poems and wrote the introduction. Spender's collaborators were comfortable in helping him transmit to English-language readers the most "authentic" Lorca yet seen: Martínez Nadal had lectured with Altolaguirre at King's College, while Gili had published in magazines such as the *Bookman* on

Catalan literature. For Spender, then, the act of translation is not an appropriation, nor is it merely a vehicle for communicating a message; it is a symbiotic practice to which the translator attaches his vision of his own relationship to the poet being translated. In this case, it is the culmination of Spender's work to make visible the fact that his transnational poetics—and those of the Auden Generation—were the poetics of his Spanish peers, too.

Martínez Nadal's lengthy introduction—itself the most robust portrait of Lorca that had appeared in English—does a good deal of literary-historical work to shape this reading of the fallen poet. Even if Lloyd, the *Daily Worker*, and the *Left Review* had stopped short of politicizing Lorca's death for the communist cause, they had stepped too close to such a reading, Spender, Gili, and Martínez Nadal imply. Lloyd especially was a foil against which these three could characterize their "Lorca" separately from any communist context. Stating that "in this book is to be found in embryo almost the whole of Lorca's world," Martínez Nadal characterizes the young Federico as a timid child absorbed in local folklore that gave a "profoundly Andalusian" element to his writing. But this Andalusianism is not a limit to Lorca's art; rather, influenced by the *modernistas*, the Generation of '14 poets, his friend Manuel de Falla, Greek theater, and much more, Lorca found his artistic voice, Martínez Nadal writes, by distinguishing himself with a "tendency to exaggerate his 'Granadismo.'" Having been present for Lorca's rise to fame, Martínez Nadal stresses that Lorca was Catholic, liberal, and not a political poet, but a "popular" poet in both senses of the term—and one who traveled around the country to bring his art to Spain's most impoverished areas to revive the forgotten forms in works like *Gypsy Ballads*, the "most widely-read book of Spanish poetry in the present century." By writing in Galician and in Catalan, too, Martínez Nadal asserts, Lorca identified himself with all of Spain, fusing diverse folk forms with classical Spanish literature and theater throughout his work. He was thus at once a poet *sui generis* and "a concentration of essential Spanish elements in a perpetual state of eruption." He represents, in other words, a cosmopolitan Spain that cannot be reduced to provincial categories.[84]

Lorca's poetry is quintessentially Spanish—a quality that proves the most difficult to translate for foreign readers. "Spain is from many points of view, a world apart," Martínez Nadal writes, "and an attempt to transfer, in Lorca's most Spanish of poetry, Spanish values of men and things meets with an almost insurmountable barrier."[85] The "Spain" represented by Lorca and his work, much like the "cultural heritage of Spain" that Spender saw in Ortega's work, must matter profoundly to its European neighbors, both for cultural and military reasons. He envisions Lorca as an embodiment of a Spain whose quest for popular democracy was halted brutally by fascist aggression, and he attributes any reading of Lorca as an "ex-officio Marxist saint" to the communists' "profoundly hypocritical attitude" toward literature, past and present.[86] Martínez Nadal quotes Lorca's claim that "I am an anarchist, communist, libertarian, Catholic, traditionalist, and monarchist" to make the point that the poet was dismayed to see "his name . . . skillfully traded on for political purposes" within Spain. His death actually bespeaks the "the latent tragedy of Spain" that had been building at least since the contentious and polarizing elections of 1934. Yet Lorca has been called unjustly an "extremist" and a "dangerous agitator" in the British media, Martínez Nadal writes. He chides the British left for distorting Lorca's reputation after his death, writing that "no less to be censured is the tendentiousness of certain English circles, who seek to . . . [use] Lorca's name for purposes of propaganda . . . [or to] disfigure the poet for political ends."[87] The fallen Republic—in fact, the cause of Spanish democracy—is noticeably absent from this volume in a way that greatly contrasts the Congress, where Lorca was the ubiquitous symbol for the endangered government. Instead, Lorca represents, for all of the writers involved in *Poems*, the extermination of Spanish poetry and culture.

Spender's identification with Lorca was not an automatic fit. His and Gili's translations are, as critics both at the time and now have noted, adequate, but too literal, sometimes awkward or inaccurate.[88] Spender misses some of the sonic and musical elements of Lorca's poetry that Lloyd, for instance, conveys much better, but it is difficult to discern any politics operating at all in the translations themselves other than Lorca's generic populism. In a review that best reflects what Spender, Gili, and Martínez Nadal sought to do, Pritchett also emphasizes that Lorca was a "non-political" and "popular" writer: "Lorca's upbringing was Catholic but his mental background was liberal. . . . There is certainly nothing proletarian about Lorca."[89] Pritchett alludes to the difficulties and paradoxes that attended the project of translating Lorca, whose work could inspire "racial" sentiments in Spain that crossed the two camps at war in Spain. He praises Spender and Gili's translations, which capture the eccentricity and jarring imagery that Lorca employs— "what we call civilisation [Lorca] called slime and wire"—and appreciates Martínez Nadal's preface, calling the volume the "first really catholic introduction to [Lorca's] work." Pritchett's invocation of "catholic[icity]" here alludes to Martínez Nadal's effort to universalize the cultural politics of Lorca's work, itself deeply rooted in Catholic themes and images. The American poet Muriel Rukeyser, who was a witness to the Spanish Civil War and a translator of Spanish texts, added in a capacious review that Lorca's poems "speak to us, in a voice that reaches with an impact that only three men of his time in Europe have had for us: Lorca, Yeats,

Rilke."[90] Lorca is not merely a tragic case for Spain, then, but for Europe as well. And for Rukeyser, he is not a regional poet or even a purely Spanish poet, but has now taken his place alongside the stalwarts of the modern European canon.

Another Lorca, Another Spain: The Battle Continues

Spender said little about why he chose to work on Lorca. He was drawn to Lorca's ability to elaborate a complex symbolic schema to local traditions and to a landscape inhabited by the poor and the oppressed. Lorca, with what Spender calls a "grammar of images," also makes an implicit critique of socioeconomic systems without being dogmatic.[91] Spender did, however, revise his portraits of the poet and his identification with him—and with "Spain." This was in part an effect of his volume's having appeared not only on the heels of Lloyd's translation in 1937, but also at the same time as a translation of *Blood Wedding* in 1939, and just before *Poet in New York* (1940), a selection of plays (1941), and Edwin Honig's biography *García Lorca* (1944), the first of its kind in English. Honig, writing at the height of World War II, claims that Lorca was killed by "Fascist terrorists" who thought that he "represented the free democracy of popular Spain which they were delivering to Hitler for target practice."[92]

These characterizations and debates were part of the expansive and variegated "afterlife" that Lorca's figure has seen in Anglophone reading publics. Spender and Gili's 1943 edition of Lorca's *Poems*, published by Hogarth Press, makes a significant revision to their original by removing Martínez Nadal's introduction and replacing it with their own foreword. This slight, banal three-page sketch of Lorca's life bears little similarity to Martínez Nadal's account. It notes that Lorca came from a family of "well-to-do farmers. From [his parents] he inherited his knowledge of the countryside, and his passionate understanding of popular and traditional themes." Spender and Gili add that Lorca's "reputation is perhaps unique in European literature." Most important, their account of his death applies no blame: the "Civil War broke out, and it was shortly followed by the brutal news of his assassination. He was Spain's popular poet in the widest sense of the word, and his political crime was not in taking sides, but in being the poet most loved by the people."[93] The Spanish Civil War was four years in the past, and while World War II raged, Spender and Gili seem resigned to Franco's permanence in Spain—if not resigned to a dread that fascism could not be stopped.

After the conclusion of World War II, Spender rewrote the Republic as a European democracy, claiming that "Fox, Bell, Caudwell and Cornford were killed in this first war for democracy in Europe."[94] He strengthened this claim in his 1951 autobiography: "the role of [Fox, Caudwell, Bell, Cornford, and other Britons killed in Spain] was to be martyrs. This martyrdom was perhaps the greatest contribution made by creative writers in this decade to the spiritual life of Europe." Earlier, poets could die for a cause, but could not be martyrs. Now, apparently, Spender believes that poets *can* be considered martyrs, when the cause is free expression—a very different ideal from that which he felt communism represented in the late 1930s. He follows this claim by reprinting in his autobiography a selection from Wordsworth on the French Revolution from *The Prelude*, returning to the connection that both he and Altolaguirre had invoked. He adds that the decline of "civilization" was not a new topic,

> but that the hope of saving or transforming it had arisen [in the 1930s], combined with the positive necessity of withstanding tyrannies. . . . The fall of the Spanish Republic symbolized the end of an epoch . . . [and] the collapse of the hope that intervention by certain groups, even by individuals, could decide the fate of the first half of the twentieth century.[95]

Spender thus retreated to developing more fully the theme of isolation that he had engaged poetically since his time in Spain in the 1930s: to "state the condition of the isolated self as the universal condition of all existence," and to emphasize that "the final horror of war is the complete isolation of a man dying alone in a world whose reality is violence. The dead in wars are not heroes: they are freezing or rotting lumps of isolated insanity."[96] His expressions of sympathy with Spanish poets was aimed at ensuring that this "condition" of isolation did not silence a generation of poets in either country.

Beyond Spender, Lorca's figure has been revised continually since 1939, too, and in ways that throw into relief Spender, Gili, and Martínez Nadal's project. In his review of Lloyd's volume of translations, Pritchett also makes an uncanny remark: "[Lloyd] has kept at least to the literal which, unless the translator is a poet of genius himself, is the best thing to do. A rhetorical poet like Roy Campbell might have managed better and saved us from the anti-climaxes of translation which sometimes salvage meaning at the expense of sound."[97] That Campbell would translate Lorca was at the time unthinkable. The expatriate South African poet Campbell had been a rising star in London's literary circles, but after recoiling from Bloomsbury liberalism, he moved to Spain and converted to a reactionary form of Catholicism in Toledo in 1935. He supported the Nationalists and claimed (falsely) to have fought for Franco's forces in the civil war. Pritchett's reference to Campbell here is particularly astounding, though, in light of a passage in *Flowering*

Rifle (1939), Campbell's benumbing 5,000-line epic tribute to Franco, that, amid slanders against Jews, homosexuals, and leftists, baldly justified Lorca's murder.[98]

After World War II, however, when Campbell was still far to the right and still belligerent—he punched Spender once during a poetry reading and assaulted Geoffrey Grigson on another occasion—he began translating Lorca's poetry. Campbell first wrote in his collection *Talking Bronco* (1946) a brief satire of Lorca's previous translators, "On the Martyrdom of F. García Lorca":

> Not only did he lose his life
> By shots assassinated:
> But with a hatchet and a knife
> Was after that—translated![99]

Then, in the essay interspersed with his translations, *Lorca: An Appreciation of His Poetry* (1952), Campbell implies why he is now associating his persona as translator with Lorca's figure. He opens with jabs at his "gullible" enemies on the left who wanted to make Lorca "a martyr for communism," but now "are belatedly trying to readjust themselves to the actual world." In reality, it "is well established that Lorca had no political tub to thump," and the communists failed to make Lorca a martyr because the poet "was by birth a landowning 'kulak' and by faith a Catholic." The failure to make Lorca a martyr is, for Campbell, a symptom of the failure of communism itself.[100]

Amid numerous digressions into diatribes against Wells and Shaw, Campbell reinterprets Lorca's career by claiming that he was "intensely and nationally Spanish, though he does not express it in patriotism." His best work is local, provincial, centered on Andalusia; his worst comes when he tries to be "cosmopolitan" (as in *Poeta en Nueva York*). Campbell argues that the Catholic grandeur of Granada, Córdoba, and Seville, not the songs of outcasts and the downtrodden, inspired Lorca. Thus, he reads Lorca's work as a protest against the tendency to look beyond regional contexts to state a poet's significance, for it "is precisely because Lorca has roots in his native soil that he can teach us what we need in spite of having no 'message;' and animate other European literatures and languages, in spite of the fact that he was ignorant of them." To be European is to be true to one's local origins, Campbell writes, not to be cosmopolitan or universalist—to celebrate one's particular culture only, not to imagine oneself as part of a larger Europe. Where Spender's volume of Lorca's poems made the Spaniard an emblem for an Andalusianism that exceeded Spain and permeated Europe, Campbell restricts him to a regional-national and Catholic context. Furthermore, Campbell asserts that "the obsessional presentiment of death is pre-eminent even in Lorca's most lush and pastoral descriptions." He also dilutes the tragedy and specificity of Lorca's death: "it is to be remembered that death was very much in the air in the twenty years that preceded the Civil war." The short biographical note at the end of the volume of translations states (also incorrectly) only that Lorca's "murder was due to a private grudge" held by some fellow Granadans and that the killing was unconnected to Falange, to political assassinations, or to any other causes beyond personal relationships.[101] Instead, Campbell writes, the greatest tragedies of Spain's war were the Republican's killings en masse of priests and nuns. Campbell's translations do not twist Lorca's poems toward any particular political end, however, and are in fact well-regarded by critics—and Eliot unsuccessfully tried to publish them at Faber and Faber.[102]

The diverging attempts of British, American, South African, and many other poets to claim Lorca's figure and his heritage have not dimmed in the present. Lorca has become, Jonathan Mayhew writes, a "multicultural hero," one who "has been invoked, at one time or another, as a patron saint of anti-Fascist and anticapitalist politics, African American and gay male identities, the poetics of the new American poetry, ethnopoetics, urban working-class experience, and the Jungian-inspired deep image."[103] Spender's groundbreaking attempt, with his Spanish collaborators, to read Lorca as a poet of a cosmopolitan and European Spain stands out in this history. And while Lorca's works did not greatly influence his poetry, Spender rewrote his understanding of Spain from the late 1930s on multiple occasions over the following decades. He revised his sense of the tragedy of the Republic's fall through the stories of individual tragedies as he came to the conclusion that communism, in fact, threatened the arts as much as fascism did. The first revision was in his autobiography, in which he called the Writers' Congress, which he celebrated when attending it in 1937, a "circus" of self-righteousness that "had something about it of a Spoiled Children's Party, something which brought out the worst in many delegates." His friendship with Altolaguirre was an exception; the Spaniard was, to Spender's mind, "a little affected, like everyone, by the prevailing hysteria, but in a way which I found sympathetic."[104] He learned much about Spain from his time with Altolaguirre: he heard some members of the Spaniard's family cheer the death of other fascist relatives; he heard Altolaguirre's somewhat comical account of his flight from the civil war to join his wife and daughter, who had escaped to France; and most enduring in Spender's memory, he heard Altolaguirre's story of surviving a shelling—alone. The Spaniard had crawled out of the rubble and sought aid for his injuries, but then saw a line consisting of an entire family, grandparents to children, waiting to have their wounds treated, at which point he felt too ashamed to seek help for his own.

Thus, when Spender reimagined his time in Spain and his view of the war, he did so through Altolaguirre, rather than through Lorca. It began with a poem that originally closed *The Still Centre*, "To a Spanish Poet (for Manuel Altolaguirre)" (1939). The poem is dedicated to Altolaguirre and develops further Spender's theme of isolation as the memorable consequence of war. It recounts through an extended address to its subject the Spaniard's solitary suffering while the "world explod[es]" around him—a scene that exemplified for Spender his notion of the "still centre."[105] Altolaguirre is trapped in a bombed-out building with "every sensation except loneliness / . . . drained out of [his] mind." He envisions Altolaguirre as being in shock, "In frozen wonder, as though you stared / At your image in the broken mirror." The other consciousness in the poem is Spender's "I." "Thus I see you" as a joyous and quixotic figure, he writes, "a man lost in the hills near Málaga." Between the two friends, who are worlds apart, the only communication is the "the violet violence of the news, / The meaningless photographs of stricken faces," which cause Spender's "imagination [to] read . . . / The penny fear that you are dead." But in this first version of the poem, Spender does not simply create an image of isolated suffering. Instead, he writes himself into Altolaguirre's world and vice versa:

> *Your heart looks through the breaking body,*
> *. . . You stare through my revolving bones*
> *On the transparent rim of the dissolving world*
> *Where all my side is opened*
> *With ribs drawn back like springs to let you enter*
> *And replace my heart that is more living and more cold.*

This corporeal personalization of sympathy and identification, though, can be for Spender little more than a "lamentation / [from a] world of happiness."[106] Altolaguirre, nevertheless honored by the poem, published it (in English) as a coda to his own collection of poetry, *Nube temporal* [*Storm Cloud*], in 1939.

When he published his collection *Ruins and Visions* (1942), Spender did not change the content of "To a Spanish Poet," only its placement, moving it away from the section of Spanish war poems and including it alongside meditations on war and loneliness. Clearly depressed by Franco's victory and the new World War, Spender writes apologetically in the foreword that he could not honestly "strike a more heroic note" in his poems on the Spanish war.[107] This walling off of "experience" is apparent when Spender alters this poem significantly for his *Collected Poems, 1928–1953* (1955). It is called "To a Spanish Poet (To Manuel Altolaguirre)," and Spender adds lines such as "(you told me later!)" and "Having heard this all from you, I see you now." He focuses less on identification and more on his communication with Altolaguirre. The Spaniard's "image in the broken mirror" now becomes "Your own image unbroken in your glass soul," yet the same fear of news of Altolaguirre's death paralyzes Spender. But now, his "imagination *breeds* /The penny-dreadful fear that you are dead"; dismissing his fancies, he adds, "Well, what of this journalistic dread?" Spender rewrites his final image, too, by removing the "we" and removing *his* body from it and leaving Altolaguirre figuratively alone: "Your heart looks through the breaking ribs—/ . . . You stare through centrifugal bones /Of the revolving and dissolving world."[108]

Spender then changed the poem again for his *New Collected Poems* (1988), which also contains a translation of another of Altolaguirre's poems. Here, the title is "To Manuel Altolaguirre," and while Spender reverts to some original lines, he revises "Your own image unbroken in your glass soul" into "Wondering if you'd turned into your soul," then adds "And no one with you there to share the joke." The new lighter, almost comical tone of the first two stanzas is broken, however, by an entirely new third stanza: "The blood! The blood! It streamed down from your forehead. /Your fingers felt to see if you were dead. /You weren't. Proud of your wound you went /To show it like a medal to your neighbours." He continues by recounting, in quotation marks to indicate Altolaguirre's voice, the Spaniard's story of his finding a family of twelve injured from the shelling, "all spread out on chairs. /—Grandparents, father, mother, children. /All twelve in bandages." The focus of this version is larger-scale suffering, not just Altolaguirre's, and Spender moves himself further away from it. He is only a correspondent; he does not have the "experience" from which to write:

> . . . *your letter which I read*
> *In London next the newspaper outspread*
> *With headlines 'Barcelona Fallen'*
> *—Panic—street fighting—thousands fled—*
> *Bringing this day each day my daily bread*
> *The penny-dreadful fear that you are dead.*

Spender's former "Well, what of this journalistic dread?" is replaced by another new, fairly long stanza introduced by "But still your stories go on running through my head." Here, Spender gives his final images from one of Altolaguirre's accounts of the funeral of his uncle, a "great general," whose wife kneeled down at his coffin. Through Altolaguirre's voice, Spender notes the scene here of a "troop of ants" who climb into the coffin and begin eating the flesh of the deceased, "each with /A morsel of the general in its teeth. /And then you saw your aunt rise from her prayers /Leaving behind a small black pool, her drawers, /As final tribute to her husband's wars."[109] This commentary on the Spanish war—a pointless war that benefited only the insects that consumed the masses of human bodies left in the aftermath of the battle—is far removed from the collaborative and corporeal sympathy that characterized the "Spain" of Spender's past. It is also far removed from the cause of a Republic and its poetic possibilities that were once Spender's own cause, too.

Conclusion: Modernism, War, and the Memory of Spain after 1939

Franco's victory in the Spanish Civil War made all but moot the bonds among British and Spanish writers that had been forming in the late 1930s. In their place came a number of works—from Spanish exiles, foreign participants in the war, and global observers alike—that were memorials or requiems for the fallen Republic, or meditations on the lessons of the Republic's loss. In the introduction to her *Delirio y destino: los veinte años de una española* [*Delirium and Destiny: A Spaniard in Her Twenties*, 1989], the Andalusian philosopher and author María Zambrano notes that she is uncertain as to why she never published this remarkable autobiographical narrative of her youth in Spain. She recalls the book's origins: having been exiled since the end of the civil war, she found herself in Havana in 1952, in need of money. She learned of "a literary prize to be awarded [by the Institut Européen Universitaire de la Culture in Geneva] for a novel or biography concerned with European culture." Zambrano wrote the entire narrative in a matter of weeks, feeling that she was "responding unconsciously to a mysterious summons from the old continent." When the jury did not choose *Delirium and Destiny* for the prize, one of its members, French writer Gabriel Marcel, protested the decision. Zambrano writes that Marcel argued that "the book deserved the prize, not only because of its literary quality but also because it was the history of Europe and of the reasons why Spain's universality was so significant."[1] Spain's history in the twentieth century, in other words, now was regarded not as Europe's anomaly, but as the history of Europe writ small.

Delirium and Destiny was awarded an honorable mention after Marcel's appeal, but it was not published for nearly four decades. In the meantime, Franco's dictatorship ended, and Spain fully joined the European cultural and economic community. Zambrano returned in 1984 and, shortly thereafter, became the first woman ever awarded Spain's prestigious Premio Cervantes (which facilitated, finally, the publication of *Delirium and Destiny*). Zambrano's writings and her career traverse José Ortega y Gasset's project for a European Spain, Victoria Ocampo's and Virginia Woolf's feminist critiques, the optimism and disillusion with the Second Republic among young Spaniards, the bonds between the Generation of '27 and the Auden generation, and the battle of interpretations over Lorca's figure. I return to her captivating intellectual and physical journeys in a moment. To understand her work fully in the Anglo- and Hispanophone contexts that this book has outlined, I turn first to the international legacies of modernism and the Spanish Republic in Britain in the 1940s.

Zambrano's work intersects here, that is, with the contemporaneous periodical work of Cyril Connolly, the most influential British critic of that decade. Connolly is perhaps best known for failing to write the great novel that his talents had signaled (as he recounts in *Enemies of Promise* [1938]), and for launching and editing the review *Horizon* from 1940 to 1950. *Horizon* attempts to fuse British late modernism with the arts of the Republicans, which became, somewhat paradoxically, the journal's model for literary intervention and efficacy during the era of widespread war. *Horizon* was founded shortly after the *Criterion* and the *London Mercury* both folded in 1939. In his concluding notes on his journal, T. S. Eliot regrets the dissolution of the periodical bonds that he had formed, for "it was the aim of the *Criterion* to maintain close relations with other literary reviews of its type, on the Continent and in America, and to provide in London a local forum of international thought."[2] A number of these reviews across the continent had folded in the late 1930s as well, leaving Eliot's and Ortega's dream of a pan-European periodical network a distant vision. *Horizon*, on the other hand, was launched precisely at this moment of despair in war. It provided a forum for Connolly and his silent editorial partner Stephen Spender to tackle an urgent set of concerns about the role of artists in the new war. The artist was more valuable than ever to Western democracies, Connolly argued, yet was grossly undervalued in Britain especially. As did Spender with his translations of Spanish writers, Connolly believed that certain elements of British modernism, when combined with the politics of foreign writers such as those in Spain, could provide a model for this sort of work.

The overriding question for *Horizon* was how to publish "imaginative writing" in a manner that was not, as Connolly writes, "middlebrow," a reversion "back to the twenties," "sameness and tameness," or a combination of "Regency smartness with Georgian mediocrity."[3] But this literature must have political valence for the moment, and a provocative essay "Why Not War Writers? A Manifesto," published in the journal's second year, outlines this challenge. A number of authors—Arthur Calder-Marshall, Bonamy Dobrée, Tom Harrisson, Arthur Koestler, Alun Lewis, George Orwell, Connolly, and Spender—argue that the sociopolitical role of writers is being threatened by Nazism, and that writers can be more effective than journalists at combating the Germans. Curiously, though, they cite Hemingway's and Malraux's works on the Spanish Civil War as evidence of this; the evidence, that is, comes from a losing cause. Writers must be put to work for the nation's cause in war, they continue:

> Why are there no novels of value about the building of shadow factories, the planning of wartime services, the operation of, shall we say, an evacuation scheme? Why are there no satires on hoarders, or the black market? Why no novels of army life? Because the writers who could write them either have the knowledge but not the time, or the time but not the knowledge to do so. . . . *Creative writers should be used to interpret the war world so that cultural unity is re-established and war effort emotionally co-ordinated.*[4]

They conclude with a proposal for the formation of an "official group of war writers" to be trained, put in contact with an "international exchange" of sympathetic writers, and "actively engaged in this war."[5] This ideal network of writers parallels the efforts that Eliot, Ortega, and their European peers launched among intellectuals after the Great War. But Connolly and his peers now want to mobilize writers in *service* to the state, rather than in a disinterested realm of culture. This argument, furthermore, is about both the topics of literary works and the free time that writers need in order to craft them.

Connolly had declared at the outset that *Horizon* would not be the voice of any cause or position, but by 1942, he had all but given up that ideal; *Horizon* was now "proud" to be "'liberal-bourgeois-intellectual.'"[6] Elaborating further the idea of authors creating propaganda for the state, Connolly turned to Spain. "Anyone would think from the way the Spanish Government is constantly referred to that they had won their war, not lost it," he writes in September 1940. Repeating the characterization of Franco's army as composed of "Moors and Foreign Legion [officers] ... from Africa," Connolly argues that despite the Republic's loss, their propaganda evinces powerfully the "essential vigour of a country which believes in democracy." He publishes in *Horizon* reproductions of four avant-garde posters that draw on familiar aesthetics from Cubism and Surrealism to make their appeals for intervention, and he introduces them by noting that the Republic's

> propaganda ... is full of certainty, not only certainty about war-aims, but certainty as to the kind of people to whom they appealed. In this number we reproduce four Spanish posters as a comment on the inadequacy of our own. They assume a high level of taste and intelligence in their audience.... [T]o them an artist or a professor was not a suspect high-brow, but someone more admirable than themselves. In England this is not the case. Our posters reflect confusion about our war-aims, suspicion about our artists, and ignorance about our public.... If the Ministry of Information does not provide encouragement, it could be given by competitions organized by the *Daily Express* or *Picture Post*.[7]

In Connolly's peculiar but powerful argument, the fact of Spain's loss in the war is outweighed and suppressed in favor of the lessons to be learned from their artists' propaganda pieces. Britain still has much to learn from Spanish arts—and now, from Spain's blunted will to democracy.

The other lesson of Spain that Connolly relates is that "the enemy is on his way" through Spain and toward England. Drawing on his knowledge of Spanish geography from his many travels there and his readings of Spanish literature, Connolly lists a number of places through which he imagines "the enemy" passing, from Algeciras, Estepona, and Almuñecar to Seville, Granada, and Córdoba, creeping northward through Andalusia and toward Madrid. "What has happened in the Peninsula will happen in France," he insists, and it will lead to an apocalyptic state of total war—"the race war, the class war, the age war, the sex war, going simultaneously." The British ought to prepare themselves, for now in London "History (the new name for Nemesis) is being uncomfortably made."[8] Soon after writing this, Connolly brought a regular Spanish voice to his journal—that of Arturo Barea, a refugee who had settled in England. Barea wrote at length on his native country; he panned Hemingway's *For Whom the Bell Tolls* for its inaccuracies, for instance, and instead praised the works of Lorca for bearing witness against fascism, "against the Right and for human rights."[9]

Horizon then directed its attention further to the Hispanophone world—especially its Spanish exiles—in order to put the fall of Spain to fascism in perspective. Connolly published articles on writers from Argentina and Mexico, then later the Philippines, then added special numbers on European literature in which Irish, Swiss, and French writers were featured. Acknowledging that the best writing was not being produced in England, and that English writers were still not taking his suggestion that they follow the lead of their Hispanophone counterparts, Connolly wrote with resignation in the final issue of *Horizon*, "we have published all too little in Spanish." He concludes that "it is a pleasure to air these fragments of delicate loneliness" by the Mexican poet Octavio Paz.[10] The memory of the Spanish war and the example of its literature and arts, however, could not provide the motivation, counterintuitive as it might have been given the Republic's loss, that Connolly sought to extract from Britain's literary peers to the south, and beyond. He reflected with greater cynicism and despair in 1969:

> When one looks back on the politics of the Civil War one sees that an immediate victory of the Spanish Government, which would have been possible if the democracies gave it the military aid which it was entitled to purchase, would have been the ideal solution, requiring only a little more courage on the part of Blum, a little more wisdom from Baldwin and Chamberlain, and rendering a European war much more unlikely, but that an eventual victory of the Communist-controlled Negrín Government might have been worse than what actually happened. . . . The defeat of the Spanish republic shattered my faith in political action. I doubt if I have written a single political article since.[11]

Connolly's dismay mirrored that of his Spanish peers, but while he turned his attention away from Spain, the Republicans in exile looked back at a lost dream.

The memory of the Republic and the painful causes of its defeat preoccupied María Zambrano for the majority of her adult life. The defining condition of her cosmopolitanism—which developed through her philosophical dialogues with Ortega and his peers, with Ocampo and other women, and with Lorca and their mutual colleagues—is exile. She spent nearly half a century exiled from her native Spain, and she kept reimagining both its past and its future constantly. Upon moving to Madrid to study philosophy in 1924, she joined the *Revista de Occidente*'s symposia and Ortega's *tertulias* with friends who would become her Generation of '27 associates. Ortega advised her thesis on Spinoza and proved an immense philosophical presence in her life, but by the late 1920s, when the emergence of the Republic seemed imminent, their differences became apparent. Juan Fernando Ortega Muñoz writes that Ortega's silence and hesitation during the Republic's early years was not only a political matter for Zambrano, but also a philosophical one that "permitted [her] to liberate herself from his tutelage and from the corset of being his disciple, and to think entirely on her own account, breaking the last link" with a philosophical inheritance that she traced all the way back to Descartes.[12] Instead, in her work she drew on the Phoenician, Greek, Roman, Arabic, and gypsy sources mingled in the history of her native Andalusia—sources that went beyond Ortega's understanding of Spain, or of Europe.

In 1930, in three open letters whose public form recalls Woolf's and Ocampo's works, Zambrano explained to Ortega her departure from his work. Ortega had offered to advise Zambrano's student group of revolutionaries informally, but he declined to join them or guide them. "You can and must do more, Señor Ortega y Gasset; your mission for Spain is higher," Zambrano writes.[13] Ortega had been the "hero" of Spain who spoke "to the world on Spain's behalf," but he was now reluctant to represent the Spain that she envisioned.[14] She and her colleagues formed the League for Social Education—a leftist revision of Ortega's past League of Spanish Political Education (1913) and a competitor to his current centrist Group in Service of the Republic. She also worked with progressive groups for women's rights. In order to revise an implicitly masculine philosophical tradition that, she believed, reached its apex in Ortega's *razón vital* ["vital reason"], Zambrano began to promulgate her own notion of *razón poética* ["poetic reason"], a fusion of intellectualism and creativity that, she believed, allowed female thinkers to enter and reshape radically the traditions of European thought.[15] In her "Por qué se escribe" ["Why one writes," 1933], Zambrano explains how this might happen, arguing that writing "only sprouts from an effective isolation, but from a communicable isolation, in which precisely through a distance from all concrete things, it becomes possible to discover the relations among them."[16] This paradoxical engaged detachment— "communicable isolation"—allows the writer to craft a philosophical position that actually unites her with "concrete" realities, she asserts. This notion that women's exclusion from the philosophical tradition is an opportunity to unite themselves with the *pueblo* presages her perspective on distance and her attitude toward writing in exile.[17] Once the civil war began, she published *Los intelectuales en el drama de España* [*Intellectuals in the Drama of Spain*, 1937], which further developed her positions on public intellectualism through a genealogy of the Spanish intellectual from Greece through the Renaissance. Retaining Ortega's distinction between official Spain and vital Spain, she writes that a Republican victory would allow vital Spain to rejoin the life of the continent and to send an anti-fascist signal to its neighbors.

Zambrano's exile, however, could not be delayed much longer. The civil war temporarily halted Zambrano's work in 1937, but she fled to Chile with her husband (an ambassador for the Republic) and continued publishing. Now reading the fallen Lorca, who had been her unrequited love in their childhood, as her ideal intellectual-poet in society, she gathered in *Federico García Lorca: antología* (1937) a collection of his poetry alongside laments on his death from Rafael Alberti, Antonio Machado, and Pablo Neruda. Zambrano's biographical sketch characterizes Lorca as a poet of the people of Granada, one whose style crosses classes. In a country where the upper classes have divorced intellectual labor from social causes—in contrast to England, France, and Germany, she believes—Lorca made a popular yet cerebral style of poetry work for social justice from the margins of politics.[18] When Zambrano returned to Spain later in 1937, she helped found the journal *Hora de España*. But less than two years later, she was forced to flee again, and as she traveled through Havana (through New York), Mexico, Paris, and South America lecturing and writing, Zambrano came to the conclusion that her exile must become the foundation of her work.

Beginning with her brief book *Isla de Puerto Rico (Nostalgia y esperanza de un mundo mejor)* [*The Island of Puerto Rica (Nostalgia and Hope of a Better World)*, 1940], Zambrano opened her engagement with Europe from her Latin American exile and worked to reclaim Spain and Europe imaginatively. She began publishing more frequently in Ocampo's *Sur*, and in her essay "Agonía de Europa" (1940), Zambrano takes up the theme of Europe's decline as an entrée into Spain's future. The same ideological forces that previously liberated Europe now have made it a slave to its past, especially its past victories over authoritarian regimes. European unity is a lost, nostalgic dream, and the previous generation's attempts to see Europe beyond national borders as a *gran unidad* failed. Despite its decline, however, Europe will not die, she insists; it cannot die. Its "resurrection" will come from a resuscitation and renovation of the principles that both sustained its life and led to its "temporary death."[19] If Europe could rediscover its Spanish roots, Zambrano believes, it could find answers to the problems of violence and persecution that have defined its recent history, since this could force the continent to consider the means by which Spain has been excluded.[20] The resurrection of Europe, then, involves a reclamation of Spain's rebirth within the continent.

All of these personal, philosophical, and political questions come to a head in Zambrano's *Delirium and Destiny* (first completed in 1952). As a record of exile and a re-reading of her own political formation, the text crosses back and forth between past dreams and present recollections, between a conviction of figurative death and an assertion of life-affirming presence. Zambrano aligns her exile with Spain's quest for a return to liberal democracy, and she sees in both the promise of destiny but the reality of delirium. Amid this existential angst, the young

Zambrano-narrator recalls looking, with Ortega, to Spain's European possibilities. Madrid calls her:

> It was the history of Spain awakening at that very hour . . . projecting itself on Madrid's implacably blue sky in 1929. . . . The dream of Spain seeped into her and she began to live this dream alone. Also the world's dream, Europe's dream—for, like her, Europe seemed to be free of obligations . . . You could say that nothing constrained this peaceful Europe. (*DD* 14–15)

She recalls searching for this "Europe" in Ortega's lectures on Kant's *Critique of Pure Reason*. Zambrano, in her reformist's spirit in the 1920s, saw spaces such as the Resi and the Institución Libre de Enseñanza as representatives of an ideal that was "simultaneously European and ancestrally Spanish; we need to unite the two definitively, reconcile the split between Spain and Europe. . . . When Spain existed, wasn't it universal?" Here and beyond, she looked for a "newly inaugurated life to keep flowing throughout the entire body of Spain"—for a plan to "transform rather than overthrow" Spain (*DD* 22). At the moment, reading Ortega "made you want to live," granted one a new vision of Europe: "Europe was no longer 'without' Spain, and one did not even have to be there to be in it. . . . Europe's wounds, and above all Europe's preoccupation, were ours as well" (*DD* 59–60). Europeans began to focus on and to understand Spain, she notes, and British writers praised their new works. The Republic would satiate the "hunger and hope" that formed Spaniards' individual provincial characters and collective national identity, and it would finally bind them to Europe. (Though Zambrano does not cite Ocampo here, she almost certainly picked up this metaphor of "hunger" for European attachments from her Argentine colleague.) The arrival of the Republic in Madrid "was the moment, the exact moment of European unity," she writes, and "[Europe's] nationalities would all have to relinquish the essences they were grasping individually. . . . [T]hey would have to pour themselves into a supranational unity" (*DD* 73, 103). The Second Republic would be the European Spain that Ortega now refused to see, she believed.

But just as Madrid begins to fulfill its destiny as "a true, great European city"—without pause in the narrative—bombs destroy the city (*DD* 134). Many of her friends and colleagues are killed; others commit suicide in exile; her hope turns to delirium. Europe becomes Zambrano's mother-Medea figure, and the philosopher asks of both Europe and of Spain, "Where does civil war originate? Will this one be the last?" In exile, she ponders, what would change "if only all Europeans could see Europe from a distance, from this continent [Latin America] born from

Europe's dream, . . . if they could see Europe from this 'afar,' which is not an 'outside' but a dimension within history" (*DD* 172). From this point, Zambrano only continues to re-view Spain from more distant points, both spatially and temporally. Her revisions to her manuscript for *Delirium and Destiny* from the 1950s through the 1980s mostly tempered her initial optimism that Europe would intervene to overthrow Franco and reestablish the Second Republic. Juxtaposing absence from Spain (exile) and presence in the New World ("I am here"), Zambrano makes her imaginative cosmopolitan attachments to Europe from afar when she declares that "at times Europe felt entirely more present than neighboring Madrid," more present "than Spanish life itself" (*DD* 71). A European Spain can only exist for her in memory, at a distance. Only decades later, long after the defeat of the Republic, would a state approximating that shape take root in the Iberian Peninsula. Her autobiography is a document that bespeaks Spain's delayed and difficult journey toward something that Ortega had hoped to bring about since the wake of the never-forgotten Disaster.

Appendix: "James Joyce in His Labyrinth [*Revista de Occidente*, 1924]"

by Antonio Marichalar, translated by Gayle Rogers

—Death? It's not interesting. What intrigues Paris at this moment surely is not Death; it is the interior monologue.
—Haven't you heard the talk about Joyce?

—J[ean] Giraudoux (1924)

The rain stops; the last drop falls on the rue de l'Odéon. Across the slick, shimmering atmosphere purrs a low, faint rumble. Suddenly, a glimmering light flows, slicing the gray glaze: in solemn silence a splendid Rolls arrives. It approaches, weightless, and dims the crystal mirage of its astonishing headlights. Like an endless sigh, it glides, seeping, stealthy, gentle. Quickly, a murmur [*rumor*] softly unglues the wheels from the damp pavement, and they take off smoothly. Cutting through the street along the stream of houses, the car moves on until it chances upon a banner that, feinting from a façade, obliges it to stop. It is detained before a bookstore whose sign reads, "Shakespeare and Company." On the picture hanging above, perpendicular and stylized, appears the sketched silhouette of Old Will.

The car is hushed to a dull snore. Its small door eases open, and from the sloping interior swirls out a faint aroma of skin, of pearls, of woman. The long, dangling rope of a necklace appears and swings deeply over the sunken curb. Just grazing the largest pearl, a foot—of the most elegant duchess in Paris—then ventures out.

Her hand on the tinted window: crystals trembling; commotion. A schoolgirl, framed stark before the bookstore, bursts forth to meet her—bow-tied boots, turned-out collar, light shawl, wild frazzled hair. She's a captain: on the shelves, the rigid volumes, aligned, ordered, obey her voice.

The two women talk, and a book—a fateful book—makes its way to the front. The lady carries it off like a trophy. Hasn't she come in search of precisely what she's been offered? She returns to the car, clutching her treasure. The prestigious J. J. emblazoned on the book's cover corresponds exactly to the R. R. that flaunts on the sparkling grille of the hawklike car. James Joyce: Rolls Royce.

Let's go. The chauffeur tips his black cap that ends in a point like a little Eton jacket. The Rolls sets sail. Now it's gone, suspended in the fog, displacing the silence—rolling along in the calm wake of its own murmur.

Legend has it that lords sold their lands to buy *Ulysses* and that a student had to spend four days in bed without food to purchase it. And this happened in our own storied times, in those lucky days that saw circulate some rare copies of this book by James Joyce—Irish author, our contemporary, better known for his cloudy legend than for his clear work. Certainly, his legend is also a work—essentially a work of its own, when we see that in the novel's gestation (as is the case at present) the artist-subject or "maker" [*hacedor*] does not intervene, but rather, working in the shadows for many long years—fifteen on *Ulysses*—abstains from all publicity generated on his behalf. No, Joyce's manner doesn't simply conform to the passing predilections of a fickle, snobbish public. Rather, something more moves him that demands our attention. Precisely, we must recognize that at the birth of Joyce's fame, Scandal, Style, and Criticism converge by consent—and, not by chance, Criticism has intervened the least thus far. But it need hardly be noted that we are dealing with prestigious and insightful criticism that merits such a name and such transcendence—and that has been so effective in this respect—that today no one is surprised to read our author's name (as in fact it already has been seen) in a chain of supreme literary "beacons" [*faros*]: Calderón, Shakespeare, Dante, Goethe, and Joyce—to the letter, a worthy signature among them.

It is curious to observe how the most cautious, sober criticism has unpacked, in Joyce's honor, the gilded themes kept in his coffers. Havelock Ellis writes in *The Dance of Life* that Joyce "marks a date in the history of British literature." And [John] Middleton Murry affirms that "*À la recherche du temps perdu* and *Ulysses* are the two invaluable documents from which one can comprehend the end of our civilization." We see, then, that, like Proust, Joyce garners superlative honors everywhere. His work both separates and links two literary generations; among the younger, he is "the greatest."

T. S. Eliot rightly assures us that "this work closes a cycle of English literature, but opens a new one in its place." Such overwhelming praise might irritate us and warn us against him, because—naturally—we resist seeing in a contemporary writer (such is the case with Anatole France)[a] the sense of absolute predestination that would designate him the indubitable representative of our epoch in the History of World Literature: "if only one of all contemporary writers could be passed on to posterity, it must be Joyce," recently declared Valery Larbaud, who has been Joyce's most fervent interpreter and biographer.

High praise, doubtless, but: Do we not risk deceiving our readers should Joyce's works not arouse such a response in them all? We must broach this question, for water so blessed must hold something marvelous. But before opening his works, let us settle a previous question: that of the supposed scandal that accompanies his texts and that, had it not been linked to such literary integrity, could have brought serious harm to this author. In facing Joyce's work, let us approach the mystery that has become his: the process of producing these very works. . . .

James Joyce published a small volume of poems, *Chamber Music* (1907),[1] that associated him with Imagism. With this he opened (and in a moment closed) his lyrical vein—with no more consequence than a faint aftertaste of them in his intercalations of verse and song in his prose since then. He next dedicated his literary activity to writing some short stories. They soon constituted a volume ready for publication, but an obstacle delayed this. Every publisher who read the manuscript declined to print it. The reason: in this series, more than a few "Dubliners" were immediately recognizable, for the author used their real names and addresses. Furthermore, the liberties he took in some scenes, and particularly the audacity that Joyce showed in one story by using certain details from the private life of Edward VII, made the publishers pull back, fearful of scandal and confiscation. In the face of such objections, Joyce went directly to the king: he sent the manuscript to the palace, laid out his complaint, and asked for a response. But royal protocol denied him an answer. Finally, one publisher, after guarantees from Joyce, launched a printing—and the very day it was printed, he received a visit from a mysterious, unknown man who bought the entire printing and burned it on the spot, saving one copy to return to the author. Who was that unknown buyer? No one knows; no one has ever known, but one might suspect without fear of error that a sovereign impulse moved him.

Time passed, and, in 1914, the collection of stories appeared, published in London with the title *Dubliners*.[2] Later, an elite London journal called the *Egoist*—like [George] Meredith's novel—began to publish *A Portrait of the Artist as a Young Man*.[3] But let us leave that work for later and move instead to the next of his works to appear: *Exiles*,[4] a three-act drama performed in Munich, and, finally, *Ulysses*,[5] the work that American puritanism has relentlessly persecuted. Four times, legal complaints forced the suspension of *Ulysses*'s publication in the *Little Review*, which in 1918 had begun serializing the novel in the United States, and demanded that Joyce appear before the high courts, defended by the famous patron of modern Irish art John Quinn, who recently died in New York [in July 1924]. Because of these delays, *Ulysses* did not appear as a book until it was printed in Paris in 1922 by Shakespeare and Company, thanks to the decision of the bold bookseller Miss Sylvia Beach.

What is it that causes Joyce's works to be persecuted with such bitter determination? Of course it is neither lewdness nor excessive liberties. Such things are absent in his books, and one would be mistaken to search through them for cheap, sinful thrills. It is well-known that good novels are not written for the average "novel reader," and this author's are so arduous and so dense that they remain long only in the hands of those who have developed a taste for philosophical and literary questions. That which might be considered scandalous matter in his work is, in fact, the same that is explored without shame in a work of medicine—and toward a purely scientific end. The rawness of expression and the desire to transcribe reality with absolute truthfulness occasioned these persecutions of Joyce and—even more damaging—motivated those who would suppose that Joyce was, like George Moore, a naturalist epigone, a faded echo of Médan.[b] Without fail, his realism—and we use the word provisionally, since we shall return to it—has no source other than his determination to bring to artistic creation elements that, through his rigorous authenticity, possess a documentary value that the modern sensibility requires; and to achieve it, he cuts through everything in his way, conventional or not. An overflow of exceedingly direct expressions and intuitions, of Greek and English classics—especially those such as *The Odyssey* and *Troilus and Cressida*—offers us a view of the true fonts of this writer's art. Those and—as Larbaud has said—the works of our Spanish casuists [Tomás] Sánchez and [Antonio] Escobar.[c]

This final point will perhaps explain the unusual fact that Joyce's works, while they were denounced by the moralizing societies of North America, received intelligent accolades from some representatives of the Catholic orthodoxy in his country;[6] and, despite a recalcitrant puritanism's branding Joyce a pornographic writer, his colleagues have seen him as a "Jesuit"—and even Joyce portrays himself as such in his works.

Of old Irish stock, James Joyce was born in Dublin in 1882. As a very young boy, he found himself boarded [*internado*] at a religious school in which he received strict instruction that made him well-versed in dead languages, Greek philosophy, and scholasticism—and made him observant of the essential elements of their tradition. But as soon as he became a man, the author of *Exiles* revealed his true calling: expatriotism. He left the oppressive surroundings of his homeland and ventured on a difficult, wandering journey. He would become an assiduous reader at the public libraries in Rome, in Trieste, in Zürich, in Paris, and by chance in Madrid, where he accidentally stayed for a time.[d] An uncloistered humanist, he buried himself in his studies of theology, medicine, and literature, and he devoted himself fully to his own prolix labor. In all his work, this religious preoccupation is always tangible: as a good Irishman, he is obsessed by religion, and echoes of his priestly training reveal themselves in his choice of themes and taste for quotations in Greek and in Latin.

But let us take up now the book that we mentioned before: *A Portrait of the Artist as a Young Man*, where we find the most authentic portrait of the definitive adolescent experience that formed this writer. Here is a book so autobiographical that it could be composed wholly of remembered elements; and in it, here is a protagonist, Stephen Dedalus, a faithful copy of the author. James Joyce traces this subtle self-re-creation [*autorecreación*] meticulously.... Stephen Dedalus ... embodies a yearning soul whose sensitivity surpasses by far the nascent possibilities of his own understanding. We see this boy, misanthropic and taciturn, pass hazardously through the chasms of school; and—turning the page—we watch how he isolates and shelters himself, this spirit given to reflection and soliloquy, and from there tries to understand his existence through sensibilities that are bleak and tarnished, but delicate and very fragile—like the clouded lenses of this sad schoolboy's glasses.

In spite of Joyce's portrayal of life in a religious school, his book does not resemble others with which we might compare it—it has no false semblance of surroundings or of place. The purpose here is distinct, and the author, limiting himself to exposition— to showing, not demonstrating—avoids interjecting any arguments between the reader and the work.... It's useless to look in literature for Stephen's spiritual brothers, even if we could find them easily in almost all "memoirs." There is one, however, that comes the closest: Arkady Dolgoruky, the protagonist of Dostoevsky's *Adolescent* [or *A Raw Youth* (1875)], who, overwhelmed by his childhood at Touchard, yearns for "personal liberty" above all else. But the humiliation that turned Dolgoruky into an egoist impels Dedalus—every child is humiliated—toward Art. Stephen, lost in thought [*ensimismado*], yearns to find the skills that he must acquire for his aesthetic flight. It has been rightly said that he who searches runs the grave risk of discovery, and Stephen, sacrificing his humanity to discover his artistry, commits—like all schoolboys in life—his corresponding attempt at escape.... Here ends an adolescence, laboriously unfolded through these copious pages. On the final page, an artist dedicated to living as "a voluntary exile" [*un destierro voluntario*] embarks on his flight invoking the aid of the authors and artisans of his homeland. Do we give Dedalus up as lost forever? His spiritual restlessness will not be merely a matter of technique.

Stephen Dedalus, lost by design [*perdidizo*], reappears in Joyce's next work, *Ulysses*, and although in it he plays the role of Telemachus and continues masking the author, he gives way to a new character who captures and reflects more fully James Joyce: Ulysses himself, here called Bloom. A difficult plot, skillfully interspersed with keys and symbols, is woven around this main character, and from the plot emerges *The Odyssey* of the real Ulysses in a manner subtle and complete. The Ulysses that Joyce now presents to us comes in modern dress—as depictions of him in other eras featured anachronistic doublets or tights—and his odyssey is reduced to a single day, a day in the life of Dublin. Meticulously laying out the arbitrary details of Dublin's quotidian existence, Joyce invites us to follow him and not to lose the thread in his complex work.

But following Bloom proves exhausting, precisely because his pace is so slow. All the action of this enormous novel takes place in several hours: from eight in the morning until three the following morning. Has a book's action ever been executed more slowly? Some extraordinary examples come to mind: Proust's winding style—not grandiose, but boundless—which recuperates, one by one, swiftly wasted seconds; the first volume of [Ivan Alexandrovich] Goncharov's *Oblomov* [1859], composed wholly of the divagations that the protagonist experiences from the time he awakens until he decides to get out of bed a little later; *Rahab* [1922], Waldo Frank's compelling novel in which Joyce's techniques have left visible footprints; and, finally, *5,000* [or *5.000, récit sportif* (1924)], the recent work by Dominique Braga in which the plot moves very slowly yet races by because the story attempts to register all the things that pass through the mind of a runner in the time taken to complete a five-thousand-meter race. . . . Art is not a falsification but an equivalence, and the slices of reality itself [in *Ulysses*], which frequently appear to be without boundaries, constitute true touchstones that signal the limits of what in reality is art and what is art in reality. There are fragments in *Ulysses* and in *Portrait* . . . (the spiritual exercises, for example) that displace a time identical to the one they occupy in real life—and furthermore retain its very nature.

In the book of Dedalus there is no real course of time because there is no plot, strictly speaking. It is a portrait, and the author does not narrate but draws out a prolonged presence: an intensification. The progress is principally psychological; we witness the development of an individual but not of a plot. "Children have neither a past nor a future: they rejoice in the present," said [Jean de] La Bruyère. . . .

It will be another matter when the painter is confronted with Bloom, who is already a man—a fleeting pose, requiring greater attention—thus, how much more swiftly his character passes by, how much more abundant and prolix will be the account of all the perceptions and observations gathered for his interior monologue.

The "interior monologue": Joyce's most discussed contribution—if it is he who contributed it. It seems that a Frenchman took it from an Englishman, who, in turn, had taken it from a Frenchman—and the tradition remains in France. Joyce himself has said to Larbaud that he had been inspired by É[douard] Dujardin's novel *Les lauriers sont coupés* [*The Bays are Sere* (1888)], which appeared at the height of the Symbolist period and went almost unnoticed by Dujardin's contemporaries, who were unable to see in its boldness another confession—one more disordered than others, perhaps. However, R[emy] de Gourmont observed that "were it written thus, *Sentimental Education* [1869] would require a hundred volumes"; and today, given that Flaubert is quoted so often in discussions of Joyce, it serves us well to remember this subtle prophecy from the critic of *The Masks* [1896–1898].

Invoking other precedents of this literary form, an array of names has been cited: Montaigne and Poe, Dostoevsky and Browning, mystics and even German Expressionists. In looking precisely at the broken and confused declarations of some of Browning's characters in *The Ring and the Book* [1868–1869] (Pompilia, Guido) or "Mr. Sludge, 'the Medium'" [1864], we find in the "dramatic monologue" a living kinship with this new "interior monologue." The same occurs within the Russian literary heritage and, in general, within the work of every writer who, having surprised himself by "talking alone," might transcribe faithfully the soliloquy that, at the moment of its production, does not suppose the presence of a listener. We can assert, without a hint of irony, that until now, those who demonstrated the "interior monologue" form did so without knowing it, or, at least, without knowing the limits and transcendence that this form implies.

For our part, having had the chance to consider possible analogies with previous forms that the style now before us might offer (complete with suggestions, evocations, perceptions, and associations of ideas, of feelings, etc.), we have noted the similarities between the norms of written introspection and the practice of experimental psychology.... There is, perhaps, one thing that signals confusion to us when we think of the "interior monologue": its very name—which seems inexact and provisional. Anyone who follows to the letter terms such as *Gothic*, *Impressionist*, *Cubist*, and so forth in order to unravel their spirits does so in error. The same occurs with the subject before us. If we focus on a soliloquy of this type, we soon perceive, in the gentle flow of its course, a thick, confused clamor caused by the plurality of voices that arise everywhere and—even though they form one voice when conjoined—that make legible the existence of a tightly woven braid of crossings and contacts in rapid succession. This explains as well the fact that in the interior monologue the narration passes from one person to another without leaving the author—as occurs in the old English ballad "Turpin Hero"[e] (which begins in the first person but ends in the third), in which we ought to find the most authentic precedent of the interior monologue, since this poem is invoked by Stephen Dedalus himself in his thesis on Saint Thomas's aesthetic rules and their derivatives.

In the rich realm of the interior monologue, we see its components parade rhythmically, blooming forth from consciousness, and we discern the most unexpected formation of pristine, natural thought. To watch this unguarded sleep is to settle oneself in the deepest and most remote fountains, then to marvel at their spontaneous integration into unified flow.... The difficulty is in aesthetically evaluating these genuine, completely wild materials. When looking at them, we tend to stumble over a preliterary crudeness because the poet (maker) [*el poeta (hacedor)*] does not make but simply feels by instinct. In such moments we tread along the boundaries between science and art. Proust's "Mes réveils" [1922], for example, delves into the confines of wakefulness and sleep, and, by transcribing the results of his analysis, he brings forth a document of dual interest: scientific and literary. By the same measure, in the last pages of *Ulysses* Joyce relates the awakening of Molly Bloom in an interior monologue—incoherent, one that, to modify Proust's *Watching her sleeping*, could be called *Listening to her sleeping*.[f] We approach it, then, with a soft step and an attentive ear; it reads:

> [E]l cuarto qué hora no de este mundo me figuro quese levantan en este momento en China peinan sus coletas para todoel día bueno pronto oiremosa las hermanas tocar elángelus no tienenadie que vengaperturbar susueño si no esun curaodós para su oficio nocturno el despertar dela gente deaquialado con su cacareo que hace estallar la cabeza vamosaver si pudiera volvermea dormir 1 2 3 4 5 quéesa specie de flor quehan inventado como las estrellas el papel de tapicería de la calle Lombard era más bonito el delantal que meha dado erauna cosasi solo que melohe puesto dos ve[c]es nadamás lo que debía hacer es bajar esta lámpara intentar otra vez para poder levantarme temprano iré a casa de los Lambes allí cerca de Findlaters y haré quenos envíen algunas flores para colocar en la casa si lo trae mañana quiero decirhoy no no el viernes esun mal día quiero arreglar la casase llena de polvo mientras duermo y podemos tocar y fumar puedo acompañarley primero hace

falta que limpie las teclas con leche qué llevaré llevaré una rosa blanca oesos pasteles de casa de Liptons me gusta el olor de una tienda grande y buena a quince perras la libra olos otros con cerezas dentro a 22 perras las dos libras naturalmente una bonita planta paraponer enmedio de lamesa la encontraría más barata en casa de vamosdondehe visto yoaver eso hace poco me gustan las flores me gustaría que todala casa nadase en rosas. . . . [Y] los que dicen no hay Dios yono daría niesto por toda su ciencia por qué no se ponen a crear alguna cosa les he preguntado yo algunas veces los ateos o como quieran llamarse quempiezean por ir aque les quiten la grasa yen seguida llamar al curagritos cuando se mueren y por qué por qué porque tienen miedo del infierno por culpa de su mala conciencia ay si que bien conozco quien hasido la primera persona enel universo que queantes que nohubiera nadie loha hecho todo que ah eso nolo saben ni yo tampoco iya podía seguneso impedir que saliera mañana por la mañana el sol brilla portí me dijo eldiaquél questábamos echados en los rhododendros en el cabo de Howth con su traje gris isusombrero de paja el día que le hice que se me declarase lehabía dado yo . . . etc.

In translation, we lose the true interweaving of Molly's words and the changes of thought prompted by analogous words as she dozes. However, we can see the transcendence of Joyce's contribution to literature of oneiric elements that others before him (Jean Paul and Hebbel, especially[8]) valued, though they employed them without such efficacy and skill.

At times, Joyce uses a technique of questions and answers, creating in them a display of his rare virtuosity. Here, to explain the relation that exists between the respective ages of the characters, he answers his question:

16 años antes, en el año 1888, cuando Bloom tenía la edad actual de Stephen, éste tenía 6 años. 16 años después, en 1920, cuando Stephen tuviese la edad actual de Bloom, éste tendría 54 años. En 1936, cuando Bloom tuviese 70 años y Stephen 54, su edad, inicialmente en la relación de 16 a 0, sería como 17 y ½ a 13 y ½, aumentando la proporción y disminuyendo la diferencia, según que fuesen añadidos futuros años arbitrarios, pues si la proporción que existía en 1883 hubiera continuado inmutable, y suponiendo que fuese posible, hasta el actual de 1904, cuando Stephen tenía 22 años, Bloom tendría 374, y en 1920, cuando Stephen tuviese 38 años, que son los que Bloom tenía actualmente, Bloom tendría 646 años; por otra parte, en 1952, cuando Stephen hubiese alcanzado el máximo de edad postdiluviana de 70 años, Bloom, habiendo vivido 1.190 años y habiendo nacido en el año 714, hubiera

> sobrepasado en 221 años el máximo de edad antediluviana, la edad de Matusalén, 969 años, en tanto que si Stephen hubiera continuado viviendo hasta que hubiese alcanzado esa edad en el año 3072 después de J. C., Bloom hubiera necesitado vivir 83.300 años, habiendo tenido que nacer en el año 81.396, antes de J. C.

Such originalities abound in Joyce. In *Ulysses*, one can search for and constantly list details (water motifs, for example) or analogies (between women and the moon), and one can find very complicated word games—untranslatable on the whole. Let us quote one:

> Simbad el Marino y Timbad el Tarino y Yimbad el Yarino y Whinbad el Wharino y Nimbad el Narino y Fimbad el Farino y Bimbad el Barino y Pimbad el Parino y Mimbad el Malino y Uinbad el Uarino y Rimbad el Rarino y Dimbad el Karino y Kimbad el Carino y Cimbad el Jarino y Ximbad el Sarino.

But, playing with the words, Joyce plays with ideas at the same time—and we are now in the realms of Surrealism and of Dada. The heavy and serious games of his rare British mentality correlate to the aesthetics of the restless modern French spirit.... Surrealism, at once born from and torn by schisms, launched its manifesto with a cry proclaiming the necessity of capturing in art all elements that might be capable of representing the subconscious as revealed in dreams. May it fare well. Its style has precedents in Apollinaire, its spirit in Freud. But Joyce worked diligently to form and incorporate these same elements in his early writings well before the Surrealists. Certainly they undergo vigorous transformations later in his work; and in Joyce—as in Valéry—the most pristine appears united with the most distilled. Their devices were not simply the first moments of something now defined by the Surrealists or the Hyperrealists as "living documents," better described as dead. They did more than risk inspiration in hazardous games to create the work of art: to create is to sacrifice oneself. "The only art is the spontaneous subjected to the conscious," as Juan Ramón Jiménez defines it.

If we group together—and then separate—Joyce and the young Surrealists, we do so to erase the label "naturalism" that weighs on his works in order to understand fully Dedalus's closing words in *Portrait*, which launch his quest to find "la realidad de la experiencia y modelar en la forja de mi alma la conciencia increada de mi raza" ["the reality of experience and to forge in the smithy of my soul the uncreated conscience of my race"]. And now, let us discuss this forging and this race.

What is it that, like a soaked cloak, confines the fervent adolescence of Stephen Dedalus? A construction; a baroque, labyrinthine order—"pure will made of stone," in Jesuit style.... [A] labyrinth is neither a tangle nor a knot but an architectural perfection: a difficult design whose only end consists precisely in finding its exit.... In the labyrinth of Crete—clear, dazzling, alabastrine—its own author became lost.... Look now at Stephen Dedalus, monster [*monstruo*[h]] of his labyrinth, buffeted by the anguish of his own struggles, desiring to rise above the indeterminate limits of his existence. His temerity will impede him from reaching the enticing feminine figure that he glimpsed in ecstasy.... When he tries to liberate himself, Faith fails him, Grace is lacking, and he falls violently both in nature and afterward in craft.

Man of flesh and bone, he wishes to detach himself and to fly above the earth—the very earth from which he is made—but his own misery denies him weightlessness. He does not have strength to find—that is, to search. *Dédalus*[i] ends with an invitation to a voyage, which is the trick solution for all who harbor a profoundly mystical discontent and believe that a definitive, permanent course exists in the ephemeral and the provisional. In the final words of the novel, Stephen has stopped invoking God and instead invokes the primitive artisan of his craft, from a distant tradition, as his patron saint. He emancipates himself from a dogma to serve the most rigorous discipline, and he does not silence his inner tormenter. Joyce's calling is artistic, but his concern is principally religious. It is not his habit that oppresses him in Ireland but his skin.

It is possible that this deep yearning also explains the vogue that this book now enjoys. Long years of persecution and of obscurity[7] give way today to moments of unprecedented esteem.... From whom follows this good favor, found in the most select cenacles? The drama of Dedalus is the effort of an obstinate spirit to overexert itself, to supersede the limits imposed on him by his birth, his education, his nationality. He proposes to himself that he will attain this ideal, and—by the love of his art—he reaches toward it. Very well; does this not seem to be snobbery?

"God made the world, and with it the snobs," writes Thackeray, their most authorized chronicler.[j] ... [The snob] is attracted ... by the incomprehensible, the monstrously ingenious [*lo inabarcable, lo monstruoso*]: Dostoevsky, Joyce, Proust. But if "snobbery" becomes a discredited word for us, we may put in its place Bovarism (in [Jules de] Gaultier's formulation), and the idea will perhaps gain precision. The characters of *Bouvard and Pécuchet*, of *Sentimental Education*, and of others are naïve beings that fail by not attaining the exalted ideals that they themselves have conceived. And in this respect—more than in technique—Joyce and Flaubert resemble one another.

In Joyce's work one must account for another factor to which we have alluded: opposition. From a certain perspective, his case could be reduced to the drama of an Irishman insistent on not being one. Attracted by the spell of Europe, he rejects the traditional elements that took root in him. But what happens to him in his country is something analogous to what happens in the United States to a Masters or to a Dreiser. The difficulty is not in reacting against one's surroundings but in escaping from them while bearing away their constitutive elements. Thus, what terrifies Dedalus when he plans his escape is his solitude, which is his only company.

In English-speaking countries, this same tension of religious problems forces out the most dynamic spirits, those most saturated with creative potential. Thus we find among religious writers [like Chesterton and Blake] such extremes of values . . . [and] in Blake a divine celebration of the naked human form. . . . The Christian who shows himself unclothed offers a spectacle of his poverty: "Ah! Seigneur! donnez-moi la force et le courage /De contempler mon cœur et mon corps sans dégoût!"[k] With its audacities, with its crudeness, Joyce's work presents to us man, abandoned and frozen stiff, because it is a work essentially Christian in its roots.

It has been said, with truth, that this work is a *Summa*. It is not only well nourished by Thomism and its modern followers [*renovadores*], who are continually cited;[8] it is also emblazoned by the most complex flora and most detailed fauna that sprout—petrified—on cathedrals. Replete with symbols, emblems, and significations, Joyce's work encompasses a world both exalted and grotesque. . . . Ezra Pound—Joyce's friend from the beginning—says of the drunken characters in *Ulysses*, "[T]he full grotesquerie of their thought appears naked; for the first time since Dante, we find harpies, living furies, symbols taken from actual reality. . . ." And this swarm of gargoyles and chimeras ends the work with its presence and fills it with unspoken meaning. Making faces in an impotent effort, the gesticulating and obscene figure that tries to uproot itself from the temple and, though permanently stuck to it, to pour through its jaws the revolting and turbulent waters—and, above all, to round out in its absurd gestures the imperturbable grandeur of the church—seems to us a finished image of this enormous and meticulous edifice that Joyce has constructed.

Like Francis Thompson (with whom he is also united through a devotion to liturgical symbolism and analytic detail, to the minute particular), James Joyce, hounded first by his persecutors, later by his enthusiasts, and by Grace always, might well revive the song of that cornered poet in "The Hound of Heaven": "I have fled from Him, through the daedal [*dédalo*] of my own spirit."[l]

Notes

Introduction

1. Valle-Inclán, *Luces de Bohemia/Bohemian Lights: Esperpento*, trans. Anthony N. Zahareas and Gerald Gillespie (Edinburgh: Edinburgh UP, 1976), 183.

2. Warner, "The Tourist Looks at Spain" [1937], in *Poems for Spain*, ed. Stephen Spender and John Lehmann, intro. Spender (London: Hogarth Press, 1939), 68.

3. Kant, *Anthropology from a Pragmatic Point of View*, trans. and ed. Robert B. Louden, intro. Manfred Kuehn (Cambridge: Cambridge UP, 2006), 151, 218, 218ng; emphases and parentheses in original. By contrast, the English and the French (and, Kant implies, the Germans) are the "*most civilized* peoples on earth," while Arabs are "pastoral peoples [who] . . . are not attached to any land, [but] cling so strongly to their way of life, even though it is not entirely free of constraint" (ibid., 214, 169; emphasis in original).

4. As I elaborate below, these are distinct debates—those of *el Ser de España, el problema de España* or *el problema español, las dos Españas*, or extra-Iberian formulations such as "Africa begins at the Pyrenees"—that share a common thread which became supremely relevant in this moment: the question of Spain's relationship to Europe.

5. Ricardo Baeza, Letter to Ortega, 27 November 1927, Fundación Ortega y Gasset-Gregorio Marañón, Madrid; hereafter cited as "FOG, Madrid." The exposition catalogue *El Madrid de José Ortega y Gasset* (Madrid: Sociedad Estatal de Conmemoraciones Culturales / Publicaciones de la Residencia de Estudiantes, 2006) gives a panoramic view of the philosopher's roles in this historical moment.

6. Regarding the danger that we lose the specificity or the definitional sense of "modernism" as we expand our modes and fields of inquiry so broadly, Mark Wollaeger invokes the Wittgensteinian notion of "family resemblance" to make the case that in "literary historical terms, the concept of modernism clearly has traveled the globe, transmitted through widely disseminated texts and transformed through multiform acts of translation and cultural consumption. Yet the sea changes effected through the agency of reception as a mode of production—repurposings, creolizations, indigenizations and the like—do not obscure the family resemblances that make multiple modernisms recognizable as members of a

class" (introduction to *The Oxford Handbook of Global Modernisms*, ed. Wollaeger [New York: Oxford UP, 2012], 11). Eric Hayot makes the point that "the solution to nationally limited approaches to modernism is not to place some other nation at modernism's center but rather to recognize the limitations of originality, to see that the influences—even apparently internal ones—on the development of such an aesthetic and cultural mode of modernism must be thought outside the boundaries of a single nation, a single historical moment, or a single national formation" (*The Hypothetical Mandarin: Sympathy, Modernity, and Chinese Pain* [New York: Oxford UP, 2009], 176).

7. Ortega, *The Revolt of the Masses*, trans. anonymous (New York: W. W. Norton, 1932), 135; hereafter cited as *RM*; Curtius, "Ortega y Gasset," in *Essays on European Literature*, trans. Michael Kowal (Princeton, NJ: Princeton UP, 1973), 304. Curtius adds that this awakening is "one of the few gratifying events of the twentieth century" (ibid.).

8. See Ann L. Ardis, "The Dialogics of Modernism(s) in the *New Age*," *Modernism/modernity* 14:3 (September 2007): 407–434. This approach to modernism was initiated in important ways by Michael North's *Reading 1922: A Return to the Scene of the Modern* (New York: Oxford UP, 1999) and Lawrence Rainey's *Institutions of Modernism: Literary Elites and Public Culture* (New Haven, CT: Yale UP, 1999). For an overview of this and other recent trends in modernist criticism, with an extensive bibliography, see Douglas Mao and Rebecca L. Walkowitz, "The New Modernist Studies," *PMLA* 123:3 (May 2008): 737–748.

9. Ocampo, "Carta a Virginia Woolf," in *Testimonios: primera serie* (Buenos Aires: Ediciones Fundación SUR, 1981), 1:11, 14.

10. Curtius, "Restoration of the Reason," trans. William Stewart, *Criterion* 6:5 (November 1927): 390.

11. Periodicals have begun to receive increased scholarly attention recently, though not often in transnational or global contexts. An exception is Eric Bulson, "Little Magazine, World Form," in *The Oxford Handbook of Global Modernisms*, ed. Wollaeger, 267–287. Several valuable resources here are Sean Latham and Robert Scholes, "The Rise of Periodical Studies," *PMLA* 121:2 (March 2006): 517–531; and *Little Magazines & Modernism: New Approaches*, ed. Suzanne W. Churchill and Adam McKible (Aldershot: Ashgate, 2007), which also contains a rich bibliography of recent works on modernist periodicals (249–262). The Modernist Journals Project, the Modernist Magazines Project, and the planned three-volume *Oxford Critical and Cultural History of Modernist Magazines*, ed. Andrew Thacker and Peter Brooker (see *Vol. 1: Britain and Ireland, 1880–1955* [2009] and *Vol. 2: North America, 1894–1960* [2012]) are some of the larger initiatives to bring these archives into more public arenas. The Magazine Modernism blog [magmods.wordpress.com] also features regular updates, articles, and notices on modernist periodicals. In Madrid, the Biblioteca Nacional has digitized and made searchable hundreds of magazines and newspapers from across four centuries; see hemerotecadigital.bne.es. I treat these critical trends at greater length in chapter 1. For the purposes of this study, I am using the terms *periodical, review*, and *journal* interchangeably, though I acknowledge that nuanced differences exist among these concepts. Those differences, however, are not crucial to the argument of this book.

12. Eliot, "A Commentary," *Criterion* 9:35 (January 1930): 182.

13. Wai Chee Dimock, "Literature for the Planet," *PMLA* 116:1 (January 2001): 175. See the discussion of modernist studies and comparative literature in Jessica Berman, "Imagining World Literatures: Modernism and Comparative Literature," in *Disciplining Modernism*, ed.

Pamela L. Caughie (New York: Palgrave, 2009), 52–70. My conception of literature in circulation here draws on David Damrosch's *What Is World Literature?* (Princeton, NJ: Princeton UP, 2003).

14. Woolf, "The Leaning Tower," in *Collected Essays* (New York: Harcourt, Brace & World, 1967), 2:181.

15. Ortega, "Spanish Letter," *Dial* 77 (October 1924): 326.

16. Ortega, *Meditations on Quixote*, trans. Evelyn Rugg and Diego Marín, intro. Julián Marías (New York: Norton, 1961), 102; hereafter cited as *MQ*. The figures that I include reflect roughly the interest among Ortega's circle in Anglo-American high modernism of the 1920s and early 1930s. American modernists, from Faulkner to Crane, did receive some treatment, but this study—for reasons of both argument and space—is primarily restricted to British and Irish figures. My contention is not, of course, that none of these exchanges would have taken place without Ortega's facilitation.

17. Martin Hume, *Spanish Influence on English Literature* (London: E. Nash, 1905), 312. Hume notes that he disagrees with this conclusion, though his study ends around 1800.

18. The bibliography of works on these and other locales or regions is now lengthy, indeed too long to list. Those that bear most on this book are Vicky Unruh, *Latin American Vanguards: The Art of Contentious Encounters* (Berkeley: U of California P, 1994); Irene Ramalho Santos, *Atlantic Poets: Fernando Pessoa's Turn in Anglo-American Modernism* (Hanover, NH: Dartmouth College/U of New England P, 2002); Tace Hedrick, *Mestizo Modernism: Race, Nation, and Identity in Latin American Culture, 1900–1940* (New Brunswick, NJ: Rutgers UP, 2003); Camilla Fojas, *Cosmopolitanism in the Americas* (West Lafayette, IN: Purdue UP, 2005); Anita Patterson, *Race, American Literature and Transnational Modernisms* (New York: Cambridge UP, 2008); and Jessica Berman, *Modernist Commitments: Ethics, Politics, and Transnational Modernism* (New York: Columbia UP, 2011). Recent titles such as *Geomodernisms: Race, Modernism, Modernity*, ed. Laura Doyle and Laura Winkiel (Bloomington: U of Indiana P, 2005); *Geographies of Modernism: Literatures, Cultures, Spaces*, ed. Peter Brooker and Andrew Thacker (London; New York: Routledge, 2005); and *Translocal Modernisms: International Perspectives*, ed. Irene Ramalho Santos and Antonio Sousa Ribeiro (New York: Peter Lang, 2008) contain a great deal of material and theorizations on modernist sites beyond the familiar Anglo-American world.

19. See, respectively, *Modernism and Its Margins: Reinscribing Cultural Modernity from Spain and Latin America*, ed. Anthony L. Geist and José B. Monleón (New York: Garland, 1999); C. Christopher Soufas, *The Subject in Question: Early Contemporary Spanish Literature and Modernism* (Washington, DC: The Catholic U of America P, 2007); José-Carlos Mainer, *La Edad de Plata (1902–1939): ensayo de interpretación de un proceso cultural* (Madrid: Ediciones Cátedra, 1983); Domingo Ródenas de Moya, *Travesías vanguardistas: ensayos sobre la prosa del Arte Nuevo* (Madrid: Devenir, 2009); Mary Lee Bretz, *Encounters Across Borders: The Changing Visions of Spanish Modernism, 1890–1930* (Lewisburg, PA: Bucknell UP, 2001); Jordana Mendelson, *Documenting Spain: Artists, Exhibition Culture, and the Modern Nation, 1929–1939* (University Park: Pennsylvania State UP, 2005). Other titles that belong with these include Susan Kirkpatrick and Jacqueline Cruz, *Mujer, modernismo y vanguardia en España: 1898–1931* (Madrid: Cátedra, 2003); Shirley Mangini, *Las modernas de Madrid: las grandes intelectuales españolas de la vanguardia* (Barcelona: Ediciones Península, 2001); Andrew A. Anderson, *El veintisiete en tela de juicio: examen de*

la historiografía generacional y replanteamiento de la vanguardia histórica española (Madrid: Gredos, 2005); Katharine Murphy, *Re-reading Pío Baroja and English Literature* (New York: Peter Lang, 2004); and articles such as C. A. Longhurst, "Coming in from the Cold: Spain, Modernism and the Novel," *Bulletin of Spanish Studies* 79 (2002): 263-283; and Brad Epps, "'Modern' and 'Moderno': Modernist Studies, 1898, and Spain," *Catalan Review* 14:1-2 (2000): 75-116. Some special issues of journals have considered Anglophone, Hispanophone, and European modernist studies together in the past decade. See the introductions to these issues: Nelson Orringer, "Introduction to Hispanic Modernisms," *Bulletin of Spanish Studies* 79 (2002), 133-148; L. Elena Delgado, Jordana Mendelson, and Oscar Vázquez, "Recalcitrant Modernities: Spain, Cultural Difference and the Location of Modernity," *Journal of Iberian and Latin American Studies* 13:2/3 (August 2007): 105-119; and C. Christopher Soufas, "Modernism and Spain: Spanish Criticism at the Crossroads," *Anales de la literatura española contemporánea* 35:1 (2010): 7-16. Brad Epps and Fernández Cifuentes point out that foreign literary histories of Spain often have ingrained further an exclusively national portrait (introduction to *Spain Beyond Spain: Modernity, Literary History, and National Identity*, ed. Epps and Fernández Cifuentes [Lewisburg, PA: Bucknell UP, 2005], 15). Mainer's *La Edad de Plata* (first published in 1975) in particular offers an invitation for paths of research into the global currents of interwar Spanish cultures that had been downplayed under Franco. But this invitation has been taken up only recently in Hispanophone criticism, and when it has been the focus has often been on influence and reception; meanwhile, it is rarely known to Anglophone critics. Mainer's editorial project, the *Historia de la literatura española* (7 vols.; Madrid: Crítica, 1973-2011), expands his reading of this era across many genres, fields, and disciplines in which modernism and vanguardism arose, tracing these movements not only in texts but also in institutions and events; see especially Mainer's own contribution (Vol. 6), *Modernismo y nacionalismo, 1900-1939* (Madrid: Crítica, 2010). Along with Mainer and the scholars cited above, valuable reconceptions of Spanish literary history have come from Jordi Gracia, Andrés Soria Olmedo, and Enrique Serrano Asenjo, and several others who are cited in this study. As do Geist and Monleón, Berman, and Alejandro Mejías-López, Bretz points to critical exclusions of Spanish modernism in volumes such as Malcolm Bradbury and James Walter McFarlane's *Modernism: 1890-1930* (New York: Penguin, 1976), which quotes Ortega throughout the introduction and at other moments when defining modernism, but which conspicuously overlooks or mischaracterizes Spanish involvement in European modernist movements. Mejías-López's *The Inverted Conquest: The Myth of Modernity and the Transatlantic Onset of Modernism* (Nashville, TN: Vanderbilt UP, 2009) also shows that Spanish modernism both has and has not been included in critical definitions of *modernism* over the past century. Within peninsular criticism, though, terms such as *transnational* and *global* do not have the popularity or currency that they do among Anglophone scholars, and the majority of studies of Spanish modernism and the avant-garde do not range beyond one language or the Spanish nation. My interest in questions of Europeanism or the Spanish problem—which are considered outdated questions by some Hispanists—is both historiographical and necessary to merging Anglo- and Hispanophone literary histories here. See also note 20.

20. I must make several qualifications and clarifications here. I am taking as given at this point that the case that national and linguistic categories alone are inadequate for literary histories has been made convincingly by many scholars. I am not suggesting, of course,

that Ortega and his circle can stand for Spanish modernism as a whole, or that there was no "Spanish modernism" until the importation of Anglo-European modernity or culture. And though strictly speaking, Ortega's "New Spain" was a plan mobilized first in 1914 and never fully fleshed out, my focus is on his post–Great War work as a public and periodical presence, and I am using "New Spain" to signify the work that grew out of it. Regarding terminology, for the purposes of my study, it makes sense to follow Geist and Monleón, who "use the term *modernism* with the broad Anglo connotation; it includes aestheticism, *modernismo*, avant-gardes, and, in general, all those artistic movements that at the end of the nineteenth and the beginning of the twentieth centuries challenged the premises of realism" (introduction *Modernism and Its Margins*, ed. Geist and Monleón, xxxii n2; emphasis in original). *Modernismo*, the potentially confusing cognate, has a distinct critical legacy that originated in the works of Spanish American writers such as José Martí and Rubén Darío in the 1880s. It shares affinities with the modernisms treated in this book, but the writers considered here did not consider themselves to be *modernistas*, nor are they classified with this group by literary historians in either language. For an overview of these issues, see Donald L. Shaw, "Hispanic Literature and Modernism," in *The Oxford Handbook of Modernisms*, ed. Peter Brooker, Andrzej Gąsiorek, Deborah Longworth, and Andrew Thacker (Oxford; New York: Oxford UP, 2010), 896–909; Cathy Jrade, "The Spanish-American *Modernismo*," in *Modernism*, ed. Astradur Eysteinsson and Vivian Liska (Amsterdam: John Benjamins Publishing, 2007), 817–830; Ricardo Llopesa, *Modernidad y modernismo* (Valencia: Instituto de Estudios Modernistas, 2000); Gerard Aching, *The Politics of Spanish American* Modernismo: *By Exquisite Design* (Cambridge; New York: 1997); and the relevant chapters in *The Cambridge History of Spanish Literature*, ed. David T. Gies (Cambridge; New York: Cambridge UP, 2004).

At the same time, I refer to the groups of leading writers and cultural figures in this study as *vanguards* and to their works as *modernist*, both in the Anglophone critical sense. The term *vanguardia*, in peninsular literary historiography, refers to movements such as Ultraism and Creationism that peaked in the late 1910s and early 1920s in Spain and had much in common with the continental avant-gardes. But as this book demonstrates, the fluidity and many overlaps between "modernist" and "avant-garde" movements that Astradur Eysteinsson, Ann L. Ardis, and others have pointed out was very much present in Spain at this time. See also Renée Silverman, "A Europeanizing Geography: The First Spanish Avant-Garde's Re-Mapping of Castile (1914–1925)," in *The Invention of Politics in the European Avant-Garde*, ed. Sascha Bru and Gunther Martens (Amsterdam; New York: Rodopi, 2006), 217–233. A fuller consideration of such groups and figures, however, is beyond the scope of this study. See Derek Harris, *The Spanish Avant-Garde* (Manchester: Manchester UP, 1995); *¡Agítese bien! A New Look at the Hispanic Avant-gardes*, ed. María T. Pao and Rafael Hernández Rodríguez (Newark, DE: Juan de la Cuesta, 2002); *Visualizing Spanish Modernity*, ed. Susan Larson and Eva Woods (New York: Berg, 2005); and for important publications from the associated figures, *Documents of the Spanish Vanguard*, ed. Paul Ilie (Chapel Hill: U of North Carolina P, 1969). Finally, the use of "generational" categories in Spanish literary historiography has a problematic record dating back to Francoist theories of national purity, and my invocation of them is not to reify them, but to draw on the historical and citational senses that were employed both by writers at the time and by contemporary critics. See Anderson, *El veintisiete en tela de juicio*; and Soufas, *Subject in Question*, both of whom call for an understanding of Spanish literary "generations" outside the national boundary that mid-twentieth-century criticism largely created.

21. Eliot, "The Man of Letters and the Future of Europe," *Horizon* 60 (December 1944): 383. Eysteinsson and Liska's *Modernism* is extensive in its nationally based approach to global modernisms, and *The Cambridge Companion to European Modernism*, ed. Pericles Lewis (Cambridge; New York: Cambridge UP, 2011), makes ties among the nations it profiles. Rebecca Walkowitz makes a strong case for integrating comparative and national methodologies in the study of contemporary literatures—a case that is apt for this book, too—in "Comparison Literature," *New Literary History* 40:3 (Summer 2009): 567–582. This issue of *New Literary History*, devoted to comparativity, has been a rich source for my thinking here; see also *boundary 2* 32:2 (Summer 2005). On modernism's engagements with the question of Europe, see *Europa! Europa?: The Avant-garde, Modernism, and the Fate of a Continent*, ed. Sascha Bru et al. (Berlin: De Gruyter, 2009).

22. To elaborate briefly, the writers in this study situate themselves somewhere between the European center of modernity and the colonial "exteriority of modernity" that Walter Mignolo identifies as the origins, respectively, of cosmopolitan projects from global designs and those from "critical cosmopolitanisms"; see Mignolo, "The Many Faces of the Cosmo-polis: Border-thinking and Critical Cosmopolitanism," in *Cosmopolitanism*, ed. Carol A. Breckenridge, Homi K. Bhabha, Sheldon Pollock, and Dipesh Chakrabarty (Durham, NC: Duke UP, 2002), 160, 159. See also Mignolo, *Local Histories/Global Designs: Coloniality, Subaltern Knowledges, and Border Thinking* (Princeton, NJ: Princeton UP, 2000); Amanda Anderson, *The Powers of Distance: Cosmopolitanism and the Cultivation of Detachment* (Princeton, NJ: Princeton UP, 2001) on the generations prior; and Rebecca L. Walkowitz, *Cosmopolitan Style: Modernism Beyond the Nation* (New York: Columbia UP, 2006) on modernism through the twentieth century.

23. Friedman, "Periodizing Modernism: Postcolonial Modernities and the Space/Time Borders of Modernist Studies," *Modernism/modernity* 13:3 (September 2006): 426. This book does not seek to define what modernism was or is, nor to settle questions such as modernism's (writ large) relation to modernity or modernization. For a discussion of scholarship on these questions, see Mao and Walkowitz, "The New Modernist Studies."

24. Sebastian Balfour and Paul Preston, introduction to *Spain and the Great Powers in the Twentieth Century*, ed. Balfour and Preston (New York: Routledge, 1999), 1. The country was also exploited economically a great deal by the major powers of Europe, including the British; see Raymond Carr, *Modern Spain: 1875–1980* (New York: Oxford UP, 1980). Regarding Anglo-Spanish relations at the time, King Alfonso XIII's engagement to Princess Victoria Eugenie (granddaughter of Queen Victoria) was hoped to signal a cooling period in Anglo-Spanish relations—until the wedding day in 1906, when Catalan anarchist Mateu Morral unsuccessfully attempted to assassinate the royal couple with an explosive attack.

25. See Franco Moretti, *Atlas of the European Novel, 1800–1900* (London: Verso, 1998) on the historical scarcity of translations of foreign literature in England compared to many European countries, too. Anthologies of Spanish writing in English translation in this era mostly were weighted toward the Golden Age and Baroque period, rarely featuring contemporary writers. See Miguel Gallego Roca, "De cómo no fueron posibles en español las traducciones vanguardistas," in *La traducción en la Edad de Plata*, ed. Luis Pegenaute (Barcelona: Promociones y Publicaciones Universitarias, 2001), 41–48, on some particular problems Spaniards encountered when translating British modernist works.

26. Douglas Little, *Malevolent Neutrality: The United States, Great Britain, and the Origins of the Spanish Civil War* (Ithaca, NY: Cornell UP, 1985), 31.

27. Tom Buchanan, *Britain and the Spanish Civil War* (Cambridge: Cambridge UP, 1997), 12; Brian Shelmerdine, *British Representations of the Spanish Civil War* (Manchester: Manchester UP, 2006), 6. "Hispanisms" are, in short, a version of Orientalisms applied to Hispanic peoples and cultures.

28. A[ubrey] F. G. Bell, "Spaniards and Spain," review of *España invertebrada* by José Ortega y Gasset, *TLS* (28 September 1922): 609; italics in original.

29. Luce López Baralt, *Islam in Spanish Literature: From the Middle Ages to the Present*, trans. Andrew Hurley (Leiden: Brill, 1992), 1.

30. Ortega to Ocampo, 31 January 1930, in Ortega, *Epistolario* (Madrid: Ediciones de la Revista de Occidente, 1974), 146.

31. Iarocci, *Properties of Modernity: Romantic Spain, Modern Europe, and the Legacies of Empire* (Nashville, TN: Vanderbilt UP, 2006), 8.

32. Dainotto, *Europe (in Theory)* (Durham, NC: Duke UP, 2007), 7.

33. "Africa begins at the Pyrenees" is variously attributed to Napoleon or to Dumas *père*. Voltaire wrote that Spain was a country with which "we are no better acquainted than with the most savage parts of Africa, and which does not deserve the trouble of being known," qtd. in Delgado, Mendelson, and Vázquez, "Recalcitrant Modernities," 107.

34. Ortega, "Preface for Germans," in *Phenomenology and Art*, trans. and intro. Philip Silver (New York: Norton, 1970), 29, 31. The most complete account of Ortega's German education is Nelson Orringer, *Ortega y sus fuentes germánicas* (Madrid: Gredos, 1979). Ortega made several trips to Germany between 1905 and 1907, and this was not uncommon among Spain's elites. He claimed to have known no German and to have read only Nietzsche in translation before his first trip there.

35. Ortega, "España como posibilidad," in *Obras completas*, 10 vols. (Madrid: Revista de Occidente, 1946–1969), 1:138; hereafter cited as *OC*; "Unamuno y Europa, fábula," in *OC* 1:128. See also Mainer, *Edad de Plata*, 139–142. An excellent and comprehensive corrected set of Ortega's *Obras completas* has been published by Taurus (Madrid; 10 vols., 2004–2011), but because it is not yet widely available, I have used the standard edition throughout this book.

36. Ortega, "La cuestion moral," in *OC* 10:73.

37. Marías, *José Ortega y Gasset: Circumstance and Vocation*, trans. Frances M. López-Morillas (Norman: U of Oklahoma P, 1970), 159; quotation marks in original. This sensibility is akin to what Bruce Robbins has described in other contexts as "situated" or "actually existing" cosmopolitanism ("Comparative Cosmopolitanisms," in *Cosmopolitics: Thinking and Feeling Beyond the Nation*, ed. Pheng Cheah and Robbins [Minneapolis: U of Minnesota P, 1998], 260).

38. Thus, to say that Ortega sought to bring "the spirit of Enlightenment . . . at last to philosophical expression in Spain," where it had only appeared dimly in the eighteenth century, as Patrick H. Dust writes, is only partially accurate ("On Reading Ortega for Our Time," in *Ortega y Gasset and the Question of Modernity*, ed. Dust [Minneapolis, MN: Prisma Institute, 1989], 66. This "spirit" had to be modified heavily. See also Pedro Cerezo Galán, *La voluntad de aventura: aproximamiento crítico al pensamiento de Ortega y Gasset* (Barcelona: Ariel, 1984).

39. See Robert Wohl, *The Generation of 1914* (Cambridge, MA: Harvard UP, 1979), 129. In fact, as early as 1907, Ortega had alluded to Germany's "cultural decadence" and its rising nationalist movement, both of which he disliked (Letter to Unamuno, 27 January 1907, in *Epistolario*, 77).

40. *MQ* 48, 97, 80. Ortega preferred the term "Mediterranean" to "Latin" because the former alluded to a broader classical world, while the latter had been restricted to language and race. Any theory of Europe, as Dainotto observes, is "a theory not only of Europe itself but of a whole series of other things," such as culture, modernity, nationalism, or secularization (*Europe*, 17). Dainotto is building on the work of Edward Said and Dipesh Chakrabarty, among others; see Chakrabarty, *Provincializing Europe: Postcolonial Thought and Historical Difference* (Princeton, NJ: Princeton UP, 2000).

41. Ortega, "Reflexiones de centenario: 1724–1924," in *OC* 4:32. Ortega uses the distinction in Spanish between "German" (referring to the nationality), which is *alemán*, and "Germanic" (referring to the ethnicity), which is *germánico*.

42. Ortega, "Reflexiones," in *OC* 4:38–39. For more on these ideas of Europe, see Robert J. C. Young, *White Mythologies: Writing History and the West* (New York: Routledge, 2004).

43. Ortega, "Reflexiones," in *OC* 4:46–47; emphases in original.

44. Kant, "Idea for a Universal History from a Cosmopolitan Point of View," in *Philosophical Writings*, trans. Lewis White Beck, ed. Ernst Behler (New York: Continuum, 1986), 259. Kant's "Idea for a Universal History" (1784) and "Perpetual Peace: A Philosophical Sketch" (1795) were written on either side of the start of the French Revolution. For an overview of Napoleon's effect on Europe, see Alexander Grab, *Napoleon and the Transformation of Europe* (New York: Palgrave, 2003).

45. Mignolo, "The Many Faces of the Cosmo-polis: Border-thinking and Critical Cosmopolitanism," in *Cosmopolitanism*, ed. Breckenridge et al., 173. See also James Tully, "The Kantian Idea of Europe: Critical and Cosmopolitan Perspectives," in *The Idea of Europe: From Antiquity to the European Union*, ed. Anthony Pagden (Washington, DC: Woodrow Wilson Center Press, 2002), 331–358); and *Europe in Crisis: Intellectuals and the European Idea, 1917-1957*, ed. Mark Hewitson and Matthew D'Auria (London: Berghahn Books, 2012).

46. Ortega, "Reflexiones," in *OC* 4:31.

47. Though I treat many of them over the course of this book, I do not have the space here to cover all of the important opposing figures, nor to account fully for why Ortega's grand project failed in the face of obstacles ranging from cultural opposition to governmental interdiction to war. For one interpretation, see Jordana Mendelson with Estrella de Diego, "Political Practice and the Arts in Spain, 1927–1936," in *Art and Journals on the Political Front, 1910–1940*, ed. Virginia Hagelstein Marquardt (Gainesville: U of Florida P, 1997), 183–214.

48. Ortega to Unamuno, 17 February 1907, in *Epistolario*, 83.

49. Thomas Mermall, "Culture and the Essay in Modern Spain," in *The Cambridge Companion to Modern Spanish Culture*, ed. David T. Gies (Cambridge: Cambridge UP, 1999), 165. Ortega, speaking in Madrid's Teatro de la Comedia, was advancing and extending the terms for the Spanish nation-state that had been laid out by Francisco Giner de los Ríos, a prominent and persecuted Krausist reformer; see chapter 3 of this volume. The works of Karl Christian Friedrich Krause, the German philosopher and student of Hegel's, were significantly influential in Spain; see Juan López-Morillas, *The Krausist Movement and Ideological*

Change in Spain, 1854-1874 (Cambridge: Cambridge UP, 1981). Ortega found, however, that the Krausists did not have what he considered a complete understanding of Europe. He writes that "all they knew of Germany was Krause. They had not even a clear notion of Kant or ... [his] contemporaries" ("Preface for Germans," in *Phenomenology and Art*, 26).

50. Ortega, "Vieja y nueva política," in *OC* 1:272, 286, 271; "Imperativo de intelectualidad," in *OC* 11:13. Ortega's faith in a vanguard dates back to his brief interest in socialism in his youth, when he championed a less conservative vanguard of leaders. His language here and at many other points is what Pheng Cheah calls "organicist;" see *Spectral Nationality: Passages of Freedom from Kant to Postcolonial Literatures of Liberation* (New York: Columbia UP, 2003). Ortega was, as I discuss in chapter 1, unapologetically Castilianist, primarily because he felt that Castile had both united and divided Spain historically. His focus on the Spanish nation was as a reform effort, not as a nationalist project, and despite his readings of Spanish history, he was a *cultural* imperialist, not a political one. Ortega called himself "ashamed" of the Spanish imperial era, in fact. See Enrique Aguilar, *Nación y estado en el pensamiento de Ortega y Gasset* (Buenos Aires: Ciudad Argentina, 1998).

51. Ortega, *The Modern Theme*, trans. James Cleugh, intro. José Ferrater Mora (New York: Harper, 1961), 19-20. A better translation of the book from which this is taken, *El tema de nuestro tiempo* (1922), is *The Task of Our Time*, given Ortega's disdain for the term *modern* (*moderno*) because of its association with the nineteenth-century's self-fulfilling prophecies of progress; see chapter 3 of this volume.

52. Spengler, *The Decline of the West*, trans. Charles Francis Atkinson (New York: Knopf, 1939), 1:16n1; emphasis in original.

53. López Campillo, *La "Revista de Occidente" y la formación de minorías (1923-1936)* (Madrid: Taurus, 1972), 55. Few scholars have treated the *Revista de Occidente*'s international profile, and the majority of studies of Ortega confine themselves either to Spain or to philosophical matters only; see chapter 1 of this volume.

54. Ortega, "Propósitos," in *OC* 6:314. Ortega admitted, in fact, that Spengler's *Decline* was "born of profound intellectual necessity," and that it "formulates thoughts that pulsate in the breast of our time" (preface to *La decadencia de Occidente: bosquejo de una morfología de la historia universal*, by Oswald Spengler, trans. Manuel G. Morente [Espasa-Calpe: Madrid, 1923], 1:i). But by the mid-1920s, Ortega believed that the "Spenglerian notion of historical pseudomorphosis is not applicable to the phenomenon of Europe," see "Preface for Germans," in *Phenomenology and Art*, 27. See also Arturo Ardao, "Los dos europeísmos de Ortega," *Cuadernos Hispanoamericanos* 403-405 (enero-marzo 1984): 493-510.

55. Ortega, "Cosmopolitismo," in *OC* 4:486.

56. Trend, *Lorca and the Spanish Poetic Tradition* (Oxford: Blackwell, 1956), 6.

57. Samuel Putnam, foreword to *European Caravan: An Anthology of the New Spirit in European Literature; Part I: France, Spain, England, and Ireland*, compiled and edited by Putnam, Maida Castelhun Darnton, George Reavey, and J[acob] Bronowski, with André Berge, Massimo Bontempelli, Jean Cassou, and E[rnesto] Giménez Caballero (New York: Brewer, Warren and Putnam, 1931), vi-vii, v.

58. Quoted in David Rubio, *The Mystic Soul of Spain* (New York: Cosmopolitan Science and Art Service, 1946), 53; translation modified.

59. J. S. Bernstein, *Benjamín Jarnés* (New York: Twayne, 1972), 36.

60. Hurtado Díaz, "La Traducción en *Residencia: Revista de la Residencia de Estudiantes*," in *La traducción en la Edad de Plata*, ed. Pegenaute, 135. The Krausist educational reformer Francisco Giner de los Ríos sent his disciple Alberto Jiménez Fraud on several trips to England in the early 1900s to study the school system that he would reproduce in Madrid. See Isabel Pérez-Villanueva Tovar, *La Residencia de Estudiantes: grupos universitarios y de señoritas, Madrid, 1910–1936* (Madrid: Ministerio de Educación y Ciencia, 1990) for a thorough documentary account of the Residencia.

61. Graham and Labanyi, "Culture and Modernity: The Case of Spain," in *Spanish Cultural Studies: An Introduction: The Struggle for Modernity*, ed. Graham and Labanyi (New York: Oxford UP, 1995), 2.

62. Manifesto of the Residencia de Estudiantes, reprinted in Pérez-Villanueva Tovar, *La Residencia*, 23.

63. Comité Hispano-Inglés, *Residencia* 1:1 (January-April 1926), 41. In London, the Anglo-Spanish Society (founded 1919) at Cambridge, Leeds, and several other schools was a parallel effort. The students at the Resi also organized post–Great War relief groups across Europe.

64. Marichalar, "Palma (lectura crítica)," in *Ensayos Literarios*, intro. and ed. Domingo Ródenas de Moya (Santander: Fundación Santander Central Hispano, 2002), 10; hereafter cited as *EL*.

65. Díez de Revenga, "Antonio Marichalar y las letras de su tiempo," review of *Ensayos Literarios*, by Antonio Marichalar, ed. Domingo Ródenas de Moya, *Quimera* 236 (2003): 79. More than any other scholar, Ródenas has been responsible for reviving the study of Marichalar's work.

66. Charles K. Colhoun, "Spanish Periodicals," *Criterion* 15:61 (July 1936): 774; Miguel Gallego Roca and Enrique Serrano Asenjo, "Un hombre enamorado del pasado: las crónicas de Antonio Marichalar en la revista *The Criterion*," *Nueva Revista de Filología Hispánica* 46:1 (1998): 71; Ródenas, "Antonio Marichalar, el embajador europeo de la generación del 27," in *EL*, ix.

67. Melchor Fernández Almagro, qtd. in Ródenas, "Antonio Marichalar," in *EL*, xxxiv.

68. See Javier Zamora Bonilla, *Ortega y Gasset* (Barcelona: Plaza Janés, 2001), 240. There is no English-language biography of Ortega that approaches the depth and quality of Zamora's account. Victor Ouimette's short sketch *José Ortega y Gasset* (Boston: Twayne, 1982); Rockwell Gray's *The Imperative of Modernity: An Intellectual Biography of José Ortega y Gasset* (Berkeley: U of California P, 1989); and Andrew Dobson's *An Introduction to the Politics and Philosophy of José Ortega y Gasset* (Cambridge: Cambridge UP, 1989) are all valuable, but somewhat limited, resources for Anglophone scholars.

69. Eliot, "Last Words," *Criterion* 18:71 (January 1939): 271.

70. Delanty and Rumford, *Rethinking Europe: Social Theory and the Implications of Europeanization* (London: Routledge, 2005), 97.

71. Brenan, preface to *The Spanish Labyrinth: Account of the Social and Political Background of the Civil War* (Cambridge: Cambridge UP, 1943), xii; Trend, qtd. in John A. Crow, *Spain: The Root and the Flower* (Berkeley: U of California P, 1985), 345.

72. Ortega, "Preface for Germans," in *Phenomenology and Art*, 75.

73. Ortega, "El error Berenguer," *El Sol*, 15 November 1930, 1.

74. Woolf, *Three Guineas* (San Diego: Harcourt Brace Jovanovich, 1966), 109.

Chapter 1

1. Trend, *A Picture of Modern Spain: Men & Music* (Boston; New York: Houghton Mifflin, 1921), 1.

2. Eliot, "A Commentary," *Criterion* 6:2 (August 1927): 98. For the sake of simplicity, I use "the *Criterion*" to refer to this review throughout, whether it was titled the *Criterion*, the *New Criterion*, or the *Monthly Criterion* at the moment, unless otherwise noted. Similarly, though the *Revista de Occidente* has been relaunched several times after World War II (and is still currently in print), my references will be to the first run, from 1923–1936, unless otherwise noted.

3. Ortega, "Un experimento europeo," *Revista de Occidente* 24:71 (May 1929): 280.

4. Eliot, "A Commentary," *Criterion* 9:35 (January 1930): 182–83; emphasis and capitalization in original.

5. See Sean Latham and Robert Scholes, "The Rise of Periodical Studies," *PMLA* 121:2 (March 2006): 517–531; Ann L. Ardis and Patrick Collier, introduction to *Transatlantic Print Culture, 1880–1940: Emerging Media, Emerging Modernisms*, ed. Ardis and Collier (Palgrave: New York, 2008), 1–12; Robert Scholes and Clifford Wulfman, *Modernism in the Magazines: An Introduction* (New Haven, CT: Yale UP, 2010); Mark Morrisson, "Mass Market Publicity—Modernism's Crisis and Opportunity," *The Public Face of Modernism: Little Magazines, Audiences, and Reception, 1905–1920* (Madison: U of Wisconsin P, 2001), 3–16; and Suzanne W. Churchill and Adam McKible, introduction to *Little Magazines & Modernism: New Approaches*, ed. Churchill and McKible (Aldershot: Ashgate, 2007), 3–18. Superb introductions to the field of Spanish periodical studies during this era can be found in Rafael Osuna's many works, including *Las revistas españolas entre dos dictaduras, 1931–1939* (Valencia: Pre-Textos, 1986); *Las revistas del 27: "Litoral," "Verso y Prosa," "Carmen," "Gallo"* (Valencia: Pre-Textos, 1993); *Las revistas literarias: un estudio introductorio* (Cádiz: U de Cádiz, 2004); and *Revistas de la vanguardia española* (Sevilla: Editorial Renacimiento, 2005). See also Francisco Javier Díez de Revenga, *Poetas y narradores: la narrativa breve en las revistas de vanguardia en España (1918–1936)* (Madrid: J. Pastor, 2005); and César Antonio Molina, *Medio siglo de prensa literaria española (1900–1950)* (Madrid: Ediciones Endymion, 1990). An overview of publications in this critical history can be found in Domingo Ródenas de Moya, "La historia en la fronda hemerográfica," *Revista de Libros* 103–104 (July–August 2005) [http://www.revistadelibros.com/articulo_completo.php?art=3663].

6. I am indebted to the major studies of both of these reviews in their national contexts: Jason Harding's *The "Criterion": Cultural Politics and Periodical Networks in Inter-War Britain* (Oxford: Oxford UP, 2002) and Evelyne López Campillo's *La "Revista de Occidente" y la formación de minorías* (Madrid: Taurus, 1972). The only comparative studies of these two journals have come from Spanish-language scholars who primarily note the affinities between them. See the documentary overview in K. M. Sibbald, "La imagen de España en *The Criterion* de T. S. Eliot" in *Luz vital: estudios de cultura hispánica en memoria de Victor Ouimette*, ed. Ramón F. Llorens García and Jesús Pérez Magallón (Alicante: Caja de Ahorros del Mediterráneo, 1999), 195–205; and the more theoretical approach of Margarita Garbisu Buesa's "*The Criterion*: su trayectoria y su vínculo europeo con la *Revista de Occidente*," *Revista de Occidente* 300 (May 2006): 147–174. Recalling these connections to Eliot, in 1982, the contemporary *Revista de Occidente* dedicated an issue to him on the centenary of his birth. See also *T. S. Eliot and Hispanic Modernity, 1924–1993*, ed. Kay Sibbald and Howard Young (Boulder, CO: Society of Spanish and Spanish-American Studies, 1994).

The coexistence of Wyndham Lewis and Herbert Read in the pages of the *Criterion*—like the coexistence of José Bergamín and Ernesto Giménez Caballero in the *Revista de Occidente*—confounds attempts to read these media as unified ideological projects, or as mouthpieces of their editors only. As does any study of a periodical's life, this chapter necessarily selects portions for analysis at the expense of others that may contradict them.

7. This is a topic that I do not have the space to address adequately in this book, but which has been treated masterfully by Christopher GoGwilt. The "idea of the West," GoGwilt argues, was significantly reoriented by the Russian Revolution, which "transformed the idea of Europe, preparing for the reactionary formation of the term 'the West'" in Spengler's use and in intellectual and literary discourse more generally; see GoGwilt, *The Invention of the West: Joseph Conrad and the Double-Mapping of Europe and Empire* (Stanford, CA: Stanford UP, 1995), 1–3; 220–242.

8. Eliot, "Last Words," *Criterion* 18:71 (January 1939): 271.

9. Eliot, "Brief Über Ernst Robert Curtius," *Freundesgabe Für Ernst Robert Curtius Zum 14 April, 1956* (Bern: Francke, 1956), 25.

10. Eliot [as "T. S. Apteryx"], "Observations," *Egoist* 5:5 (May 1918): 69.

11. Waugh, qtd. in *T. S. Eliot: The Contemporary Reviews*, ed. Jewel Spears Brooker (Cambridge: Cambridge UP, 2004), xv. Kevin J. H. Dettmar calls *Catholic Anthology* "a calculated insult to the Georgian sensibility" (introduction to *Rereading the New: A Backward Glance at Modernism*, ed. Dettmar [Ann Arbor: U of Michigan P, 1992], 4).

12. Eliot to John Quinn, July 9, 1919, in *Letters of T. S. Eliot*, 2 vols., ed. Valerie Eliot and Hugh Haughton (London: Faber and Faber, 2009), 1:375.

13. Eliot, "London Letter," *Dial* 72 (May 1922): 510.

14. Eliot, "A Commentary," *Criterion* 2:5 (October 1923): 104; emphasis in original. Despite the resistance in London, there was a small window of opportunity in this moment. In a survey of Spanish literature in England in the 1920s and 1930s, David Callahan notes that "the period following the First World War appears to have been somewhat more receptive to the passage of a certain number of foreign works into English than had previously been the case" ("Material Conditions for Reception: Spanish Literature in England, 1920–1940," *New Comparison* 15 [Spring 1993]: 101).

15. Eliot, "Tradition and the Individual Talent," in *Selected Prose of T. S. Eliot*, ed. and intro. Frank Kermode (New York: Farrar, Straus and Giroux, 1975), 39, 38.

16. Eliot to Mary Hutchinson, 11[?] July 1919, in *Letters* 1:379; emphasis in original. The Greek term *metic* was specifically Athenian in the classical era, connecting Athens to London as Eliot will in *The Waste Land*.

17. Eliot, "In Memory of Henry James," *Egoist* 1:5 (January 1918): 1.

18. Eliot, "The Three Provincialities," *Tyro* 2 (1922): 12.

19. Eliot to Larbaud, 12 March 1922, in *Letters* 1:643.

20. Eliot to Middleton Murry, 3 October 1922, in *Letters* 1:756. Eliot confessed his nervousness to Richard Aldington: "You know that I have no persecution mania, but that I am quite aware how obnoxious I am to perhaps the larger part of the literary world of London and that there will be a great many jackals swarming about waiting for my bones" (Eliot to Aldington, 13 July 1922, in *Letters* 1:699).

21. Pound to Eliot, 14 March 1922, in *Letters* 1:648; [sic]. Pound adds that "No Englishman's word is worth a damn.... I have published nothing there since I left.... I dont want

to appear in England. I have no belief in their capacity to understand anything. They still want what I was doing in 1908" (ibid., 647, 648).

22. Eliot, "A Commentary," *Criterion* 4:1 (January 1926): 4. Eliot wanted everything in the journal published in English; it was, save one short story, Cocteau's "Scandales."

23. Eliot, "A Commentary," *Criterion* 8:33 (July 1929): 577.

24. Bush, T. S. *Eliot: A Study in Character and Style* (New York: Oxford UP, 1983), 103.

25. Eliot, letter in *Transatlantic Review* 1:1 (January 1924): 95. Pollard examines Eliot's "complementary" cosmopolitanism in *New World Modernisms*, 5–13. On reactionary politics in several periodicals of the era, see Paul Peppis's *Literature, Politics, and the English Avant-garde: Nation and Empire, 1901–1918* (New York: Cambridge UP, 2000).

26. Eliot, Circular for the *Criterion*, 1922. See Eliot, "Foreign Exchanges," *Lloyds Bank Monthly* (October 1923): 360.

27. Eliot did have in mind Ford Madox Ford's editorship at the *English Review*, no doubt, and its valorization of the *Mercure de France*, but Ford had been replaced by Austin Harrison in 1910 and the review had become explicitly partisan; see Morrisson, *Public Face*, 51–53.

28. Eliot, "The Social Function of Poetry" [1945], in *On Poetry and Poets* (New York: Farrar, Strauss, and Giroux, 1957), 13; emphasis in original.

29. Eliot to Trend, 9 July 1924; in *Letters* 2:457.

30. Britain already had a *Review of Reviews* published by W. T. Stead, but Eliot aimed for a more elite and cosmopolitan audience. More similar was the established *Littell's Living Age*, a Boston-based publication that had British circulation. Eliot's idea, however, was to review sympathetic foreign periodicals by giving a sense of their cultural politics (rather than by reprinting selected pieces from them, which the *Criterion* did not do).

31. Eliot to *La Revue de France*, 28 October 1924, in *Letters* 2:522; Eliot to E. R. Curtius, 28 August 1922, in *Letters* 1:734. This section also allowed Eliot's staff to take small jabs at its American competitors, such as those Herbert Read offered against the *Dial*. It was expanded over time to include Latin American periodicals, for instance, and there was never an equivalent space for reviewing British journals.

32. Eliot to Pound, 9 July 1922, in *Letters* 1:693; emphases and parentheses in original; Eliot to Aldington, 4 May 1923, in *Letters* 2:122.

33. L. Higgin, "Spanish Novelists of To-Day," *Fortnightly Review* 90:536 (August 1911): 287; Ramiro de Maeztu, qtd. in S. Verdad [J. M. Kennedy], "Foreign Affairs," *New Age* 8:8 (22 December 1910): 172; Gilbert Seldes, "The Theatre Abroad," *Dial* 81 (October 1926): 322. Some reviews featured letters or dispatches from correspondents in New York, Paris, and Berlin, but Madrid was rarely, if ever, included. Of titles roughly similar to the *Criterion*, the *Fortnightly Review* and the *English Review* printed irregular notes on Spanish literature, but only the *Athenaeum* (which merged with the *Nation* in 1921) and the American *Dial* (which had British circulation) treated Spanish literature with any consistency. The *Athenaeum's* columns from the Spanish figure Rafael Altamira are generally list-like and give little sense of Spanish letters. Despite employing Maeztu, A. R. Orage's *New Age* barely covered Spanish matters. In 1918, Ezra Pound, who had maintained some Spanish contacts from his graduate studies in Madrid, planned a bilingual "Spanish number" of the *Little Review* with the help of Tomás Morales, a poet from the Canary Islands. This ambitious project was never realized; see *Pound/The "Little Review": Letters of Ezra Pound to Margaret Anderson: The "Little Review" Correspondence*, ed. Thomas L. Scott, Melvin J. Friedman, and Jackson R. Bryer (New York: New Directions, 1988), 203.

34. Eliot to Aldington, 4 July 1922, in *Letters* 1:691. Aldington, a critic and Imagist poet, initially handled French reviews.

35. Eliot to Flint, 29 January 1923, in *Letters* 2:26. Flint had made his name as an expert on foreign letters with an influential review, "Contemporary French Poetry," in Harold Monro's *Poetry Review* in 1912. In 1920, he collaborated with Eliot and Aldous Huxley on *Three Critical Essays on Modern English Poetry*.

36. Orlo Williams, "Modern Spain," *TLS* (23 June 1921): 399; Williams, review of *The Origins of Modern Spain* by J. B. Trend, in *Criterion* 13:53 (July 1934): 665.

37. Trend, *Picture of Modern Spain*, 1, 39.

38. Eliot to Marichalar, 5 April 1922, in *Letters* 1:659. Eliot wanted to include *Índice* in the *Criterion*'s reviews of foreign periodicals, but it folded in 1922 (Eliot to Aldington, 27 May 1923, *Letters* 2:143). Larbaud wrote to Marichalar that he gave Eliot the Spaniard's address; Larbaud to Marichalar, 5 April 1922, Archives of Antonio Marichalar, Marqués de Montesa, Real Academia de la Historia, Madrid; hereafter cited as "Marichalar, RAH, Madrid."

39. Larbaud, "The *Ulysses* of James Joyce," in *James Joyce: The Critical Heritage*, ed. Robert H. Deming (New York: Barnes and Noble, 1970), 1:253; translation modified. See also Pascale Casanova, *The World Republic of Letters*, trans. M. B. DeBevoise (Cambridge: Harvard UP, 2004), 128–129.

40. Eliot to Flint, 13 July 1922, in *Letters* 1:698.

41. Hesse, "Recent German Poetry," *Criterion* 1:1 (October 1922): 89.

42. Marichalar, "Contemporary Spanish Literature," *Criterion* 1:3 (April 1923): 277, 278 283, 288, 290, 286; capital letters in original. Notably, Marichalar dismisses the playwright Jacinto Benavente, one of the few Spanish writers discussed in Britain at the time. When Benavente, a very conservative figure, was the surprise winner of the Nobel Prize in 1922, Marichalar was forced to append to his article a humble note expressing his appreciation that Benavente's work has drawn foreign attention to Spanish arts.

43. Marichalar, "Madrid Chronicle," *Criterion* 6:4 (October 1927): 355. Roberta Johnson treats the multiple sexualized and gendered valences of the Don Juan figure in literary-political debates in Spain at this moment in *Gender and Nation in the Spanish Modernist Novel* (Nashville, TN: Vanderbilt UP, 2003), 111.

44. Eliot to Marichalar, 9 August 1922, in *Letters* 1:719. Eliot had studied some Spanish at Harvard. This relationship was not without disagreements, as when Eliot, on the advice of Flint, rejected one of Marichalar's contributions in 1926.

45. Eliot to Trend, 18 January 1923, in *Letters* 2:16–17. Eliot's letters show that he had already read Marichalar's as yet unpublished chronicle.

46. Eliot to Trend, 15 February 1923, in *Letters* 2:57; Eliot to Marichalar, 3 August 1926, FOG, Madrid.

47. The misunderstanding between Eliot and Ramón occurred over the writer's original manuscripts, which he claimed Eliot never returned, igniting a series of angry letters from the Spaniard. Ramón first asks for, then reiterates his request—then angrily demands—the return of his notebooks from Eliot. These unpublished letters from May 1922 are held in Harvard's Houghton Library. Furthermore, Flint found the stories extraordinarily difficult to translate, and Eliot found them bizarre and disappointing, too much like the iconoclastic avant-gardes that did not interest him. This might have been predictable to some degree: Ramón had translated Marinetti's Futurist manifesto into Spanish in 1910, and he had

greater sympathy with the avant-gardes of the continent than with Eliot's neoclassical Europeanism. Juan Ramón Jiménez perhaps would have been a better choice. Eliot wrote that he preferred Marichalar's "straightforward *chronique* of Spanish letters" to Ramón's work (Eliot to Flint, 15 August 1922, in *Letters* 1:724). Ramón's stories appear in "The New Museum," *Criterion* 1:2 (January 1923): 196–201. The little magazine *Broom* (1921–1924), an Anglophone periodical originally printed in Italy, actually had printed three of Ramón Gómez de la Serna's short pieces in May 1922, but its circulation and audience were very different.

48. Trend to León Sánchez Cuesta, 14 August 1927; 12 October 1928, Archives of the Residencia de Estudiantes, Madrid.

49. Trend, "The Moors in Spanish Music," *Criterion* 2:6 (February 1924): 206, 208, 215. For Eliot's suggestions to Trend, see Eliot to Trend, 23 August 1923, in *Letters* 2:193.

50. Trend, "Music Chronicle," *Criterion* 4:1 (January 1926): 155. Trend's letters with Falla are gathered in Trend and Falla, *Epistolario (1919–1935)*, ed. Nigel Dennis (Granada: U de Granada, 2007). Dainotto studies a similar argument by the eighteenth-century Jesuit thinker Juan Andrés, who conceived of European modernity through the "oriental" influences in Sicily and Andalusia (*Europe (in Theory)*, [Durham, NC: Duke UP, 2007], 101–133).

51. Trend, "Music Chronicle," *Criterion* 9:34 (October 1929): 101, 100. See also Trend, "Music Chronicle," *Criterion* 3:12 (July 1925): 567–569.

52. Trend, "Music Chronicle," *Criterion* 3:9 (October 1924): 118, 117.

53. Eliot, qtd. in Leslie Paul, "A Conversation with T. S. Eliot," *Kenyon Review* 27 (1965): 14. Ortega's homage, "Le Temps, la distance et la forme chez Marcel Proust," appeared in the *NRF*, alongside similar pieces from most every prominent French writer and from international figures ranging from Curtius to Middleton Murry, one month after Eliot's latest "Lettre d'Angleterre." David Chinitz remarks on some instances in which Eliot and Ortega have been wrongly coupled as antagonists of mass culture in his *T. S. Eliot and the Cultural Divide* (Chicago: U of Chicago P, 2003), 195n7. In a column for *The New Age* in 1916, Maeztu had briefly introduced Ortega's thought to British audiences simply by noting that "Señor Ortega y Gasset does not know the English. My friendship could not induce him to try to understand them. And yet his observation[s on the Great War are . . .] typically English" ("A Visit to the Front," *New Age* 20:4 [23 November 1916]: 77).

54. Eliot to Marichalar, 23 August 1923, in *Letters* 2:189.

55. Flint, "Spanish Periodicals," *Criterion* 2:5 (October 1923): 109. As David Callahan notes, "such respect for a Spanish journal from [Eliot,] a leading member of the most dynamic literary circles in England[,] would have been inconceivable" even ten years earlier; in "The Early Reception of Ortega y Gasset, 1920–1939," *Forum for Modern Language Studies* 26:1 (1990): 77.

56. Curtius, "Ortega y Gasset," in *Essays on European Literature*, 282.

57. Eliot to Trend, 9 July 1924, in *Letters* 2:457; Trend to Eliot, ibid., n2.

58. Eliot to Ortega, 13[?] July 1924, in *Letters*, 2:466; capital letters in original.

59. Ortega, "Spanish Letter," the *Dial* 77 (October 1924): 324, 325, 326. Ortega's article is excerpted mostly from his essay on El Escorial. Alyse Gregory secured this "Spanish Letter" earlier that year (Gregory to Ortega, 28 April 1924, FOG, Madrid). Gregory hoped that Ortega would produce another piece, perhaps on Baroja or on Waldo Frank, but Ortega's life in the *Dial* was brief: Ortega and the *Revista de Occidente* are mentioned only once, and the notion of a European Spain is mostly absent from the American review's pages. As editor,

Marianne Moore also wrote Ortega several times in 1926–1927 asking for columns and/or book reviews, without success. It may be asked if Eliot's anti-Semitism and his increasing anti-liberalism might have dissuaded Ortega from taking on such a role, but Eliot's views on Jewish people were not known to Ortega; anti-Semitism per se did not offend him (see his exchanges with Trend below); and even Eliot's conversion did not prevent Ortega from participating in the fiction competition in 1929–1930.

60. Paul Morand, "Paris Letter," *Dial* 78 (March 1925): 221. Morand believes that Ortega is an ideal match for the *Dial*, but this relationship did not pan out. The *Dial* had secured through John Dos Passos a contribution from Unamuno in 1920. Pound, the Paris correspondent at the time, hoped it would be the first of four regular pieces from the philosopher, and James Sibley Watson, one of the new owners of the review, advertised Unamuno as a member of the journal's new "foreign staff" (Pound to Scofield Thayer, 4–5 July 1920, in *Pound, Thayer, Watson, and the "Dial": A Story in Letters*, ed. Walter Sutton [Gainesville: U of Florida P, 1994], 63). Unamuno contributed only one piece, however, which was delayed until 1924 and does not treat Spanish culture at all. The journal printed articles by Dos Passos on Pío Baroja and Antonio Machado, but little followed. Dos Passos's early articles on Spanish figures of the Generation of '98 were collected in his *Rosinante to the Road Again* (1922).

61. Ortega, "Propósitos," in *OC* 6:313. The *Revista* never had a circulation of greater than 3,000, yet its influence on major cultural figures and centers across the Hispanophone world was immense.

62. Claudio de la Torre and Pedro Salinas had studied at Cambridge; Luis Cernuda and Manuel Altolaguirre would spend significant time in England and in America; and Ramón Pérez de Ayala was the future Spanish ambassador to England. Baeza, who had taught at Cambridge and had written extensively on Irish literature, translated works by D'Annunzio, Ibsen, Conrad, Galsworthy, and Wilde. Díez-Canedo had published translations in a variety of media including *Faro*, *España*, *El Liberal*, and the weekly arts supplement *Los Lunes de El Imparcial*, and he helped found *Índice* with Juan Ramón Jiménez. On the evolving group of collaborators at the *Revista*, see López Campillo, *La "Revista de Occidente,"* 71–76.

63. Some *modernistas* and members of the Generation of '98 had brought significant works of French literature in translation to Spain, while the vanguardists of the 1910s translated famous texts of Dadaism and Italian Futurism into Spanish. Translations from English, which were less frequent, had appeared in vanguard periodicals, but often came from figures with singular interests in it, such as Unamuno, Pérez de Ayala, Juan Ramón Jiménez, Gregorio Martínez Sierra, Salvador de Madariaga, and José Pablo Rivas. Despite their restricted cultural politics, two regional journals were cutting-edge outlets for criticism on British literature in the late 1910s and early 1920s. *Hermes*, a Spanish-language Basque publication, published notable pieces of criticism on modernist figures, including several by Pound. *Nós* [*Ourselves*, or *Us*] a Galician-language journal that advocated for that province's autonomy, followed Irish politics and literature assiduously at the time, too—especially the works of the Irish Revival and of Wilde and Shaw. Ortega's former review *España* published some commentaries on British literature, including essays by Ortega himself on Wells and Chesterton. The Catalan publication *La Revista* (unrelated to Ortega's) ran some similar articles, as did Manuel Azaña's *La Pluma*. The Spanish daily press published translated material and commentary on foreign literatures, in newspapers like *El Sol*, *El Heraldo de Madrid*, *ABC*,

and in *Los Lunes de El Imparcial*. Shakespeare was a far greater presence than any modern English-language writer, but gradually, the works of Victorian and Edwardian writers—Dickens, Hardy, Wells, Chesterton, Conan Doyle, Wilde, Shaw, and Yeats—all appeared in Spain before 1920. But Ortega, himself a regular presence in these papers, saw limited spaces for such work in daily media. My work on this subject has been aided valuably by Antonio Raúl de Toro Santos and David Clark's *British and Irish Writers in the Spanish Periodical Press 1900–1965. Escritores británicos e irlandeses en la prensa española 1900–1965* (Oleiros: Netbiblo, 2007), which contains a very rich bibliography. See also Jean Andrews, *Spanish Reactions to the Anglo-Irish Revival in the Early Twentieth Century: The Stone by the Elixir* (Lewiston, NY: Edwin Mellen P, 1991). For an overview of translation from the era of vanguards through to the civil war, see Miguel Gallego Roca, "De las vanguardias a la Guerra Civil," in *Historia de la traducción en España*, ed. Francisco Lafarga and Luis Pegenaute (Salamanca: Ambos Mundos, 2004), 479–526.

64. Gallego Roca, "De las vanguardias," in *Historia de la traducción*, ed. Lafarga and Pegenaute, 519. See also Gallego Roca, "De cómo no fueron posibles en español las traducciones vanguardistas," in *La traducción en la Edad de Plata*, ed. Pegenaute, 41–48.

65. Baeza, "El espíritu de internacionalidad y la traducciones," in *Teoría y práctica de la traducción en la prensa periódica española (1900–1965)*, ed. Antonio Raúl de Toro Santos and Pablo Cancelo López (Soria: Diputación Provincial de Soria, 2008), 117–118. More has been translated in the past 10 to 12 years than had been in the previous 70 or 80, Baeza claims.

66. Ortega, "Cosmopolitismo," in *OC* 4:487, 489.

67. Ortega, "Reforma de la inteligencia (1)," in *OC* 4:498–499.

68. Ortega, *The Dehumanization of Art and Other Writings on Art and Culture*, trans. anonymous (Garden City, NY: Doubleday Anchor, 1956), 3, 12, 40. Ortega argues that this trend should raise the awareness of the elite that they should lead their countries and their continent.

69. López Campillo lists the Revista de Occidente press's translators in her *La "Revista de Occidente,"* 257. Almost all of the papers and letters concerning Ortega's founding of the journal were lost when its offices were bombed during the Spanish Civil War, so accounts such as hers and my own are based primarily on published materials, memoirs, and the letters preserved at Ortega's home.

70. Marichalar, "Estela de Joseph Conrad," in *EL*, 219.

71. Marichalar, "Las 'vidas' y Lytton Strachey," in *EL*, 132.

72. Marichalar, "Último grito," in *EL*, 261. Marichalar is quoting Middleton Murry.

73. Marichalar, "James Joyce in His Labyrinth" ["James Joyce en su laberinto," 1924], see appendix page 210.

74. Marichalar, "Mutaciones," in *EL*, 225, 227.

75. Marichalar, Review of *El alba y otras cosas* by Ramón Gómez de la Serna, *Revista de Occidente* 3:7 (January 1924): 122.

76. Marichalar, "Madrid Chronicle," *Criterion* 4:2 (April 1926): 357. Flint also mentions in this number that the *Revista*, whose issues have not made it to his desk recently, is surging back with strong issues.

77. Marichalar, "La joven literatura," in *EL*, 193, 194. See Domingo Ródenas de Moya, "La joven literatura española ante la 'petite chapelle' francesa: Larbaud, Marichalar e *Intentions*," *Hispanogalia* I (2004–2005): 107–133. Marichalar also organized the commemoration

in Seville of the 300th anniversary of baroque Spanish poet Luis de Góngora's death. This event marked the public coalescence of the Generation of '27. Enrique Díez-Canedo followed with a survey of the "young literature" of Spain in *Intentions* in 1925. See especially Anderson, *El veintisiete en tela de juicio*, 13–66, for a recovery of the many ways in which "generación" was used in the twenties to refer to these poets.

78. Baeza, "Samuel Butler, 'dilettante' consumado," *Revista de Occidente* 15:43 (January 1927): 71.

79. Several presses had begun printing collections of translated texts in the late 1910s and early 1920s, including Biblioteca Nueva, the Compañía Ibero Americana de Publicaciones, and Calpe, but contemporary Anglophone writers were not often included in these series. Zeus and Cénit were two of the presses that published many translations in the early 1930s.

80. Eliot to Richard Cobden-Sanderson, 1 December 1922, in *Letters* 1:604.

81. Marichalar, "Último grito," in *EL*, 261. The *Revista* did not offer reviews of foreign periodicals like those in the *Criterion*, only a list of titles received ("Mementos de revistas"). However, notes like these are common, and there are reviews of foreign literatures that often refer to journals, such as Enrique Díez-Canedo's "El país donde florece la poesía: USA" ["The Country Where Poetry Flourishes: USA"], *Revista de Occidente* 7:21 (March 1925): 353–359. See my "A Spanish View of Modernist Poetry in American Periodicals (1925)," in the *Journal of Modern Periodical Studies* 3:1 (2012): 10–18.

82. "Well said," writes the reporter, José Luis Salado, "our *Revista de Occidente* does seem very much like the *Criterion*" (Salado, "Antonio Marichalar tiene en su despacho un retrato del duque de Osuna," *El Heraldo de Madrid*, 3 April 1930, 8).

83. Guillén, *Lenguaje y poesía: algunos casos españoles* (Madrid: Alianza, 1972), 191.

84. "Current Reviews," *transition* 2 (May 1927): [n.p.].

85. "Glossary," *transition* 4 (July 1927): 181. I thank Lori Cole for pointing me to this issue of *transition*.

86. Pastor, "Spain," in *Contemporary Movements in European Literature*, ed. William Rose and Jacob Isaacs (London: G. Routledge and Sons, 1929), 89–124.

87. Pierre de Lanux, "Notes from France," *The Bookman* 59:6 (August 1924): 756; emphasis in original.

88. Schulten, "Mainake [sic], una ciudad griega en el extremo Occidente," *Revista de Occidente* 10:28 (October 1925): 88.

89. Bosch Gimpera, "Los pueblos primitivos de España," *Revista de Occidente* 9:26 (August 1925): 156. See also Bosch Gimpera, "Problemas de la colonización fenicia de España y del Mediterráneo occidental," *Revista de Occidente* 20:60 (June 1928): 314–348. Bosch Gimpera follows the line of argument that "East" and "West" began to separate themselves across the Mediterranean in the fifth and sixth centuries A.D.

90. García Gómez, "Oriente y Occidente: el eterno problema," *Revista de Occidente* 33:98 (August 1931): 121, 125; emphasis mine. See also Lino Novás Calvo's essay on Singapore, "Donde el Oriente se encuentra con Occidente" ["Where East Meets West"], *Revista de Occidente* 50:148 (October 1935): 122–128.

91. See, for instance, Maya Soifer, "Beyond *convivencia*: Critical reflections on the historiography of interfaith relations in Christian Spain," *Journal of Medieval Iberian Studies* 1:1 (January 2009): 19–35.

92. Menéndez Pidal, "De la vida del Cid," *Revista de Occidente* 11:32 (February 1926): 149–150; emphasis in original.

93. Menéndez Pidal, *The Cid and His Spain*, trans. Harold Sunderland (London: J. Murray, 1934), 452, 453, 15; translation modified.

94. Mainer, "Reconstruir la España contemporánea (entre la literatura y la historia)," in *España: la mirada del otro*, ed. Ismael Saz (Madrid: Marcial Pons, 1998), 90. These matters are discussed in Joan Ramon Resina, "Whose Hispanism? Cultural Trauma, Disciplined Memory, and Symbolic Dominance," in *Ideologies of Hispanism*, ed. Mabel Moraña [Nashville, TN: Vanderbilt UP, 2005], 160–186); and Thomas Harrington, "Rapping on the Cast(i)le Gates," in *Ideologies of Hispanism*, 107–137. The latter essay, however, ascribes an imperialist position to Ortega that is inaccurate. Resina shows in "From Crowd Psychology to Racial Hygiene: The Medicalization of Reaction and the New Spain," that Ortega, even while condemning fascism, provided some building blocks of the racialized ideologies of Spanish fascism in his *Invertebrate Spain* and *Revolt of the Masses* (in *Crowds*, ed. Jeffrey T. Schnapp and Matthew Tiews [Stanford, CA: Stanford UP, 2006], 225–248). The ideas in these texts, however, are ones that Ortega came to regret and revise greatly throughout the 1920s and 1930s.

95. Castro, "An Introduction to the *Quijote*," in *An Idea of History: Selected Essays of Américo Castro* (Columbus: Ohio State UP, 1977), 112. This essay grew out of Castro's reflections on *Don Quixote* that he first published in the *Revista de Occidente*.

96. Sánchez-Albornoz, "España y el Islam," *Revista de Occidente* 24:70 (April 1929): 1, 6, 4, 3, 6, 30. As Patricia Grieve points out, Sánchez-Albornoz's vision of continuity in Spanishness from its Christian origins in Asturias later were appropriated by the Franco regime, who molded it into its own ideal of Spain as a Christian state unaffected essentially by the Moorish invasions (Grieve, *The Eve of Spain: Myths of Origins in the History of Christian, Muslim, and Jewish Conflict* [Baltimore: Johns Hopkins UP, 2009], 30). This occurred despite the fact Franco had exiled Sánchez-Albornoz, who had served as ambassador to Portugal in the liberal Republican government. The debate between Castro and Sánchez-Albornoz came to a head in the 1950s, when the former was teaching at Princeton in his own exile and the latter was at the University of Buenos Aires.

97. In fact, despite his earlier criticism of Bertrand Russell, in 1924 he began publishing in translation the first of many of the philosopher's books through his Revista de Occidente press. Antonio Espina, in an exemplary moment, criticized Ivan Goll's new anthology *Les cinq continents* for not reflecting the fact that "the Orient, with its nucleus Slavic and Asiatic, is the most interesting and full of promise" of all literatures, more so than those of British, American, or "Latin civilizations" (Espina, review of *Les cinq continents: Anthologie mondiale de poésie contemporaine* by Ivan Goll, *Revista de Occidente* 1:2 [August 1923]: 251).

98. Frank, *Virgin Spain* (New York: Boni and Liveright, 1926), 241.

99. Keyserling, "España y Europa," *Revista de Occidente* 12:35 (May 1926): 133–134, 144, 138. Like Ortega, and like the *Criterion*, Marichalar chided Russell alongside the Keyserling, Rolland, and other thinkers for their "dilettante Orientalism," asking, "will we have to say this is the 'Orientalization' rather than the 'Decline' of the West?" (Marichalar, review of *El nuevo glosario: los diálogos de la pasión meditabunda*, by Eugenio d'Ors, in *EL*, 188; "La panacea de Darmstadt," *Revista de Occidente* 23:67 [January 1929]: 103).

100. Ángel González Palencia, " 'La Divina Commedia' y el Islam," *Revista de Occidente* 9:25 (July 1925): 109.

101. Letter to Stanley Rice, 1 October 1923, in *Letters* 2:229. Like the ambivalent turn to the East that he made in *The Waste Land*, Eliot's sense was split. Publicly, he wanted an

open-ended debate; privately, he worried about those "forms of Oriental influence which seem to me conducive to hysteria and barbarism," and he pointed to Germany as the "gate" through which they were coming. Eliot, who said he had "dabbled in Oriental languages," wrote all of this to Rice and confessed that he feared that the continent might "relax our hold on those European traditions without which I believe we should relapse into a state of barbarism equal to that of America or Russia." Furthermore, Eliot pointed to Hermann Hesse as an example of the dangerous "Orientalist" strain in contemporary writing—a trend that wrongfully pulls young writers toward Dostoevsky. Yet, he proudly published both of these writers in the inaugural issue of the *Criterion* (Letter to Rice, ibid., 2:230, 229).

102. Zulueta, "El enigma de Rusia," *Revista de Occidente* 9:27 (September 1925): 278.

103. Eliot, "A Commentary," *Criterion* 4:2 (April 1926): 222; Eliot to Marichalar, 20 January 1926, FOG, Madrid; Eliot to Ortega, 3 August 1926, FOG, Madrid. Eliot's first letter, in fact, was in part a response to Ortega's about a review-exchange. Ortega's brother Eduardo Ortega y Gasset, a well-known figure in the center-left opposition to Primo de Rivera's rule, had also been exiled by the dictator.

104. Massis, *Defence of the West*, Pt. I, trans. Flint, *Criterion* 4:2 (April 1926): 224, 225, 224, 227, 237.

105. Codrington, letter to the *Criterion* 7:4 (June 1928): 435.

106. Spengler was not a major presence, however, in the *Criterion*, as he had been in the *Revista de Occidente*. Eliot had read *Decline of the West* and was unimpressed; in his commentary, he dismissed Spengler as an "abstract philosopher ... of history" whose work merits little attention ("A Commentary," *Criterion* 2:8 [July 1924]: 491).

107. Trend, review of *El pensamiento de Cervantes*, by Américo Castro, *Criterion* 5:1 (January 1927): 146.

108. Trend to Ortega, 29 August 1933, FOG, Madrid; emphasis in original. There is some truth to Trend's statement, given that, despite the labor of generations of Hispanists, Cambridge, for one, had no chair in Spanish until Trend's appointment in 1933.

109. Trend, "Music Chronicle," *Criterion* 8:32 (April 1929): 485. Apuleius was a North African Berber who wrote in Latin during the Roman occupation, thus he distantly prefigures Falla's Andalusian music.

110. Trend, "Music Chronicle," *Criterion* 3:11 (April 1925): 435.

111. Trend, "Music Chronicle," *Criterion* 8:31 (December 1928): 308.

112. Trend, "Music Chronicle," *Criterion* 11:45 (July 1932): 704. In the same breath, though, Trend is worried by German nationalistic suppressions of Jewish music and musicians at a festival in Vienna.

113. Stanley Rice, "Hindu Music," *Criterion* 4:3 (June 1926): 551. Likewise, to approach the topic of the "West" in the *Criterion* only through Eliot's own views and his publication of French reactionaries is to miss other authors such as May Sinclair, a regular contributor early in the journal's life. Her short story "Jones's Karma," for instance, is told through Buddha-figures.

114. Flint, "Spanish Periodicals," *Criterion* 4:4 (October 1926): 812, 813. Trend's new book on Spain, *Alfonso the Sage*, is also reviewed positively in this issue.

115. Marcelle Auclair, "Los dos últimas obras de Valery Larbaud: *Allen* y *Jaune bleu blanc*," *Revista de Occidente* 18:54 (December 1927): 407.

116. Eliot, "A Commentary," *Criterion* 6:2 (August 1927): 97–98.

117. Marichalar, "Ideas and Beliefs of José Ortega y Gasset," *Criterion* 17:69 (July 1938): 714. Ortega criticized the League on several occasions for amplifying rather than stemming nationalist aggression; see especially "La Paz y España," in *OC* 10:451–453; and "España y la Liga de Naciones," in *OC* 10:502–504.

118. Eliot, "Brief Über Ernst Robert Curtius," 26; emphasis in original. On Ortega and Curtius's collaborations in the *Revista*, see Andrés Soria Olmedo, *Vanguardismo y crítica literaria en España (1910-1930)* (Madrid: Istmo, 1988), 157–189. Harding reads the "defence of the West" in the *Criterion* through its German connections and Curtius's role in it; see *The "Criterion,"* 202–226.

119. Curtius, "Ortega y Gasset," in *Essays on European Literature*, 288.

120. Curtius, "Restoration of the Reason," *Criterion* 6:5 (November 1927): 397, 396, 390, 397.

121. Curtius, "T. S. Eliot," in *Essays on European Literature*, 358.

122. Eliot, "A Commentary," *Criterion* 6:2 (August 1927): 97, 98, 99; capital letters in original.

123. Eliot, "A Commentary," *Criterion* 7:3 (March 1928): 194.

124. Trend, "Music Chronicle," *Criterion* 8:31 (December 1928): 307. Flint wrote that "even M. Henri Massis may become aware of [English history] one of these days, and he may then, perhaps, rewrite his *Defence of the West*, introducing the chief character, this country, that is busily defending what he both misunderstands and just talks at" ("French Periodicals," *Criterion* 6:4 [October 1927]: 381).

125. Fletcher, "East and West," *Criterion* 7:4 (June 1928): 306, 322–323.

126. Eliot, "A Commentary," *Criterion* 6:1 (July 1927): 3; emphasis in original.

127. Eliot, *Dante* (London: Faber & Faber, 1929), 18–20; emphasis in original.

128. Pound to Eliot, 4 November 1922, in *Letters* 1:772; [sic], emphasis in original.

129. Eliot, "East Coker" V:1–2, in *Complete Poems and Plays, 1909-1950* (New York: Harcourt Brace, 1980), 128.

130. Harding, *The "Criterion,"* 225. See Peter Ackroyd, *T. S. Eliot: A Life* (New York: Simon & Schuster, 1984), 248. Jeroen Vanheste's *Guardians of the Humanist Legacy: The Classicism of T. S. Eliot's "Criterion" Network and Its Relevance to Our Postmodern World* (Leiden; Boston: Brill, 2007) is an ambitious attempt to characterize these periodicals as engaged in humanist practices derived from the classical Greek tradition. However, it is largely a disorganized index of overtures without analysis that seriously misreads both Eliot and Ortega. Vanheste's chapter, "The idea of Europe," in *T. S. Eliot in Context*, ed. Jason Harding (Cambridge: Cambridge UP, 2011) outlines the argument of his book and the figures upon whom he depends (52–59).

131. Eliot, "The Unity of European Culture," in *Notes toward the Definition of Culture* (New York: Harcourt, Brace, and Co., 1949), 120.

132. Eliot, "Last Words," 271. Few archives remain to explain the sudden disappearance of this competition; see Garbisu, "The *Criterion*," 155.

133. The two met on several occasions when the Spaniard traveled to London, and later, Marichalar translated Eliot's *For Lancelot Andrewes* (1928) for the Spanish journal *Cruz y Raya* [roughly, *Yes and No*, with the additional sense of *Enough!*] in 1934, but I have found no correspondence between them after the civil war.

134. Eliot, "Brief Über Ernst Robert Curtius," 26; Curtius, "Hermann Hesse," in *Essays on European Literature*, 170.

135. See J. H. Copley, " 'The Politics of Friendship': T. S. Eliot in Germany Through E. R. Curtius's Looking Glass," 243–267; and William Marx, "Two Modernisms: T. S. Eliot and *La Nouvelle Revue Française*," in *The International Reception of T. S. Eliot*, ed. Elisabeth Däumer and Shyamal Bagchee (London: Continuum, 2007), 25–35.

136. Trend to Ortega, 15 November 1925, FOG, Madrid.

137. Trend to Ortega, 1 December 1926, FOG, Madrid.

Chapter 2

1. Larbaud, *Lettres à Adrienne Monnier et à Sylvia Beach, 1919–1933*, ed. Maurice Saillet (Paris: Institut Mémoires de l'édition contemporaine, 1991), 97; parentheses in original. Monnier owned the Parisian La Maison des Amis des Livres, sister-store to Beach's Shakespeare and Company. Cf. Molly's line, "*O Maria Santissima* he did look a big fool . . .," in Joyce, *Ulysses* (New York: Vintage Press, 1986), 18.306–307; hereafter cited as *U*. The readings I offer below bring together what Franco Moretti calls "*space in literature*" and "*literature in space*," which he suggests "may occasionally (and interestingly) overlap"; he dismisses these overlaps too quickly, however, by arguing that the two "are essentially different" (*Atlas of the European Novel, 1800–1900* [New York: Verso, 1998], 3; emphases in original).

2. Anonymous, review of *El Artista Adolescente (Retrato), novela de James Joyce, traducción de Alfonso Donado, prólogo con varias ilustraciones de Antonio Marichalar* (Madrid: Biblioteca Nueva, 1926), *Criterion* 5:1 (January 1927): 158. The unsigned review was likely written by Conrad Aiken, or perhaps J. B. Trend.

3. Joyce to Harriet Shaw Weaver, 28 May 1929, in *Letters of James Joyce*, ed. Stuart Gilbert (London: Faber, 1957), 1:281.

4. Joyce, "The Day of the Rabblement," in *Occasional, Critical, and Political Writings*, ed. and intro. Kevin Barry (Oxford: Oxford UP, 2000), 50; hereafter cited as *OCPW*.

5. Letter to Mrs. William Murray, 14 October 14, 1921, in *Letters* 1:174. This letter and Joyce's acknowledgment of a response (which apparently did not mention Mamy) some three weeks later are both dated after Joyce had completed "Penelope," making Galway—which Brenda Maddox rightly accentuates, too—more likely as a deeper source for Molly's imagined Hispanicity; see note 8.

6. Joyce, "The Mirage of the Fisherman of Aran" (1912), in *OCPW* 203, 201. The English destruction of Galway during Cromwell's conquest of Ireland was said to be particularly brutal after the local population sided with the Catholic confederates and against the English garrison in the Irish Rebellion of 1641–1642.

7. Joyce, "The City of the Tribes" (1912), in *OCPW* 197. Molly also connects Ireland, Gibraltar, and Spain through Stephen's name: "Dedalus I wonder its like those names in Gibraltar Delapaz Delagracia they had the devils queer names" (*U* 18.1463–1464). This trip in the late summer of 1912 was Joyce's last to Ireland.

8. *U* 18.1587–1589. On Galway and Gibraltar, see Brenda Maddox, *Nora: The Real Life of Molly Bloom* (Boston: Houghton Mifflin, 1988), 8, 206.

9. *U* 4.211–212. The "Levante" also refers in Spain to the country's eastern Mediterranean coast.

10. *U* 18.864–865, 13.969, 16.873, 5.594–595, 11.732–733, 13.1114–1115, 16.879. Joyce's proofs reveal that he added several "Spanish" elements on revision to strengthen this portrait of Molly. Philip Herring details the means by which "Molly's Gibraltar was created out of

books" in "Towards an Historical Molly Bloom," *ELH* 45:3 (1978): 501. Molly's origins are notoriously difficult to pin down, primarily because her father Brian Tweedy's stories are at best dubious. The traditional reading is that her father was an Irishman in the British army stationed in Gibraltar, where he met her mother, a possibly Jewish Spaniard named Lunita Laredo, who might also have been a prostitute (cf. Molly in "Penelope," "my mother whoever she was might have given me a nicer name Lord knows after the lovely one she had Lunita Laredo" [*U* 18.846–848]). See also Jonathan Quick, "Molly Bloom's Mother," *ELH* 57:1 (1990): 223–240.

11. John Henry Raleigh explains the likely (and convoluted) origin of this conjecture in his *The Chronicle of Leopold and Molly Bloom: Ulysses as Narrative* (Berkeley: U of California P, 1977), 112.

12. *U* 16.1429–1430. This moment mirrors an earlier one in "Eumaeus" in which Murphy "fumble[s] out a picture postcard from his inside pocket" that depicts natives in Bolivia. Bloom "unostentatiously" flips over the card to see an address from Chile (*U* 16.472, 16.487).

13. *U* 16.1414–1415. Besides referring to a popular rhyme, the "king of Spain's daughter" is possibly an inside reference to Lucia, whose summer camp had been visited by the royal; see Maddox, *Nora*, 215.

14. Buchanan, *Britain and the Spanish Civil War* (New York: Cambridge UP, 1997), 12.

15. Hume, *Spain: Its Greatness and Decay (1479–1788)*, intro. Edward Armstrong (Cambridge: Cambridge UP, 1898), v. Hume's account aims to be sympathetic to Spain, in actuality.

16. See *La Época* and *El Imparcial* of 5 May 1898, both available digitally through the Hemeroteca digital de la Biblioteca Nacional de España (hemerotecadigital.bne.es).

17. The "wild geese" were former Irish soldiers who, exiled from Ireland, joined continental armies. The exiled Fenian and wild goose Kevin Egan, based on Joseph Casey, is twice described as having "Spanish tassels," abutting such connections (*U* 3.230, 15.4498).

18. Joyce, *OCPW* 118–19; *Finnegans Wake*, intro. John Bishop (New York: Penguin, 1999), 309; hereafter cited as *FW*.

19. Buchanan, *Britain and the Spanish Civil War*, 12.

20. Andrew Gibson details these critiques on both political and cultural levels in *Joyce's Revenge: History, Politics, and Aesthetics in* Ulysses (Oxford; New York: Oxford UP, 2002). See also Richard Begam, "Joyce's Trojan Horse: *Ulysses* and the Aesthetics of Decolonization," in *Modernism and Colonialism: British and Irish Literature, 1899–1939*, ed. Begam and Michael Valdez Moses (Durham, NC: Duke UP, 2007), 185–208; and Willard Potts, *Joyce and the Two Irelands* (Austin: U of Texas P, 2000).

21. John McCourt, "Trieste," in *James Joyce in Context*, ed. McCourt (Cambridge: Cambridge UP, 2009), 230. He notes that Joyce eventually came to see the Austro-Hungarian empire with more sympathy (237). See also McCourt, *The Years of Bloom: James Joyce in Trieste, 1904–1920* (Madison: U of Wisconsin P, 2000); and Andras Ungar, *Joyce's* Ulysses *as National Epic: Epic Mimesis and the Political History of the Nation State* (Gainesville: U of Florida P, 2002). Ungar especially focuses on Joyce's revision of the epic tradition that had been associated with empires. On Joyce and the notion of British "civilization," see Brian Shaffer, *The Blinding Torch: Modern British Fiction and the Discourse of Civilization* (Amherst: U of Massachusetts P, 1993), 101–120.

22. Gibson, *James Joyce* (London: Reaktion, 2006), 81.

23. Michael Groden, Ulysses *in Progress* (Princeton, NJ: Princeton UP, 1977), 133–134. Groden refers to several pages of the Buffalo Mss. V.A.8 and V.A.6.

24. Joyce, *A Portrait of the Artist as a Young Man*, ed. John Paul Riquelme (New York: Norton, 2007), 13.

25. The novel opens in a tower built by the British in Ireland and closes in Molly's dreamscape of British-occupied Gibraltar. A number of Martello towers were built in Ireland and England to guard against French invasion in the early nineteenth century, while Gibraltar provided the military base for Admiral Lord Nelson's decisive victory over the Franco-Spanish naval forces in the Battle of Trafalgar in 1805. Between these two pillars stands Dublin's Nelson's Pillar in "Aeolus," erected in 1808 "IN THE HEART OF THE HIBERNIAN METROPOLIS," where the "one-handled adulterer" Nelson, mocked in the opening pages of the novel by Buck Mulligan, looks over Dublin and completes the triad of colonial spaces (*U* 7.1, 7.1072).

26. Bazargan, "Mapping Gibraltar: Colonialism, Time, and Narrative in 'Penelope,'" in *Molly Blooms: A Polylogue on "Penelope" and Cultural Studies*, ed. Richard Pearce (Madison: U of Wisconsin P, 1994), 119. Joyce's early critics followed Stuart Gilbert in seeing Gibraltar as Joyce's symbolic margin of Europe and edge of the Homeric world—one of the pillars of Hercules. Andrew Gibson has detailed also the ways in which Britain's occupation of Gibraltar fueled Irish anti-colonialist sentiment in *Joyce's Revenge*, 252–260. See also Ralph W. Rader, "The Logic of *Ulysses*: Or, Why Molly Had to Live in Gibraltar," *Critical Inquiry* 10:4 (June 1984): 567–578.

27. Field, *Gibraltar* (New York: Charles Scribner's Sons, 1888), 113, 129, 4, 32, 111, 104. See James Van Dyck Card, "A Gibraltar Sourcebook for 'Penelope,'" *James Joyce Quarterly* 8 (1971): 163–175.

28. Ford, *A Hand-Book for Travellers in Spain and Readers at Home* [1845] (Carbondale, IL: Southern Illinois UP, 1966), 2:513; emphases in original. See also Rafael I. García León, "Richard Ford's *Gatherings from Spain* and Joyce: A Possible Source for Some Spanish Words in *Ulysses*," *Papers on Joyce* 12 (2006): 85–92. Pound worked briefly in Gibraltar in 1908 and thus could have provided Joyce with some information informally, but I have found no record of such an exchange.

29. Ford, *A Hand-Book for Travellers in Spain*, 2:512, 507, 512; emphases in original.

30. Buchanan, *Britain and the Spanish Civil War*, 10. The name "Gibraltar" derives from the Arabic *Jebel Tariq* ["Tariq's Mountain"], named for the general of the Moorish troops who took the Rock. Cf. Joyce's wordplay early in *Finnegans Wake*: "Otherways wesways like that provost scoffing bedoueen the jebel and the jpysian sea" (*FW* 5).

31. See Ernle Bradford, *Gibraltar: The History of a Fortress* (London: Rupert Hart-Davis, 1971), 158–170. Bradford quotes a 1901 British Parliamentary Committee on Gibraltar, which stated that "no great power of imagination is required to conjure up the situation that might face us if Spain's unending grievance at our occupation of her ancient territory led her to join with other Powers, seemingly chivalrous to help her, but fighting really for their own hands" (ibid., 169–170).

32. Balfour, *The End of the Spanish Empire* (Oxford: Clarendon Press, 1997), 48.

33. Ganivet, *Spain: An Interpretation*, trans. J. R. Carey, intro. R. M. Nadal (London: Eyre & Spottiswoode, 1946), 44, 86, 87, 89–90, 119; translation modified. See also *Spain's 1898 Crisis: Regenerationism, Modernism, Post-colonialism*, ed. Joseph Harrison and Alan

Hoyle (Manchester; New York: Manchester UP, 2000); and Brad Epps, "'No todo se perdió en Cuba': Spain between Europe and Africa in the Wake of 1898," in *National Identities and European Literatures/Nationale Identitäten und Europäische Literaturen*, ed. J. Manuel Barbeito et al. (Bern: Peter Lang, 2008), 160–167. Incidentally, Ganivet thinks comparatively through the figure of Ulysses about national mythologies and destinies over two decades prior to Joyce, writing that "Ulysses is the Greek *par excellence*, in him are united all the Aryan—prudence, constancy, effort, self-control, with Semitic astuteness and fertility of resource.... Our Ulysses is Don Quixote ... If we look outside Spain for a modern Ulysses, we shall find none to surpass the Anglo-Saxon Ulysses, Robinson Crusoe. The Italian Ulysses is a theologian, Dante himself in his *Divina Commedia*; the German Ulysses is a philosopher, Doctor Faustus" (*Spain*, 134–135).

34. Quoted in "La guerra del Rif," iEspaña, enlamemoria.iespana.es/africa/africa03.htm (Accessed 8 December 2009). Alfonso XIII was called "the infant king" because his father, King Alfonso XII, died of tuberculosis just before he was born, so he technically assumed the throne at birth.

35. Ródenas, "Antonio Marichalar," in *EL*, xii.

36. José Ortega Munilla to el Marqués de Montesa [Pedro Marichalar y Monreal], 17 March 1921. Marichalar, RAH, Madrid.

37. Casanova, *The World Republic of Letters*, 142, 39, 172, 21.

38. Larbaud, *An Homage to Jerome: Patron Saint of Translators* (Marlboro, VT: Marlboro P, 1984), 21, 87. Curtius and Larbaud discuss their respective cultural work and mention their journalistic relations with Eliot and Ortega in their correspondence, which is collected in *Deutsch-französische Gespräche, 1920–1950: La Correspondance de Ernst Robert Curtius avec André Gide, Charles Du Bos et Valery Larbaud*, ed. Herbert and Jane M. Dieckmann (Frankfurt am Main: Klostermann, 1980), 341–376.

39. Larbaud, letter to Marichalar, 18 March 1922, RAH, Madrid.

40. Larbaud, qtd. in Ródenas, *Travesías vanguardistas*, 193.

41. Quoted in Ródenas, "Antonio Marichalar," in *EL*, xv.

42. Carlos G. Santa Cecilia meticulously traces the translation and reception of Joyce's work in the Spanish press from 1921–1976 as it circled out from Marichalar's article in his *La recepción de James Joyce en la prensa española (1921–1976)* (Sevilla: U de Sevilla, 1997).

43. Pound indicated to John Quinn that he would work to disseminate *Ulysses* in Spain and Italy, but that he did not expect much success. He says that he wrote to Miguel de Unamuno about Joyce, but I have found no record of their correspondence. See Letter to John Quinn, 19 June 1920, in *Letters of Ezra Pound*, ed. D. D. Paige (New York: Harcourt, Brace, 1950), 153.

44. Díez-Canedo, "La vida literaria," *España* 9:399 (8 December 1923): 4. See also Goldring, "Letras inglesas," *La Pluma* 17 (September 1921): 246.

45. Marichalar, "James Joyce in His Labyrinth" ["James Joyce en su laberinto," 1924], see appendix pages 209, 210; hereafter cited in text.

46. Marichalar removes this speculation from the later editions of the essay. The claim was not his alone; see Antonio Raúl de Toro Santos, "Noticias de Joyce y su obra en la prensa española," in *Silverpowdered Olivetrees: Reading Joyce in Spain*, ed. Jeffrey Simons, José María Tejedor Cabrera, Margarita Estévez Saá, and Rafael I. García León (Sevilla: U de Sevilla P, 2003), 19–25; and Santa Cecilia, *La recepción*, 44. An apocryphal rumor that Joyce visited Barcelona in 1926 circulated for some time, too.

47. The sections of "Penelope" that Marichalar translates are *U* 18.1540–1558 and 18.1564–1574. He stops just short of the final lines of the novel; because of this, his translated passages overlap incompletely with Borges's. He notes, too, Joyce's works have been translated, or are being translated, into a host of European languages, from Italian to Swedish.

48. Several contemporary critics have addressed other such problems: María Ángeles Conde-Parrilla, for instance, has provided a capacious analysis of the problems encountered when the Spanish translator attempts to capture Joyce's "subver[sions of] standard English grammatical rules"—when, for instance, he uses double negatives or reversed word order, which are grammatically wrong in English but correct or inconsequential in Spanish; see in Conde-Parrilla, "James Joyce's *Ulysses*: The Style of Molly's Soliloquy in Spanish," in *Rimbaud's Rainbow: Literary Translation in Higher Education*, ed. Peter Bush and Kirsten Malmkjær (Amsterdam: John Benjamins Publishing Company, 1998), 83. María Luisa Venegas Lagüéns, too, has written of individual words such as "plump" and structural elements such as repetitions that bring forth similar problems, in Venegas Lagüéns, "Translating Repetitions in *Ulysses*," in *The Scallop of Saint James: An Old Pilgrim's Hoard. Reading Joyce from the Peripheries*, ed. Mla. Susana Domínguez Pena, Margarita Estévez Saá, and Anne MacCarthy (Weston, FL: Netbiblo, 2006), 141–152; see also Francisco García Tortosa, "*Ulysses* as Translation," in *Silverpowdered Olivetrees*, ed. Simons et al., 45–55. The new translation of *Ulysses* that García Tortosa and Venegas Lagüéns published in 1999 re-creates anew Joyce's inventiveness and corrects a number of errors in previous editions. On Spanish translations of Joyce's works generally, see Patrick O'Neill, *Polyglot Joyce: Fictions of Translation* (Toronto: U of Toronto P, 2005) 29, 71–75; and *James Joyce in Spain: A Critical Bibliography (1972–2002)*, ed. Alberto Lázaro and Antonio Raúl de Toro Santos (A Coruña: Universidade da Coruña, 2002). See also Francisco García Tortosa and Carmelo Medina Casado, preface to *Papers on Joyce* 9 (2003): 1–6. On translating the place-names of "Ithaca" into Spanish (Castilian dialect), Galician, and Catalan, see Helena Buffery and Carmen Millán-Varela, "Translations of Joyce in Spain: The Location of 'Ithaca'," *Modern Language Review* 95:2 (April 2000): 399–414.

49. Borges, "El *Ulises* de James Joyce," *Proa* 6 (January 1925): 3.

50. See Waisman, *Borges and Translation: The Irreverence of the Periphery* (Lewisburg, PA: Bucknell UP, 2005), 167–169. See Borges, "El Ulises de James Joyce" and "La Última Hoja del *Ulises*," *Proa* 6 (January 1925): 3–9. See also Dora Battistón, Carmen Trouvé, and Alto Reda, "Borges y la traducción de las últimas páginas del *Ulysses* de Joyce," *Anclajes* 5:5 (December 2001): 55–70.

51. Marichalar's "Penelope" is perhaps less known, too, because he deleted, without explanation, his translations in reprints of the essay; only the versions of "James Joyce en su laberinto" in the *Revista de Occidente* and in the volume *Joyce en España II* contain it. Instead, when he published revised versions, Marichalar added to his existing outline of the interior monologue a note on the making of the form as aesthetic artifact:

> the interior monologue constitutes a pure artistic creation that appears to us deceptive because it is the imaginative equivalence of a reality that does not permit control. It is compiled without punctuation, and it operates with the regularity of a machine that needs no human intervention; if we try to capture it, we awaken, and the natural interior monologue ceases ("James Joyce en su laberinto" [1933], in *EL*, 79).

52. This reading of "Penelope" is constructed by male readers. Ewa Ziarek provides an overview and analysis of this topic in "The Female Body, Technology, and Memory in 'Penelope,'" in *James Joyce's* Ulysses: *A Casebook*, ed. Derek Attridge (New York: Oxford UP, 2004), 103–128. Many of the essays in the collection *James Joyce in Context*, ed. McCourt, also address gender and the public/private spheres of Dublin as Joyce portrayed and revised them. Enda Duffy treats "Penelope" in its colonial contexts in *The Subaltern* Ulysses (Minneapolis: U of Minnesota P, 1994), 165–191.

53. Joyce to Mademoiselle Guillermet, 5 September 1918, in *Letters* 1:120; Joyce to Carlo Linati, 21 September 1920, in *Letters*, 1:146; italics in original.

54. Budgen, *James Joyce and the Making of* Ulysses, intro. Hugh Kenner (Bloomington: Indiana UP, 1960), 17.

55. Joyce to Harriet Shaw Weaver, 11 July 1924, in *Letters of James Joyce*, ed. Richard Ellmann (New York: Viking Press, 1967), 3:99.

56. Casanova, *The World Republic of Letters*, 249, xii.

57. Joyce (speaking to Arthur Power), qtd. in Richard Ellmann, *James Joyce* (New York: Oxford UP, 1982), 505; Joyce to William Heinemann, 23 September 1905, in *Letters of James Joyce*, ed. Richard Ellmann (New York: Viking Press, 1966), 2:109; Letter to Stanislaus Joyce, 24 September 1905; in *Letters*, 2:111.

58. See Walkowitz, *Cosmopolitan Style*, 56–77; and Vincent J. Cheng, "Nation Without Borders: Joyce, Cosmopolitanism, and the Inauthentic Irishman," in *Joyce, Ireland, Britain*, ed. Andrew Gibson and Len Platt (Gainesville: University of Florida Press, 2006), 212–233.

59. Larbaud, "The *Ulysses* of James Joyce," in *James Joyce*, ed. Deming, 1:253; translation modified.

60. Lernout, introduction to *The Reception of James Joyce in Europe*, ed. Lernout and Wim van Mierlo (London: Thoemmes Continuum, 2004), 1:11.

61. Latham, "Twenty-first Century Critical Contexts," in *James Joyce in Context*, ed. McCourt, 152.

62. Eliot, "*Ulysses*, Order, and Myth," in *Selected Prose*, ed. Frank Kermode (New York: Harcourt Brace Jovanovich, 1975), 177.

63. Eliot, "The Three Provincialities," 11.

64. Pound, "T. S. Eliot," in *Literary Essays of Ezra Pound*, ed. and intro. T. S. Eliot (New York: New Directions, 1968), 420. See also Joseph Kelly, *Our Joyce: From Outcast to Icon* (Austin: U of Texas P, 1998), 63–84.

65. Pound, "*Dubliners* and Mr James Joyce," in *Literary Essays*, ed. Eliot, 407.

66. Pound, "The Non-existence of Ireland," *New Age* 16:17 (25 February 1915): 452; "*Dubliners* and Mr James Joyce," *Literary Essays*, ed. Eliot, 400–401.

67. Brooker, *Joyce's Critics: Transitions in Reading and Culture* (Madison: U of Wisconsin P, 2004), 40.

68. Antonio Raúl de Toro Santos, "La huella de Joyce en Galicia," in *Joyce en España II*, ed. Francisco García Tortosa and Toro Santos (A Coruña: Universidade da Coruña, 1997), 32. For a fuller overview of the Spanish critical reception of Joyce, see my "Spain, Galicia, and the 'Atlantic' Joyce," *JJQ* 47:2 (Winter 2010): 563–572.

69. Lázaro, "A Survey of Spanish Critical Response to James Joyce," in *The Reception of James Joyce in Europe*, ed. Lernout and van Mierlo, 2:425. See also María Teresa Caneda Cabrera, "Translation, Literature and Nation: The *Xeneración Nós* and the Appropriation of Joyce's Texts," in *Trasvases culturales: literatura, cine, traducción*, ed. José Miguel Santamaría et al. (Vitoria: Universidad del País Vasco: 1997), 71–79.

70. Antonio Raúl de Toro Santos, *La literatura irlandesa en España* (Universidade da Coruña: Netbiblo, 2007), 48. Toro Santos also notes that Joyce eventually influenced the fiction of Risco, Otero Pedrayo, and other Galician writers.

71. Teresa Irabarren, "The Reception of James Joyce in Catalonia," in *The Reception of James Joyce in Europe*, ed. Lernout and van Mierlo, 2:446. See also John Beattie, "Joyce's Work and Its Early Reception and Translation in Catalonia (1921–1936)," in *La Traducción en la Edad de Plata*, ed. Luis Pegenaute (Barcelona: Promociones y Publicaciones Universitarias, 2001), 15–25.

72. See Carlos G. Santa Cecilia, *La recepción de James Joyce en la prensa española* (Sevilla: U de Sevilla, 1997), 42. See Ortega, *Dehumanization*, 33. The *Revista* did not unquestioningly celebrate Joyce: Benjamín Jarnés's review of *Portrait*, for instance, is lukewarm.

73. Joyce to Harriet Shaw Weaver, 28 May 1929, in *Letters* 1:281; Joyce to Marichalar, 4 February 1925, Marichalar, RAH, Madrid. See also Joyce's letter to Dámaso Alonso, 31 October 1925, in *Letters* 3:128–130. John Nash studies the ways in which Joyce engages with the reading and reception of his work in *James Joyce and the Act of Reception: Reading, Ireland, Modernism* (Cambridge: Cambridge UP, 2006).

74. See, for instance, Ernesto Giménez Caballero, "Del morbo gaélico," *El Sol*, 14 May 1926, 2; Melchor Fernández Almagro's notes in *La Época*, 3 July 1926, Suplemento [n.p.]; and a discussion of Joyce in *El Heraldo de Madrid*, 25 May 1926, [n.p.].

75. Morales Ladrón, "Joycean Aesthetics in Spanish Literature," in *The Reception of James Joyce in Europe*, ed. Lernout and van Mierlo, 2:434–444; on Latin American writers, see César Augusto Salgado, *From Modernism to Neobaroque: Joyce and Lezama Lima* (Lewisburg, PA: Bucknell UP, 2001) and R. W. Fiddian, "James Joyce and Spanish-American Fiction: A Study of the Origins and Transmission of Literary Influence," *Bulletin of Hispanic Studies* 66:1 (January 1989): 23–39.

76. Chacel, "El loco," in *Obra Completa*, ed. Carlos Pérez Chacel and Antonio Piedra (Valladolid: Fundación Jorge Guillén, 2000), 5:70.

77. Chacel, "Ortega a otra distancia," in *La lectura es secreto* (Madrid: Ediciones Júcar, 1989), 150.

78. Marichalar, "James Joyce en su laberinto," in *EL*, 77, 86. Much of this additional text comes from another essay, "Nueva Dimensión," that Marichalar published in the *Revista de Occidente* in 1929.

79. Marichalar to Beach, 1 November 1924, Archives of Sylvia Beach, Poetry Collection of the State University of New York at Buffalo.

80. Letter to Beach, 16 June 1931, Archives of Sylvia Beach, Poetry Collection of the State University of New York at Buffalo. Ocampo did not sponsor the first translation of *Ulysses*, which appeared in 1945.

81. Lázaro, "James Joyce's Encounters with Spanish Censorship, 1939–1966," *Joyce Studies Annual* 12 (Summer 2001): 38–54. See *James Joyce in Spain*, ed. Lázaro and Toro Santos, 27–41, for an overview of these trends, along with an impressive compendium of statistics and data. See also Antonio Raúl de Toro Santos and David Clark's *British and Irish Writers in the Spanish Periodical Press (1900–1965)*; and Toro Santos, *La literatura irlandesa en España*.

82. See Vila-Matas, *Dublinesque*, trans. Anne McLean and Rosalind Harvey (New York: New Directions, 2012). Spanish is now, Patrick O'Neill notes, the only European language

with three different translations of *Ulysses* (*Polyglot Joyce*, 73–74). See Alberto Lázaro, "A Survey," 422–433. The first complete translation of *Ulysses* into Spanish, the Argentine J. Salas Subirat's 1945 version, was banned in Spain until 1962; see Lázaro, "James Joyce's Encounters with Spanish Censorship (1939–1966)," *Joyce Studies Annual* 12 (Summer 2001): 38–54.

83. García Tortosa, "España y su función simbólica en la narrativa de *Ulises*," *Revista Canaria de Estudios Ingleses* 8 (April 1984): 24. See also J. M. Fiol and J. C. Santoyo, "Joyce, *Ulysses* y España," *Papeles de Son Armadans* 197 (August 1972): 121–140.

84. José M. Ruiz, "El componente hispánico en la lengua y en la obra literaria de James Joyce," *Letras de Deusto* 14:28 (1984): 110.

85. See, for example, *Silverpowdered Olivetrees*; *An Old Pilgrim's Hoard*; and *Vigorous Joyce: Atlantic Readings of James Joyce*, ed. M. Teresa Caneda Cabrera, Vanessa Silva Fernández, and Martín Urdiales Shaw (Vigo: Universidad de Vigo, 2010).

86. Pound, "Ulysses," in *Literary Essays*, ed. Eliot, 403.

87. Wollaeger, "Reading *Ulysses*: Agency, Ideology, and the Novel," in *James Joyce's Ulysses: A Casebook*, 146.

88. Ortega, *Meditations on Quixote*, 102.

89. Beach to Marichalar, 11 January 1927. Marichalar, RAH, Madrid.

Chapter 3

1. Marichalar, "Las 'vidas' y Lytton Strachey," in *EL*, 131; hereafter cited as "LLS."

2. Valdeavellano, "Marichalar y el duque de Osuna," *La Época*, 1 February 1930: 6.

3. Connolly, *Enemies of Promise* (Chicago: U of Chicago P, 2008), 47; *The Modern Movement* (London: Deutsch, 1965), 41.

4. Richard Holmes, qtd. in Michael Holroyd, *Lytton Strachey: The New Biography* (London: Chatto & Windus, 1994), 429.

5. Johnston, qtd. in Laura Marcus, "The Newness of the 'New Biography,'" in *Mapping Lives: The Uses of Biography*, ed. Peter France and William St. Clair (Oxford: Oxford UP, 2004), 195. Johnston overstates the case relative to other literary forms of the era, but his point generally holds. Marcus has been one of the few contemporary scholars to study modernist biography in a sustained manner; see her *Auto/biographical Discourses: Theory, Criticism, Practice* (Manchester: Manchester UP, 1994), 90–134, on Woolf and Strachey.

6. Enrique Montero describes this political movement as the "new liberalism," which was oriented more toward the "social organism" and was "interventionist in social questions," whereas traditional liberalism had focused primarily on individual freedoms ("Reform Idealized: The Intellectual and Ideological Origins of the Second Republic," in *Spanish Cultural Studies: An Introduction: The Struggle for Modernity*, ed. Helen Graham and Jo Labanyi [New York: Oxford UP, 1995], 124).

7. Review of *Riesgo y ventura del duque de Osuna (ensayo biográfico)* by Antonio Marichalar, in *Nueva España* 2 (February 1930): 17. On *Nueva España*, see José-Carlos Mainer, *La Edad de Plata (1902–1939): ensayo de interpretación de un proceso cultural* (Madrid: Ediciones Cátedra, 1983), 272–276; the journal was the successor to *Post-guerra* (1927–1928).

8. Gustavo Pérez Firmat uses this term in *Idle Fictions: The Hispanic Vanguard Novel, 1926–34*, expanded ed. (Durham, NC: Duke UP, 1993), 169–177. For an overview of the "biografía vanguardista" element of *la nueva biografía*, see Francisco M. Soguero García's lucid

account, "Los narradores de vanguardia como renovadores del género biográfico: aproximación a la biografía vanguardista," in Francis Lough, ed., *Hacia la novela nueva: Essays on the Spanish Avant-Garde Novel* (Oxford: Peter Lang, 2000), 199–217.

9. Ortega, "El error Berenguer," *El Sol*, 15 November 1930, 1.

10. Marcus, "The Newness of the 'New Biography,'" in *Mapping Lives*, ed. France and St. Clair, 194.

11. Max Saunders, "Biography and Autobiography," in *The Cambridge History of Twentieth-Century English Literature*, ed. Laura Marcus and Peter Nicholls (Cambridge: Cambridge UP, 2004), 287; Regenia Gagnier, *Subjectivities: A History of Self-representation in Britain, 1832–1920* (New York: Oxford UP, 1991), 39. Matthew Sweet's *Inventing the Victorians* (London: Faber, 2001) joins Gagnier in studying Strachey's role in distorting our contemporary views of the Victorians. See also *Biographical Passages: Essays in Victorian and Modernist Biography*, ed. Joe Law and Linda K. Hughes (Columbia: U of Missouri P, 2000); Saunders's taxonomy on pp. 302–303 is especially useful for scholars of modernist biography.

12. Letter to Virginia Woolf, 8 November 1912, in *The Letters of Lytton Strachey*, ed. Paul Levy (London: Viking, 2005), 211.

13. See Barry Spurr, "Camp Mandarin: The Prose Style of Lytton Strachey," *English Literature in Transition* 33 (1990): 31–45. Spurr is quoting Anthony Kenny. A much less sympathetic account is John Halperin's "*Eminent Victorians* and History," in *The Virginia Quarterly Review* 56:3 (Summer 1980): 433–454.

14. Strachey, *Eminent Victorians* (San Diego: Harvest/Harcourt, 1969), viii; hereafter cited as *EV*.

15. Quoted in Holroyd, *Lytton Strachey*, 307–308, 48.

16. Letter to E. M. Forster, 24 May 1917, in *Letters*, 352.

17. Bell, qtd. in *Lytton Strachey by Himself: A Self-Portrait*, ed. and intro. Michael Holroyd (London: Heinemann, 1971), 135; Garnett, "Keynes, Strachey and Virginia Woolf in 1917," *London Magazine* 2 (September 1955): 53.

18. Woolf, *Sowing: An Autobiography of the Years 1880–1904* (New York: Harcourt, Brace & World, 1960), 175.

19. Letter to Lady Ottoline Morrell, 19 May 1915, in *Letters*, 251.

20. Quoted in Holroyd, *Lytton Strachey*, 311. Here, Ruth Hoberman's claim in her important work *Modernizing Lives* that "Strachey's subjects are actors denying their artifice" resonates most fully (*Modernizing Lives: Experiments in English Biography, 1918–1939* [Carbondale: Southern Illinois P, 1987], 42).

21. Strachey, *Queen Victoria* (New York: Harcourt, Brace, 1921), 414.

22. One notable project inspired indirectly by Strachey's work was the "Republic of Letters" series that Routledge launched in 1925 under the joint editorship of Eliot and Richard Aldington. This short series presented critical biographies of figures such as Voltaire, Pushkin, and Gogol, but its impact was not great.

23. Pérez Firmat marks the years 1926–1934 as bookends of this period of experimentation in Spanish novels; the second date marked the publication of the second edition of Jarnés's *El profesor inútil*; see *Idle Fictions*. See also Luis Fernández Cifuentes, *Teoría y mercado de la novela en España: del 98 a la República* (Madrid: Gredos, 1982), esp. 342–351 on biography; Roberta Johnson, *Crossfire: Philosophy and the Novel in Spain, 1900–1934*

(Lexington: U of Kentucky P, 1993); Domingo Ródenas de Moya, *Los espejos del novelista: modernismo y autorreferencia en la novela vanguardista española* (Barcelona: Ediciones Península, 1998), and *Travesías vanguardistas*; María Soledad Fernández Utrera, *Visiones de estereoscopio: paradigma de hibridación en el arte y la narrativa de la vanguardia española* (Chapel Hill: U of North Carolina P, 2001); and José Manuel del Pino, *Montajes y fragmentos: una aproximación a la narrativa española de vanguardia* (Amsterdam: Rodopi, 1995). In addition to those mentioned below, texts such as Ramón Gómez de la Serna's *El incongruente* (1922), Ramón del Valle-Inclán's *Tirano banderas* (1926), Juan Chabás's *Puerto de sombra* (1928), Jarnés's *Locura y muerte de nadie* (1929), Rosa Chacel's *Estación. Ida y vuelta* (1930), Francisco Ayala's *Cazador en el alba* (1930), and Maurice Bacarisse's *Los terribles amores de Agliberto y Celedonia* (1931), also highlight (and in the case of Ramón, antedate) this movement.

24. Dennis, "Prose: Early twentieth century," in *The Cambridge History of Spanish Literature*, ed. Gies, 573.

25. Pérez Firmat, *Idle Fictions*, 170.

26. For a history of biography in the context of Ortega's work, see Ana Rodríguez-Fischer, "Un proyecto de Ortega y Gasset: la colección *Vidas españolas e hispanoamericanas del siglo XIX*," *Scriptura* 6–7: 133–144.

27. Ángel Sánchez Rivero wrote in a review of Maurois's *Disraeli*, for instance, that the new interest in biography was apiece with a renewed interest in novels, and that this had occurred in the unlikely post-war environment of anti-heroism and mass anonymity (review of *Disraeli*, by André Maurois, *Revista de Occidente* 18:54 [December 1927]: 299). López Campillo and Serrano Asenjo both note that statistically, articles on biographies and reviews and translations of them spiked between 1927 and 1932. See also Manuel Pulido Mendoza, *Plutarco de moda: la biografía moderna en España (1900–1950)* (Mérida: U de Extremadura, 2009).

28. Marichalar, "Escuela de Plutarcos," in *EL*, 241, 242.

29. His translation is very straightforward, a task made somewhat easier by Strachey's Latinate style, which itself was influenced by the Briton's admiration of French essayists. Holroyd notes that *Eminent Victorians* sold well in both Britain and in the United States—over 90,000 hardback copies in Strachey's lifetime alone—which helped lead to its being translated into French, Polish, Romanian, Italian, Japanese, and Spanish (*Lytton Strachey*, 427).

30. "LLS," 133. As usual, no translator was given when "The End of General Gordon" appeared in the *Revista* in March 1928 (29:57), but it was almost certainly Marichalar. Marichalar's article was translated into German for the *Neue Schweizer Rundschau* in 1929 (Cifuentes, *Teoría y mercado*, 345.) Benjamín Jarnés also praised Strachey's work in the *Revista de Occidente* in 1929.

31. Woolf, "The New Biography" [1927], in *Collected Essays* (London: Hogarth Press, 1967), 4:231; emphasis mine. Woolf is reviewing Harold Nicolson's *Some People* (1927).

32. Chabás, "Resumen Literario. Noticias Literarias.—Libros Nuevos.—Revistas," *La Libertad* (11 August 1928) [n.p.], qtd. in Pulido Mendoza, *Plutarco de moda*, 12. Ludwig's publisher claimed that his *July '14* sold 10,000 copies in Spain in its first two months alone.

33. Baeza, "Este florecimiento de la literatura biográfica," *El Sol*, 5 May 1927, 5.

34. The title of the series was changed to *Vidas españolas |e hispanoamericanas del siglo XIX* when Spanish-American figures were added, beginning with Bolívar in 1930.

Biographies of Sarmiento, Martí, and Morelos were among those that appeared by 1936. Chacel's *Teresa*, begun in 1930 for the *Vidas* series, was not finally published until 1941 in Buenos Aires.

35. See Gallego Roca, "De las vanguardias," in *Historia de la traducción*, ed. Lafarga and Pegenaute, 482.

36. Benjamín Jarnés coined this term in his review of Ramón's biographies, "Vidas oblicuas," *Revista de Occidente* 26:77 (November 1929): 251–256.

37. Translations and Spanish originals including F. A. Kirkpatrick's *Los conquistadores españoles* (1932), Manuel Altolaguirre's *Garcilaso de la Vega* (1933), Hillaire Belloc's *María Antonieta* (1933), Clennell Wilkinson's *Nelson* (1934), and D. B. Wyndham Lewis's *Carlos de Europa. Emperador de Occidente* (1934) highlighted this series, too.

38. Dennis, "Prose," in *Cambridge History of Spanish Literature*, ed. Gies, 574.

39. Eugenio Montes, qtd. in Soguero García, "Los narradores," 209n31; translation modified.

40. Primo de Rivera suspended the Constitution of 1876 and ended the Restoration parliamentary system of *turno pacífico*, or "peaceful rotation." This had been a system by which Liberals and Conservatives, through rigged elections and secret alliances, rotated holding power. Antonio Cánovas had devised this system as a way of preventing substantive reform, especially from below, in Spain. Primo de Rivera also banned all political parties but his own Unión Patriótica, paved the way for Franco's banning of regional languages, and paid a much-publicized visit to Mussolini in Rome. In 1929 he briefly closed down the University of Madrid, prompting the resignations of Ortega and several other prominent chairs (Rockwell Gray, *The Imperative of Modernity: An Intellectual Biography of José Ortega y Gasset* [Berkeley: U of California P, 1989], 186). See Genoveva García Queipo de Llano, *Los intelectuales y la dictadura de Primo de Rivera* (Madrid: Alianza, 1988). On Primo de Rivera's positioning himself between London and Rome, see Ismael Saz (trans. Susan Edith Núñez), "Foreign Policy under the Dictatorship of Primo de Rivera" and "The Second Republic in the International Arena," in *Spain and the Great Powers in the Twentieth Century*, ed. Sebastian Balfour and Paul Preston (New York: Routledge, 1999), 53–95.

41. Though he saw an enlightened minority as a state's leaders, Ortega in his adult life was a steadfast liberal whose very reading of modernity depended on liberal assumptions. For a masterful account of liberalism in this era of Spanish history, including Ortega's role in it, see Victor Ouimette, *Los intelectuales españoles y el naufragio del liberalismo (1923–1936)*, 2 vols. (Valencia: Pre-textos, 1998). That Ortega was seen as the spokesman for liberalism might surprise some contemporary readers who associate his work—especially *Revolt of the Masses*—with an anti-democratic elitist strain of modernist thought, as does John Carey in *The Intellectuals and the Masses: Pride and Prejudice among the Literary Intelligentsia, 1880–1939* (New York: St. Martin's Press, 1993). Ouimette gives the best point-by-point explication of Ortega's liberalism and defends him against charges of anti-liberalism in "Ortega and the Liberal Imperative," in *Ortega y Gasset Centennial/Centenario Ortega y Gasset*, (Madrid: Turanzas, 1985), 57–68. See also Ignacio Sánchez Cámara, *La teoría de la minoría selecta en el pensamiento de Ortega y Gasset* (Madrid: Tecnos, 1986).

42. Montero, "Reform Idealized," in *Spanish Cultural Studies*, ed. Graham and Labanyi, 126.

43. Carta abierta [Open Letter], signed by 25 Spanish writers, April 1929, qtd. in Federico García Lorca, *Epistolario Completo*, ed. Andrew A. Anderson and Christopher Maurer (Madrid: Cátedra, 1997), 607–608.

44. Ben-Ami, *The Origins of the Second Republic in Spain* (Oxford: Oxford UP, 1978), 34. José-Carlos Mainer's *La corona hecha trizas: una literatura en crisis (1930–1960)* (Barcelona: Editorial Crítica, 2008) is a valuable resource on the literature of Spain's transitional phases of post-monarchy, including the cultures of Republicanism and fascism. On the politics of Spain's writers during the rise of fascism, see Jordi Gracia, *La resistencia silenciosa: fascismo y cultura en España* (Barcelona: Anagrama, 2004).

45. Ortega, "Nada 'moderno' y 'muy siglo XX,'" in *Obras completas* 2:22, 23, 24.

46. Chacel, qtd. in Serrano Asenjo, *Vidas oblicuas: aspectos teóricos de la nueva biografía en España* (Zaragoza: Prensas universitarias de Zaragoza, 2002), 109.

47. Payne, *Spain's First Democracy: The Second Republic, 1931–1936* (Madison: U of Wisconsin P, 1993), 3.

48. Tuñón de Lara, *La España del siglo XX* (Madrid: Ediciones Akal, 2000), 1:411. See Jean Bécarud and Evelyne López Campillo, *Los intelectuales durante la II República* (Madrid: Siglo Veintiuno, 1978); and Javier Tusell and Genoveva García Queipo de Llano, *Los intelectuales y la República* (Madrid: Nerea, 1990).

49. Anonymous reviewer, qtd. in Pérez Firmat, *Idle Fictions*, 18.

50. Ortega, "La pedagogía social," in *OC* 1:506. Marichalar had taken up biography in shorter form previously, and with a somewhat similar figure. In the *Revista de Occidente* in February 1925, he provided a short sketch of the life of Count Boni de Castellane, a French noble of the Belle Époque who married into the wealthy American family of Jay Gould. After the Count burned through millions of dollars, his wife Anna left him—in financial ruin, as he recounted in his memoir *The Art of Being Poor*.

51. Sánchez Rivero, review of *Disraeli*, 305; Gabriel Jackson, *The Spanish Republic and the Civil War, 1931–1939* (Princeton, NJ: Princeton UP, 1972), 178.

52. José Luis Salado, "Antonio Marichalar tiene en su despacho un retrato del duque de Osuna," *El Heraldo de Madrid* (3 April 1930): 8.

53. On Strachey's ambivalent relationship to his family's past and its wealth, see Barbara Caine, *From Bombay to Bloomsbury: A Biography of the Strachey Family* (Oxford: Oxford UP, 2005). Ródenas calls Marichalar a "man of sober contradictions" such as these, in "Antonio Marichalar," in *EL*, x.

54. Marichalar, *The Perils and Fortune of the Duke of Osuna*, trans. Harriet de Onís (Philadelphia: J. B. Lippincott, 1932), 15; hereafter cited as *O*. I quote from the English text throughout, but will modify Onís's translation and will refer to the Spanish at times, which will be noted. All references to the Spanish edition are from Marichalar, *Riesgo y ventura del duque de Osuna* (Madrid: Espasa-Calpe, 1930). The first four titles in the *Vidas* series were Wenceslao Ramírez de Villa-Urrutia's *El general Serrano, Duque de la Torre*, Jarnés's *Sor Patrocinio*, Espina's *Luis Candelas*, and Tomás Domínguez Arévalo, Count of Rodezno's *Carlos VII*. Domingo Ródenas has published a new edition of *Riesgo y ventura* with an introduction and index (Madrid: Palabra, 1998).

55. *O* 150. *Riesgo y ventura* is a technical legal term that translates roughly to "assuming all risk and responsibility" against potential catastrophes.

56. The line from Montaigne is given in French in the text. In later editions, Marichalar changes "God" to "Honor."

57. Serrano Asenjo, "Los Osuna de Antonio Marichalar (1): El Malogrado," *Revista Hispánica Moderna* 55:2 (December 2002): 343.

58. Torres Bodet, review of *Riesgo y ventura del duque de Osuna*, by Antonio Marichalar, *Revista de Occidente* 27:80 (February 1930): 281, 282, 291.

59. American publishers William Bradley and J. B. Lippincott in fact competed for the rights to translate *Osuna*. Letter from William Bradley to Marichalar, 29 April 1931, Ransom Center for the Humanities, University of Texas at Austin.

60. Colhoun, review of *The Perils and Fortune of the Duke of Osuna*, by Antonio Marichalar, trans. Harriet de Onís, *Criterion* 13:50 (October 1933): 163–164. Colhoun misreads Marichalar's account, however, in attributing too great an amount of blame for Osuna's debts and ill health to his marriage late in life to Princess Leonor.

61. Trend, review of *The Perils and Fortune of the Duke of Osuna*, by Antonio Marichalar, trans. Harriet de Onís (Philadelphia: J. B. Lippincott, 1932), *TLS* (3 August 1933): 521.

62. Alfred von Dohna, review of *The Perils and Fortune of the Duke of Osuna*, trans. Harriet de Onís (Philadelphia: J. B. Lippincott, 1932), in *Bookman* (September 1932): 511.

63. López Campillo, *La "Revista de Occidente,"* 131. Gonzalo Santonja's *La República de los libros: el nuevo libro popular de la II República* (Barcelona: Anthropos, 1989) provides a sociological account of shifts in reading practices during the Second Republic.

64. Osuna, *Las revistas españolas entre dos dictaduras, 1931–1939* (Valencia: Pre-Textos, 1986), 50.

65. Ródenas de Moya, "Antonio Marichalar," in *EL*, xl–xli.

66. J. Jefferson Jones of J. B. Lippincott Company, Letter to Marichalar, [n.d.], RAH, Madrid.

67. Marichalar, *Riesgo y ventura del duque de osuna* (Madrid: Espasa-Calpe, 1959), 9, 11, 12.

68. Serrano Asenjo, "El malogrado," 483, 484.

69. This insight belongs to Juan Herrero-Senés, whom I thank for sharing it with me.

70. Salado, "Antonio Marichalar tiene en su despacho," 8.

Chapter 4

1. Ocampo, "Carta a Virginia Woolf," in *Testimonio: primera serie* (Buenos Aires: Editorial Fundación SUR, 1981), 1:14.

2. Woolf, "Memoir of Julian Bell," in Woolf, *The Platform of Time: Memoirs of Family and Friends*, ed. S. P. Rosenbaum (London: Hesperus Press, 2007), 28. Rosenbaum's collection reproduces Woolf's entire memoir of Julian, including several parts that Quentin Bell cut when he printed it as "Reminiscences of Julian" in his *Virginia Woolf: A Biography* (1972). The text is dated 30 July 1937, 12 days after the news of Julian's death reached London.

3. Woolf, *Three Guineas* (San Diego: Harcourt Brace Jovanovich, 1966), 33, 103; hereafter cited as *TG*. The American (Harcourt) edition that scholars and readers have used for a number of years omitted the photographs of Englishmen from the text. Most newer editions have replaced them; see note 116.

4. Ocampo, "Carta a Virginia Woolf," in *Testimonios*, 1:11. Ocampo's six-part *Autobiografía* (1979–1984), published posthumously, supplements the *Testimonios* with her own family's history. See Sylvia Molloy, *At Face Value: Autobiographical Writing in Spanish America* (Cambridge; New York: Cambridge UP, 2005).

5. Jayne Marek's *Women Editing Modernism: "Little" Magazines and Literary History* (Lexington: U of Kentucky P, 1995) provides an overview of this work. The volume *Gender*

in Modernism: New Geographies, Complex Intersections, ed. Bonnie Kime Scott (Urbana: U of Illinois P, 2007) contains an excellent set of contexts for a chapter such as this one, and it includes a brief section on Ocampo as well. See also Susan Stanford Friedman, *Mappings: Feminism and the Cultural Geographies of Encounter* (Princeton, NJ: Princeton UP, 1998).

6. Ocampo, "Virginia Woolf, Orlando y Cía," in *Testimonios: segunda serie* (Buenos Aires: Ediciones SUR, 1941), 2:17.

7. Woolf, Diary, 28 March 1905, in *A Passionate Apprentice: The Early Journals, 1897–1909*, ed. Mitchell Leaska (London: Hogarth Press, 1990), 257. All spelling and grammar from Woolf's diaries and letters [sic]. Some of Woolf's travel writings are collected in *Travels with Virginia Woolf*, ed. Jan Morris (London: Hogarth Press, 1993).

8. Borrow, *The Bible in Spain, or, The journeys, adventures, and imprisonments of an Englishman, in an attempt to circulate the Scriptures in the peninsula* (London: J. Murray, 1843), 1:x–xi, xii, xiv.

9. Diary entries, 5 April 1905, in *Passionate Apprentice*, 261; 8 April 1905, and 9 April 1905, in *Passionate Apprentice*, 262.

10. Diary entry, 28 April 1905, in *Passionate Apprentice*, 268.

11. Woolf, "An Andalusian Inn," in *The Essays of Virginia Woolf*, ed. Andrew McNeillie (San Diego: Harcourt Brace Jovanovich, 1986–1994), 1:50, 51, 52.

12. Woolf to Violet Dickinson, 30 April 1905, in *The Letters of Virginia Woolf*, ed. Nigel Nicolson and Joanne Trautmann (New York: Harcourt, Brace, Jovanovich, 1975–1980), 1:189; hereafter cited as *L*. See Woolf, "Journeys in Spain," in *Essays* 1:44–46. The books she reviews are Rowland Thirlmere's *Letters from Catalonia* (1905) and Somerset Maugham's *The Land of the Blessed Virgin* (1905). Woolf's judgments of both works were unenthusiastic and she seems to have incorporated little, if anything, from them into her fiction.

13. Woolf to Lytton Strachey, 1 September 1912, in *L* 2:5.

14. Woolf, *The Voyage Out*, ed. and intro. Jane Wheare (London: Penguin, 1992), 31, 85.

15. Woolf to Gerald Brenan, 25 December 1922, in *L* 2:597.

16. Woolf to Mary Hutchison, 18[?] April 1923, in *Congenial Spirits*, 162. In the same letter, she mentions the "deformed Catalans" that she and Leonard had encountered. Woolf also read Roger Fry's artistic travelogue *Sampler of Castile* (1923), which records images of Spain mostly similar to Woolf's own, but without the "violent" imagery. Woolf later joked to Gerald Brenan that she "heard from Saxon [Sydney-Turner] yesterday from Madrid, where, as far as I can tell, Bloomsbury is now conglomerated" because Sydney-Turner, Barbara Bagenal, Ralph Partridge, Frances Marshall, and Thérèse Lessore were all there (Woolf to Brenan, 4 October 1929, in *L* 4:98).

17. Woolf to Vanessa Bell, 1 April 1923, in *L* 3:25–26.

18. Woolf, "To Spain," in *Essays of Virginia Woolf*, 3:361, 362, 363, 364.

19. Woolf, *Flush: A Biography*, intro. Trekkie Ritchie (San Diego: Harcourt Brace Jovanovich, 1983) 3–4; parentheses in original. The actual etymology of "Spain"—more specifically, the origin of the Latin "Hispania"—remains disputed.

20. [César Falcón?], "Una mujer con importancia," *La Gaceta Literaria* 1:7 (1 April 1927): 5.

21. Russell, "Literatura masculina y literatura femenina," *El Sol*, 18 February 1930, 3.

22. Montes, "El arte de matar tiempo," *El Sol*, 2 September 1931, 2. Montes, a vanguard writer who would become a Falangist in a few years, reveals his skepticism toward Woolf's

fictional project in his "Cuando zozobra un imperio" ["When an Empire Capsizes"], *El Sol*, 20 October 1931, 2.

23. Marichalar, "Último grito," in *EL*, 259–260. On the Hispanic reception of Woolf's texts to the present, see Alberto Lázaro, "The Emerging Voice: A Review of Spanish Scholarship on Virginia Woolf," in *The Reception of Virginia Woolf in Europe*, ed. Mary Ann Caws and Nicola Luckhurst (London: Continuum, 2002), 247–62. A Catalan translation of *Mrs Dalloway* was published in Spain in 1930 and made its way into Woolf's hands (Letter to Ocampo, 28 December 1934, in *L* 5:358).

24. Marichalar, "De la novela contemporánea," in *EL*, 304. He also links Proust, Miró, and Woolf again briefly in this essay (309).

25. Lojo Rodríguez, "'A gaping mouth, but no words': Virginia Woolf Enters the Land of Butterflies," in *The Reception of Virginia Woolf in Europe*, ed. Caws and Luckhurst, 245. See also María José Gámez Fuentes, "Virginia Woolf and the Search for Symbolic Mothers in Modern Spanish Fiction: The Case of *Tres Mujeres*, in *The Reception of Virginia Woolf in Europe*, ed. Caws and Luckhurst, 263–280; and Mónica Ayuso, "Virginia Woolf in the Spanish-American Imagination," in *Virginia Woolf and Communities: Selected Papers from the Eighth Annual Conference on Virginia Woolf*, ed. Jeanette McVicker and Laura Davis (New York: Pace UP, 1999), 97–102. The connection between Ortega's and Woolf's writings has been picked up by contemporary critics, too. Laura Doyle and Laura Winkiel connect Ortega's argument in *The Dehumanization of Art* that "artists on the margins of modernity are best positioned to reconfigure art's functions" to Woolf's call for a intellectual anti-fascist union: "In a sense Ortega y Gasset indicates that the Society of Outsiders [Woolf] yearns for [in *Three Guineas*] already exists, and its members readily, almost necessarily, craft the kind of art she envisions" (introduction to *Geomodernisms: Race, Modernism, Modernity*, ed. Doyle and Winkiel [Bloomington: U of Indiana P, 2005], 2–3). Frank Gloversmith traces some aesthetic affinities among the thought of Ortega and several figures of the Bloomsbury circle in his "Autonomy Theory: Ortega, Roger Fry, Virginia Woolf," in *The Theory of Reading*, ed. Gloversmith (Totawa, NJ: Harvester Press, 1984), 147–198.

26. [No translator given], "El Tiempo Pasa," *Revista de Occidente* 31:93 (March 1931): 283–297. This anonymous translation is not Marichalar's; see Lázaro, "The Emerging Voice," 248. The same issue contains a translation of portions of Aldous Huxley's *Vulgarity in Literature* (1930).

27. Marichalar, "Spanish Chronicle," *Criterion* 12:47 (January 1933): 252, 253.

28. On Ortega's impressions and their friendship, see Zamora Bonilla, *Ortega y Gasset*, 269, 396–402 *passim*.

29. Ocampo, qtd. in Patricia Owen Steiner, *Victoria Ocampo: Writer, Feminist, and Woman of the World* (Albuquerque, NM: U of New Mexico P, 1999), 32.

30. Frank [unsigned], Editorial, *Seven Arts* 1:1 (November 1916): 52–55. For more on Frank's circulation in Hispanophone modernist cultures, see my "The Circulation of Interwar Anglophone and Hispanic Modernisms," in *The Oxford Handbook of Global Modernisms*, ed. Mark Wollaeger (New York: Oxford UP, 2012), 461–477.

31. Bourne, "Trans-National America," in *The History of a Literary Radical and Other Papers*, intro. Van Wyck Brooks (New York: S. A. Russell, 1956), 271, 272, 276. *Seven Arts* was absorbed by the *Dial*.

32. Ibid., 283, 278, 283, 281.

33. Frank, *Our America* [1919] (New York: Boni and Liveright, 1921), xi, x; emphases in original.

34. Frank, *Memoirs of Waldo Frank*, ed. Alan Trachtenberg and intro. Lewis Mumford (Amherst: U of Massachusetts P, 1973), 94–95.

35. Frank, *Our America*, 3, 9, 8, 232. Dos Passos published his article on "Young Spain," which mostly treats the Generation of '98, in *Seven Arts* in August 1917.

36. Frank to Ortega, 23 July 1922, FOG, Madrid; capital letters in original.

37. See Arnold Chapman, "Waldo Frank in the Hispanic World: The First Phase," *Hispania* 44:4 (December 1961): 626–634, and "Waldo Frank in Spanish America: Between Journeys, 1924–1929," *Hispania* 47:3 (September 1964): 510–521.

38. Reyes, introduction to Waldo Frank, *España virgen: escenas del drama espiritual de un gran pueblo*, trans. León Felipe (Buenos Aires: Editorial Losada, 1947), 12.

39. Frank, *Virgin Spain: Scenes from the Spiritual Drama of a Great People* (New York: Boni and Liveright, 1926), [n.p.], 193.

40. Frank, *America Hispana. South of Us; The Characters of the Countries and the People of Central and South America* (New York: Garden City Publishing, 1940), viii; capital letters in original. Frank writes that he prefers "America Hispana" to "Latin America" because the former captures the degree to which this area was formed by a distinctly Hispanic character that differs from French or Italian cultures. On "American" and "Hemispheric" understandings of "the Americas" in contemporary critical discourses, see, *inter alia*, *Do the Americas Have a Common Literature?*, ed. Gustavo Pérez Firmat (Durham, NC: Duke UP, 1990); and Diana Taylor, "Remapping Genre Through Performance: From 'American' to 'Hemispheric' Studies," *PMLA* 122:5 (October 2007): 1416–1430.

41. Frank, *The Re-discovery of America: An Introduction to a Philosophy of American Life* (New York: Charles Scribner's Sons, 1929), 194, 15.

42. Frank, *America Hispana: A Portrait and a Prospect* (New York: Charles Scribner's Sons, 1931), 317, 357, 127.

43. Strong, *The Poetic Avant-garde: The Groups of Borges, Auden, and Breton* (Evanston, IL: Northwestern UP, 1997), 101, 107.

44. Reyes to Ocampo, 15 January 1931, in Reyes and Ocampo, *Cartas echadas: correspondencia 1927–1959*, ed. and intro. Héctor Perea (México, D.F.: Universidad Autónoma Metropolitana, 1983), 19.

45. See Vicky Unruh, *Latin American Vanguards: The Art of Contentious Encounters* (Berkeley: U of California P, 1994), 21–26.

46. King, *"Sur": A Study of the Argentine Literary Journal and Its Role in the Development of a Culture, 1931–1970* (Cambridge: Cambridge UP, 1986), 34. On the origins and cultural politics of the journal, see also Nora Pasternac, *"Sur," una revista en la tormenta: los años de formación 1931–1944* (Buenos Aires: Paradiso, 2002); Rosalie Sitman, *Victoria Ocampo y "Sur": entre Europa y América* (Tel Aviv: U of Tel Aviv, 2003); and María Esther Vázquez, *Victoria Ocampo: el mundo como destino* (Buenos Aires: Seix Barral, 2002), 167–177.

47. Ortega to Ocampo, 31 January 1930, in Ortega, *Epistolario*, 145.

48. King, *"Sur,"* 4.

49. Ocampo, qtd. in Meyer, *Victoria Ocampo: Against the Wind and Tide* (Austin: U of Texas P, 1990), 61.

50. Ocampo, "Carta a Waldo Frank," *Sur* 1:1 (Summer 1931): 11–12.

51. Ibid., 17, 18, 14, 18, 17.

52. Woolf, in *The Diary of Virginia Woolf*, ed. Anne Oliver Bell (New York: Harcourt, Brace, Jovanovich, 1977–1984), 4:263, 26 November 1934; hereafter cited as *D*. The transcription of Woolf's diary prints "Vasta" for "Rasta"; it is unclear whether the mistake was Woolf's or her editors'—or perhaps Roger Fry's. In any case, the term in question is "rasta," or "Rasta," a shortened form of *rastaquouère*. This was, at the time, a usually derogatory term for "a person (esp. one from a Mediterranean or South American country) regarded as a social interloper and freq. considered to be nouveau riche or excessively ostentatious in manners or dress; a foreign upstart" (*OED*). The two also shared a mutual acquaintance, Julio Irazustra, an Argentine aristocrat who met Woolf when he studied at Oxford in 1924–1925 (King, *"Sur,"* 74). For more on Ocampo and Woolf's letters and interactions, see Fiona G. Parrott, "Friendship, Letters and Butterflies: Victoria Ocampo and Virginia Woolf," *STAR: Scotland's Transatlantic Relations Project Archive* (April 2004): 1–7.

53. Ocampo, "La Historia Viva," in *Domingos en Hyde Park* (Buenos Aires: Ediciones SUR, 1936), 13–14. Doris Meyer has translated this essay in full in her *Victoria Ocampo*, 217–222.

54. Ocampo, "Virginia Woolf, Orlando y Cía," in *Testimonios*, 2:79.

55. Woolf, *A Room of One's Own*, intro. Susan Gubar (Orlando, FL: Harcourt, 2005), 36.

56. Ocampo, "La Historia Viva," in *Domingos*, 17.

57. Ocampo, "La Historia Viva," in *Domingos*, 16. "La Historia Viva" originally ended with cautious optimism that Mussolini would change his attitude. By the time of its publication in *Domingos en Hyde Park* in August 1936, however, Italy had invaded Abyssinia. Ocampo appended a note to the essay declaring that all hope was lost and criticizing Catholics in Argentina who decried anti-clericism in Spain while tacitly supporting Mussolini's war in Africa (24).

58. Ocampo, "Gabriela Mistral in Her Letters," in *This America of Ours: The Letters of Gabriela Mistral and Victoria Ocampo*, ed. and trans. Elizabeth Horan and Doris Meyer (Austin, TX: U of Texas P, 2003), 296. This is a calculated refutation of Ortega, who had written in the first issue of the *Revista de Occidente* on the conservative poet Anna de Noailles.

59. Ocampo, "Carta a Virginia Woolf," in *Testimonios*, 1:7, 8.

60. Ibid., 9, 11–12, 12, 13, 14; emphasis in original. Ocampo's rewriting of Woolf's line is in English in the original.

61. See Meyer, *Victoria Ocampo: Against the Wind and Tide*, 293n46, on this unpublished letter's date and provenance (probably early 1935).

62. Ocampo, "Carta a Virginia Woolf," in *Testimonios*, 1:13, 8.

63. Ibid., 1:8.

64. Woolf asked Ocampo about her lectures, "Is it your Latin blood [that makes them exciting]?" (Woolf to Ocampo, 2 September 1937, in *L* 6:167).

65. Woolf to Ocampo, 26 February 1935, in *L* 5:372.

66. Woolf to Hugh Walpole, 5 December 1934, in *L* 5:350; parentheses in original; Woolf to Sackville-West, 19 December 1934, in *L* 5:355. Woolf jokes in the same letter to Walpole that Ocampo is "immensely rich, amorous; has been the mistress of Cocteau, Mussolini—Hitler for anything I know" (ibid.).

67. Woolf to Ocampo, 5 December 1934, in *L* 5:349. Woolf perhaps refers to the sense among some native English speakers that words in Spanish run together quickly without the familiar glottal stops.

68. Woolf to Ocampo, 29 October 1935, in *L* 5:439.

69. Woolf to Ocampo, 29 October 1935, in *L* 5: 438–39. Woolf adds, regarding the butterflies Ocampo sent her, "What could have been more fantastically inappropriate!" Urmila Seshagiri treats Woolf's Orientalisms in her "Orienting Virginia Woolf: Race, Aesthetics, and Politics in *To the Lighthouse*," in *Virginia Woolf: An "MFS" Reader*, ed. Maren Linett (Baltimore: Johns Hopkins UP, 2009), 300–326.

70. Woolf to Ocampo, 22 December 1934, in *L* 5:356. On the possibility that Woolf read "Carta," see Bernice L. Hausman, "Words Between Women: Victoria Ocampo and Virginia Woolf," in *In the Feminine Mode: Essays on Hispanic Women Writers*, ed. Noël Valis and Carol Maier (Lewisberg, PA: Bucknell UP, 1990), 207. This essay discusses Ocampo's ideals of feminine authorship at length.

71. Woolf, *D* 5:141, 20 May 1938.

72. Woolf to Ocampo, 29 October 1935, in *L* 5:439.

73. Woolf to Ocampo, 21 June 1935, in *L* 5:405.

74. Woolf to Ocampo, 2 May 1936, in *L* 6:35. In *The Reception of Virginia Woolf*, both Nicola Luckhurst (introduction, 2–8) and Laura María Lojo Rodríguez ("A gaping mouth") note that Woolf's level of involvement with the translations of her work that Ocampo organized, while still minor, indeed was rare. Lojo Rodríguez's excellent essay is especially useful in its treatment of the translations of Woolf's texts and their Hispanophone contexts.

75. Graciela Queirolo, "La década de 1930 a través de los escritos feministas de Victoria Ocampo," in Alicia N. Salomone, Gilda Luongo, Natalia Cisterno, Darcie Doll, and Graciela Queirolo, *Modernidad en otro tono: escritura de mujeres latinoamericanas* (Santiago: Editorial Cuarto Propio, 2004), 221–222. See Meyer, *Victoria Ocampo*, 132–138. See Steiner, *Victoria Ocampo*, 121–32, for a series of Ocampo's statements on feminist issues over several decades. Argentine women did not gain suffrage until 1947.

76. Ocampo, "La mujer, sus derechos y sus responsabilidades," in *Testimonios*, 2:253. See Meyer, *Victoria Ocampo*, 184.

77. Ocampo, "La mujer," in *Testimonios*, 2:259, 264, 267.

78. Auden, "Impressions of Valencia," *New Statesman and Nation* 13:310 (30 January 1937): 159.

79. Greaves, *The Spanish Constitution* (London: Hogarth Press, 1931), 7, 20. Greaves's pamphlet includes a history of the revolution and a bibliography of works on the Second Republic, such as Ortega's *Rectificación de la república* (1931). Other studies and commentaries were published by Leonard Woolf, H. G. Wells, C. L. R. James, Viscount (Lord Robert) Cecil, Edgar H. Brooks, R. M. Fox, John S. Stephens, Florence Wilson (of the Association for International Understanding), Freud (*Civilization and Its Discontents*), Louis Golding (*Letter to Adolf Hitler*), and the Friends Anti-War Group. For a full account of Hogarth's publications and social agenda, see J. H. Willis, *Leonard and Virginia Woolf as Publishers: The Hogarth Press, 1917–1941* (Charlottesville: U of Virginia P, 1992).

80. Leonard and Virginia were not always in step on political matters at this time; see Laura Moss Gottlieb, "The War Between the Woolfs," in *Virginia Woolf and Bloomsbury: A Centenary Celebration*, ed. Jane Marcus (Bloomington: Indiana UP, 1987), 242–52. See also Wayne K. Chapman and Janet M. Manson, "Carte and Tierce: Leonard, Virginia Woolf, and the War for Peace," in *Virginia Woolf and War: Fiction, Reality, and Myth*, ed. and intro. Mark Hussey (Syracuse, NY: Syracuse UP, 1991), 58–78; *Virginia and Fascism: Resisting*

the Dictators' Seduction, ed. Merry M. Pawlowski (New York: Palgrave, 2001); and Melba Cuddy-Keane, *Virginia Woolf, the Intellectual, and the Public Sphere* (Cambridge; New York: Cambridge UP, 2003).

81. Leonard Woolf, *Barbarians Within and Without* (New York: Harcourt, Brace and Co., 1939), 15, 170. The British version of the book, published by Victor Gollancz's Left Book Club, was titled *Barbarians at the Gate*.

82. "The Vortex in Spain," *Times*, 19 August 1936, 6. I have not been able to identify the primary author(s) of the letter. On the racist element of pro-Republican rhetoric in England, see Tom Buchanan, *The Impact of the Spanish Civil War on Britain: War, Loss and Memory* (Brighton: Sussex Academic Press, 2007), 1–22. For comprehensive histories of the war, see Hugh Thomas, *The Spanish Civil War* (New York: Penguin, 1977); Gabriel Jackson, *The Spanish Republic and the Civil War, 1931–1939* (Princeton, NJ: Princeton UP, 1965); and Michael Alpert, *A New International History of the Spanish Civil War* (New York: St. Martin's Press, 1994).

83. Neal Wood, *Communism and British Intellectuals* (New York: Columbia UP, 1959), 57. The Labour Party intervened in the massive international propaganda battle concerning Spain with pamphlets such as *Madrid, the "Military" Atrocities of the Rebels: A Record of Massacre, Murder, Mutilation* (London: Labour Publication Department, 1937). The Left Book Club, too, printed calls for aid and relief money. These efforts were widely seen as failures, however; see Tom Buchanan, *The Spanish Civil War and the British Labour Movement* (Cambridge: Cambridge UP, 1991), 227–228.

84. Brenan, preface to the first edition of *The Spanish Labyrinth: Account of the Social and Political Background of the Civil War* (Cambridge: Cambridge UP, 1950), xvii. Brenan opens this preface by quoting Marx's comment that there is "no country except Turkey, so little known to and so falsely judged by Europe as Spain" (xi).

85. Though Cunard spearheaded the effort, the questionnaire included 12 signatories, Louis Aragon, Pablo Neruda, Auden, Spender, and José Bergamín among them. For a discussion and summary of opinions, see Valentine Cunningham, "Neutral? 1930s Writers and Taking Sides," in *Class, Culture, and Social Change: A New View of the 1930s*, ed. Frank Gloversmith (Brighton, Sussex: Harvester Press, 1980), 45–69. For Joyce's non-response, see Ellmann, *James Joyce*, 704, 693. Pound responded with typical venom, "Questionnaire an escape mechanism for young fools who are too cowardly to think, too lazy to investigate the nature of money, its mode of issue.... You are all had. Spain is an emotional luxury to a gang of sap-headed dilettantes" (*Authors Take Sides on the Spanish War* [London: Left Review, 1937] 27). Elsewhere, Pound contradicted his own vision of Spain in *The Spirit of Romance* and voiced the prejudice that "as to Spain it cannot be too frequently reiterated that Europe ENDS with the Pyrenees" ("Race," *New English Weekly* 10 [16 October 1936]: 1; emphasis in original). Among other well-known modernists, G. B. Shaw wrote an introductory response for the Republic but only offered mild support elsewhere; Ford Madox Ford was "for" the Republic but did and wrote little on its behalf; H. G. Wells was "neutral" but wrote letters requesting aid for the Republic through his PEN Club office; and Yeats was forced to question and finally abandon his fascist leanings publicly, renouncing Franco and supporting the Second International Writers' Congress in Spain (see Elizabeth Cullingford, *Yeats, Ireland and Fascism* [New York: New York UP, 1981], 220–223). In New York, the Communist-backed League of American Writers produced a counterpart pamphlet,

Writers Take Sides: Letters about the War in Spain from 418 American Authors (1938), also overwhelmingly in favor of the Republic.

86. Woolf, *D* 5:114, 13 October 1937.

87. Woolf to Margaret Llewellyn Davies, 4 July 1938, in *L* 6:250. The "subject" in reference is not made clear by Woolf, but the context is a discussion of anti-fascism while the war in Spain was ongoing.

88. Froula, *Virginia Woolf and the Bloomsbury Avant-Garde: War, Civilization, Modernity* (New York: Columbia UP, 2005), 266. I am indebted here to Froula's exposition of Woolf's account of the formation of the public sphere.

89. See Hermione Lee, *Virginia Woolf* (New York: Knopf, 1997), 661; and Jane Dunn, *A Very Close Conspiracy: Vanessa Bell and Virginia Woolf* (Boston: Little, Brown and Company, 1990), 281. David Bradshaw scrupulously documents Woolf's involvement with various anti-fascist groups in his "British Writers and Anti-Fascism in the 1930s, Part One: The Bray and Drone of Tortured Voices," in *Woolf Studies Annual, Vol. 3* (New York: Pace UP, 1997), 3–27. Woolf signed a letter of support for "measures for the maintenance of cultural freedom" that the first Congress of the Anti-fascist Writers in Paris hoped to initiate; see Amabel Williams-Ellis and Edgell Rickword, "A Writer's Congress," *New Statesman and Nation* 9:220 (11 May 1935): 673.

90. Woolf, *D* 5: 97, 23 June 1937; *D* 5:203. Bilbao indeed had just fallen. Maggie Humm counts 24 references to the Spanish war in Woolf's diary (*Modernist Women and Visual Cultures: Virginia Woolf, Vanessa Bell, Photography, and Cinema* [New Brunswick, NJ: Rutgers UP, 2003], 200).

91. Lee, *Virginia Woolf*, 676. Mussolini had sent over 10,000 Italian troops to Spain in January 1937.

92. Woolf to Elizabeth Bowen, 28 February 1939, in *L* 6:319.

93. Information Service No. 31, June 1939, 6, in *A Bibliography of Virginia Woolf*, 4th ed., ed. B. J. Kirkpatrick and Stuart N. Clarke (Oxford: Clarendon Press, 1997), Item E20: 409.

94. Woolf, *D* 5:32, 10 November 1936.

95. Woolf, *D* 4:307, 28 April 1935.

96. Woolf to Vanessa Bell, 17 August 1937, in *L* 6:159.

97. Woolf to Bell, 28 June 1936, in *Congenial Spirits: The Selected Letters of Virginia Woolf*, ed. Joanne Trautmann Banks (San Diego: Harcourt Brace Jovanovich, 1989), 37.

98. Woolf to Julian Bell, 28 July 1936, in *Nineteen Letters to Eleven Recipients*, ed. Joanne Trautmann Banks, *Modern Fiction Studies* 30:2 (Summer 1984): 192.

99. Woolf to Julian Bell, 14 November 1936, in *L* 6:83–85. Bell was teaching in China at the time. Bell, like other international observers, feared that the new war in Spain would bring about Fascist attacks in France, where nationalist uprisings and attacks on the Popular Front had been increasing. On the discord within and failure of the pacifist contingent at the Labour Party's 1935 conference in Brighton, which angered Leonard and Virginia, see Martin Ceadel, *Pacifism in Britain, 1914–1945: The Defining of a Faith* (Oxford: Oxford UP, 1980), 197ff. Lord Robert Cecil was instrumental in founding the League of Nations and remained a passionate advocate of its work.

100. Woolf, *D* 5:29, 30 October 1936.

101. Leonard Woolf to Julian Bell, 15 November 1936, in *Letters of Leonard Woolf*, 409.

102. Woolf, *D* 5:79–80, 15 April 1937. Julian edited a set of essays by conscientious objectors to the Great War, *We Did Not Fight: 1914–1918*, in 1935; see Peter Stansky and

William Abrahams, *Journey to the Frontier: Two Roads to the Spanish Civil War* (Stanford, CA: Stanford UP, 1994), 115–117. He still leaned toward pacifism as late as April 1936. See also Patricia Laurence, *Julian Bell: The Violent Pacifist* (Cecil Woolf, Bloomsbury Heritage Series, 2006). Woolf felt that Julian was a different person upon his return from China: "I felt him changed," she writes, "taut, tense, on the defensive: yet affectionate: but no longer spontaneous. . . . Set & rather self centred" (*D* 5:68, 69, 14 March 1937). For an insightful reading of the dynamic between the two, see Emily Robins Sharpe, "Pacifying Bloomsbury: Virginia Woolf, Julian Bell, and the Spanish Civil War," in *The Theme of War and Peace in Virginia Woolf's War Writings: Essays on Her Political Philosophy*, ed. Jane M. Wood, intro. Karen Levenback (Lewiston, NY: Edwin Mellen Press, 2010), 153–170.

103. Woolf, *D* 5:101, 11 July 1937.

104. Quentin Bell, *Bloomsbury Recalled* (New York: Columbia UP, 1995), 213.

105. Woolf, *D* 5:126, 3 February 1938. Julian Bell begins his poem "Autobiography": "I stay myself—the product made /By several hundred English years, /[. . .] Of high Victorian intellects, /Leslie, Fitzjames."

106. Woolf to Ocampo, 2 September 1937, in *L* 6:166.

107. Woolf, *D* 5:104, 8 June 1937.

108. Woolf, "Reminiscences of Julian," 258–259.

109. Woolf, *D* 5:199, 17 January 1939.

110. Woolf, *D* 5:206, 28 February 1939. She had written earlier, "dreamt of Julian one night: how he came back: I implored him not to go to Spain. He promised. Then I saw his wounds," (*D* 5:172, 17 September 1938).

111. *TG* 30, 137; Woolf, *D* 5:148, 3 June 1938.

112. Transcribed from third scrapbook, item 39, in *Virginia Woolf: Major Authors on CD-ROM*, ed. Mark Hussey (Woodbridge, CT: Primary Source Media, 1997); capital letters in original.

113. Delaprée, *Martyrdom of Madrid* (Madrid, 1937 [no press given]), 14, 17, 45. Patricia Laurence treats this source and Woolf's Monk's House papers at greater length in "The Facts and Fugue of War: From *Three Guineas* to *Between the Acts*," in *Virginia Woolf and War*, ed. Hussey, 225–245.

114. See Marcus, *Virginia Woolf and the Languages of Patriarchy* (Bloomington: Indiana UP, 1987), 78–79.

115. Sontag, *Regarding the Pain of Others* (New York: Farrar, Strauss, and Giroux, 2003), 9.

116. Dalgarno, *Virginia Woolf and the Visible World* (Cambridge: Cambridge UP, 2001), 169; Humm, *Modernist Women and Visual Cultures*, 196. See also Sonita Sarker, "*Three Guineas*, the In-corporated Intellectual, and Nostalgia for the Human," in *Virginia Woolf in the Age of Mechanical Reproduction*, ed. Pamela Caughie (New York: Garland, 2000), 37–66; Diane Gillespie, "'Her Kodak Pointed at His Head': Virginia Woolf and Photography," in *The Multiple Muses of Virginia Woolf*, ed. Diane F. Gillespie (Columbia: U of Missouri P, 1993), 113–147; and Julia Duffy and Lloyd Davis, "Demythologizing Facts and Photographs in *Three Guineas*," in *Photo-Textualities: Reading Photographs and Literature*, ed. Marsha Bryant (Newark: U of Delaware P, 1996), 128–140.

117. Woolf, *TG* 141; Woolf, *D* 5:162, 17 August 1938.

118. Woolf, *D* 3:145, 4 July 1927.

119. Woolf, Letter to Elizabeth E. Nielsen, in *Nineteen Letters to Eleven Recipients*, 199.

120. *TG* 4. This aspect of *Three Guineas* has been expanded through work such as Anna Snaith's publication of 82 letters that Woolf received in response to the book, which Snaith notes "extend Woolf's argument about cultural and intellectual freedom" beyond the borders of the text ("Wide Circles: The *Three Guineas* Letters," in *Woolf Studies Annual 6* [New York: Pace UP, 2000], 8). See also Brenda Silver, "*Three Guineas* Before and After: Further Answers to Correspondents," in *Virginia Woolf: A Feminist Slant*, ed. Jane Marcus (Lincoln: U of Nebraska P, 1983), 254–276. Several editions of *Three Guineas* with various paratextual materials are now in circulation; for an overview and analysis of the mass of Woolf's papers, see Rebecca Wisor, "Versioning Virginia Woolf: Notes toward a Posteclectic Edition of *Three Guineas*," *Modernism/modernity* 16:3 (September 2009): 497–535.

121. Mangini, *Memories of Resistance: Women's Voices of the Spanish Civil War* (New Haven, CT: Yale UP, 1995), 4.

122. Ocampo, "Cartas abiertas," *Sur* 7:32 (May 1937): 71.

123. Ocampo, "Posición del *Sur*," *Sur* 7:35 (August 1937): 8.

124. Mistral to Ocampo, 21 August 1936, in *This America of Ours*, 43; italics in original; translation modified. Mistral had been skeptical of Ocampo's European-American feminism prior to reading this text.

125. Ocampo, "Prólogo," in *Testimonios*, 2:10.

126. Ocampo, "Virginia Woolf, Orlando y Cía," in *Testimonios*, 2:72.

127. Ocampo, "La mujer y su expresión," in *Testimonios*, 2:271, 286. On Ocampo's early cosmopolitanism, see Gorica Majstorovic, "Cosmopolitanism and the Nation: Reading Asymmetries of Power in Victoria Ocampo's 'Babel,'" *A Contracorriente* 3:3 (Spring 2006): 47–64; and Majstorovic, "An American Place: Victoria Ocampo's Editorial Politics, the Foundation of *Sur*, and Hemispheric Alliances," *Arizona Journal of Hispanic Cultural Studies* 9 (2005): 171–180.

128. Ocampo, qtd. in Steiner, *Victoria Ocampo*, 160.

129. Letter to Angelica Ocampo, 29 October 1975, in *Cartas a Angélica y otros*, ed. Eduardo Paz Leston (Buenos Aires: Editorial Sudamericana, 1997), 226.

130. Rockwell Gray, *The Imperative of Modernity: An Intellectual Biography of José Ortega y Gasset* (Berkeley: U of California P, 1989), 112.

131. Woolf to Vita Sackville-West, 19 August 1939, in *L* 6:351.

132. Ayuso, "Virginia Woolf in Mexico and Puerto Rico," in *Woolf Studies Annual* 14, ed. Mark Hussey (New York: Pace UP, 2008), 1.

133. Ocampo, "Carta a Virginia Woolf," in *Testimonios*, 1:13.

Chapter 5

1. Lehmann, *New Writing in Europe* (New York: Penguin Books, 1940), 13.

2. Spender, *World Within World* (New York: St. Martin's Press, 1994), 251.

3. Maurice Percy Ashley, "Eternal Spain: The Problem of Disunion," *TLS* (27 November 1937): 897.

4. Esty, *A Shrinking Island: Modernism and National Culture in England* (Princeton, NJ: Princeton UP, 2004), 9. Jessica Berman makes a compelling case for integrating Spanish Civil War writing and propaganda within the study of modernism, rather than "segregating

it within the Spanish tradition or in the category of war writing," in her wide-ranging comparative study *Modernist Commitments: Ethics, Politics, and Transnational Modernism* (New York: Columbia UP, 2011), 35; see also 184–188.

5. Quoted in John Sutherland, *Stephen Spender: A Literary Life* (New York: Oxford, 2005), 209.

6. Lawrence Venuti, introduction to *The Translation Studies Reader* (New York: Routledge, 2004), 11. See also Susan Bassnett, *Translation Studies* (New York: Routledge, 2002), on the "survival of a text" in translation (9).

7. I borrow this phrase from Francis Mulhern, *The Present Lasts a Long Time: Essays in Cultural Politics* (Notre Dame, IN: U of Notre Dame P, 1998), 165. Mulhern is drawing on the work of scholars of translation, such as André Lefevere and Susan Bassnett, who have focused on the role of culture in translation.

8. Heard to Ortega, 12 July 1929, FOG, Madrid. The journal folded shortly after this date, with no contribution from Ortega.

9. [Sender's name missing] to Ortega, 6 March 1934, FOG, Madrid.

10. See Zamora Bonilla, *Ortega y Gasset*, 327–347.

11. "Choice before Spain," *Times*, 18 November 1933, 11; "Critical Week for Spain, *Times*, 23 June 1931, 17. The *Times* repeated the former phrase in its account, "The Spanish Struggle," *Times*, 11 February 1939, 13; and the latter in "Spanish Crisis," *Times*, 10 June 1933, 12. The *Times* had mentioned in 1929 Ortega's resignation, along with other professors at the University of Madrid, in protest of Primo de Rivera; see "Resignation of Five Spanish Professors," *Times*, 5 August 1929: 15. David Callahan notes that "Ortega's political stance, an unfamiliar mixture of liberalism and proto-existentialism, possessed an idealistic drift which was out of place in the left-wing intellectual climate of the 1930s" (Callahan, "The Early Reception of Ortega y Gasset, 1920–1939," *Forum for Modern Language Studies* 26:1 [1990]: 82).

12. Quid Nunc [unknown alias], "Club Gossip," *English Review* (May 1931): 529.

13. Petrie, "Foreign Affairs," *English Review* (June 1931): 335, 334, 335.

14. Pankhurst, review of *The Revolt of the Masses*, by José Ortega y Gasset, *New Statesman and Nation* 4:73 (16 July 1932): 74; capital letters in original.

15. Marichalar, "Spanish Chronicle," *Criterion* 11:43 (January 1932): 296, 297, 298, 300–301, 302; capital letters in original.

16. A year later, Frank McEachran in a *Criterion* review of *Revolt*, both praised Ortega's desire for a "supernational state" that simultaneously can do domestic economic work and serve as a model for all of Europe, and condemned the Spaniard for allegedly fascist tendencies in his thought. See McEachran, review of *The Revolt of the Masses*, by José Ortega y Gasset, *Criterion* 12:46 (October 1932): 144–146.

17. Kerrigan, introduction to *Revolt of the Masses*, by José Ortega y Gasset, trans. and intro. Kerrigan (Notre Dame, IN: U of Notre Dame P, 1985), xxi.

18. Letter to Helene Weyl, 19 November 1934, in *Correspondencia: José Ortega y Gasset, Helene Weyl*, intro. Jaime de Salas, trans. María Isabel Peña Aguado (Madrid: Biblioteca Nueva/Fundación Ortega y Gasset, 2008), 183; emphasis in original.

19. Marichalar to Ortega, 10 December 1936, forwarding a letter from the Junta Técnica del Estado, Comisión Cultura y Enseñanza (Burgos), FOG, Madrid.

20. Furthermore, Ortega, already horrified at Hitler's Germany, received word from Count Keyserling that his works were being suppressed by the Nazis because of rumors

that he was organizing "red militias" in Spain (Keyserling to Ortega, 24 May 1934, FOG, Madrid). Keyserling says that he received warning of the suppression from the Ministry of Propaganda of the Reich. Ortega's anger at this situation caused him to withhold publication of *Revolt*'s planned "Preface for Germans" in 1934.

21. Marichalar, "Spanish Chronicle," *Criterion* 17:69 (July 1938): 713.

22. Ortega, "Epílogo para ingleses," in *OC* 4:283. He also added a Prologue for the French to later editions of *Revolt*.

23. Ibid., 285, 284, 285.

24. Ortega, "Concerning Pacifism," trans. A. R. Pastor, *The Nineteenth Century* 124 (1938): 27.

25. Crispin, *Quest for Wholeness: The Personality and Works of Manuel Altolaguirre* (Valencia: Albatros Hispanófila, 1983), 27.

26. Juan Manuel Rozas, qtd. in Molina, *Medio Siglo*, 137. On '27 and its magazines, see Anthony L. Geist, *La poética de la generación del 27 y las revistas literarias: de la vanguardia al compromiso (1918–1936)* (Madrid: Guadarrama, 1980). See also James Valender, Azucena López Cobo, and Almudena de la Cueva, *Viaje a las islas invitadas: Manuel Altolaguirre, 1905–1959* (Madrid: Publicaciones de la Residencia de Estudiantes, 2005); Gabriel Morelli, *Manuel Altolaguirre y las revistas literarias de la época* (Viareggio [Lucca]: M. Baroni, 1999); and Julio Neira, *Manuel Altolaguirre, impresor y editor* (Málaga; Madrid: Publicaciones de la Residencia de Estudiantes, 2008).

27. Rafael Martínez Nadal describes the flat on Warwick Road in this manner in his "Manuel Altolaguirre en Londres (Apuntes para unas viñetas)," *Ínsula* 41:475 (June 1986): 11. Altolaguirre was invited to give lectures at a number of universities, including Oxford, Cambridge, Liverpool, Birmingham, and Manchester. I have not been able to determine how many of these offers he accepted (Altolaguirre, *Epistolario, 1925–1959*, ed. James Valender [Madrid: Residencia de Estudiantes, 2005], 306).

28. See *1616* 1 (1934), reprinted as a bound volume (Madrid: Turner, 1981). The contents and the styles of poetry represented in *1616* are irregular. Certain themes prevail in any given issue, and topics such as nature, romance, and the heavens recur, but the authors and languages continually juxtaposed in the journal best evince Altolaguirre's innovations, especially as he drew on the history of the sonnet.

29. See Diego Saglia, *Poetic Castles in Spain: British Romanticism and Figurations of Iberia* (Amsterdam: Rodopi, 2000).

30. See J. de Oliveira E. Silva, "Sir Philip Sidney and the Castilian Tongue," *Comparative Literature* 34:2 (Spring 1982), 130–145. This topic is an emerging area of interest among early modern scholars: the *Journal for Early Modern Cultural Studies*, for instance, devoted an issue in 2010 to "Anglo-Spanish cultural exchange." British critics of the early 1900s such as James Fitzmaurice-Kelly and Martin Hume had begun studying the intersections of British and Spanish letters in history, but their work rarely treated anything published after 1800.

31. Drummond's Scottishness does technically alter Altolaguirre's conception of "English" literature, but given Drummond's participation and investment in the English tradition of Sidney, Spenser, and Shakespeare, the difference for the purposes of *1616* is minor. Altolaguirre published a biography of Garcilaso de la Vega in 1933; see chapter 3.

32. Letter to Concha Méndez, [?] March 1935, in *Epistolario*, 316.

33. Richardson, "Spanish Poetry, 1935," *Contemporaries* 2:1 (Summer 1935): 239.

34. Altolaguirre, "Percy B. Shelley," in *Obras Completas*, ed. James Valender (Madrid: Istmo, 1986), 1:395.

35. Orwell to Cunard, 6 August 1937, qtd. in D. J. Taylor, *Orwell: The Life* (New York: H. Holt, 2003), 245.

36. Orwell, review of *Invertebrate Spain*, by José Ortega y Gasset, in *Complete Works of George Orwell*, ed. Peter Davison (London: Secker and Warburg, 1998), 11:103–105.

37. Spender, "The Spanish Mind," *London Mercury* 37 (1937): 203–204. On the competitions among scholarly reviewers and translators of Spanish literature to claim authority in such forums, see Sebastiaan Faber, *Anglo-American Hispanists and the Spanish Civil War: Hispanophilia, Discipline, and Commitment* (New York: Palgrave Macmillan, 2008).

38. Spender, diary entry of 29 November 1932, in *Letters to Christopher*, ed. Lee Bartlett (Santa Barbara, CA: Black Sparrow Press, 1980), 152–53.

39. Spender to Christopher Isherwood, 28 March 1936 and 2 April 1936, in *Letters to Christopher*, 107, 109. Spender notes that "politics are also very interesting here; they sound very like Irish politics, with a perpetual struggle between the Castilians and the Catalans" (109).

40. Ibid., 110, 119, 110. Spender sent a translated stanza of Lorca's "Romance of the Spanish Civil Guard" to Isherwood.

41. Spender, "Heroes in Spain," 48; "Tangiers and Gibraltar *Now*," 44; "I Join the . . . Communist Party," 60, in *The Thirties and After: Poetry, Politics, and People, 1933–1970* (New York: Random House, 1978).

42. Spender, *Forward from Liberalism* (New York: Random House, 1937), 280–81.

43. Spender, "Stephen Spender (Inglaterra)," *II Congreso Internacional de Escritores Antifascistas (1937)*, ed. Manuel Aznar Soler and Luis Mario Schneider (Barcelona: Editorial Laia, 1979), 3:57, 58. Robert Stradling notes that "Rafael Alberti and Miguel Hernández were among the approved 'warrior poets'" whose work was distributed to the International Brigades on Spanish fronts (*History and Legend: Writing the International Brigades* [Cardiff: U of Wales P, 2002], 150). "Caudwell" was the pseudonym of Christopher St. John Sprigg. See also Valentine Cunningham, *British Writers of the Thirties* (Oxford: Oxford UP, 1988); Katherine Bail Hoskins, *Today the Struggle: Literature and Politics in England during the Spanish Civil War* (Austin: U of Texas P, 1969); and Stanley Weintraub, *The Last Great Cause: Intellectuals and the Spanish Civil War* (New York: Weybright and Talley, 1968). On journals during the war, see *Magazines, Modernity and War*, ed. Jordana Mendelson (Madrid: Ministerio de Cultura, 2008).

44. Spender, *World Within World*, 241.

45. See D. Trevor, "Poets of the Spanish War," *Left Review* 3:8 (September 1937): 455. On the aesthetics of '27, see Francisco Javier Díez de Revenga, *Las vanguardias y la Generación del 27* (Madrid: Editorial Síntesis, 2004).

46. See Serge Salaün, *La poesía de la guerra de España* (Madrid: Castalia, 1985), 187–233.

47. Spender, "Heroes in Spain," 49, 50. Spender also recorded his impressions of the conference in the article "Spain Invites the World's Writers: Notes on the International Congress, Summer 1937," in *The Thirties and After*, 50–57.

48. Spender, *World Within World*, 231.

49. Valender, "Biografía de Manuel Altolaguirre," in *El espacio interior: Manuel Altolaguirre, 1905–1959* (Andalucía: Junta de Andalucía, 2005), 64.

50. Alberti et al., "Propósito," *Hora de España* 1 (January 1937): 5. Spender's "Not to you," "The uncreating chaos," "An 'I' can never be a great man," and "After they have tired of the brilliance of cities," translated by Altolaguirre and Denis Campkin, appear in *Hora de España* 11 (November 1937): 47–50.

51. "Dos Sonetos de William Wordsworth," trans. Richardson and Cernuda, *Hora de España* 16 (April 1938): 11–12.

52. Lehmann, "Manifesto," *New Writing* 1 (Spring 1936): 1.

53. Lehmann, *The Whispering Gallery: Autobiography I* (London: Longmans, Green and Co., 1955), 279.

54. Ibid., 273, 279.

55. Lehmann, *New Writing in Europe*, 129.

56. Lehmann, *Whispering Gallery*, 279.

57. Lehmann, *New Writing in Europe*, 112, 127.

58. M. J. Benardete, foreword to . . . *And Spain Sings: Fifty Loyalist Ballads Adapted by American Poets*, ed. Benardete and Rolfe Humphries (New York: The Vanguard Press, 1937), viii.

59. Spender, introduction to *Poems for Spain*, ed. Spender and John Lehmann (London: Hogarth Press, 1939), 7, 11; emphasis in original; hereafter cited as *PS*.

60. Spender, *PS* 10; Callahan, "Stephen Spender, the 1930s, and Spanish Writing," *Miscelánea: A Journal of English and American Studies* 32 (2005): 39.

61. Spender, *PS* 9. Spender's own poetry has been translated into Spanish in a bilingual edition of Spanish Civil War poems, alongside texts by Auden, Campbell, Cornford, Langston Hughes, Day-Lewis, MacNeice, Herbert Read, and many others, in a volume published on the 50th anniversary of the war, *Poesía anglo-norteamericana de la guerra civil española: antología bilingüe*, ed. Román Álvarez Rodríguez and Ramón López Ortega (Valladolid: Junta de Castilla y León, 1986).

62. MacNeice, "Remembering Spain," *PS* 100. An homage to Lorca by his compatriots was similarly generic in its laments; Bergamín says ignorance killed him, and even Alberti is not overtly political, but focuses on the tragic aspects of Lorca's death (*Homenaje al poeta Federico García Lorca* [Valencia: Ediciones Españoles, 1937], 25).

63. Quoted in Sutherland, *Stephen Spender*, 244. Spender's other projects at the moment included his novel *The Backward Son*, his play *Trial of a Judge*, his essay on Picasso's *Guernica*, his translations of Rilke's *Duino Elegies* and Lorca's *Poems*, and his pamphlet *The New Realism*.

64. Willis, *Leonard and Virginia Woolf as Publishers: The Hogarth Press, 1917–1941* (Charlottesville: U of Virginia P, 1992), 340.

65. See Marichalar, "Madrid Chronicle," *Criterion* 4:2 (April 1926): 357.

66. Lloyd, qtd. in Callahan, "Negotiating Spanish Poets," 160.

67. Lorca, interviewed by *La Gaceta Literaria*, 15 January 1931, in *Treinta entrevistas a Federico García Lorca*, ed. and intro. Andrés Soria Olmedo (Madrid: Aguilar, 1989), 43.

68. Lorca, qtd. in Edwin Honig, *García Lorca* (Norfolk, CT: New Directions, 1944), 18.

69. Gibson, *Federico García Lorca: A Life* (New York: Pantheon Books, 1989), 425. Lorca, whose family was connected to various figures in the new government, did sign a declaration condemning Hitler, and he canceled a trip to Italy because of Mussolini's invasion of Abyssinia. But he remained at heart a humanitarian, refusing many invitations to join the communist party.

70. Lorca, quoted in Martínez Nadal, introduction to *Poems*, by Federico García Lorca, trans. Stephen Spender and J. L. Gili, intro. R. M. Nadal (London: The Dolphin Press, 1939), xxv. Geist also cites an interview that Ernesto Giménez Cabellero gave in 1982 in which he claims that Falange would almost certainly have eventually appropriated and elevated Lorca's work if he had lived ("Recycling the Popular: Lorca, *Lorquismo*, and the Culture Industry," in *Modernism and Its Margins*, ed. Geist and Monleón, 158–159).

71. Gibson, *Federico García Lorca*, 469–470. See *Times*, 12, 14, and 23 September and 5 October 1936, for reports on Lorca's death. For a full account, see Ian Gibson, *The Death of Lorca* (Chicago: J. P. O'Hara, 1973).

72. Stradling, *History and Legend*, 6.

73. *Times*, "Defiance at Toledo," 14 September 1936, 12. The newspaper's coverage of this story, however, was scarce for the following years.

74. *Daily Worker*, "Fascists Murder Poet," 11 September 1936, [n.p.].

75. *Daily Worker*, 16 September 1936, [n.p.].

76. *Left Review* 3:2 (March 1937): 71–72. Lloyd includes a translation of "The Faithless Wife," a poem that incorporates elements of class but is otherwise apolitical. The ephemeral propaganda papers (*Spain Illustrated*, *Revolt!*, *Volunteer for Liberty*) made no sustained effort to make Lorca a communist martyr, nor did likely outlets like Gollancz's *Left News* and Left Book Club. It remains possible, however, that Stalinists in Spain did claim such a reading.

77. Lloyd, preface to Lorca, *Lament for the Death of a Bullfighter, and Other Poems*, trans. Lloyd (Oxford: Oxford UP, 1937), ix, xv.

78. Lloyd, introduction to Lorca, *Lament for the Death of a Bullfighter, and Other Poems*, trans. Lloyd (London: William Heinemann, 1937), xv, vii, vii, viii.

79. Edgell Rickword [unsigned editorial], *Left Review* 3:7 (September 1937): 460.

80. Muir, review of *Lament for the Death of a Bullfighter, and Other Poems*, by Federico García Lorca, trans. A. L. Lloyd, *Criterion* 17:66 (October 1937): 153–154.

81. Pritchett, "The Bullfighter," review of *Lament for the Death of a Bullfighter, and Other Poems*, by Federico García Lorca, trans. A. L. Lloyd, *New Statesman and Nation* 14:336 (31 July 1937): 189.

82. Spender, *Life and Letters To-Day* 17 (Winter 1937): 144.

83. Sultana Wahnón traces Lorca's reception in post-war Spain, where his name was taboo throughout the 1940s but his work was slowly reappropriated toward new ends by the Franco regime beginning in the 1950s, in "La recepción de García Lorca en la España de la posguerra," *Nueva revista de filología hispánica* 43:2 (1995): 409–430. The Francoists also disseminated several fabrications of the circumstances of Lorca's death.

84. Martínez Nadal, introduction to *Poems*, ix, x, xv–xvi, xxv. Neither Spender's autobiography nor his biographers' accounts of his life give details on how he came to collaborate with Martínez Nadal and Gili.

85. Martínez Nadal, introduction to *Poems*, xxiv.

86. Spender, *World Within World*, 251.

87. Martínez Nadal, introduction to *Poems*, xxv, xxvii.

88. For example, *oscuro* is rendered "obscure," instead of "dark," or *manzana* is "apple" instead of "block." The most substantive (and comical) is Lorca's "Gacela del mercado matutino," whose title—because *gacela* is both "ghazal" and "gazelle"—appears "Gazelle of the Morning Market." *Poeta en Nueva York* had not been published in Spanish, and the choice

to include his phantasmagoric portrait of Harlem and his ode to Whitman was bold. Still, the references to homosexual cultures in the latter poem were omitted from the translation. It is unclear whether Spender knew of Lorca's sexual orientation; and if he did, whether he—having recently left Tony Hyndman and married Inez Pern—identified with Lorca is a matter of speculation.

89. Pritchett, "Lorca," review of *Poems*, by Federico García Lorca, trans. Stephen Spender and J. L. Gili, intro. R. M. Nadal, *New Statesman and Nation* 18:440 (29 July 1939): 192.

90. Ruykeyser, "Lorca in English," review of translations of *Blood Wedding* by Gilbert Neiman; *Poems* by Stephen Spender and J. L. Gili; and *The Poet in New York* by Rolfe Humphries, *Kenyon Review* 3:1 (Winter 1941): 127.

91. Spender made the comment to Paul Binding; see Binding, *Lorca: The Gay Imagination* (London: GMP Publishers, 1985), 51.

92. Honig, *García Lorca*, 18

93. Spender and Gili, introduction to F. G. Lorca, *Poems*, trans. Spender and Gili (London: Hogarth Press, 1943), 6, 7, 8. This edition ends with "The Lament," which includes the lines, "I have shut my balcony /because I do not want to hear the weeping" (56). Gili returned to Lorca's work in 1960, when he published prose translations of over 70 poems in *Lorca*, intro. and ed. Gili (Harmondsworth: Penguin, 1960).

94. Spender, *Poetry since 1939* (London: Longmans, Green and Co., 1948), 29.

95. Spender, *World Within World*, 203, 249, 261.

96. Spender, *World Within World*, 255; "Heroes in Spain," in *The Thirties and After*, 49.

97. Pritchett, "The Bullfighter," 189.

98. In a review, Spender calls *Flowering Rifle* an "incoherent, biased, unobjective, highly coloured and distorted account of one man's experiences of the Spanish war, seen through the eyes of a passionate partisan of Franco" ("The Talking Bronco," review of *Flowering Rifle*, by Roy Campbell, *New Statesman and Nation* 17:420 [11 March 1939]: 370). *Flowering Rifle* also includes several jabs at "MacSpaunday," as Campbell called MacNeice, Spender, Auden, and Day-Lewis collectively.

99. Campbell, *Talking Bronco* (London: Faber and Faber, 1946), 70. See Peter Alexander, *Roy Campbell: A Critical Biography* (Oxford: Oxford UP, 1982), 213–215.

100. Campbell, *Lorca: An Appreciation of His Poetry* (New Haven, CT: Yale UP, 1952), 7.

101. Campbell, *Lorca*, 8, 9, 71, 33, 7. Campbell's complete translations of Lorca can be found in his *Collected Works* (Craighill: A. D. Donker, 1985–1988). Campbell cites as evidence that "death was very much in the air" the slogan "'Viva la muerte,' the cry of the anarchists" (33). In fact, this was a slogan of the nationalist rebels and was made famous by the Francoist military leader José Millán Astray.

102. The Scottish poet Hugh MacDiarmid, still a communist in 1957, then attempted to wrest Lorca back for the left. He published his own epic, propagandistic rejoinder to Campbell, "The Battle Continues." Amid his own equally partisan (and equally benumbing) attacks on the "Fascist henchman" Campbell, MacDiarmid compared the two poets: "Lorca, dead, lives forever. /Campbell, living, is dead and rots." MacDiarmid included an "Author's Note" stating that the "fact that Mr Roy Campbell (still wearing his political and religious convictions like a bull-fighter's *traje de luces*) died, appropriately enough in Portugal, while this book was a-printing has not called for any alteration of the text" (MacDiarmid, *The Battle Continues* [Edinburgh: Castle Wynd, 1957], 15).

103. Jonathan Mayhew, *Apocryphal Lorca: Translation, Parody, Kitsch* (Chicago: U of Chicago P, 2009), 27.

104. Spender, *World Within World*, 241, 246; capital letters in original. See Robert Thornberry, "Writers Take Sides, Stalinists Take Control: The Second International Congress for the Defense of Culture (Spain 1937)," *The Historian* 62:3 (March 2000): 589–605.

105. See A. Kingsley Weatherhead, *Stephen Spender and the Thirties* (Lewisburg, PA: Bucknell UP,) 180.

106. Spender, *The Still Centre* (London: Faber and Faber, 1939), 105–107.

107. Spender, *Ruins and Visions: Poems, 1934–1942* (New York: Random House, 1942), 11. Spender also included his translations of works by Altolaguirre, such as "My Brother Luis," in later editions of his own collected poems.

108. Spender, *Collected Poems, 1928–1953* (New York: Random House, 1955), 108–109; emphases mine. More precise dating for these revisions is difficult. On this poem's inspiration, see also Gabriel Insausti, "Spender y Altolaguirre: una amistad en un poema," *Cuadernos hispanoamericanos* 643 (2004): 87–99.

109. Spender, *Collected Poems, 1928–1985* (Boston: Faber and Faber, 1985), 76–77.

Conclusion

1. Zambrano, introduction to *Delirium and Destiny: A Spaniard in Her Twenties*, trans. Carol Maier (Albany: State U of New York P, 1999), 1–2; hereafter cited as *DD*.

2. Eliot, "Last Words," 271.

3. Connolly, "Comment," *Horizon* 1:2 (February 1940): 68.

4. Connolly et al., "Why Not War Writers? A Manifesto," *Horizon* 22 (October 1941): 237–238; emphasis in original. Spender disagreed here, writing that "it would be impossible, of course, for a poet to enter into an undertaking to write poetry about war in the same way that a painter can paint scenes of war. It would also have been impossible for a government in conducting total war to give poets complete freedom without any obligation to write propaganda or, indeed, to write anything; for these are the conditions of freedom which most poets require" (*Poetry since 1939*, 10).

5. Ibid., 238. See also Sean Latham, "Cyril Connolly's *Horizon* and the End of Modernism," in *The Oxford Critical and Cultural History of Modernist Magazines*, ed. Peter Brooker and Andrew Thacker (New York: Oxford UP, 2009), 1:865–874.

6. Connolly, "Comment," *Horizon* 34 (October 1942): 225.

7. Connolly, "Comment," *Horizon* 9 (September 1940): 85–86.

8. Connolly, "Comment," *Horizon* 15 (March 1941): 159–160; capital letters in original.

9. Barea, "Notes on Federico García Lorca," *Horizon* 27 (March 1942): 197.

10. Connolly, "Comment," *Horizon* 120–121 (December 1949–January 1950): 359.

11. Connolly, "The Spanish Civil War (2)," in *The Evening Colonnade* (New York: Harcourt Brace Jovanovich, 1975), 357, 359.

12. Ortega Muñoz, *María Zambrano: la aurora del pensamiento*, ed. Ortega Muñoz (Junta de Andalucía, Consejería de Cultura, 2004), 14.

13. Zambrano to Ortega, 11 February 1930, in *Revista de Occidente* 120 (May 1991): 15.

14. Zambrano, review of *Obras de José Ortega y Gasset (1914–1932)*, by José Ortega y Gasset, *Cruz y Raya* 2 (1933): 154.

15. Clare E. Nimmo develops this point in the context of the historiography of feminist criticism and, in particular, Cixous's "The Laugh of the Medusa," in her "The Poet and the

Thinker: María Zambrano and Feminist Criticism," *Modern Language Review* 92:4 (October 1997): 893–902. See also *María Zambrano: la razón poética o la filosofía*, ed. Teresa Rocha Barco (Madrid: Tecnos, 1998).

16. Zambrano, "Por qué se escribe," *Revista de Occidente* 44:132 (June 1934): 318.

17. In reality, Zambrano had begun formulating a theory of exile even before the war. In "Nostalgia de la tierra" (1933), she extended Ortega's work to claim that "dehumanized art is nothing other than deterritorialized art" (in *Documents of the Spanish Vanguard*, ed. Paul Ilie [Chapel Hill: U of North Carolina P, 1969], 235).

18. Zambrano, "La poesía de Federico García Lorca," in *Federico García Lorca: Antología* (Vélez-Málaga: Fundación María Zambrano, 1989): 15–16.

19. Zambrano, "La agonía de Europa," *Sur* 72 (1940): 30, 35.

20. Zambrano, "La violencia europea," *Sur* 78 (1941): 9–20.

Translator's Notes to Appendix

a. Anatole France, who won the Nobel Prize in Literature in 1921, died on 12 October 1924, only weeks before this article appeared and almost certainly after it was finalized for publication. Marichalar deleted this reference in the later editions of the article.

b. The Irish poet and novelist George Moore (1852–1933), a self-made disciple of French realism and a social provocateur, was an important early influence on Joyce. "Médan" refers to a group of six French naturalist authors (named after Émile Zola's residence near Paris) who published the collection *Les soirées de Médan* (1880).

c. Tomás Sánchez (or Thomas Sanchez [1550–1610]) was an early Spanish Jesuit, the author of controversial works on marriage and lying; Antonio Escobar y Mendoza (1589–1669) was a Spanish Jesuit and the author of treatises on morality condemned by Pascal and others.

d. In the later editions of this article, Marichalar retracts the speculation that Joyce spent time in Madrid.

e. "Turpin Hero" or "The Ballad of Dick Turpin" tells of the rogue English highwayman Dick Turpin and his fugitive ride on his horse Black Bess. Joyce's title for the earlier version of *Portrait* was *Stephen Hero*. Both *Portrait* and *Ulysses* refer to the ballad and character.

f. Marichalar refers to Proust's "La regarder dormir" and "Mes réveils," published in the *Nouvelle Revue Française* in November 1922, the month of the author's death.

g. Johann Paul Friedrich Richter (1763–1825) was a German writer of eccentric and imaginative novels and stories. Christian Friedrich Hebbel (1813–1863) was a German poet and dramatist known for his psychological and sometimes grotesque themes.

h. *Monstruo* means "giant," "genius," or "monster," a play on the enormity (literal and figurative) of Joyce's work, the genius of writers like those Marichalar discusses, and the minotaur in Daedalus's labyrinth.

i. As was fairly common in Spanish and French criticism at the time, Marichalar refers here to *Portrait* by its protagonist's name.

j. In Thackeray's *Book of Snobs* (1848), the original reads, "First, the World was made: then, as a matter of course, Snobs" (2). Marichalar alters Thackeray's line by beginning with "Dios hizo el mundo" (literally, "God made the world"), thus extending the thematic tension between divine creation and hubris that he treats in the article.

k. The closing lines of Baudelaire's "A Voyage to Cythera" (1857): "O Lord! Give me the strength and the courage /To contemplate my heart and my body without disgust!"

l. Marichalar revises in translation two lines from the English poet Thompson's "The Hound of Heaven" (1890), which explores Catholic and ascetic themes. Thompson's poet/speaker attempts in vain to hide from God's calling: "I fled Him, down the labyrinthine ways /Of my own mind." Marichalar translates the title as "Lebrel celestial" and rewrites these lines as "He huído de El, a través del dédalo /de mi propio espíritu," also playing on *través*, "misfortune" or "travesty."

Author's Notes

1. *Música de cámara*.
2. A French version is being prepared: *Gens de Dublin*.
3. *Retrato del artista de joven*, entitled *Dédalus* in the 1924 French translation by Ludmila Savitzky. There is also a Swedish translation and one in Spanish in preparation.
4. There is an Italian version.
5. Several fragments have been translated in the new journal *Commerce* (Paris, 1924).
6. A biographical truth must be noted here: the most favorable critical article with which *Portrait* was welcomed appeared in a journal inspired by the Irish clergy: *Dublin Review*.
7. [Herbert] Gorman is publishing a book about the first 40 years of Joyce's life.
8. Especially P[adre Francisco] Suárez, Jesuit of Granada (1548–1617).

Index

1616: English and Spanish Poetry (periodical), 5, 7, 11, 28, 164, 170–174, 265nn28, 31
  and Anglo-Spanish modernism, 170–174
  see also Altolaguirre
advertising: in periodicals, 34, 37, 96, 110, 134, 174
Africa/Africanism, 54–57, 108, 146, 193
  see also Moors/Moorishness; Arabs/Arabic cultures; Spain
Alberti, Rafael, 50, 51, 173, 176, 179, 186, 187, 205, 266n43, 267nn50, 52
Aldington, Richard, 35, 36, 42, 232n20, 233n32, 234nn34, 38, 250n22
alliance politics, 6–7, 16, 21, 26, 42, 46, 66, 92, 93, 126, 158, 167
Alonso, Dámaso, 49, 50, 89, 248n73
Altamira, Rafael, 233n33
Altolaguirre, Manuel, 5–7, 27–28, 44, 165, 170–174, 177–178, 181–183 passim, 193, 195–198, 236n62, 252n37, 265n27, 28
  and *1616: English and Spanish Poetry*, 170–174
  collaborations with Stephen Spender, 177–178, 181–183
anarchism, 12, 76, 86, 95, 167, 175, 182, 185, 226n24, 269n101
Anderson, Andrew A., 223n19, 225n20, 238n77, 253n43
Anglo-Saxon, 33, 71, 129, 245n33
Anglo-Spanish relations: *see* Britain; Spain
anti-Europeanism, 7, 9
  see also nativism
anti-fascism, 5–8, 27, 126, 147, 149, 156–160, 162, 164–167, 169, 182, 195, 204, 256n25, 261n89
anti-Semitism, 63, 236n59

Arabs/Arabic cultures, 3, 4, 40, 52–56, 68–69, 105, 136, 171, 204, 221n3, 244n30
Ardis, Ann L., 222n8, 225n20, 231n5
Argentina, 84, 127, 135–139, 142–144, 157–161, 206, 259n75
  Buenos Aires, 8, 27, 126, 137–138
  women's rights in, 142–144
  see also Ocampo
arts and the state: *see* censorship; Second Republic
Asia/"Asiatic," 16, 19, 29, 53–58
  see also East
Asín Palacios, Miguel, 55–57
assimilation, 40, 53, 134
Atlantic/transatlantic, 6, 11, 87, 135
Auden Generation, 8, 27, 163–198 passim
  connections to Spanish writers, 178–184
Auden, W. H., 24, 145, 174–176, 181–182, 188, 259n78, 260n85, 267n61, 269n98
autarky, 24, 90
Authors Take Sides on the Spanish War, 146–147, 260n85
autobiography: modernist, 27, 98, 143, 186, 193, 195, 199, 203–207, 213, 254n4, 262n105
avant-garde literature, 7, 34, 37, 45, 77–80, 84–85, 105–106, 114, 177, 224n19, 225n20
Ayuso, Mónica G., 162
Azorín (José Martínez Ruíz), 39, 45, 79, 93, 135

Baeza, Ricardo, 9, 25, 44–45, 50, 109, 133, 221n5, 236n62
  "The Spirit of Internationalism and Translation," 45

273

INDEX

barbarism, 4, 26, 58, 75, 102, 145–146, 154, 157, 168, 240n101
  see also Black Legend
Baroja, Pío, 45, 110, 135, 236n60
Baroque era: see Spain
Bartók, Béla, 41, 58
Basque country: see Spain; Picasso; Wordsworth
Bassnett, Susan, 264nn6, 7
Bazargan, Susan, 74
Beach, Sylvia, 66, 79, 88, 90, 93, 133, 212
Bell, Julian (nephew of Woolf), 27, 125–126, 148–152, 254n2, 261n102, 262n105
  death in Spanish Civil War, 125–126, 148–152
Bell, Quentin, 101, 149, 150, 254n2
Bell, Vanessa, 130, 141, 153
Benda, Julien, 47, 93
Benavente, Jacinto, 93, 234n42
Berber cultures, 40, 55, 136, 240n109
Bergamín, José, 39, 50, 106–107, 173, 176, 179
Berlin, 11, 35, 46, 47, 96, 169
Berman, Jessica, 10, 222n13, 223n18, 224n19, 263n4
bilingualism, 5, 11, 139, 170–174, 189, 233n33, 267n61
biography: modernist, 5, 12, 23, 26–27, 95–124 passim
  see also New Biography; la nueva biografía
Black Legend, 4, 22, 70, 128, 135
Blake, William, 107, 114, 163, 170, 220
Bloomsbury Group, 49, 101, 132–133, 144–150, 161, 193
  politics regarding Spain, 144–150
Bolshevism, 57, 146, 161, 167, 168
Bonaparte, Napoleon, 12, 30, 95, 109, 126, 140, 165, 171–172, 178, 181, 227n33, 228n44
  depicted by modernists, 126, 165, 181
  see also Napoleonic Wars
Borges, Jorge Luis, 26, 84, 137, 139, 158, 160, 246n47
Bourne, Randolph, 134, 136
Brenan, Gerald, 24, 130, 146
Bretz, Mary Lee, 10, 223n19
Britain, 6, 26–27, 60–62, 101–105, 145–146, 171–172, 182–184
  as European, 33, 60–62
  empire, 6, 12–13, 60–62, 67–76, 101–105, 108, 130–132
  relationship with Spain, 6–7, 12–13, 67–76, 149, 152, 171–172, 182–184, 202–203
  exceptionalism, 61
Browning, Robert, 82, 131, 133, 142, 215
Buchanan, Tom, 70, 72, 75
Buenos Aires: see Argentina
Buñuel, Luis, 13, 22, 185
Byron, Lord: and Spain, 164, 171

Callahan, David, 232n14, 235n55, 264n11
Cambridge University, 22, 58, 230n63, 236n62, 265n27
Campbell, Roy, 28, 193–195, 267n61, 269n102
  translations of Lorca 194–195
Caneda Cabrera, María Teresa, 247n69, 249n85
cante jondo, 40–41, 185
capitalism, 9, 21, 34, 47, 144, 176
Casanova, Pascale, 77, 85
Castile: see Spain; Madrid
Castro, Américo, 53–55, 57, 169, 239nn95, 96
Catholicism/Catholic church, 4, 12, 17, 23, 26, 37, 54–56, 66–70, 74, 81, 87, 101, 123, 158–160, 187–188, 191, 193–194, 212
  see also clergy and clericism
Celtic/Celto-Iberian, 14, 71, 87–88, 136
censorship, 79–81, 87, 90, 110, 124, 186–189, 248n82
Cernuda, Luis, 41, 171, 173, 178, 236n62
Cervantes, Miguel de, 20, 48, 54, 79, 97, 135, 171
  Don Quixote, 66, 79, 118–119, 245n33
Chacel, Rosa, 89, 109, 124, 251n23, 252n34
Chakrabarty, Dipesh, 228n40
Cheah, Pheng, 229n50
Chesterton, G. K., 22, 114, 174, 220, 236n63
China, 46, 60, 102–103, 159, 179, 261n99
Cid, El, 53, 185
civilization (concept), 6, 30, 33, 40, 54–60, 72, 75, 98–104, 130–131, 138, 146, 155, 180, 193, 239n97, 243n21
clergy and clericism: in Spain and in Ireland, 12, 21, 71, 81, 89–90, 110–111, 123, 213
Colhoun, Charles K., 23, 122
collaboration (Anglo-Spanish), 4–8, 21, 31, 127, 164–174, 178–182, 189
collectivity, 8, 34, 127, 168, 206
colonialism, 11–13, 17, 52, 65–67, 73–78, 92, 98, 127, 144, 158, 161, 226n22, 244nn25, 26
  see also Spain; Ireland; Argentina
communism, 12, 28, 146, 161, 163–165, 176, 182, 185–187, 190–194, 268n76, 269n102
  see also Spender
comparative literatures, 5–11 passim, 226n21
competitions: literary, 11, 24, 29–32, 59, 61, 199–200, 202
Connolly, Cyril, 6, 9, 28, 95, 161, 200–203
  see also Horizon
Conrad, Joseph, 48–49, 99
conservatism, 17, 87, 113, 119, 144, 161, 167, 234n42
Córdoba: see Spain
Cornford, John, 176, 182, 192–193
cosmopolitanism 4–8, 13–16, 19–21, 25–28
  see also Eliot; Ortega; Joyce; Marichalar; Strachey; Woolf; Ocampo; Spender; Altolaguirre

Criterion, The (periodical), 8, 11, 25, 29–43, 49–50, 56–63
  collaborators, 29–43, 56–63
    see also Marichalar; Trend; Larbaud; Flint
  debates on Europe and the West, 56–63
  and foreign periodicals, 29–32, 42–43, 50–51
  on Spain and Spanish literature, 36–43, 58–59
    see also Eliot
Cruz y Raya (periodical), 123, 173, 241n133, 270n14
Cubism, 47, 50, 202, 215
cultural politics, 5, 6, 25–26, 44–46, 74–78, 108, 133, 143, 165, 170, 191
Cunard, Nancy, 147, 174, 179–180, 260n85
Curtius, E. R., 7, 20, 29, 38, 39, 42, 58, 60–61, 63, 93, 245n38
  Europeanism (in *Criterion* and *Revista de Occidente*), 29, 60–61

Dada, 82, 218, 236n63
Daily Worker (newspaper), 149, 186, 190
Dainotto, Roberto M., 13, 228n40, 235n50
Dalí, Salvador, 13, 22, 185
Damrosch, David, 223n13
dandy figure, 116, 118–120
Dante, 33, 50, 55–57, 61, 79, 133, 210, 220, 245n33
Day-Lewis, Cecil, 161, 175, 182, 183
decadence/decline, 16, 19–20, 38, 43, 55, 59, 67–77, 91–92, 97, 114–115, 117–120, 136–138, 205, 229n54
  see also Spain; Spengler; Ortega; Joyce
democracy, 17–18, 23, 27, 92, 96–97, 100–101, 104, 111–113, 120, 127, 144, 160, 164, 176, 181, 186, 190–193, 200–205
  see also liberalism
Dennis, Nigel, 106, 110
Dial, The (periodical), 43, 50, 135, 233n31, 235n59, 236n60, 256n31
dictatorship: *see* Primo de Rivera; Franco; Mussolini; Hitler
Dictionary of National Biography (DNB), 98, 106, 108
Díez de Revenga, Francisco Javier, 23, 230n65, 231n5, 266n45
Díez-Canedo, Enrique, 44, 79, 106, 236n62, 238nn77, 81
Donado, Alfonso (translator of Joyce): *see* Alonso, Dámaso
Don Juan figure, 39, 69, 118, 234n43
Dos Passos, John: on Spanish literature, 236n60, 257n35
Dostoevsky, Fyodor, 38, 80, 99, 109, 135, 213, 215, 240n101
Doyle, Laura, 223n18, 256n25
Dust, Patrick H., 227n38

East, 38, 40–41, 48, 53–58, 61, 239n101
Eliot, T. S., 4–8, 11, 24–25, 29–40, 56–63, 86–87, 146, 176, 195, 200–201, 211, 235n59, 239n101
  on Asia and the East, 56
  collaborators, 29–32, 35–40, 49
  cosmopolitanism, 33–35, 232n16
  on Europe and the West, 33–35, 56–63
  founds *Criterion*, 29–35
  reception and translation in Spanish, 49–50, 173
  relationship with Larbaud, 34, 37, 63
  relationship with Marichalar, 37–39, 42, 49
  relationship with Ortega, 43, 56, 63
  Works:
  Criterion commentaries, 33–35, 56–63
  Dante, 61
  Four Quartets, 62
  "Tradition and the Individual Talent," 33, 47
  The Waste Land, 32–33, 37, 49, 232n16
elitism, 9, 18, 25, 44, 46–47, 85, 97, 112, 114, 121, 133, 137, 229n50, 252n41
empire: *see* imperialism; Britain; Spain
England: *see* Britain
English Review, The (periodical), 167, 233nn27, 33
Enlightenment, 4, 8, 14, 16, 21, 47, 77, 97, 111, 113, 156, 170, 227n38
epistolary genre: *see* essay-letter
Epps, Brad, 224n19, 245n33
España (periodical), 18, 54, 79, 236n63
Espasa-Calpe, 106, 109
Espina, Antonio, 44, 50, 51, 96, 106, 110, 239n97, 253n54
essay-letter (public letter), 5, 27, 125, 127, 141, 157
Esty, Jed, 163
Eurocentrism, 8, 12, 16, 67
Europäische Revue, Die (periodical), 29
Europe:
  and Africa, 3–4, 12
  as cosmopolitan, 3–10, 15–16, 20–21, 23
  literature and periodicals, 6–10, 13, 20–28
  and modernity, 3–6, 10, 13, 18
  northern/Southern countries, 4, 9–10, 13–15, 19
  wars, 6, 10, 12–13, 23–28
  see also Britain; Spain; Ireland; West; East
exceptionalism: *see* Spain
exile, 6, 26, 28, 80, 158, 164, 169, 171, 199, 202–207, 239n96, 240n103, 243n17, 271n17
experimentation, 37, 83, 110, 172, 185, 250n23
Expressionism, 47, 50, 82, 215

Falange: *see* Spain
Falla, Manuel de, 39–41, 48, 190, 235n50

fascism, 6, 9, 12, 17, 20, 21, 23, 27, 60, 125–127, 139–161, 168, 176–188, 191, 192, 195, 202, 253n44, 269n102
  see also Spain; Nazism; anti-fascism
feminism, 5, 6, 7, 27, 125–127, 139–162
  see also Woolf; Ocampo
Fernández Almagro, Melchor, 44, 110, 230n67
Fernández Cifuentes, Luis, 224n19, 250n23, 251n30
Flaubert, Gustave, 32, 82, 85, 87, 108, 215, 219
Flint, F. S., 9, 25, 35–37, 42, 55, 58–59, 234nn35, 44, 47, 241n124
foreign literatures, 4–11 passim, 31, 33, 35, 37–42, 48, 55–59 passim, 77, 97, 100, 107, 136, 138, 164–166, 172, 178, 190, 201, 226n25, 232n14, 236n63
Forster, E. M., 98, 101, 146, 147, 176
Fox, Ralph, 176, 179, 182, 183, 192, 193
France and French literature, 13, 15, 21, 29, 35, 45, 49–50, 53–54, 57–58, 71, 78, 82, 86, 99, 107, 130, 133–135, 156, 160, 215, 228n44, 235n53, 236n63
  see also Paris
Franco, Francisco, 28, 146, 150–152, 170, 178–188 passim, 192–194, 199–201, 207
  see also Franco regime; Spanish Civil War; Woolf; Lorca; Spender
Francophilia/gallophilia, 31, 35, 45
Frank, Waldo, 6, 11, 27, 55, 63, 126–127, 133–139, 141, 160–161
  relationship with Ocampo, 136–137, 141, 160–161
  relationship with Ortega, 55, 63, 160–161
  view of "America Hispana," 136–137, 161
  view of Spain, 135–136
Freud, Sigmund, 84, 108, 218, 259n79
Friedman, Susan Stanford, 11, 255n5
Froula, Christine, 147, 156
Fry, Roger, 38, 98, 140, 255n16

Gaceta Literaria, La (periodical), 21, 50, 131
Gallego Roca, Miguel, 45, 226n25
Galway: as "Spanish city": see Joyce
Ganivet, Ángel, 76, 244n33
Garbisu Buesa, Margarita, 231n6, 241n132
García Gómez, Emilio, 52
García Lorca, Federico: see Lorca
García Tortosa, Francisco, 91, 246n48
Garnett, David, 101, 132, 147
Geist, Anthony L., 10, 223n19
Generation of '27, 8, 22, 28, 45, 47, 49–52, 58, 67, 76–78, 83, 89, 164, 176–184, 193, 200
  and Auden Generation, 177–182
  in Criterion, 49–52
  see also Lorca; Spender

Generation of '98: and Ortega, 17, 38, 76–77, 236nn60, 63
genre, 5, 27, 44, 52, 95–97, 105–108, 122–124, 141, 157
geography, 11, 12, 68, 76, 93, 127
Germany and German-language writers, 4, 7, 13–15, 19–20, 29–31, 36–38, 44–46, 53–61 passim, 84, 86, 96, 107, 109, 152–156, 227n34, 228nn39, 41, 49, 264n20
  see also Curtius; Kant
Gibraltar: and Spain: see Joyce
Gibson, Andrew, 73, 243n20, 244n26
Gibson, Ian, 186, 268n71
Gili, J. L., 165, 188–193, 269n93
  collaborations with Spender, 188–193
Giménez Caballero, Ernesto, 17, 51, 232n6, 248n74, 268n70
Giner de los Ríos, Francisco, 113, 145, 228n49, 230n60
Goethe, Johann Wolfgang, 20, 79, 89, 163, 210
Golden Age [Siglo de Oro] (early modern Spain): see Spain
Gómez de la Serna, Ramón, 9, 37–39, 45, 47, 49–51, 78, 86, 88, 90, 93, 107, 110, 138, 234n37, 251n23
  as biographer, 107, 110
  in Criterion, 37–39
  in Revista de Occidente, 45, 49–51
Góngora, Luis de, 20, 36, 37, 39, 177, 185, 186, 238n77
Goya, Francisco, 20, 97, 107, 122
Gracia, Jordi, 224n19, 253n44
Great War (World War I): see Europe
Greece, 11, 33, 52, 73, 155, 212, 232n16, 245n33
  and Hellenism 19, 91
Grieve, Patricia, 239n96
Guernica: see Spain
Guillén, Jorge, 50, 51, 173
Gypsies (Roma of Spain): see Spain

Harding, Jason, 62, 231n6, 241n118
Harvard University, 166, 234nn44, 47
Hayot, Eric, 222n6
Heard, Gerald, 166
Hegel, G. W. F., 4, 15, 19, 58, 228n49
Heinemann (publisher), 187
Hemans, Felicia: translations from Spanish, 171
Hemingway, Ernest, 132, 154, 163–164, 201, 202
Hermes (periodical), 79, 236n63
Hernández, Miguel, 176, 179, 182, 266n43
Hesse, Hermann: in Criterion, 38, 240n101
Hispanicity [hispanidad], 12, 25, 54, 65, 67–70, 74, 91–92, 128, 167, 185
Hispanism (stereotype), 12, 69–70, 143, 146, 227n27, 239n94

Hispanism (profession), 22, 36, 51, 171, 174, 224n19, 240n108, 266n37
Hispanizantes: see Spain
Hitler, Adolf, 145–146, 151, 155, 160, 168, 192, 264n20, 267n69
Hogarth Press: and Spanish Republic, 143, 145, 180, 259n79
Hora de España (periodical), 181, 205, 267n50
Horizon (periodical), 9, 28, 200–203
Hughes, Langston, 48, 139
humanitarianism, 59, 100, 148, 157, 202, 267n69
Hume, Martin, 70, 243n15, 265n30
Hungary, 41, 58, 72, 92, 243n21
Huxley, Aldous, 48, 49, 132, 138, 139, 143, 147, 158, 161, 256n26
Huxley, Julian, 146, 160, 161
hybridity, 3–4, 15, 40, 53, 54, 58, 68, 72, 75, 92, 133, 136, 167
Hyndman, Tony, 178, 182, 269n88

Iarocci, Michael, 13
Iberian Peninsula: *see* Spain
Ibsen, Henrik, 85, 86, 89, 236n62
idealism (Kantian), 15–16
Imparcial, El (newspaper), 70, 77, 236n62, 237n63, 243n16
imperialism (British and Spanish), 14, 16–17, 26, 34, 46, 59–62, 65–67, 70–77, 84–87, 91–93, 100–105, 109, 161, 175–176, 229n50, 243n21
 and decadence/decline, 70–77, 84–87, 91–93
 neo-imperialism, 17, 23, 76–77
 post-imperialism, 6, 7, 26, 65–66, 84, 92, 161
 see also Joyce; Strachey; Frank
impressionism, 26, 79, 97, 99, 132
Índice (periodical), 37, 65, 66, 78, 234n38, 236n62
Inquisition: *see* Spain
Institución Libre de Enseñanza, 22, 111, 206
intellectuals, 4, 8, 10, 13, 16–22, 30–31, 34–37, 42–50, 56, 59–61, 65, 77–78, 80, 91, 95, 106, 111–113, 125, 127, 138, 144–147, 150, 154, 158, 166–169, 176, 183, 201, 204–205
 as international vanguard, 16–22, 60
 and nationalism, 16, 42
 and the state, 46, 56, 111–113, 123, 138, 158
interior monologue, 26, 65, 82–84, 215–216, 246n51
International Brigades, 150, 178, 180, 184, 186
internationalism, 19–20, 23, 34, 45–47, 60, 97–99, 113, 144, 165, 169–171
Ireland: *see* Joyce; Marichalar
Islam, 32, 51–55, 60
 see also Arabs/Arabic cultures; Moors/Moorishness

Italy, 13, 15, 17, 41, 46, 55–56, 61, 126, 131, 140, 145, 154, 155, 156, 172
 see also Europe; Mussolini

Jarnés, Benjamín, 22, 44, 106, 110, 124, 138, 252n36
Jesuits (Society of Jesus), 11, 81, 212, 219
Jewish history and cultures, 52, 61, 93, 136, 161, 243n10
Jiménez, Juan Ramón, 37–39, 45, 49, 65, 84, 93, 106, 218, 235n47
Johnson, Roberta, 234n43, 250n23
journalism, 8, 25, 28, 50, 68, 152, 164, 176, 197, 201
Joyce, James, 4–11 passim, 23, 25–26, 37, 39, 47, 49, 65–93, 98, 108, 132, 135, 146, 209–220
 characterizations of Ireland, 11, 67, 85, 92, 214, 244n25
 on Galway as "Spanish," 68, 70, 71, 242nn5, 6, 8
 cosmopolitanism, 87
 cultural politics, 67, 73, 85–87
 interactions with Spanish writers, 88–89
 in periodicals, 78–79, 85–89
 and Trieste, 68, 72, 85, 243n21
 Works:
 Italian journalism, 68, 71
 Ulysses
  the citizen: and Mrs Rubio, 71, 74
  Leopold Bloom, 68–72
   as cosmopolitan subject, 91–92
  Molly Bloom, 74
   as cosmopolitan subject, 91–92
   origins in Gibraltar, 68, 74
   as "Spanish type," 65, 67–69, 91–92
  readings of empires, 71–72
  reception and translation in Spanish, 65–67, 78–84, 87–88
  representations of Gibraltar, 74–77, 92
  representations of Spain, 68–72, 91–92
  Stephen Dedalus, 69, 70, 73
  Spanish-Irish connections, 66–67, 71, 81, 91–92
Juan Ramón: *see* Jiménez, Juan Ramón
justice, 8, 16, 103, 156, 181, 205

Kant, Immanuel, 3–4, 6, 9, 10, 13–16, 21, 22, 25, 32, 53, 58, 156, 208, 221n3, 228n44
 on cosmopolitanism and Europe, 13–16, 25
 on Spaniards, 3–4, 14–15, 32
 see also Ortega
Keyserling, Count, 22, 51, 55, 138, 139, 264n20
King, John, 138
Krause, Karl Christian Friedrich (and Krausism), 22, 113, 228n49

Labanyi, Jo, 22
Labour Party, 145, 150, 260n83, 261n99
Landor, Walter Savage: and Spain, 172
Larbaud, Valery, 9, 11, 25, 37–39, 42, 50–51, 59, 63,
    65–66, 77–79, 85–86, 211–212, 234n38,
    245n38
  and *Criterion*, 34, 37–39, 42
  relationship with Joyce, 65–66, 77–78, 85–86,
    211–212
  relationship with Marichalar, 37, 50, 66, 77–78,
    234n38
Latham, Sean, 86, 222n11, 231n5, 270n5
Latin (race), 13–16, 53, 58, 61, 68, 129, 141, 166,
    258n64
Latin America, 16, 28, 136–137, 157–161, 205, 257n40
Lawrence, D. H., 49, 89, 132, 138
Lázaro, Alberto, 88, 90
League of Nations, 9, 17, 18, 20, 41, 59–60, 113,
    145, 150, 261n99
Left Review (periodical), 147, 149, 180, 186–188
Lehmann, John, 8, 28, 163, 175, 178–181, 183, 184
  and Spanish writers, 178–181
Lewis, Wyndham, 36, 48, 146, 232n6
liberalism, 7, 12, 17–18, 22, 26–27, 53, 57, 95–124,
    144–146, 160, 176, 181, 190–191, 201,
    249n6, 252n41
literary history, 10–13, 31–33, 96–98, 163–164,
    170–174, 224n19, 225n20
literary space, 8, 11, 24, 27, 85, 95–96, 242n1
Lloyd, A. L., 179, 183, 185–190, 191, 192, 193,
    268n76
  translations of Lorca, 185–190
London, 7, 11, 31–33, 37, 127, 157, 160, 170–171, 200
López Campillo, Evelyne, 19, 237n69, 251n27
Lorca, Federico García, 5, 6, 7, 16, 27–28, 135, 159,
    163–166, 171–192 passim
  in *1616: English and Spanish Poetry*, 171–174
  cosmopolitanism, 185–186, 190–192
  and Generation of '27, 50, 176–178
  as martyr-figure, 165–166, 176–180, 183–189
  and music, 41
  reception and translation in English, 41, 50,
    175–176, 179–195
  see also Spender; Spanish Civil War
Ludwig, Emil, 95, 109, 251n32

MacDiarmid, Hugh, 269n102
Machado, Antonio, 17, 38, 49, 176, 188, 205,
    236n60
MacNeice, Louis, 161, 175, 182, 183, 188, 269n98
Madariaga, Salvador de, 145, 169, 236n63
Madrid, 7, 11–13, 20, 31, 35, 43, 47, 67, 92, 96, 127,
    129–130, 149–152, 206–207
  as European, 7, 11, 13, 67, 92
  and Spanish Civil War, 149–152

Maeztu, Ramiro de, 17, 37, 135, 235n53
Mainer, José-Carlos, 10, 53, 224n19, 253n44
major/minor languages and states, 10, 35, 44–45,
    48, 67, 84–87
Mangini, Shirley, 157
manifestos, 22, 34, 99, 138, 147, 148, 154, 153, 171,
    178, 201, 218
Marcus, Jane, 153
Marcus, Laura, 98, 249n5
marginality, 4–8, 11–12, 25, 31–32, 51–52, 65–70,
    87, 92–93, 127, 185, 256n25
Marías, Julián, 14
Marichalar, Antonio (Marqués de Montesa), 6, 7,
    11, 23, 37–43, 44, 48–51, 57, 60–62,
    65–67, 77–93, 95–98, 107–110, 113–124,
    132–135, 158, 166, 168–169, 174,
    209–220, 234n42, 235n47, 246n51
  in *Criterion*, 37–43, 57, 60
  and Generation of '27, 37–43, 185
  on Joyce, 77–93 passim
  and liberalism, 113–114
  and New Biography/*nueva biografía*, 95–98,
    109–110, 113–124
  relationship with Beach, 90, 93
  relationship with Eliot, 37, 39, 60
  relationship with Larbaud, 37, 39, 65–66, 77–78
  relationship with Ocampo, 90, 158
  relationship with Ortega, 77, 93, 109–111, 117,
    166–169
  in *Revista de Occidente*, 44, 48–51
  and Second Republic, 95–98, 107–110,
    113–124
  on Strachey, 107–109
  as translator, 82–85, 107–108, 158
  on Woolf, 132–133, 158
  Works:
    "James Joyce in His Labyrinth," 66–67, 79–92,
      209–220
      influence, 88–92
      and Joycean criticism, 85–92
      reading of Joyce, 79–81
      translations of *Ulysses*, 82–85
    "'Lives' and Lytton Strachey," 107–109
    The Perils and Fortune of the Duke of Osuna,
      95–98, 113–124
      as commentary on Spain, 120–122
      influenced by Strachey, 114–118
      reception (in English and in Spanish),
        121–124
    "School of Plutarchs," 107–109
    Spanish chronicles (*Criterion*), 37–43
    see also Eliot; Joyce; Strachey; Ortega
Martínez Nadal, Rafael, 165, 189–193, 265n27
masculinity, 27, 127, 133, 136, 140–141, 144, 150,
    153, 154, 204

Massis, Henri, 34, 57–59, 63, 146, 241n124
Maurois, André, 95, 107, 109, 251n27
Maurras, Charles, 34, 57, 63, 146
McCourt, John, 243n21
medieval era, 30, 41, 53, 54, 55, 136, 177
Mediterranean cultures, 14–15, 53, 91, 228n40, 238n89, 242n9
memoir, 125, 140–141, 151, 213, 254n2
Méndez, Concha, 170, 172
Menéndez Pidal, Ramón, 53, 55–56, 168, 177
metropole/colony, 6, 12, 47, 67
Mignolo, Walter, 16, 226n22
minority/vanguard cultures, 9, 21, 46, 48, 60, 157, 187, 252n41
Miró, Gabriel, 39, 51, 78, 86, 132
Mistral, Gabriela, 158, 159, 160
modernism (general), 4–12, 223n19, 225n20
modernismo, 21, 45, 190, 225n20, 236n63
modernist studies (Anglo-and Hispanophone), 10–13, 223n18, 224n19, 225n20
modernization, 12, 14, 22, 97, 226n23
monarchism: *see* Britain; Spain
Montemayor, Jorge de: translated by Sidney, 172
Montes, Eugenio, 132, 255n22
Moors/Moorishness, 3, 4, 25, 32, 40–41, 51–54, 69–71, 75, 128, 136, 146, 165, 185, 188, 201, 244n30
 see also Arabs/Arabic cultures; Berber cultures; Spain; Race
Moretti, Franco, 226n25, 242n1
Morocco, 71, 76, 77
Morrisson, Mark, 231n5, 233n27
Mulhern, Francis, 264n7
multiculturalism, 6, 41, 54, 55, 195
music: *see* Trend; Lorca
Mussolini, Benito, 114, 126, 140–141, 145–146, 148, 252n40, 258n57, 267n69
 meeting with Ocampo, 140–141
mysticism, 17, 36, 51, 55–56, 138, 154, 161, 215

Napoleon: *see* Bonaparte, Napoleon
Napoleonic Wars (inc. Peninsular War), 30, 74, 171–172, 244n25
nation-state, 11, 46, 126, 145, 157, 228n49
nationalism, 6, 9, 16, 19, 26, 30, 41–42, 47, 58–61, 74, 86, 229n50
nationality, 8, 18, 33, 78, 80, 91, 126, 134, 157
nativism, 17, 19, 21, 71, 76, 87, 134
Nazism, 151, 160, 201, 264n20
neoclassicism, 35, 37, 235n47
New Biography, 12, 26–27, 95–98, 105–109, 113–114, 121,
New Liberalism, 27, 96–97, 11, 121, 249n6
New Spain: *see* Ortega; Spain

New World, 4, 18, 76, 126, 135–138, 161, 196, 207
 see also Latin America; Argentina; United States
New Writing (periodical), 9, 163, 178–180
New York City, 8, 134, 137
Nietzsche, Friedrich, 38, 86, 89
nineteenth century, 26, 30, 46, 59–60, 78, 86, 95–124 passim
Non-Intervention Agreement, 150, 164, 169
North, Michael, 222n8
northern/southern countries: *see* Europe
Nós (periodical), 87–88, 236n63
Nouvelle Revue Française, La (periodical), 29, 35, 43, 44, 51, 63, 134, 137, 235n53
nueva biografía, la, 97, 105–110, 121–124
Nueva España (periodical), 96, 249n7

Ocampo, Victoria, 4–8, 11, 27, 90, 126–128, 133, 136–144, 151, 157–162, 200, 204–206, 258n57
 and essay-letters, 157–160
 meets Mussolini, 140–142
 politics and dissidence, 139–144, 157–160
 relationship with Frank, 136–139
 relationship with Ortega, 136–137, 161
 relationship with Woolf, 126, 139–143, 151, 160–162
 Works:
 "Carta a Virginia Woolf," 8, 141–142
 Sur (as editor and publisher), 136–139, 158
occupation (colonial), 54, 73, 74, 75, 171, 244nn26, 31
oligarchy, 20, 112
Orientalism, 41, 58, 138, 227n27, 239n99, 259n69
Ortega y Gasset, José, 25–28, 230n68
 on British modernism, 46–47, 132–133
 cosmopolitanism, 20–21, 46–47
 and Eliot, 7, 29–30, 32, 41, 47, 58–63, 235n53
 elitism, 17–18, 112
 on Europe and the West, 3–10, 12–21, 29–32, 51–53, 127, 138, 161
 and foreign periodicals, 7, 51, 56
 and Generation of '27, 96–98, 111, 124
 and Generation of '98, 76–77
 and Germany, 4, 13–16, 227n34, 228n39, 264n20
 and *la nueva biografía*, 106–110
 and Joyce, 77–80, 88, 92–93
 and Kant, 3, 9, 13–16
 and modernism, 20–21, 224n19, 225n20
 and the New Spain, 3, 9, 16–18, 31, 67, 96–98, 112, 127, 225n20
 on the nineteenth century, 111–112
 politics, 17, 46–47, 111, 239n94, 252n41
 and Primo de Rivera regime, 23–24, 46, 111

Ortega y Gasset, José (*continued*)
  as public intellectual, 3–5, 18, 185, 203
  as publisher, 12–14, 19–20, 43–45, 106–110, 122–123, 133–135, 185, 236n63
  reception and translation in English, 12, 39, 42–43, 51, 58, 145, 164–170, 174–175, 235n53, 264nn11, 16
  relationship with Frank, 55, 63, 160–161
  relationship with Marichalar, 77, 93, 109–111, 117, 166–169
  relationship with Ocampo, 136–137, 161
  relationship with Zambrano, 200–207
  and *Revista de Occidente*, 7–8, 19–20, 24, 29–63 passim
  and the Second Republic, 161, 166–170, 204
  on Spain, 3–10, 12–21, 51–53, 96–98, 111–112, 229n50
  and the Spanish Civil War, 169–170
  on Spengler, 19–20, 161, 229n54
  "United States of Europe," 93, 138
  Works:
  "Cosmopolitismo," 46–47
  The Dehumanization of Art, 47, 80, 106
  Meditations on Quixote, 18, 77
  "Nada 'moderno' y 'muy siglo XX,'" 111–112
  "Propósitos," 20, 30, 43
  Revolt of the Masses, 42, 138, 161, 166–169, 252n41
  "Spanish Letter," (*Dial*), 43
  "Vieja y nueva política," 17, 96
  see also Eliot; Marichalar; Joyce; Ocampo; Zambrano
Orwell, George, 139, 163–164, 174–175, 201
Osuna, Rafael, 123, 231n5
Otero Pedrayo, Ramón, 88, 248n71
Ouimette, Victor, 230n68, 252n41

pacifism, 102, 108, 145–147, 150, 156, 170, 261n99, 262n102
pan-Europeanism, 15, 20, 25, 47, 56, 60, 106, 139, 155
pan-Hispanism, 17, 37, 139
Pankhurst, Sylvia: on Ortega, 168
Paris, 12–13, 51, 77–79, 118–119, 134–135, 160, 209, 212, 242n1
parliamentary system, 18, 46, 112, 123
Pater, Walter, 99, 107
patriarchy, 125, 150–154 passim, 159–160
pedagogy (social and cultural), 4, 22, 121–122
Pérez de Ayala, Ramón, 44, 45, 51, 89, 135, 169, 171
Pérez Firmat, Gustavo, 106, 249n8, 250n23
periodicals (general), 6–10, 29–32, 50–51, 62–63, 123, 133, 137, 171, 200, 222n11, 231n6, 232n6, 236n63
  international periodical communities, 8–10, 20, 25, 29–32, 34–37

periodical networks, 50, 61, 127, 133, 200–201
  see also Criterion; *Revista de Occidente*; Sur; *1616: English and Spanish Poetry*; *New Writing*; *Horizon*; *Hora de España*
periphery, 4, 6, 12–13, 33, 67, 92, 96
  see also marginality
Perón, Juan, 27, 139, 160
philosophy, 4–5, 9–10, 13–19, 44, 46, 111–112, 168–169, 203–205
  see also Kant; Ortega; Zambrano
Picasso, Pablo, 13, 79, 89, 107, 148, 178, 267n63
populism, 28, 112, 170, 182, 183, 191
postcolonial criticism, 8, 13, 65, 67, 74–75, 84–86, 91, 98, 127, 143
Pound, Ezra, 6, 33–34, 36, 38, 62, 79, 85–87, 89, 92, 98, 146, 188, 220, 233n33, 236n60, 244n28, 245n43, 260n85
  contacts in Spain, 79, 89, 233n33, 236nn60, 63, 245n43
  and periodicals, 33–34, 36
  readings of Joyce, 79, 85–87
prestige (international), 9, 79, 96, 137, 173, 177, 200
Primo de Rivera, José Antonio, 114, 169
Primo de Rivera, Miguel: dictatorship, 23–24, 39, 46, 56, 78, 96, 110–113, 121–122, 167, 168, 252n40, 264n11
Pritchett, V. S., 179, 188, 191, 193
Proa (periodical), 84, 137
progressivism, 17, 22, 27, 36, 96–97, 100, 112, 204
  see also Ocampo; New Liberalism
propaganda, 154, 176, 182, 191, 201–202, 263n4, 268n76, 269n102, 270n4
Protestantism, 13, 81
Proust, Marcel, 11, 42, 48, 79, 80, 82–83, 84, 88, 131–132, 210, 214, 216, 219, 235n53, 271nf
provincialism, 9, 18, 31, 43, 54, 58, 59, 61, 86–89, 93, 95, 169, 190, 194
psychology, 48–49, 80, 84, 90, 100, 108, 117, 139, 142, 148, 214, 215, 271ng
public sphere, 4, 9, 11, 16–18, 31, 42, 55, 56, 95, 123, 127, 140–141, 152, 156, 160, 164
Pyrenees, 13, 21, 23, 55, 227n33, 260n85

race: in Europe and Spain, 10, 17, 43, 53, 69–71, 130, 228n40
radicalism, 134, 145, 150, 169
Rainey, Lawrence, 222n8
Ramón: *see* Gómez de la Serna, Ramón
rationalism, 14–15
reactionaries, 17, 57, 58, 163, 178, 193, 233n25, 240n113
  see also Massis; Maurras
realism, 78, 80, 87, 106, 212, 271nb

reciprocity (literary), 6–8, 12–13, 31–32, 40, 66–67, 78, 133–134
  see also collaboration
reformism, 4–10, 16–17, 22, 43–46, 67, 96–101, 110–124, 145, 206, 229n50
regeneracionismo, 17, 76–77
regeneration (cultural, political), 6–7, 17, 25, 42, 55, 65–67, 76–77, 92, 134–136
Renaissance, 5, 13–14, 16, 172, 204
  see also Spain
"Republic of letters," 6, 9, 13, 21, 51, 79, 95, 98, 165, 250n22
Residencia de Estudiantes, 22, 36, 40, 56, 106, 111, 113, 170, 185, 188, 230n60
Revista de Occidente, La, 5, 8, 11, 19–21, 24–27, 66, 77, 79–93 passim, 121–123, 138–139, 229n53, 231n2, 231n6
  biography in, 97, 106–110, 112, 121–122
  book press, 106–110, 122–123, 133, 135, 185, 237n69, 239n97
  British modernism in, 46–51, 66, 79–81, 84, 88–89, 106–110, 127, 132, 141
  characterizations of Spain, Europe, and the West, 19–21, 43–45, 51–56
  collaborators, 43–45
  and Primo de Rivera regime, 24
  relationships with foreign periodicals, 5, 8, 11, 29–32, 56–58, 60–62, 238n81
  translations in, 43–45
  see also Ortega; Marichalar
Reyes, Alfonso, 44, 78, 135, 137
Rice, Stanley, 58, 239n101
Richardson, Stanley, 172–174, 178
Rickword, Edgell, 176, 182, 186, 188
Risco, Vicente, 87–88
Ródenas de Moya, Domingo, 10, 223n19, 230n65, 231n5, 237n77, 251n23, 253n54
Rolland, Romain, 51, 59, 106, 134, 239n99
Roman empire, 15, 53, 54, 57, 60–61
Romance (Spanish ballad), 165, 171, 177–185
Romantic poets: sympathy with Spain, 12, 171–174, 178
Rome, 33, 35, 47, 73, 140, 213, 252n40
Russell, Bertrand, 46, 48, 55, 102, 147, 149, 161, 239n97, 239n99
Russia (inc. USSR), 11, 17, 29, 46, 55–58, 61, 83, 119–120, 138, 139, 161, 175, 179, 232n7
  and Europe/the West, 55–58, 61

Sackville-West, Victoria (Vita), 142, 147, 161
Sánchez-Albornoz, Claudio, 53–55, 239n96
Sánchez, Tomás (Spanish casuist), 81, 212, 271nc
Santa Cecilia, Carlos G., 88, 245n42, 248n72
Santayana, George, 49
Scholes, Robert, 222n11, 231n5

Second International Congress of Writers for the Defense of Culture (Valencia, 1937), 150, 164, 176–178, 191, 195
Second Republic (Spain, 1931–1939), 6, 22, 24–28, 96–98, 110–114, 127–128, 144–154, 158–162, 164–198, 199–207, 260n85
  and British writers, 144–154, 176–192
  as "New Spain," 96–98, 110–114, 144–154
  see also Spanish Civil War; Generation of '27
secularism, 6, 12, 17, 21–22, 85, 86, 100, 113
Semitic peoples and cultures, 16, 55, 245n33
  see also Jewish history and cultures
Serrano Asenjo, Enrique, 109, 121, 124, 251n27
Seven Arts (periodical), 134, 256nn30, 31, 257n35
  see also Frank
Shakespeare, William, 59, 79, 142, 162, 163, 171, 177, 209, 237n63
Shaw, G. B., 48, 49, 50, 79, 137, 158, 194, 236n63, 260n85
Shelley, Percy Bysshe: and Spain, 171–174 passim
Sidney, Sir Philip: translates Montemayor, 188–189
Silver Age [Edad de Plata, 1898–1939], 5, 16, 65, 85
  see also Spain
Sinn Féin, 87
social reform: see reformism
Socialism, 17, 34, 59, 77, 145, 164, 175, 229n50
Sol, El (newspaper), 18, 50, 109–110, 111, 132, 236n63
Soufas, C. Christopher, 10, 223n19, 225n20
South America, 4, 128–129, 136–139, 141, 143, 158, 159, 185
Spain:
  Baroque era, 177, 185, 219, 226n25, 238n77
  Catholicism, 4, 12, 17, 23, 26, 37, 54–56, 66–70, 74, 81, 87, 101, 123, 158–160, 187–188, 191, 193–194, 212
  connections to Ireland, 66–68, 70–71, 91–92, 242nn5, 6, 8
  as cosmopolitan, 3–10, 13–24 passim, 91–92, 96–97
  as declining/decadent, 16, 19–20, 38, 43, 55, 59, 67–77, 91–92, 97, 114–115, 117–120, 136–138, 205, 229n54
  exceptionalism/non-Europeanness, 4–24, 29–59
  Moorish presence, 3, 4, 25, 32, 40–41, 51–54, 69–71, 75, 128, 136, 146, 165, 185, 188, 201, 244n30
  Golden Age [Siglo de Oro], 5, 13–14, 16, 172, 204
  Gypsies (Roma), 40, 165, 177, 183, 185, 204
  hispanizantes, 7, 19, 53
  and Iberian history, 41, 53, 75, 136

Spain: (*continued*)
  as the "New Spain," 3, 9, 16–18, 31, 67, 96–98, 110–114, 127, 144–154, 225n20
  relationship with Britain, 6–7, 12–13, 67–76, 149, 152, 171–172, 182–184, 202–203
  relationship with Africa, 54–55, 57, 108, 146, 193
  relationship with New World, 4, 18, 76, 126, 135, 136, 138, 161, 196, 207
  Silver Age [*Edad de Plata*]: *see* Silver Age
  typologies, 3–4, 12–14, 69–70, 143, 146, 227n27, 239n94
  political history and movements:
    Carlism (monarchism), 76, 112, 114, 118, 120
    civil war: *see* Spanish Civil War
    empire, 68, 72–77, 108, 135, 229n50
    Falange (fascism), 114, 165, 195, 268n70
    First Republic, 26, 97, 112–113, 120, 124
    Franco regime, 23–24, 90, 124, 152, 163, 186, 189, 200, 225n20, 239n96, 268n83, 269n101
    Inquisition, 4, 54, 72
    liberalism, 7, 12, 17–18, 22, 26–27, 53, 57, 95–124, 144–146, 160, 176, 181, 190–191, 201, 249n6, 252n41
    medieval era, 30, 41, 53–55, 136, 177
    monarchs, 18, 23, 54, 68, 76–77, 89, 111–112, 226n24, 253n44
    Primo de Rivera regime: *see* Primo de Rivera
    Restoration, 18, 112, 252n40
    Second Republic: *see* Second Republic
    Spanish-American War of 1898, 4, 16, 76, 207
    women's rights, 127, 145, 152
  provinces and cities:
    Andalusia, 16, 39–40, 52, 70, 128, 165, 185–190, 194, 199, 204, 235n50, 240n109
      Córdoba 40, 54, 194, 202
      Granada, 41, 130, 184–186, 190, 205
    Asturias, 54, 239n96
    Basque Country 55, 131, 147, 181, 236n63
      Guernica, 148, 178, 267n63
    Castile (and Castilianism), 16, 44, 54, 84, 132, 169, 181, 229n50, 246n48
      see also Madrid
    Galicia, 71, 86–87
Spanish Civil War, 7, 10, 12, 22, 23, 24, 93, 125–126, 133, 146–147, 150, 151, 155, 157–158, 169, 174–175, 179–180, 189, 191–198, 199–203, 204, 206, 260n82, 262n102, 266n43
  see also Spain; Ortega; Marichalar; Woolf; Ocampo; Spender; Altolaguirre; Connolly; Zambrano

Spanish-language (Hispanophone) criticism, 5, 6, 7, 66–67, 85–93, 109, 134, 224n19, 231n6
"Spanish problem," The [*el problema español*], 4, 221n4
"Spanish type": *see* Hispanism; Joyce
Spender, Stephen, 5, 6, 8, 27–28, 149, 163–166, 174–198
  and the Auden Generation, 175–180
  collaborations with Spanish writers, 164–166, 182–193
  on Ortega, 175
  and Orwell, 174–175
  relationship with Generation of '27, 164, 177–184
  relationship with Manuel Altolaguirre, 164–165, 177–178, 182, 196–198
  on Romantic poets, 181
  and Roy Campbell, 194
  on Spanish Civil War, 179–184, 195–198
  translations of Lorca, 164, 177, 184–193
  travels in Spain, 174–178
  Works:
    Poems for Spain, 178–184
    "To a Spanish Poet"/"To Manuel Altolaguirre," 196–198
Spengler, Oswald, 19–20, 52, 55, 57, 59, 137, 161, 229n54, 232n7, 240n106
St. John of the Cross, 20, 36, 173
Starkie, Walter, 23, 51
stereotypes: *see* Hispanism
Strachey, Lytton, 4, 5, 11, 23, 26, 48, 95–105, 107–110, 113–119, 122, 132, 154
  and New Biography, 95–105
  Reception and translation in Spanish, 107–109
  Works:
    Eminent Victorians, 99–105
Steiner, Patricia Owen, 256n29, 259n75
Supervielle, Jules, 48, 51, 137
supranationalism, 8, 24, 31, 49, 78, 80, 133, 157, 168, 206
Sur (periodical), 8, 27, 136–139, 141, 158, 160, 205
  and Anglo/Spanish modernism, 136–139
  see also Ocampo
Surrealism, 82, 202, 218
Sutherland, John, 184, 264n5
sympathy, 20, 22, 31, 35, 40, 42–43, 125–128, 144–148, 157, 161, 167, 172, 174, 178–181, 193, 196, 198
  see also translation

tertulias (intellectual conversation groups), 18, 185, 203
Teuton (race), 33, 61
Thompson, Francis, 81, 170, 220, 272n1
Times (London newspaper), 28, 146, 186

Times Literary Supplement (*TLS*), 12, 36, 122, 129, 163
Toro Santos, Antonio Raúl de, 237n63, 245n46, 247n68, 248n70
Torres Bodet, Jaime, 44, 121–122
Transatlantic: *see* Atlantic
translation (general), 4–7, 12, 23
  see also Criterion; *Revista de Occidente*; Marichalar; Ocampo; Spender; Altolaguirre
transnationalism (concept), 4, 7, 9, 23, 24, 66, 84, 126, 134, 152, 182, 190, 222n11, 224n19
  and modernism, 4–13
travelers in Spain: *see* Woolf; Spender
Trend, J. B., 9, 20–21, 23, 24, 25, 29, 36–41, 42, 43, 57, 58, 61, 63, 122, 185
  anti-Semitism, 63
  in *Criterion*, 39–41, 57–58
  on Spanish-Moorish music, 36–41
Trieste, 34, 68, 72, 85, 213
Two Spains, The [*las dos Españas*], 17, 221n4

Unamuno, Miguel de, 17, 56, 76, 77, 93, 135, 168, 236n60, 236n63, 245n43
United States, 22, 47, 61, 70, 76, 80, 93, 134–136, 138, 159, 212
universalism, 6–8, 15–16, 24–28
universities, 11, 14, 18, 22, 111, 113, 173

Valéry, Paul, 22, 23, 29, 34, 49, 50, 59, 84, 114, 137, 218
vanguard biography: *see* New Biography; *la nueva biografía*
Vidas españoles del siglo XIX series, 109, 110, 115, 122, 253n54
  see also la nueva biografía
Visigoths: in Spain, 15, 53, 54

Walkowitz, Rebecca L., 222n8, 226nn21, 22, 247n58
Wells, H. G., 22, 135, 137, 146, 166, 194, 236n63, 260n85
West, 12, 15, 19–20, 25, 40–47, 52–62, 134, 137, 155, 180, 200, 232n7, 238n90, 241n124
  see also Spain; Europe

Western Europe, 15, 29, 38, 41, 60–61
Winkiel, Laura, 223n18, 256n25
Wollaeger, Mark, 92, 221n6
women's writing: *see* Ocampo; Woolf
Woolf, Virginia (Stephen), 5–9, 27, 38, 90, 98, 109, 125–133, 140–162, 178, 204
  activism, 144–148
  anti-fascism, 125, 140, 143, 146–148
  cosmopolitanism, 127, 156–157
  on English culture, 126, 130, 148–149
  Hispanism, 128–129, 142–143, 153
  reception and translation in Spanish, 127, 131–133, 157–160
  relationship with Julian Bell, 125, 148–152
  relationship with Ocampo, 126, 139–143, 151, 160–162
  on Spain and Spanish Civil War, 125, 128–131, 147–150
  travels to Spain, 128–129
  Works:
    "An Andalusian Inn," 128–129
    "The Art of Biography," 109
    "Memoir of Julian Bell," 125–126
    A Room of One's Own, 141, 160
    Three Guineas
      composition history, 143, 148–151
      Dictator-Creon figure, 126, 154–155
      feminism, 144–157
      on English tyranny, 126, 154–156
      on Spanish Civil War, 126–127, 152–154
      photographs in, 126, 152–156
    "To Spain," 130–131
    "Vortex in Spain," 146
Woolf, Leonard, 101–102, 129, 131, 145–146, 149–150, 154, 161, 180, 259n80, 261n99
  influence on *Three Guineas*, 145, 150
Wordsworth, William: Spanish sonnets, 171, 181, 193
World War II, 6, 24, 28, 160, 161, 192, 196

Yeats, W. B., 79, 191, 260n85

Zambrano, María, 6, 24, 28, 199–200, 203–207